A NATURAL HISTORY OF
BELIZE

NUMBER FIFTY-TWO
The Corrie Herring Hooks Series

A NATURAL HISTORY OF

BEL

SAMUEL BRIDGEWATER

Foreword by Stephen Blackmore

IZE

INSIDE THE MAYA FOREST

UNIVERSITY OF TEXAS PRESS, AUSTIN

in association with the

NATURAL HISTORY MUSEUM, LONDON

Requests for permission to reproduce material
from this work should be sent to:
    Permissions
    University of Texas Press
    P.O. Box 7819
    Austin, TX 78713-7819
    www.utexas.edu/utpress/about/bpermission.html

The paper used in this book meets the minimum requirements
of ANSI/NISO Z39.48-1992 (R1997) (Permanence of Paper). ∞

Designed by Lindsay Starr

LIBRARY OF CONGRESS CATALOGING-IN-PUBLICATION DATA

Bridgewater, Samuel, 1968–
    A natural history of Belize : inside the Maya forest / Samuel
Bridgewater ; foreword by Stephen Blackmore. – 1st ed.
        p. cm. – (The Corrie Herring Hooks series; no. 52)
    Includes bibliographical references and index.
    ISBN 978-0-292-72671-0 (cloth : alk. paper)
    1. Natural history–Belize. 2. Forests and forestry–Belize.
3. Land use–Belize–History. I. Title.
    QH108.B43B75 2011
    508.7282–dc23   2011024357

    ISBN 978-0-292-73900-0 (e-book)

CONTENTS

Dedicated to the memory of
Nicodemus ("Chapal") Bol
(1961–2011)

FOREWORD

FOR MANY YEARS BIOLOGISTS tended to overlook Belize as a focus of their research and flocked instead to neighboring countries in Central America. During the 1980s, while working for the Natural History Museum in London, I began to get to know Central America through two visits to Honduras collecting herbarium specimens for the international project Flora Mesoamericana. I often heard it said that the most interesting places for biologists in Central America were the Mosquitia region of Honduras, Barro Colorado Island in Panama, and the wonderful national parks of Costa Rica. Belize, in contrast, was not worth visiting because the forests had been destroyed by logging and the impact of frequent hurricanes. What remained, apparently, was uninteresting secondary forest and monotonous swamps.

Fortunately for me, I was persuaded to make a visit to Belize in 1990 by David Sutton, a colleague at the Natural History Museum who knew better. Taking part in the Programme for Belize workshop to develop the management plan for the Rio Bravo Conservation and Management Area swiftly replaced misguided prejudice with a deep impression of an extensively forested country full of wildlife. In a visit of just one week we saw the extraordinary diversity of forest types that are crammed into Belize: pine ridge, rain forest, seasonally dry forests, savanna, and mangrove. The abundance of birds, mammals, reptiles, and amphibians was remarkable. I was astonished to discover that Belize has the world's finest zoo and ecotourism facilities of the quality of Chaa Creek and Chan Chich. I met key players from the worlds of government, business, ecotourism, education, and NGOs and could never again fly to Belize without recognizing at least a few old friends at the airport. I found that the history of human occupation of Belize adds layer upon layer of interest to the nature of the country. The density of ancient Mayan sites is extraordinary, although, like everything else in Belize, they are, for no good reason, much less famous than those of Guatemala, Honduras, or Mexico. The diversity of the present-day people of Belize and the warmth of their welcome made a permanent impression. In that week I was hooked. I left feeling that I must have been the victim of a conspiracy of deception intended to keep the place secret. David Sutton was pleased, too. He had utterly convinced me that this was the place for the NHM to establish its proposed tropical field station. The only question was, in a land of so many possibilities, where should it be located?

During our next visit, in 1991, Earl Green, the chief forest officer, and John Howell, the Tropical Forestry Action Plan advisor, suggested that we might do well to build the research station in the Chiquibul Forest. The Chiquibul was then more or less inaccessible, and although it offered the most exciting opportunity of all, it seemed, in every respect, to be beyond our wildest dreams. Attempting to get there in a Forest Department Land Rover proved impossible; we became hopelessly bogged down shortly beyond the Guacamallo Bridge. Undeterred, the decision was made for the Forest Department and the Natural History Museum to build a research station at Las Cuevas. Marcus Matthews was recruited to lead the project, ably supported by Nicodemus "Chapal" Bol and his wife, Celia. My first night at Las Cuevas was at the end of the second Joint Services Expedition to the Upper Raspaculo River in 1993. The excitement of exploring the forest and caves, together with the chorus of frogs, made it impossible to sleep. Thanks to extraordinary support from the British Forces, the research station was grander than we could have imagined and soon established itself as a superb base for research and conservation projects. Later, John Howell came out of retirement to head up Las Cuevas Research Station, and he was followed in turn by Chris Minty, who was awarded an MBE for his work there, and Sam Bridgewater.

Today Las Cuevas is thriving under the leadership of Chapal and is managed, as it should be, by the Las Cuevas Trust, a Belizean NGO. Scientists from the NHM continue to be involved, but now a cluster of international organizations, including the Conservation Management Institute of Virginia Polytechnic Institute and State University, Acadia University, and the Royal Botanic Garden Edinburgh work alongside the University of Belize, Friends for Conservation and Development, and the Belize Forest Department to keep Las Cuevas thriving. When I last visited Belize, in 2004, I was delighted to hear several representatives of the Belize government say what a significant part the station had played in the conservation of the Chiquibul Forest. The accumulated scientific papers and reports testify to the importance of the Chiquibul and Belize. But until the publication of this new book there has been no synthesis of the biodiversity and ecology of what is now, at long last, properly recognized as one of the most significant centers of biodiversity in Central America. Thanks to Sam Bridgewater, the secret is now out!

Professor Stephen Blackmore,
Regius Keeper, Royal Botanic Garden Edinburgh
FELLOW OF THE ROYAL SOCIETY OF EDINBURGH

ACKNOWLEDGMENTS

THIS BOOK COULD NOT HAVE BEEN WRITTEN without the help of a great many people. First and foremost are the staff members of Las Cuevas Research Station, who have kept the facility operational over the years despite considerable financial and logistical challenges. Particular thanks are due to Nicodemus ("Chapal") and Celia Bol, who have been the heart and soul of the station, always providing a warm welcome to visitors, keeping them safe, and catering tirelessly to their needs. Chapal's tragic death in 2011 is a great loss to the facility. His love of, respect for, and knowledge of the jungle made him uniquely adapted to the position of Operations Manager and, subsequently, Station Manager. With him, the station and the Chiquibul forest have lost their staunchest supporter and a tireless campaigner.

The book's foundation is the science of the researchers who have visited the facility over the years, and it is hoped that the contents does justice to their endeavors. The author takes responsibility should there be any misrepresentation of their research findings. The science underpinning the book is credited to the original authors through endnotes. Numerous individuals have provided photographs for the book and are credited alongside their images.

Las Cuevas was established with financial assistance from the British High Commission (BHC) in Belize and constructed by the Royal Engineers of the British Army. The station has enjoyed support from the British government and the British Army Training Support Unit Belize (BATSUB) throughout its life. Thanks are specifically due to His Excellency Gordon Baker of the BHC, the Right Honorable David Gibson of the Belize government, and Earl Green of the Belize Forest Department, all of whom were instrumental in establishing the operating memorandum of understanding between the NHM and the government of Belize.

Thanks are due to the libraries of the Natural History Museum in London and the Royal Botanic Garden Edinburgh, and to individual researchers who have contributed sections to the book, including Chris Minty, Steve Javorek, and Bruce Miller. The book has also benefited from discussions with many other people. In particular, thanks are due to Jim Ratter, Peter Furley, Vanessa Plana, Elizabeth Graham, Percival Cho, Zoë Goodwin, David Harris, William Milliken, and Julie Jones. The author has also benefited from the friendship and knowledge of many people in Belize who encouraged the completion of this work. Thanks are due to Judy and Heather Duuploy and Brett Adams of the Belize Botanic Gardens; Jan Meerman; Paul Walker; Elma Kay; and Steven Brewer.

Finally, I would like to thank Carolyn Petersen and my parents for their continuous support throughout the book's preparation.

A NATURAL HISTORY OF

BELIZE

INTRODUCTION

CHRIS MINTY & SAMUEL BRIDGEWATER

THE MAYA FOREST IS THE SECOND-LARGEST continuous expanse of moist tropical forest in South and Central America after Amazonia. Battered by hurricanes for millions of years, occupied by Maya Indians for thousand of years, and logged for hundreds of years, the continued existence of this forest into the twenty-first century is a testament to its remarkable ecological resilience.

Despite its history of disturbance, or maybe because of it, the Maya Forest is ranked as an important global biodiversity hotspot. It occurs within the confines of Central America, which itself is recognized as one of the most significant ecological areas in the world on account of its great biological diversity and the unusually high number of animals and plants unique to the region. Stretching across the Yucatán region of southern Mexico, Belize, and northern Guatemala and extending into peripheral areas of southern Guatemala, Honduras, and El Salvador, the Maya Forest is known locally as La Selva Maya. Its wildlife includes a range of animal species unknown even from other parts of Central America, including eleven species of mammals, twenty species of birds, thirty-nine species of reptiles, and eleven species of amphibians. It is also a center of plant diversity; provides some of the last regional habitats for endangered species such as the jaguar, the scarlet macaw, Baird's tapir, and Morelet's crocodile; and forms a critical component of the internationally supported Mesoamerican Biological Corridor, which was conceived with the aim of maintaining regional ecological connectivity across Central America. As such, La Selva Maya is considered a top priority for conservation protection by many international organizations.

View across the rolling forest landscape of the Chiquibul. © William Milliken.

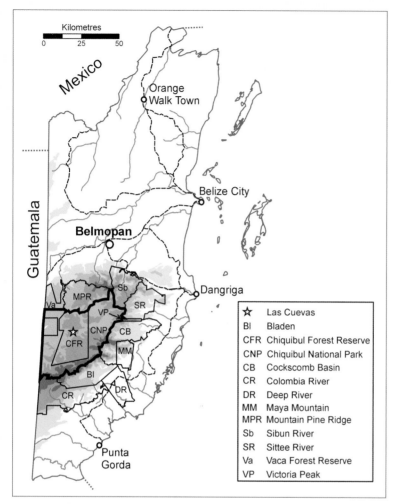

Topographical map of Belize showing the location of all reserve areas within the Maya Mountains Key Biodiversity Area. The extent of the Chiquibul Forest is highlighted in bold. © Iain Cameron. Courtesy of the Geography Department, School of Geosciences, Edinburgh University.

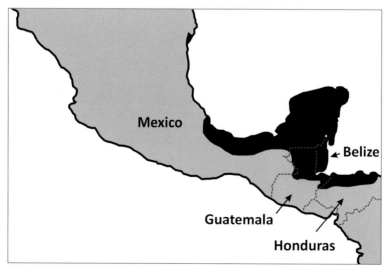

Map showing the extent of the core area of the lowland "Maya Forest" (La Selva Maya). The location of Belize on the Caribbean coast of Central America to the east of Guatemala and south of the Yucatán region of southern Mexico is shown.

When combined with the Caracol Archaeological Reserve that lies within its confines, the Chiquibul Forest covers 177,000 hectares of the Maya Mountain Massif of Belize and is an integral part of the wider international Maya Forest. Bordered and buffered by eight complementary national Belizean reserves, the Chiquibul Forest is also contiguous with adjacent protected areas in the Petén region of Guatemala. Together these conservation units cover an area of outstanding natural beauty in excess of 500,000 hectares and encompass what is known as the Chiquibul-Maya Mountains Key Biodiversity Area (CMMKBA).

HISTORICAL CONTEXT

Three centuries ago the Spanish and British fought over Belize's natural resources. Spain claimed territorial rights over this entire section of Central America, although Britain held colonial settlements in the small coastal territory that would later become known as British Honduras and eventually Belize. In 1859 a treaty between Guatemala (which had become independent from Spain in 1821) and Britain sought to end the dispute over the boundaries between Guatemala and British Honduras. The agreed frontier ran north to south directly through the dense forest now known as the Chiquibul. The treaty obligated both parties to jointly improve trade and establish communication between the countries by means of a road from Guatemala City in the west to the British settlement on the coast in the east. Eighty years later, however, Guatemala declared the treaty void, claiming that Britain had not upheld its part of the agreement. Dispute and conflict over the border has dominated the politics of the region ever since and remains a cause of fluctuating tension today. While the border is still contested, its general location is visible when viewed from space, with satellite images revealing a reasonably clear demarcation line: forest generally occurs on the Belizean side to the east, with urban development and agricultural areas tending to define the Guatemalan side to the west.

Long before any border disputes, in fact long before any demarcated borders, the forest was home to the sophisticated and culturally advanced Maya civilization. Even during this era, however, territorial conflicts existed between adjacent city-states, with regional centers of power waxing and waning in their sphere of influence. With a population believed to have reached close to four million at its peak, the lowland Maya dominated the land for three thousand years. Their traditional territory extended from the southeastern Mexican states into Guatemala and included Belize, northern Honduras, and parts of El Salvador. This was a civilization that rose from the very depths of the tropical forest and initially flourished within it, although the Maya undoubtedly cleared great tracts of forest as their civilization grew. Archaeologists have discovered Mayan settlements, temples, and great cities throughout the region, with the center of this culture focused on the southern lowlands of the Yucatán Peninsula. The large, internationally famous Caracol Maya archaeological site, for example, is located within the heart of the Chiquibul Forest. Reputedly stretching over sixty-five square miles, at its height this city and its immediate environs had a population of more than 120,000. Indeed, it is difficult to walk anywhere in the Chiquibul jungle today without stumbling across the crumbling remains of past Mayan occupation. The evidence suggests that much of the area we know as forest today was replaced by an agricultural landscape during this period. As the Maya Classic period progressed from ca. AD 250 onward, large-scale agriculture, construction, and urbanization initiated a period of unprecedented cultural and religious development. The Maya developed an empire that consisted of numerous independent and interdependent states, including the famous archaeological sites of Palenque (Mexico), Copán (Honduras), and Tikal (Guatemala). They participated in long-distance trade, not just among themselves but also with other neighboring Amerindian groups. Goods such as salt, cotton, fish, cacao, jade, and obsidian fueled their growing economies. As their population grew, they learned how to make marginal land agriculturally productive and farmed steep hillsides and swamps. They domesticated animals. They had scientists, astronomers, and teachers who studied the skies and seasons and developed complex systems for reading, writing, and arithmetic. They had rulers, statesmen, and priests, who made laws, formed governments, initiated wars, and predicted catastrophic events.

However, during and subsequent to the ninth century, in a period known as the Terminal Classic, many lowland cities went into decline and were subsequently abandoned. The reasons for this remain shrouded in mystery and form part of the great Maya enigma. While no theory is universally accepted, some researchers support environmental and political explanations for the fall of regional city-centers, with warfare, crop failure, epidemic disease, and drought all variously invoked.

By the time the Spanish arrived in Central America six hundred years later in the early sixteenth century, some of the major centers of Maya population in Belize had been abandoned, leaving the lowland to be reclaimed by forest, although smaller towns and villages persisted in favored areas. In the 1600s British pirates and buccaneers who had previously been plying their trade pillaging Spanish ships in the Bay of Honduras discovered they could make a good living by cutting and selling logwood and, later, mahogany and Spanish cedar. These hardy men became known as the Baymen and originally settled to the north of what is now Belize City. The British and Spanish continued to have numerous disputes over ownership of the territory, but after the Baymen successfully won the Battle of St. George's Caye against the Spanish in 1798, the British gained full control of the settlement, affirmed by its subsequent appointment as a fully fledged colonial state in 1862. Forestry dominated the economic activity of the colony throughout much of its subsequent life, and as it flourished, logging pushed ever deeper into the inland territory, eventually encroaching into the Chiquibul in the early decades of the twentieth century. The influence of forestry suppressed the development of other social and economic activities, such as agriculture, although overexploitation of the country's timber resources and the appearance of new markets for natural wild-harvested products resulted in moderate diversification of forest use. Exports of chicle, the basis of chewing gum, extracted from the sapodilla tree (*Manilkara* spp.), strengthened the economy from the late 1800s. Indeed, the Chiquibul Forest derives its name from its association with the sapodilla (also known as chicle) tree. The fruits of allspice (*Pimenta dioca*) were also collected and exported as a preservative and culinary flavoring. However, over time these resources also became uneconomical to harvest and have not been extracted from Belize in significant quantities since the 1950s. With little financial incentive to keep them there, the British began to withdraw.

Maya pyramid at Caracol. The population of this abandoned city is thought to have exceeded 120,000 prior to the Maya "collapse." © William Milliken.

Mahogany logs are unloaded from the Chiquibul railway at Vaca Falls before they are floated down the Macal River, ca. 1925. © Belize Archives and Records Service.

In 1964 British Honduras attained self-government and in June 1973, in recognition of its developing national identity, the official name of the country was changed to Belize. Full independence, however, was not achieved until September 21, 1981. On this date George Price—the "father of the nation"—became the country's first prime minister. The government of Belize has alternated periodically ever since between the two main political forces, the People's United Party (PUP) and the United Democratic Party (UDP).

Today Belize has a population of approximately 300,000 and one of the lowest population densities in the region. Most of the country's populace live within the coastal and lowland zones centered upon the towns of Corozal, Orange Walk, Belize City, Dangriga, and Punta Gorda. Relatively few sizable settlements occur inland, with the notable exceptions of San Ignacio and Belmopan, the capital. The country is culturally diverse: much of the population consists of Mopan, Yucatec and Kekchi Maya and Mestizo, Creole and Garifuna peoples of Mesoamerican, European, and African extraction. In part, the current ethnic mix of Belize relates to the early days of the timber industry, when slaves were brought from Africa to cut logs. Over the last four decades there has been a steady increase in the population and cultural diversity of the country due to immigration from Guatemala and other neighboring Latin American countries, North America, Europe, the Middle East, and Asia. With this population increase there has been an associated increase in deforestation due to a rise in both intensive and traditional slash-and-burn agricultural practices. Part of the former is driven by the Mennonites, a group originating in the Netherlands that arrived in Belize via Mexico in 1958. Despite the forward march of development, Belize—unlike many Central American countries—still has much of its natural resources intact, with about a quarter of its territory under some form of protection, including ca. 167,000 hectares (4 percent) designated as National Park and ca. 380,000 hectares (9 percent) as Extractive Forest Reserve.

GEOGRAPHY

Belize is one of the smallest countries in Central America, measuring ca. 280 kilometers from north to south and 100 kilometers from east to west, with a land area of approximately 22,960 square kilometers. It is located on the eastern seaboard of the Yucatán Peninsula, with Mexico to the north and Guatemala to the south and west. The climate is subtropical, tempered by trade winds coming off the Caribbean Sea. The mean annual temperature ranges from 27°C in coastal districts to 21°C in the Maya Mountains, although there is considerable annual variation. Temperatures at Las Cuevas, for example, can fall below 10°C at night during the first three months of the year and rise as high as 39°C during the hottest month (May), although the average annual daily temperatures typically vary between 19°C (January) and 27°C (May). For the most part, across the country temperatures generally remain consistently hot, except when

Modern-day descendants of the ancient Maya frequently practice a form of slash-and-burn agriculture known as milpa cultivation. The forest is cut and burned before crops are planted. © Stephen Blackmore.

Belize experiences short-lived weather systems from the north (northers). The humidity of the country is also high, due in part to the influence of the trade winds collecting moisture over the Caribbean Sea before reaching the country. Despite its small size, annual precipitation varies greatly across the territory, with the south receiving four times as much as the north. Rainfall is not even throughout the year but highly seasonal—especially in the north of the country—with the dry season typically lasting between February and May. The annual rainfall at Las Cuevas varies between 1,500 and 1,800 millimeters, with the wettest months being July through to October.

Geographically the country can be divided into four distinct regions: the northern lowlands, the coastal plain, the offshore cays and atolls, and the Maya Mountains and their foothills.

The northern lowlands are characterized by broadleaf forest on limestone-derived alkaline soils, and pine savanna on sandy acidic soils of granitic, fluvial (riverine), and marine origin. Wetland swamps, freshwater rivers, and lagoons are also common throughout this region. One of Belize's most important export crops is sugarcane, with the industry centered in the northern districts of Orange Walk and Corozal. This region is also home to significant communities of agriculturally productive Mennonites, who have converted large tracts of forest to grow a broad range of crops, including rice, millet, corn, and sorghum and who supply much of the local markets with poultry and eggs.

Rice farming in Orange Walk District (northern Belize). © Sam Bridgewater.

Much of the coastal plain region is formed from erosional deposits of the rocks that form the Maya Mountains. Across this area the soils are frequently acidic and infertile and covered by various forms of pine savanna; however, soils of high fertility also exist, and such pockets in Stann Creek and Toledo Districts are often farmed for citrus and bananas, two other important export commodities. Mangrove forests line the country's coastal edge, although much of this ecosystem has been heavily cleared in recent years to make way for coastal developments.

Despite the wildlife attractions of the inland territory, the majority of Belize's tourists come to spend time exploring the offshore cays and atolls that form part of the second largest barrier reef in the world. Extending for 281 kilometers, this biodiverse ecosystem is one of Belize's greatest natural resources and the principal lure for the 250,000 international travelers that visit annually. Tourism is the country's most important service sector and represents over a fifth of the gross domestic product. The landscape of this region is dominated by sandy cays, and mangrove forest.

The Maya Mountains are a complex amalgamation of sedimentary, metamorphic, and igneous rocks, dominated by submontane and montane broadleaf forest. The area also includes the Mountain Pine Ridge, a region largely defined by dense forms of pine savanna over granitic and acidic metamorphic rocks. The geology of the inland part of this region dates back to the mid-Paleozoic era ca. 400 million years ago (MYA) and includes the area known as the Chiquibul. This national park and forest reserve area covers much of the northwestern part of the Maya Mountains and is underlain largely by metamorphosed sedimentary mudstones and shales supporting acidic soils of low fertility. Limestone was deposited over these substrates in all but the highest mountain areas during the Cretaceous era, when Belize lay under a shallow tropical sea. However, much of this calcium-rich bedrock has long since eroded. The resulting complex mosaic of lime-rich (to the west) and acid soils provides the canvas for the development of the rich assemblage of plant species characteristic of the Chiquibul today. Rolling karst hills with numerous subterranean caves dominate the western expanse of the area, with sloping mountainous terrain underlain by sedimentary and metamorphic bedrock defining the eastern region.

Belize is renowned for having one of the highest national proportions of its territory under some degree of protection. Although there is an extremely comprehensive network of conservation areas, in reality, some have become what the literature refers to as "paper parks" in the sense that they are legally designated but either lack strategic long-term visions and management plans or suffer from inadequate funding and protection. Many have also been encroached on by landless refugees from neighboring countries, are exploited legally and illegally for timber and extractive products, or suffer from internal agricultural incursions and settlements. Some are even threatened with losing their protected status altogether. Belize is currently experiencing relatively high rates of deforestation (about 2 percent per annum), and it is predicted that just under 60 percent of original forest cover will remain by 2020.

The management of protected areas in Belize is the subject of increasing debate as the country struggles to reconcile social and economic development with environmental protection. The pressures on protected areas are increasing as consumption of natural resources, coupled with agricultural expansion, fuels the demand for the release of land previously designated as conservation areas. The most recent manifestation of development threatening the ecological integrity of the Chiquibul region was the completion of the controversial hydroelectric Chalillo Dam in 2005. The main rivers of note running through the Chiquibul are the Raspaculo River, the Macal River, the Chiquibul River, the Ceibo Grande River, and the Ceibo Chico River. Together they provide the lifeline to many terrestrial species as well as to aquatic animals, particularly during the dry season, when food shortages and lack of water create particularly challenging conditions. The Chalillo Dam, located on the Macal River in the north of the region where it borders the Mountain Pine Ridge, has permanently inundated a significant proportion of the area's riverine habitat and altered the aquatic ecology of the region. Without doubt, the dam has had a serious environmental impact in the area, not least of which is the loss of crucial areas of habitat for endangered species, such as the Baird's tapir and the scarlet macaw. The dam has also greatly increased access into this previously remote region, and it is highly likely that other infrastructure projects will follow. This project was the second of three dams planned for this river system. The governmental rationale for the project was to increase the country's independence in electrical energy, much of which is currently imported from Mexico.

Aerial view of Five Blues Lake National Park, 2005. The lake famously drained away in 2006. © Sam Bridgewater.

THE CHIQUIBUL

Construction of the Chalillo Dam on the Macal River, 2004. After completion of the dam, the valley upstream was flooded. © William Milliken.

The western region of Belize known as the Chiquibul covers an area of some 177,000 hectares and is the largest protected area in the country. It includes the Caracol Archaeological Reserve (CAR), designated in 1995; the Chiquibul Forest Reserve (CFR), designated in 1956; and the Chiquibul National Park (CNP), designated in 1991. The CFR initially covered the majority of the area and was managed primarily for timber production. Mahogany (*Swietenia macrophylla*) and Spanish cedar (*Cedrela odorata*) were the primary species extracted, along with smaller amounts of other, secondary hardwoods, such as Santa Maria (*Calophyllum brasiliense*) and nargusta (*Terminalia amazonia*). Pine (*Pinus* spp.) has also been logged from islands of pine savanna occurring within the broadleaf forest. Intense lobbying by conservationists in the 1980s, however, led to part of the reserve being reclassified as a national park under the National Parks System Act in 1991. It remains legal to extract timber and other natural resources from the CFR under government license, although the national park area is theoretically inviolate. In the late 1990s, both boundaries were once again reevaluated, with the entire area redesignated in May 1998. These subsequent changes have been made to account for environmental, biodiversity, and timber production characteristics under the auspices of the Forest Planning and Management Project (FPMP). The boundaries have now been redrawn to encapsulate not only the core timber production area in the reserve and the protective buffer zone in the national park, but also a 100-hectare working circle around Las Cuevas Research Station, designated specifically to conduct research.

In addition to logging and large-scale governmental development projects, multiple critical issues face the conservation of biodiversity in the Chiquibul, including hunting, looting of Maya archaeological sites, and Guatemalan incursions for milpa farming. Some of these activities are associated with the *Chamaedorea* industry, which supplies a source of greenery for the international floricultural industry through the collection of the leaves of this widespread understory palm. This activity has occurred in the region throughout much of the last decade. Leaf harvesting was initially undertaken primarily by Guatemalans crossing the border illegally, although legal Belizean concessions were granted within the CFR in 2004. However, even in its legalized form, doubt remains regarding the sustainability of the industry.

It is clear that if conserved areas are to be managed sustainably, they need to compete effectively with other land uses in contributing to both the economic and social development of the country as well as in fulfilling Belize's obligations under the Convention of Biodiversity. Agencies with management responsibilities for protected areas therefore face a challenging situation requiring a strategic, multiuse approach that is both socioeconomically and ecologically sustainable. Accordingly, the management of protected areas in Belize has shifted considerably in recent years away from governmental control. A relatively new development is the appearance of joint-management agreements between nongovernmental organizations (NGOs) and the state, with a

diverse range of stakeholders involved in decision making. On June 1, 2007, one such agreement was signed between the Belize Forest Department and Friends for Conservation and Development (FCD), providing a continuous management presence in the Chiquibul for the first time. With funding from Conservation International through the Critical Ecosystem Partnership Fund (CEPF) and the Belizean Protected Areas Conservation Trust (PACT), FCD provides rangers who conduct patrols and man checkpoints within the forest to ensure that the environmental laws of Belize are being monitored and enforced. Previously, the limited resources of the Belize Forest Department meant that the state could maintain only a sporadic presence in this remote region. FCD has also facilitated formal discussions among key Belizean institutions and bilateral partners in Guatemala to produce a common vision for the Chiquibul and neighboring forest ecosystems. In addition, the Belize Forest Department is keen to consolidate many of the country's existing protected units into larger, ecologically resilient management areas; in the future it is possible that the fourteen national protected areas that cover the Maya Mountain Massif may be managed as a single entity.

TOP: The main accommodation and research block at Las Cuevas. © Sam Bridgewater. BOTTOM: A fruiting branch of *Trichilia erythrocarpa*, a member of the mahogany family (Meliaceae), ready to be pressed by a field botanist. © Sam Bridgewater.

LAS CUEVAS

In 1992 a Memorandum of Understanding was signed between the government of Belize and the Natural History Museum of London (NHM). Under its terms, a research station, with financial assistance from the British High Commission in Belize, was to be established in the Chiquibul Forest. Its mission was to document and make known the biological diversity of the area and contribute practical knowledge to the sustainable

FACING: Las Cuevas Research Station. © Sam Bridgewater.

development of the region. Constructed by British Army Engineers, Las Cuevas Research Station became operational two years later. The varied topography, geology, and hydrology and strong seasonality of rainfall within the region have combined to create a complex mosaic of ecosystems that has excited the interest of scientists. Since its establishment, researchers from around the world have visited the station to study the region's biodiversity. Operated by the Natural History Museum for the first decade of its life, management of the station is now the responsibility of the Las Cuevas Trust, a consortium of Belizean and international partners. In its early days the work at Las Cuevas focused on describing and recording the constituent species of the forest, playing to the taxonomic strengths of the NHM. In more recent years, however, there has been a rise in applied ecological projects. The importance of the scientific work conducted at Las Cuevas and at Belize's other ecological research stations is highlighted by the sobering fact that in the last fifty years more than 70 percent of Central America's natural vegetation cover has been cleared, and the wildlife that once occupied the region's vast swaths of jungle now survive in only a few fragmented pockets of forest, with the Maya Forest acting as a particularly important oasis of biodiversity within a sea of cultivated land. As Central America's population grows, agriculture devours ever more forest each year. There are many disturbing examples of countries that have almost entirely lost their biological heritage due to these pressures, compounded by urban expansion and the production of internationally traded commodities such as beef, coffee, and sugar. The Chiquibul and associated Belizean forest areas are unusual in that they still represent an area of outstanding biodiversity and are one of the last remaining true wilderness areas of Central America. It is here, more than anywhere in the region, that there is still a chance for nature in its full glory to be conserved and there exists the possibility of finding a balance between conservation and development—a balance that not only provides for the needs of the Belizean people but also safeguards the forest's rich biological heritage.

This book illustrates how science can help us understand the ecological foundations of the forest ecosystem and, in so doing, improve our ability to protect and manage it wisely. It draws on local and regional research findings to provide a popular portrait of the biodiverse and resilient Chiquibul. It does not provide the last word on the matter—no natural history book ever can—as much remains to be discovered. There are also considerable disciplinary biases related to the focus of the scientists that have visited the area. Research in the region is ongoing, and every year scientists return to Las Cuevas to continue their studies. As new data is collected, theories are amended and species records updated. Of necessity, much subject matter has been omitted from the book due to the constraints of space. Thus, for example, insects are not included. This super-diverse and ecologically important group deserves a book in its own right, although it may be many years before the information exists for such a book to be written. As in most tropical regions, insects remain among the poorest studied and the least understood class of animals, despite being of critical conservation significance. Nevertheless, regardless of its shortcomings, this book provides what we believe is a useful summary of the current state of ecological knowledge for the area, interpreting and presenting information from an extensive series of specialist peer-reviewed papers, reports, and theses of wide taxonomic, ecological, and conservation focus and placing this information in the public domain. In so doing, it is hoped that this book will stimulate further research within the Chiquibul and facilitate enjoyment, understanding, and the conservation of this fabulous region.

Dawn breaks over the Chiquibul. © Sam Bridgewater.

OUT OF THE OCEAN

THE ORIGINS OF BELIZEAN LIFE

1

AS A SMALL COUNTRY territorially squeezed into a few hundred kilometers of Caribbean coast, Belize cannot boast about its size. However, its rich biological diversity is world-renowned and the envy of countries many times its area. From the fringing mangroves of the low-lying coastal areas to the elfin woodlands of its highest peaks, Belize has an estimated eighty-five terrestrial ecosystems encompassing many forms of forest, savanna, and swamp vegetation. They harbor an impressive range of plant and animal species, and it is no surprise that ecotourists and researchers from around the world choose Belize as their preferred location for leisure or as a center for scientific study.

The great diversity of life found in many subtropical and tropical countries poses fundamental scientific questions that have been puzzling researchers for generations. Not least of these is why, for example, are tropical countries often so biologically diverse while temperate regions are comparatively poor in species, and when and how did this multitude of species arise? Belize has a part to play in providing insights into the origin and maintenance of our planet's diversity. Its varied terrain, heterogeneous patchwork of vegetation types, and plant and animal diversity reflect not only its current and past climate but also its underlying bedrock and soils. These in turn owe their existence to millions of years of dynamic geological and climatological history.

To understand why Belize is so biologically fascinating today, we must trace its history back through time. We must go beyond the era of the multiple ice ages starting 2 MYA, when the world's temperate regions lay largely under ice, and even beyond the Jurassic era of the dinosaurs 200 MYA, when much of Belize's territory lay accumulating lime-rich sediment under a shallow tropical sea. To begin at the beginning, we must travel, if not back to the origins of the earth itself (ca. 4.6 billion years ago), then at least deep into the Paleozoic era over 359 MYA—a time when most of the world's continents were joined into a single massive super-landmass called Pangaea and when the world's flora was dominated not by flowering plants, as it is today, but by flowerless primeval forests of club mosses and horsetails.

This chapter provides an overview of the origin of Belize and Belizean life. It begins with a brief geological history of Belize and continues with an examination of the scientific evidence that has helped to clarify the relative antiquity and varying geographic origins of its plant groups. The chapter concludes with a discussion of the major events that have shaped Belize's existing fauna. This includes an examination of the Great American Interchange and an explanation of the theories that seek to explain why tropical biotas are so diverse.

THE BIRTH OF BELIZE:
A BRIEF GEOLOGICAL HISTORY

The existence and characteristic shape of Central America is a relatively recent phenomenon. The stretch of land that now unites North and South America, and of which Belize forms a part, initially existed only as a series of islands. As a result of tectonic activity and drops in sea level during the Pliocene epoch (ca. 5.3–1.8 MYA), these islands became connected over time into a single landmass, with the Panamanian land bridge finally complete 3 MYA. However, many of the component geological parts of Central American landforms were created by more ancient processes. At the time the rocks that now form Belize's Maya Mountains were being laid down in the Devonian period over 359 MYA, the two prehistoric continents Laurasia and Gondwana were beginning to converge to form the "super landmass" of Pangaea. Gondwana comprised all the landmasses of the present-day Southern Hemisphere (Antarctica, South America,

Africa, Madagascar, New Guinea, Australia, and New Zealand, as well as India and Arabia), with Laurasia including what we now know as North America, Europe, Siberia, and China and parts of Southeast Asia. Since the formation of Pangaea, continental drift, changes in sea level due to climate fluctuations, and geological activity have interacted to produce the landscapes we can identify today. Pangaea began to split apart through plate tectonics during the Jurassic period (ca. 200–146 MYA), with the component Gondwana and Laurasia reforming and beginning to fragment themselves in the Cretaceous era (146–66 MYA), marking the beginning of the birth of the continents as we know them today. South America began to split apart from Africa about 100 MYA.

The fruiting structure of *Heliconia latispatha*, a common species of disturbed areas. The bright-colored bracts are characteristic of the Heliconiaceae family, which is believed to have diverged from its closest evolutionary ancestors about 60 MYA.
© Sam Bridgewater.

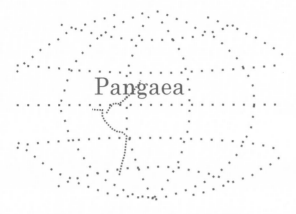

Pangaea

Permian ca. 225 MYA

Laurasia

Gondwana

Triassic ca. 200 MYA

Jurassic ca. 135 MYA

Cretaceous ca. 65 MYA

Present day

The approximate positions of the world's continents through geologic time to the present day.

There is a great amount of scientific literature listing dates for the earth's major geological periods and events. Although different academic sources are in general agreement over approximate dates, there is considerable variation in the finer details. For geological dates, this book follows the 2004 edition of *A Geologic Time Scale*, published under the auspices of the International Commission on Stratigraphy.[1] Dates for major movements of the earth's crusts (tectonic events) follow those given by Stephen McLoughlin in his 2001 research paper on the breakup of Gondwana.[2] It is hard for those not familiar with the geological time scale to associate actual dates with the terms used by academics to define distinct periods. In addition, few of us are familiar with geological sequences. For this reason, when a geological period (e.g., Jurassic) is mentioned in the text, it is followed by the dates that define it, with the time scale used being "millions of years ago" (MYA). Thus, "Jurassic" will appear in the text as "Jurassic (200–146 MYA)." The defining dates are rounded up to the nearest million years.

Humans are relatively short-lived, and few of us will ever survive to celebrate our hundredth birthday. Our general concept of time reflects our transience on this planet, and seconds, minutes, hours, days, weeks, months, and years are the basic measures we use to track our passing through life. When we discuss human history, we need to expand our concept of time; centuries and millennia are the intervals used by scientists when describing our ancestors. Geologists, however, must use a completely different clock,

since the history of our planet is measured in thousands of millions of years and almost surpasses our comprehension. To this end, a precise terminology has been developed to help communicate the time periods and associated events that have defined the earth's history. The largest period of time is called an aeon (e.g., Mesozoic aeon). This can be divided into two or more periods (e.g., Cretaceous period), which in turn can be further subdivided into two or more epochs (e.g., Lower Cretaceous epoch), which itself can be split into ages (e.g., Aptian age). The use of the geologic terminology can be confusing. A chart visually representing geologic time is indispensable when considering the earth's history, and a simplified one is provided on page 23. Traditionally, geological strata have been identified through the unique assemblages of fossils they contain. The existence of similar suites of fossils in rocks from around the world can be used to correlate them to similar geologic periods. Visible changes in fossil sequences allow relative age estimates of rocks. For example, rocks containing ammonites are always older than those containing mammal bones. This is known because the geologic strata within which ammonites are found occur below the first rocks where mammals first appear; as a general rule of thumb for sedimentary rocks, younger rocks overlie older ones. The development of radiocarbon dating now enables relatively precise estimations of age to be given to rock formations, and the earth's history is known to date back about 4.6 billion years.

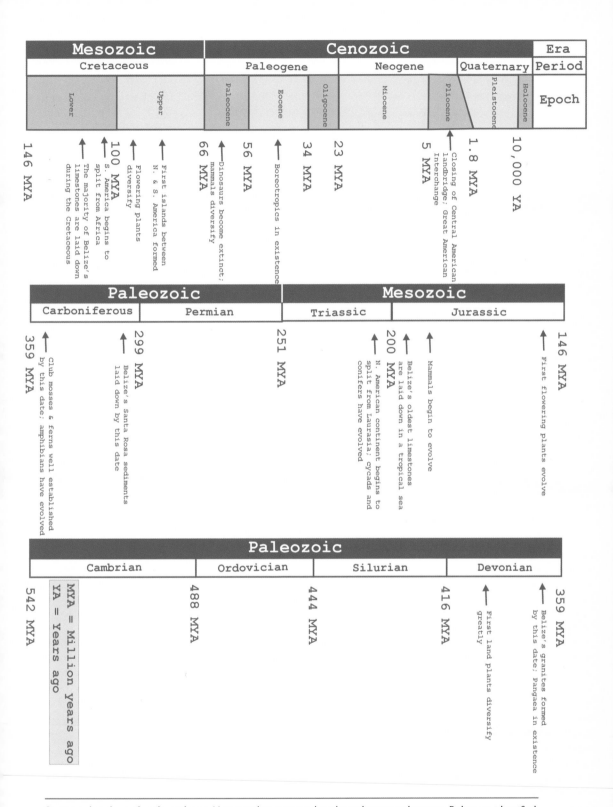

Stratigraphic chart of geological eras. Major evolutionary and geological events relevant to Belize are identified.

GRANITE AND LIMESTONE:
FROM THE OLD TO THE NEW

The oldest rocks in Belize are granites believed to date back to the Devonian (416–359 MYA) or even Silurian period (444–416 MYA).[3] These earliest rock formations now underlie the Mountain Pine Ridge and much of the Cockscomb Basin, and they outcrop in parts of the Hummingbird and Mullins Rivers. Granite is an igneous rock, formed when magma from the earth's interior cools and solidifies. These earliest Belizean granites are predominantly found as structures known as plutons, meaning that the magma cooled and solidified below the earth's surface rather than above it.

The second-oldest rocks belong to what regional geologists call the Santa Rosa Group and date back to the Carboniferous and Permian periods (359–251 MYA) at the time the supercontinent Pangaea was beginning to form.[4] These comprise a mixture of sedimentary rocks, including sandstones, conglomerates, mudstones, and shales, although much has been physically and chemically altered (metamorphosed) by a combination of heat and/or pressure. Most famously associated with the bedrock of the Maya Mountains, outcrops of these rocks can also be seen elsewhere in southern Belize,[5] and they likely underlie many more recent geologic formations. The different Santa Rosa rock formations were formed by the erosion of other preexisting rock materials by wind or water, with the subsequent deposition of the debris in lakes, lagoons, and oceans. Over time, the layers of sediment built up, forming rock as the lower layers became compacted by the pressure of the material above. The specific type of rock created depended on the type of compacted sediment. Sandstones are made from quartz and feldspar minerals, and these can be seen, for example, at Baldy Beacon. In contrast, mudstone is formed by the deposition of much finer-grained clay material and is typical across much of the Maya Mountain region. The exact origin of these Santa Rosa sedimentary rocks is uncertain, although the material will have derived from erosion of the rocks that formed the supercontinents. Recent research comparing the chemical composition of the Santa Rosa rocks and Belize's older granitic plutons suggests that in some areas erosion of the plutons may have led to the formation of the sedimentary rock.[6]

Subsequent to their formation, large areas of these sedimentary rocks became metamorphosed. This may have been due to contact with molten magma, tectonic forces in the earth's crust, or the weight of overlying rock formations. During the period when the Santa Rosa sediments were being formed and altered, there was also volcanic activity producing lava flows and ash, which later consolidated into volcanic rock. A good example of this is the solidified lava flows and tuffs (compressed ash) that can be seen today as a strip of rock on the southern boundary of the Maya Mountains to the north of Bladen Branch.[7] Unlike granitic plutons, these subsequent igneous formations were extruded (i.e., they cooled above ground rather than below it), and hence their form and structure is smaller grained. Sometime at the end of the Jurassic period and the beginning of the Cretaceous (146 MYA), further sedimentary deposits occurred during a time when the climate was hot.[8] These make up Belize's "continental red beds" and are part of what geologists call the Todos Santos formation. Their distinctive color is due to iron oxide in their mineral structure. They can be seen only in a few isolated places in Belize today, including close to Punta Gorda.

Belize is perhaps best known for its limestone and dolomite, which cover over 50 percent of its territory.[9] These were the last major rock formations to be laid down. Limestone is a special sedimentary rock formed by the compacted calcite (calcium carbonate) shells of marine organisms and corals typically laid down in shallow tropical seas. Under special conditions favored by the presence of magnesium-rich water, calcite deposits can change structurally and chemically to produce dolomite— $CaMg(CO_3)_2$. This differs from limestone in containing magnesium.

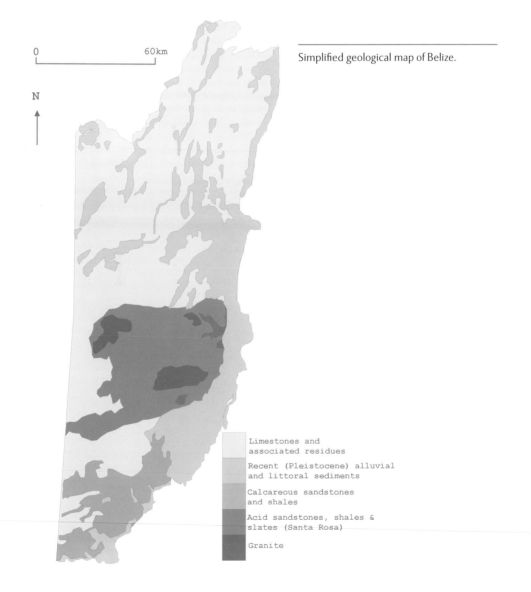

0   60km

N

Simplified geological map of Belize.

Limestones and associated residues

Recent (Pleistocene) alluvial and littoral sediments

Calcareous sandstones and shales

Acid sandstones, shales & slates (Santa Rosa)

Granite

For much of geological history Belize was submerged under sea, and its lime-rich rocks were laid down during these episodes. The oldest limestones date back to the start of the Jurassic period, 200 MYA, when Pangaea was beginning to fragment, although most were laid down during the subsequent Cretaceous period (146–66 MYA). The most recent limestones arose during the Paleogene and Neogene periods (66–1.8 MYA)[10] during times of regional land subsidence when the world's continents were almost in their current positions. The majority of Belize's older limestone occurs primarily in an arc to the north, west, and south of the Santa Rosa sediments of the Maya Mountains, the largest continuous extension comprising the Vaca Plateau, the western and southernmost portions of the Chiquibul Forest Reserve, and the western areas of the Chiquibul National Park. The younger limestones occur principally in the north and south of the country.

Although Belize's main rock formations were all laid down by 1.8 MYA, in more recent times, during the Quaternary period (1.8 MYA–present), there has been constant erosion of all the preexisting rocks by rain and river action. This has transferred and deposited sediments from higher to lower-lying regions. However, there has been insufficient time for the majority of these sediments to consolidate and form solid rock. Much of the coastal plain occurs on such relatively recent alluvial deposits, and some of Belize's savanna formations, for example, occur on recently deposited infertile sands eroded from the Maya Mountains.

Limestone cliffs in Cayo District. For much of geological history, Belize was submerged under a shallow tropical sea. During this time limestone was laid down, with this bedrock defining large areas of the national landscape. © Sam Bridgewater.

Publications describing Belize's geology date back over one hundred years. Although not the earliest written account, one of the first classic and detailed texts to be published was produced by Karl Sapper, a German explorer, geographer, and polymath who traveled across Central America at the end of the nineteenth century. Despite traveling largely by foot, Sapper explored and documented the region's forests, mountains, and indigenous cultures. His astute observations and maps provided an important source of geological information for the next fifty years.[11] In 1928 another classic text focusing on Belize was published by Leslie Ower, a geologist assigned to the colony by the British government.[12] His "Geology of British Honduras" summarized the existing knowledge about Belize's rock forms and provided the first geological map for the country. Between 1951 and 1955, C. G. Dixon, another British geologist, prepared an updated geological map of the country and investigated the country's mineral potential.[13] Belize's classic geological text, however, and one still frequently cited was published in 1977 by geologists James Bateson and Ian Hall.[14] Focusing on the Maya Mountains, their work is regarded as one of the seminal geological publications of the country. Although their findings have since been updated and the last thirty years have seen great advances in our understanding of Belizean geology, this work still stands as a superb contribution to our understanding of Belize's ancient history.

CURIOUS KARST

The calcite (calcium carbonate–$CaCO_3$) that forms limestone is readily dissolved by water. Rainwater is generally lightly acidic in nature due to the combining of moisture in the air with atmospheric CO_2 to create carbonic acid (H_2CO_3). This natural acidity can be further elevated once rain has fallen and run over acid rocks and soils. If this water passes over limestone, it starts to dissolve the rock over which it flows, eventually forming striking and often curious features, such as caves, rolling hills, cliffs, towers, sinkholes, and underground rivers. Geographers call this kind of landscape karst, and in the case of Belize, the limestone areas most conspicuously sculpted by water in this way are those of the Cretaceous age.[15] It is believed that much of the karstification of the limestone occurred relatively recently during the last 10,000 years (i.e., the Holocene). However, one age estimate for the Chiquibul Cavern, based on a study of the decay of uranium isotopes in stalagmites, suggests that this system was forming at least 700,000 years ago.[16]

The western Chiquibul and Vaca Forest Reserves form the largest karstic areas in Belize, although significant areas can also be seen, for example, to the east of the Western Highway in the vicinity of Gracie Rock and the Manatee Forest Reserve, within the Columbia River Forest Reserve, and at Caves Branch along the Hummingbird Highway. Some of these areas are defined by many small dome-shaped hills with depressions (dolines or sinks) of varying sizes between them. Such areas are called cockpit karst, first described and named from similar formations in Jamaica. It is said that the name derives from the clandestine cockfighting that used to take place, hidden in the depressions of the rock.

Belize has a large quantity of world-famous cave systems scattered throughout its karst. Although over 150 kilometers of underground passages have been surveyed, many remain a mystery and have yet to be fully explored. Limestone caves often contain stalactites and stalagmites, which sometimes join to create beautiful and striking pillar formations. Both stalactites and stalagmites are formed by the deposition of calcite from dripping water, with the former descending from the roof of a cave and the latter rising from its base. Belize's caves share a number of features that are considered relatively rare elsewhere in the world.[17] These include "shields" or "palettes," which are disk-shaped depositions of calcite resulting from water slowly seeping from cracks in cave walls, and bellholes, which are upward-tapering cavities in the cave ceilings. It is believed that the latter are due to long-term localized and concentrated bat-roosting. Such is the preponderance of caves in Belize that many place-names refer to them. Las Cuevas Research Station itself is named in recognition of the preponderance of caves (*cuevas*) in the surrounding area, and a large nearby cave supplies its water. The most famous of the area's caves is the Chiquibul Cavern (see boxed text), which lies to the west of the field station. This was the subject of a National Geographic article in 2000.[18] That there are so few readily available sources of water in the Chiquibul region is due to its karstic nature, with the majority of streams and rivers flowing underground.

A view into the forest from the cave that supplies Las Cuevas Research Station with its water.
© William Milliken.

Nohoch Ch'en sinkhole, Chiquibul Forest Reserve. © Alastair Rogers.

THE CHIQUIBUL CAVERN AND THE GREAT WELL

The immense, meandering Chiquibul Cavern forms a subterranean link between Belize and Guatemala and extends for over sixty-five kilometers deep beneath the forest floor.[19] Within its network of passages, underground canals, chambers, and sumps lies the magnificent Belize Chamber. At 1,600 feet long by 600 feet wide, this cathedral-like space is the largest known cave room in the Western Hemisphere.[20] The presence of artifacts within the accessible areas of the cave proves that the ancient Maya once used it as a source of water and as a sacred place for conducting rituals. The cave was rediscovered only as late as 1984, and since that time it has been the focus of numerous caving and scientific expeditions. Biologists, for example, have discovered the skeletons of extinct animals within it, including a species of vampire bat (*Desmodus draculae*) and a female cub of a species of bear (*Tremarctos floridanus*). Another famous karstic site situated in the limestone area of the Chiquibul is the sinkhole called Nohoch Ch'en (Maya for "great well"). This dramatic feature represents a collapsed cave system in which the walls have remained but the roof has fallen, creating a lost world hidden deep below the jungle floor. This landform was first explored scientifically by the New Millennium Expedition in 2000.[21]

CONTINENTAL COLLISION:
BELIZE'S TECTONIC HISTORY

Belize's rock formations are a physical testament of its dynamic origins. Many separate, complicated tectonic and climatic events have combined through geologic time to mold Belize's current form. These are still imperfectly understood but have involved continental drift and the collision, uplifting, and deformation of regional rock formations due to movements in the earth's crust. In addition, volcanic activity, subsidence, and sedimentation, the shearing and faulting of land due to tectonic pressure, and changes in sea level during global interglacial periods have all played incisive roles.

Belize forms part of what geologists call the Maya Terrane. This land block was originally part of the great Pangaea landmass and, subsequently, the most southerly North American part of Laurasia after the breakup of the supercontinent during the Jurassic period (200–146 MYA). After North America split from the remainder of Pangaea and Laurasia, it moved westward, driven by the formation of new rock along the Mid-Atlantic Ridge. The Maya Terrane moved with the North American plate, eventually to underlie the Yucatán of Mexico, Belize, and the Petén region of Guatemala. For most of this period of continental drift, the Maya Terrane was submerged under the sea, and it was during this period that limestones were deposited, forming a sequence of rock more than three thousand meters thick in places. This would originally have covered almost all of the earlier-formed granites and Santa Rosa sedimentary and metamorphic rocks comprising the bedrock of what we now know as the Maya Mountains. However, much of the limestone has since been eroded to reveal these more ancient geological features.

As the worlds' continents continued to move apart during the Cretaceous period (146–66 MYA), there was no land connection between North and South America, which remained separated from each other by ocean. Around 80 MYA, a complex series of collisions and associated subductions between the oceanic Farallón plate, the North American plate, and the Caribbean plate formed a series of volcanic islands that would eventually form the Greater Antilles (Hispaniola, Jamaica, and Cuba) and, from about 11 MYA, parts of mainland Central America. At this time, the global climate was cooling and the ice caps at the poles were beginning to expand, causing the sea level to drop and increasing the land areas above water between North and South America. By the late Miocene (7–5 MYA), Central America still comprised a region of scattered islands, but the depth of the sea between them was becoming increasingly shallow. A further drop in sea level, the deposition of sediments into the shallow stretches of sea between the island areas, and tectonic uplift conspired to close the last remaining sea gaps between the islands, and about 3 MYA Central America as we know it today was born.

Few episodes in the world's ancient history have excited as much scientific curiosity as the cataclysmic event, or series of events, that precipitated the extinction of the dinosaurs ca. 65 MYA. This extinction episode is of particular interest to our species, as the demise of the dinosaurs heralded the rise of the time of mammals, the taxonomic group to which we belong. The point that marks this monumental change in our fossil record distinguishes the Cretaceous (K) from the Tertiary (T) geological periods and is called the K-T boundary. Its presence can be seen in certain geological formations of that age as a distinct layer of clay. One widely accepted theory put forward in part to explain this event is that the earth was hit by a meteor north of Belize adjacent to the Yucatán Peninsula (Mexico), forming the 150-kilometer-wide Chicxulub Crater. Evidence supporting this theory is the presence of iridium in rock formations associated with the K-T boundary. This element is rare in terrestrial rocks but relatively common in asteroids. In addition, tiny glass-like structures called spherules are also common at the geological boundary layer, and these are typically produced by explosive events involving rocks. Such spherules have been found in Belize's Albion Island quarry, 360 kilometers to the south of the Chicxulub Crater, and have been interpreted as ballistic fallout from an asteroid's impact. It is not known exactly what the effects of such an impact might have been, but global fires, acid rain, short- and long-term climate change, and tsunami effects have all been intimated as possible factors causing widespread extinctions. A tidal wave caused by the impact may have flooded the entire Caribbean region, extirpating all life below a certain altitude, with the highest peaks of the Maya Divide hypothesized as remaining unaffected, acting as potential refugia for species wiped out elsewhere.

The Maya Mountains of Belize are particular interesting in terms of their tectonic history. In addition to representing the only exposed outcrop of rocks of ancient Paleozoic age in the region, the whole massif has been folded by tectonic pressure, and it dips to the west at an angle of approximately 10 degrees. The area also represents what geologists call a horst, which is an uplifted block of the earth's crust between parallel faults. It is believed that this occurred sometime during the Cretaceous period (146–66 MYA).

There has been tectonic movement elsewhere in Belize, and its rocks are bisected by numerous fault lines. For example, relatively recent faulting of limestone during the Paleogene and Neogene periods (66–1.8 MYA) can be seen in northern Belize at such sites as the Booth River and Rio Bravo Escarpments. Here fault lines run in an approximately northerly direction, the rock to the east of the fault having been thrown downward in relation to those rocks to the west.[22]

Interpreting the Belizean landscape is complicated but can be a hugely enjoyable experience for those with a detective's temperament. Not everything is as it might seem at first sight, however, and those conducting fieldwork, geological hammer in hand, would be wise to leave their preconceptions at home. As a rule of thumb, rocks that lie above others are generally younger, but tectonic movement and folding can quite literally turn the world on its head. In addition, although we take our bearings from what we see around us now, many of these features would not have been around at the time the rocks being investigated were formed. Areas now under the sea, for example, may once have been above water, while the sandstone rocks we now find far inland may have been formed along a relict coastline.[23]

The geology and climate of an area define the type of soil found, and the soils of the Chiquibul are discussed in chapter 2 (see "The Soil of the Chiquibul Forest Reserve"). Vegetation essentially maps soils, and the many plant species that together make up the regional flora each has its own evolutionary tale.

GOLD, OIL, AND DOLOMITE

Although Belize's rocks are not of the correct variety to yield precious gems such as diamonds, rubies, and emeralds, other valuable minerals can be found. Yet few occur in sufficient quantities to make their extraction economically viable. Molybdenum, for example, which is used in the production of steel alloys, has been found in the Maya Mountains associated with shales close to granite outcrops. Another mineral, barite, used in the manufacture of paints and paper, has been found associated with quartz veins in the Mountain Pine Ridge, while copper, lead, and zinc are known from similar veins occurring close to the Sibun River. Tin, in the form of its mineral oxide cassiterite, occurs in alluvial granite-derived gravels in the Maya Mountains; gold, occurring as small flakes associated with quartz veins, has been found in stream deposits, including at the Ceibo Grande and Ceibo Chico in the Chiquibul Forest.

Although there are tales of the ancient Maya working gold in some fabled part of the Maya Mountains, no significant lodes warranting a gold rush have been found in modern times, although since the late 1980s some successful prospecting has been undertaken under license in the alluvial fan of the Ceibo Chico area of the Chiquibul National Park.

Limestone and dolomite rocks are also economically valuable. Numerous small kilns along the Hummingbird Highway, for example, are used to convert limestone to lime for use as a fertilizer, and a dolomite mine exists close to Punta Gorda. Dolomite stone can be used ornamentally and in the manufacture of cement. Like lime, it is also used agriculturally and horticulturally for lowering the acidity of soil mixes, with the Belizean citrus and banana plantations benefiting from its application. The most recent excitement relating to the economic potential of Belize's geological formations is the discovery of oil at Spanish Lookout. Although prospectors have been searching for oil reservoirs hidden within Belize's limestone for over fifty years, it was only subsequent to 2004 that a commercial operation commenced. The relative quantities are believed to be small when compared with the much larger oil deposits held by Mexico, but they are significant nevertheless and are capable of producing a few thousand barrels per day. As Belize does not have its own refinery, the crude oil is currently loaded onto barges and shipped to the United States.

The most recent assessment of the Belizean vascular flora—which includes conifers, cycads, flowering plants, ferns, and club mosses but excludes mosses, liverworts, and lichens—lists 3,408 species for the territory.[24] This number would be significantly increased if nonvascular plants and lichens were included. However, botanists have yet to catalog accurately how many species of these poorly studied groups occur. If all of Belize's land plants are considered, then its flora comprises elements whose ancestral lines are of vastly different ages.

Club mosses and ferns, for example, are represented in Belize by 255 species. These two groups had already become well established on the planet before the onset of the Carboniferous period (359–299 MYA). Thus, present-day Belizean species represent the end of lineages lasting over 359 million years! Cycads and conifers, although appearing more recently in evolutionary history when compared with either club mosses or ferns, had already evolved as distinct groups by the Jurassic period (200 MYA). They are now represented in Belize by seven species. Today flowering plants (angiosperms) dominate Belize's flora, with 3,145 species represented. These are evolutionary youngsters, relatively speaking. Although they appear in the fossil record for the first time only at the end of the Jurassic period (146 MYA), it was not until the Cretaceous (146–66 MYA) that they diversified greatly to become the biggest and most successful group of plants on earth. Thus, Belize's flora can be considered to be a mixture of families of ancient and more recent lineages.

Certain periods of history have witnessed apparent explosions in species' evolution rates. For plants, these include the Devonian period (416–359 MYA), when the first land plants diversified greatly in form,

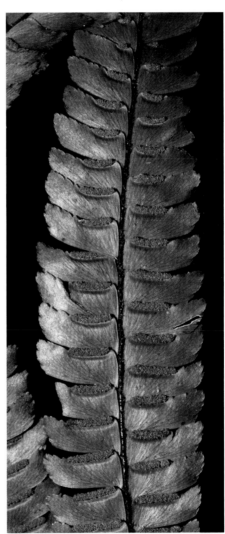

The typical arrangement of the spore-producing structures (sporangium) on the fern genus *Adiantum*. Ferns were well established by the Carboniferous period. © David Harris.

and the Cretaceous period (144-66 MYA), when flowering plants first became evident, radiating quickly to become the dominant group of the world's flora. The incredible diversification and ecological success of the angiosperms, in particular, have fascinated scientists for hundreds of years. Just as new species have periodically appeared, other groups have become extinct, and our knowledge of them is confined to the fossil record. Of all the species—both plants and animals—that have ever lived, only a tiny proportion can be seen alive today. Recreating the complete tree of life, therefore, is hugely problematic. The fossil record is only partially complete and thus gives us only glimpses into the past. Modern techniques for investigating the evolutionary relationships of organisms, including the use of DNA sequences and molecular clocks, are also imprecise, and disagreements continue as to when, and how, certain plant groups evolved.

Belize's major terrestrial plant groups are discussed in this section as they appear in the evolutionary record.

KINGDOMS AND DOMAINS: CLASSIFYING LIFE ON EARTH

The earliest biological classification systems developed by scientists such as Carl Linnaeus (1753) recognized two major forms of life—plants and animals—and the broad shoehorning of organisms into those that "move and eat" and those that "take root and photosynthesize" is one that most nonscientists intuitively understand. However, as our knowledge of the natural world improves and our ability to study it becomes more sophisticated, it has become apparent that this two-tiered classification system cannot comfortably accommodate all life on earth. For example, we now know that fungi are closely related, both chemically and structurally, to neither plants nor animals. Where, then, does one place them in the tree of life? There are many further complications; one of these relates to DNA. Every organism on earth has its own distinct genetic constitution held in its DNA. Biologists now classify all organisms as belonging to one of two

groups—prokaryotes and eukaryotes—based in part on how DNA is contained within the cell. Eukaryotes are single- or multicelled organisms whose DNA is stored within a distinct membrane-enclosed compartment within the cell called a nucleus. Prokaryotes differ in that they lack a distinct nucleus. Most prokaryotes are single-celled organisms and can be further divided into two groups: the bacteria and the archaea, which differ from each other in their metabolism and chemical composition.

In an attempt to reconcile all the broad forms of life into one classification system, scientists now generally place all organisms into one of three domains, Bacteria, Archaea, and Eukarya. The eukaryote domain can conveniently be thought to comprise four kingdoms—animals, plants, fungi, and protists, with the latter effectively a bunch of biological misfits largely defined by their dissimilarity to all other groups.

Epidendrum ciliare. The Orchidaceae family is famous for its range of pollination mechanisms. Orchid diversification is often explained in terms of the closely evolved association between pollinators and individual species of orchids. This group is believed to have evolved around 100 MYA. © Brett Adams. Courtesy of the Belize Botanic Garden.

CLUB MOSSES AND FERNS: LAND PLANTS OF ANCIENT EVOLUTIONARY LINEAGE

Seven species of club moss (Lycopodiopsida) are recorded for Belize,[25] of which three (*Huperzia dichaeoides, H. linifolia,* and *Lycopodiella cernua*) are recorded as growing within the Chiquibul.[26] Club mosses are an ancient group of plants that evolved just before the start of the Devonian era over 400 MYA, and despite their ancient origin, direct descendants of this group still exist, with 1,500 species known worldwide. Although comprising less that one percent of the world's current flora, in the Devonian and Carboniferous periods club mosses were one of the dominant groups of plants. The name "club moss" is misleading in that these plants are not a kind of moss at all but are more closely related to ferns and horsetails. Club mosses have simple scalelike leaves and basic internal transport systems; although existing species are small, during the Carboniferous era (359–299 MYA) some grew to heights in excess of thirty meters. Yet these "giant" club mosses were not as structurally sophisticated as our existing

The club moss *Lycopodiella cernua.* © Sam Bridgewater.

tree species. In addition, they had no flowers and depended on spore dispersal to re-produce. One famous example of an ancient club moss is the now-extinct genus *Lepido-dendron*, which represented one of the dominant plant groups at the time. Coal deposits are derived from the pressurized remains of this and other club mosses, together with other plant groups such as horsetails and ferns that thrived in the swamp forests of that era.

DIVERSIFICATION OF PLANT LIFE: THE DEVONIAN EXPLOSION

The Devonian period (416-359 MYA) wit-nessed an incredible diversification in plant life. At the onset of this period, land plants were typically prostate, simple, and small and showed little variety in shape. However, by its end, many different forms had evolved—with some tree species attaining twenty meters in height—and structurally diverse forests had developed. Important plant groups that arose during the Devonian, and which we still rec-ognize today, include the club mosses, mosses, and ferns. The Devonian is known as one of the key time periods for plant evolution, and this dramatic expansion in the variety of plant life occurred over a period of about fifty million years—unfathomably long by our own perception but, geologically speaking, relatively brief.

One of the most recognizable and graceful groups of plants existing today are the ferns. The checklist of Belize lists 234 species for the country,[27] and 107 are currently known for the Chiquibul.[28] Although they evolved after the club mosses and horse-tails, fernlike fossils are present by the end of the Devonian (ca. 360 MYA). Among the evolved characteristics that helped ferns to be hugely successful were their leaves, which were broad and feathery, presenting a large surface area to the sun and thereby maximizing their ability to photosynthesize. However, like club mosses and horsetails, reproduction was still dependent on spores and required two distinct independent but mutually dependent life cycles. Although not found in Belize, one fossil from the late Devonian that has revealed much about plant evolution is *Archaeopteris*. Although its leaves are fernlike in form and, like ferns, it produces spores to reproduce, unlike ferns, *Archaeopteris* produces a woody trunk akin to those usually associated with coniferous trees, which are known to have evolved later during the Carboniferous period (359-299 MYA). It thus potentially represents a now-extinct link between these two important plant groups and was an important component of the world's first forests.

SOWING THE SEEDS OF SUCCESS

One of the major evolutionary breakthroughs in land plants and a factor in their sub-sequent success was the evolution of seed. This occurred during the Devonian. Prior to this point, the dominant plant groups of the time, such as club mosses and ferns, had

The extinct genus *Archaeopteris* is known only from the fossil record. This plant group appears to represent an intermediate form between ferns and conifers and may be a distant evolutionary cousin to species such as Caribbean pine (*Pinus caribaea*), found in Belize today. © The Natural History Museum, London.

two separate autonomous phases to their reproductive life cycle, increasing the chance that the process could be disrupted. In addition, part of the reproductive process relied on the presence of water and was thus problematic in dry conditions. The evolution of the seed increased reproductive efficiency, reduced dependency on water, and dispensed with the need for two distinct phases to reproduction.

The first known seed-producing plants are called "seed ferns," a group similar in general form to some existing ferns but now entirely extinct. Their existence is known only from the fossil record. Another significant evolutionary development that occurred during the Devonian and Carboniferous periods was improvement to plant rooting systems, which provided a stronger means of anchoring the plant to the ground and increased ability to absorb water and nutrients.[29] The development of roots was of vital importance in the breakdown of rock, and by the end of the Devonian period well-developed, fertile soils were in existence.

THE GYMNOSPERMS

Fossil evidence proves that forests of tall, nonflowering, seed-bearing plants existed by 380 MYA, with competition for light driving the increase in size experienced by many of the plant groups of that era. During the Triassic (251–200 MYA) and Jurassic (200–146 MYA) periods, gymnosperms–plants producing unprotected seed, a group to which present-day conifers and cycads belong–dominated much of the world's existing forests.

One important group of known fossil seed plants, representatives of which have been found preserved in Belizean rocks, is the extinct group Cordaitales. Like existing gymnosperms, the Cordaitales produced cones and seed, although their leaves differed from those we know today by being significantly broader and larger. The gymnosperms shared their heyday with the dinosaurs, and the evolutionary lineage has survived to the present era. In addition to the exotic monkey puzzle *Araucaria heterophylla*, which can be found cultivated in many Belizean gardens, Belize has native representatives of three other different types of gymnosperm: cycads (four species), pines (two species), and podocarps (one species). Members of the Podocarpaceae family (mountain cypress or yellow wood), for example, would have been one of the dominant trees during the era of the dinosaurs; in Belize and the Chiquibul region the one existing species known (*Podocarpus guatemalensis*) is now largely confined to high-elevation forests.

Fossils of seed ferns, such as *Neuropteris,* have been found in the Santa Rosa rocks of the Maya Mountains. This was one of the first known plant groups to produce seed and dates back to the Carboniferous period (359–299 MYA). © The Natural History Museum, London.

THE CHIQUIBUL'S FOSSIL PLANTS

A number of well-preserved plant fossils have been found in Belize. Some of the first described were collected by the geologist Dixon in the 1950s.[30] These include impressions of *Cordaites, Neuropteris,* and *Calamites* found in the Chiquibul's Santa Rosa rock. Flourishing in the tropical swamp conditions that existed at the time, these were among the most highly evolved plants of the Carboniferous era (359–299 MYA), although they are now all extinct. *Cordaites* was a woody plant similar in form to our present-day conifers, whereas *Neuropteris* was a seed fern. *Calamites* was a giant tree horsetail similar to the modern-day genus *Equisetum* but attaining great heights in excess of ten meters.

Flowers are among the most exquisite manifestations of natural beauty, and biological diversity in Belize is reflected in the great variety of flower form and color that can be witnessed across its territory. Every flower has evolved in response to specific ecological pressures, with each designed to facilitate the dissemination of pollen and the reproductive process. Although flowers are often thought of as being synonymous with plants, many of the plants with older lineages, including mosses, cycads, ferns, and conifers, do not produce them.

Geologically speaking, flowers evolved only relatively recently in the earth's history. Just as the fossil record reveals an explosion in plant diversification during the Devonian, so too is a second period of rampant plant evolution encountered during the Cretaceous era (146-66 MYA). This is considered the great era of flower evolution. Although it is believed that flowering plants (angiosperms) evolved prior to the Cretaceous, perhaps diverging from a group of gymnosperms called the gnetales,[31] it was during the Cretaceous that they diversified greatly, and within a relatively short period of time most of the flowering plant lineages we know today had evolved. Their subsequent success was such that they eventually came to dominate the flora of most of the world, taking primacy in many geographical locations. Today over 80 percent of all land plant species produce flowers, and angiosperms comprise an estimated 250,000 species.[32]

Although the reasons behind the origin of angiosperms remain an unsolved mystery, various theories have been put forward to explain their rapid rise to ecological dominance. One hypothesis suggests that chance duplications in chromosome numbers during reproduction might have been important, dramatically increasing the number of genes coding for different physical characters and hence increasing diversification rates.[33] Changes in the browsing behavior of dinosaurs, the evolutionary driving influence of insect pollinators and

Angelonia ciliaris is a common species of the savanna and one of the estimated 3,265 flowering plants known to occur in Belize. © Zoë Goodwin.

herbivores, and geological activity that precipitated elevated levels of carbon dioxide, resulting in increased plant growth rates and expanded habitat colonization opportunities, have also been suggested as significant factors.[34]

With the evolution of the flower, the means by which plants reproduced changed dramatically. For example, gymnosperms usually require wind to carry pollen from male cones to female cones for fertilization to occur, and this is a largely wasteful endeavor, with pollination left to chance and the vagaries of local wind patterns. With the advent of the flower, however, a greater proportion of plants became dependent on animal pollination, and many groups subsequently developed complex interactions with their pollinating vectors (see "Honey Guides, Tongue Tubes, and Love Chambers:

The fruits of *Hampea stipitata* open to reveal the bird-dispersed black seed and its surrounding white aril. © Sam Bridgewater.

The Pollination Ecology of the Chiquibul" in chapter 5). Flower adaptations to early insect pollination, for example, included the development of sticky pollen that could adhere to the body of the pollinating visitor, facilitating its transport, and the production of nectar to provide a sugary reward. Insect pollination is more reliable than wind pollination, with a greater chance that pollen is transferred from one flower to another. Unlike gymnosperms, early angiosperm seeds were also enveloped within a structure known as a carpel. The carpel itself protects the seed while it develops and was thus an important evolutionary improvement. Together with surrounding tissues, the carpel also develops into the fruit as the seed matures. Although early angiosperm fruits were initially small, as mammal and bird groups diversified greatly after the Cretaceous era (66 MYA–present day), they provided a new means of seed dispersal to help plants colonize new areas. Capitalizing on these new potential dispersal vectors, the fruits of many angiosperm species coevolved with the emerging warm-blooded stars of the animal kingdom, becoming edible and attractive and resulting in the myriad of fruit forms we know today.

Over one thousand flowering plant families exist. Some of these are thought to have evolved relatively early in the history of angiosperms, while others are more recently derived. Existing Belizean flowering plant families belonging to broad groups, such as the Magnoliales, Laurales, and Piperales, and believed to have appeared early in flowering plant history (before the onset of the Palaeogene 66 MYA) include the Nymphaceae (the water lilies), the Magnoliaceae (the magnolias), the Piperaceae, the Chloranthaceae, and the Lauraceae (avocado family). Only one species of magnolia is known from Belize (*Magnolia yoroconte*), and this occurs naturally only at higher elevations in the Maya Mountains. Likewise, the one Belizean representative of the Chloranthaceae is *Hedyosmum mexicanum*. This, too, is frequently found in forests of altitude. The Lauraceae is an extremely important component of Belizean forests. Represented by over thirty-one species in Belize, this is one of the defining tree groups of the Chiquibul Forest. With their jointed stems, spikelike inflorescence, and often peppery-smelling leaves, the Piperaceae are also an important component of the Chiquibul's vegetation, although most species are shrubs or herbs.

Some angiosperm plant groups started to appear in the fossil record only relatively recently in the Paleogene period (66–23 MYA). One good example is provided by the families belonging to the order Zingiberales. These include the Musaceae (the banana family), the Zingiberaceae (the gingers), the Heliconiaceae (the heliconias), and the Costaceae. These are all important components of Belize's understory forest flora and are believed to have originated less than 50 MYA,[35] with the ginger family itself dated to the Miocene epoch (23–5 MYA). Grasses and sedges are also relatively young, with evidence suggesting that these families also arose around the same time.

Palynology is the study of pollen grains (produced by gymnosperms and angiosperms) and spores (produced by ferns and lower plants). All plants produce vast amounts of these minute genetic propagules during the reproductive process, much of which falls to the ground as a kind of invisible biological rain. The outer coats of both spores and pollen are composed of a highly resistant substance called sporopollenin, and this has aided their preservation in the fossil record. Much of what we can infer about the evolution of plants and vegetation history is derived from an examination of the type and relative quantity of fossilized pollen and spores occurring in rocks of different ages. For example, encompassing 175,000 species representing 75 percent of all existing flowering plant species, the eudicots are the most diverse group of flowering plants recognized by taxonomists. Although the many families that together make up this group vary greatly in form, they all produce a similar kind of pollen that has three microscopic pores. This is very different from the pollen forms of other plant groups. The first fossil evidence for this group, based on an examination of fossilized pollen, has been dated to ca. 125 MYA, midway through the Cretaceous period.[36] However, the earliest evidence of angiosperms has been dated somewhere between 141 and 132 MYA.[37] An examination of fossil pollen has also clearly illustrated the trend of increasing abundance and diversification of angiosperms as the Cretaceous period progressed. The same period coincided with little change in gymnosperm diversity but a marked decline in fern species. Angiosperms were therefore already dominant by this time. In addition, pollen evidence suggests that angiosperms first appeared and became prominent at relatively low to middle latitudes (20°N to 20°S), appearing subsequently only at higher latitudes.[38]

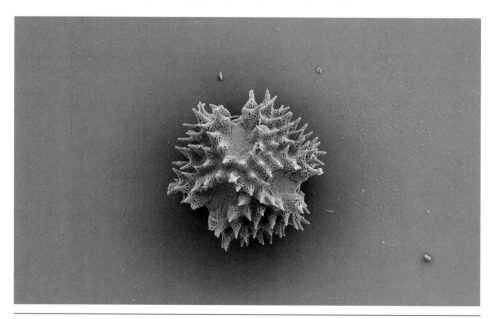

Pollen grain of *Rafinesquia* (Asteraceae) showing the three pores typical of plants belonging to the eudicot group. © Alex Wortley.

In recent decades scientists have developed various molecular techniques allowing them to compare differences in DNA gene sequences between species. In the early years of the development of molecular clocks it was thought that changes in DNA sequences between species accumulate at a roughly constant rate through time. Although it is now known that this is not always necessarily the case and that DNA in different taxonomic groups does not always mutate at the same rate, the technique is still highly useful in creating dated evolutionary trees and shedding light on how biological groups relate to one another. For molecular clocks to work, they need to be calibrated, and fossils are used to provide "minimum oldest dates" for specific characters, providing fixed date estimates that can be used to infer evolutionary rates. The use of such techniques has suggested that angiosperms first evolved during the Jurassic (200–146 MYA), significantly prior to the dates suggested by fossil evidence.[39]

THE ORIGIN OF THE BELIZEAN FLORA

Every hemisphere produces plants of a different species; and it is not by the diversity of climates that we can attempt to explain, why equinoctial Africa has no laurineae, and the New World no heaths. . . . In the vegetable as well as the animal kingdom, the causes of the distribution of the species are among the mysteries, which natural philosophy cannot reach.   A. VON HUMBOLDT AND A. BONPLAND, *Personal Narrative of Travels to the Equinoctial Regions of the New Continent, during the Years 1799–1804*

The Neotropics are considered one of the "megabiodiversity" regions of the world, and an estimated 90,000 plant species grow within its confines.[40] Mesoamerica, which includes all of the Central American countries as well as the Yucatán Peninsula of Mexico, has a vascular flora in excess of 17,000 species;[41] of this, Belize is known to have at least 3,408 species. In addition to plants, over 150 species of mammals, 540 species of birds, 600 species of freshwater and marine fishes, 151 species of amphibians and reptiles, and a huge but currently undocumented number of insects occur within Belize's territory.[42] But when and how did the great diversity of Belize and the Neotropics arise? This question has been puzzling scientists for hundreds of years and continues to intrigue modern researchers.

It has long been known that distributions of organisms have changed through time. The rocks that would eventually form Belize, for example, lay under the ocean for much of evolutionary history. The land plant and animal groups that now inhabit it, therefore, must either have evolved in situ after the sea withdrew or have colonized it as it appeared from the shallow seas, either arriving overland or by long-distance dispersal from preexisting populations in other geographic regions. Historical bioge-ography is the scientific discipline that attempts to explain how and when biota devel-oped and to clarify how current species patterns originated. Of critical importance to this endeavor is understanding where and at what time a particular taxon or group of taxa evolved.

Historically, a number of criteria have been used to clarify origins of taxa. It was once thought, for example, that the location of the greatest diversity of species for a particular genus was the center of evolutionary origin of that group. However, it has since been shown that such premises are flawed. Initially our knowledge of species ori-gins was based solely on their first appearance in the fossil record. But there have been tremendous scientific advances in the last few decades, including the development of molecular clocks and rigorous mathematical analyses, that enable evolutionary trees to be depicted and dated. To begin to understand the origins of biotas has required as-sembling evidence from many disparate scientific disciplines, including paleontology (the study of fossils), systematics (the study of diversity and species relationships), mo-lecular biology, geology, and ecology. Many aspects of these disciplines have recently been used in the field of phylogenetics. This has become one of the most powerful tools in unraveling the histories of biotas. However, although some of the mysteries that puzzled early tropical naturalists like Humboldt and Bonpland, Wallace, and Darwin are being explained, many more continue to perplex.

PHYLOGENETICS: A MODERN TOOL IN UNDERSTANDING THE ORIGIN OF FLORAS

The earliest scientists who attempted to classify life on earth believed that the species they discovered, named, and grouped together, based on physical similarity, had each been uniquely created by God. However, following the publication of Darwin's theory of evolution in the latter part of the nineteenth century, it became widely accepted that all taxa are related to one another and that relationships between them can be depicted through an evolutionary tree. Most modern taxonomists generally try to en-sure that their classifications represent evolutionary groupings. In addition to describ-ing species, they attempt to clarify evolutionary relationships. The currently accepted means of doing this uses an approach called phylogenetics. The discipline of modern phylogenetics was first conceived by the German Willi Hennig in 1950 and requires a taxonomic group to be "monophyletic," which means it contains all the modern de-scendants of a common ancestor. Fundamental to constructing a phylogenetic tree is an understanding of which characters are derived through evolution and shared be-tween taxa. The methodology for ascertaining this is complex but is based on examin-ing evolutionary characters against other less closely related groups of taxa (termed "outgroups"). It assumes that shared characters between taxa are generally due to a

common ancestor, and can thus define a monophyletic group, rather than to convergent evolution, and that characters shared with outgroups are likely to be more ancestral. Parsimony, the principle that evolution is generally straightforward rather than
complex, is used to choose the most likely phylogenetic tree that reflects all the diversity observed in a group in the fewest number of evolutionary "steps" from the ancestor.

Phylogenetic trees are proving of fundamental importance in understanding the
origins and patterns of diversity. In addition to allowing inference of the pattern of ac-
cumulation of species lineages through time, they can help reveal when lineages first
arrived in different geographical areas.

Initially, phylogenetic (evolutionary) trees were based on visible morphological
characters such as flower structure. However, the advent of molecular techniques has
made it possible to look at differences in DNA gene sequences and use these as characters as well. This has resulted in a comprehensive review of plant classification. In
the 1990s the first draft phylogenetic tree based on such molecular data was produced
for all flowering plants.[43] Most modern classification systems now have molecular underpinnings, following the structure outlined by the Angiosperm Phylogeny Group
in 2003.[44] Although there has been some disquiet among traditionalists, the basic
structure of evolutionary trees based on DNA and their corresponding classification
systems are similar to those formerly based on morphology, reinforcing rather than
undermining them. However, some fundamental rearrangements of taxonomic groups
have been required. For example, using DNA data, scientists found that the family
Flacourtiaceae was in fact an artificial grouping, as it was not derived from the descendants of a single common ancestor. Therefore, it was disbanded and its component taxa
reassigned to natural evolutionary groupings. This is why the published *Checklist of the
Vascular Plants of Belize* recognizes twenty-three species as occurring in Flacourtiaceae,[45]
whereas more recent examinations of the flora reassign them to other families, with
many now placed in Salicaceae (the willow family).

THE GONDWANAN VS. LAURASIAN DEBATE

After the theory of continental drift was widely accepted during the 1960s and 1970s,
one of the dominant scientific theories of the 1980s and 1990s was that the current
neotropical flora comprised a mixture of plant families derived from two historical
geographic origins: Gondwana and Laurasia. These included "southern elements" presumed to have originated in Gondwana (e.g., Annonaceae, the custard apple family)
and "northern elements" that had a Laurasian origin (e.g., Scrophulariaceae, the fox-
glove family).[46] The essential assumption was that families assigned to one of these origins had first evolved and spread across the landmass of origin prior to its breakup due
to tectonic movement. The observation that separate landmasses (e.g., South America
and Africa) had characteristic families in common provided evidence supporting the

theory that these areas were once joined. Taxonomic differences between them at the generic and species level were attributed to divergence and speciation subsequent to the splitting of the supercontinents. Only at a much later date was it suggested that Laurasian (represented by North America) and Gondwanan (represented by South America) plant taxa intermingled in the Neotropics in places such as Belize to form the composite floras we know today. It was initially believed that intermingling started with the establishment of the first island links between North and South America (11 MYA), with the development of the solid land bridge drastically increasing subsequent migration rates between these two continents.

One seminal scientific study published in 1982, for example, assigned 145 neotropical plant families to either a Laurasian or Gondwanan origin, with Laurasian elements making up less than 10 percent of the flora of South America.[47] This study suggested that Belize, whose geological history is more closely allied with North than South America, has a flora that appears to be dominated by putative Gondwanan taxa, an indication that the northerly migration into Central America of these species of "southern origin" swamped the preexisting Laurasian elements. More recent research, much of it based on molecular evidence, suggests that the story is considerably more complicated.

HISTORICAL BIOGEOGRAPHY: DISPERSAL OR VICARIANCE?

A number of theories have been proposed to explain the observed global distribution of biota, especially observed disjunctions in plant and animal groups. Of these, two have been hugely influential: the dispersal and vicariance theories. In essence, the dispersal theory suggests that species arise in one locality and subsequently disperse to others across a barrier, such as a mountain chain or an ocean, where they may diverge from the parent population. In the case of plants, for example, this might be caused by seeds being carried a long distance from an original population area by a bird or mammal. Where the newly established population is reproductively separated from the original population, it may change genetically and evolve into new species. Dispersal is believed to have been important in the development of the biota of many oceanic islands, with the classic example often cited being that of Darwin's finches. In this case, all the many forms of finches to be found on the Galápagos archipelago, each with its distinct physical characteristics, are believed to have all evolved from a single species that first colonized one of the islands from mainland South America about 3 MYA.

However, with the general acceptance of plate tectonics from the 1960s onward, the theory of vicariance gained momentum. This suggests that many plant and animal distribution patterns can be explained by the fragmentation of once previously widespread populations by such events as continental drift and the creation of mountain chains. According to this theory, the development of barriers, which split apart existing populations and caused them to be reproductively isolated, is often the driving force behind both species divergence and observed disjunctions in closely related plant and animal groups. A common example often cited historically is the plant family Proteaceae, which occurs in Australia, Africa, and South America—areas all now separated by oceans. In Belize the family is represented by a single species: *Roupala montana*, a common shrub of savanna areas. Vicariance theory argues that the most plausible explanation for the occurrence of this family in all of the world's southern landmasses is that they were connected long in the past as a single landmass (Gondwana). The current observed generic and species-level differences on each continent are explained by genetic isolation and divergence within each of the areas subsequent to their geographic separation. The presence of *Roupala* in Belize would be attributed

Finches collected by Darwin in the Galápagos Islands during the voyage of the *Beagle*. These finches are a model of evolution in action, their beak shape having adapted to food. © The Natural History Museum, London.

Roupala montana, a member of Proteaceae. The family occurs in the Neotropics, Africa, and Australia, strongly suggesting that these continents were once connected to one another. © Sam Bridgewater.

to its migration northward from South America. Vicariance is a popular paradigm supported by scientists, as it provides a convenient explanation for the observed global distribution of many plant and animal groups.

These two theories are not incompatible and provide an important starting point when attempting to unravel the origins of regional floras and faunas, such as those found in Belize.

UPDATING THE MODEL: EVIDENCE FOR RECENT EVOLUTION, HISTORICAL MIGRATION, AND LONG-DISTANCE DISPERSAL

Recent advances in molecular biology have helped clarify the evolutionary relationships and biogeographic history of many plant families. Partly as a result of an improved knowledge of fossils, it is now known that certain neotropical families once assumed to have had a Gondwanan distribution are in fact relatively recent in origin and were not in existence before the great southern landmass broke apart. Thus, their distribution patterns across the world's existing southern continents cannot be explained by vicariance. One example of this is Bignoniaceae, an important element of neotropical rain forests. This family is represented by forty-six species in Belize—many of which are forest vines—and includes the characteristic mayflower tree (*Tabebuia guayacan*). Of these, twenty species occur in the Chiquibul Forest. The family also occurs in many other regions of the world, including Africa and Asia. The Bignoniaceae has been dated to 50 MYA, which is significantly younger than the date of the known split of Gondwana (ca. 100 MYA), which undermines the theory that its broad present distribution across the world in geographically disjunct localities is due to this tectonic event.[48]

The evolutionary pattern of Bignoniaceae appears to be repeated for many quintessential plant groups that together define the contemporary floras of countries like Belize. Thus, classifying plant families into those of Gondwanan or Laurasian origin would appear to represent an oversimplified view. It cannot even be assumed that all the representative genera of families of known antiquity dating prior to the split of Gondwana—such as the Lauraceae or Annonaceae, for example—have evolved completely in situ. In the former case, some of the most diverse neotropical genera, including *Ocotea* (200 species worldwide, 7 species in Belize) and *Nectandra* (100 species worldwide, 11 species in Belize) are believed to have evolved relatively recently (ca. 23 MYA) and from African ancestry. A 2004 study reevaluated the seminal neotropical plant origin work of 1984, cited earlier, and concluded that over 20 percent of 1,104 Amazonian tree species known for

The mayflower tree (*Tabebuia guayacan*). Although the Bignoniaceae family occurs in Latin America, Asia, and Africa, its current distribution cannot be due to continental drift and vicariance, as it evolved considerably after Gondwana began to split apart. © Sam Bridgewater.

an area of Ecuador belonged to genera and families that could be classified as relatively recent immigrants from other continents. This is a much greater proportion than was previously thought. The same is almost certainly true for Belize.

If the existing combination of plant groups in the world's tropical regions cannot be explained by vicariance alone, then long-distance dispersal across oceans or migration across landmasses must be invoked instead. One example of long-distance migration might be provided by Malphigiaceae, which occurs throughout the world's tropical regions and is represented in Belize by thirty-six species (including the craboo tree, *Byrsonima crassifolia*). It was once suggested that this was a Gondwanan family due to its pantropical distribution. However, like Bignoniaceae, the maximum age of the family is now believed to be ca. 70 MYA, much younger than the split of Gondwana. Molecular studies also show that the ancestral groups of this family occur in northern South America. Although it is possible that the family might have colonized Africa and Asia through long-distance dispersal events across the Atlantic, an analysis of species evolutionary patterns suggests that they are best explained by migration of this plant group northward through Laurasia and, from there, eastward and then southward into Africa and Asia.[49]

Trophis racemosa. The fig family (Moraceae) is believed to have evolved in Laurasia ca. 74–110 MYA before migrating into other parts of the world. © Sam Bridgewater.

Overland migration theories have become increasingly popular since evidence has suggested that subsequent to its split from Gondwana, South America did not exist in isolation from all other continents, with its species evolving only from the stock inhabiting it after its break from Africa. It is highly probable, and in some cases certain, that there were intermittent island links with Africa (until 76 MYA) and with North America (from about 50 MYA). It is also believed that there was even a continuous land bridge connecting it with Australia and New Zealand via Antarctica about 65 MYA. These all provided multidirectional historical migration pathways for a broad range of plant and animal taxa. It is hard to conceive today how tropical taxa could possibly migrate between Asia, Africa, and South America through temperate Europe and North America. However, many regions of the world that are currently too cold to support a tropical flora and hence provide a likely migration pathway for tropical species were once considerably hotter prior to changes in the earth's climate. One example is the Boreotropics of Laurasia (see boxed text).

Another example of a plant family believed to have dispersed widely is provided by the fig family, Moraceae. This includes the Belizean breadnut tree (*Brosimum alicastrum*), which is abundant in the Chiquibul. The existing global distribution of this plant family was also once attributed to the breakup of Gondwana. Molecular evidence, however, suggests that it is just as likely to have evolved in Laurasia (ca. 74–110 MYA), with multiple migrations of taxa occurring subsequently into South America, Africa, and Asia.[50]

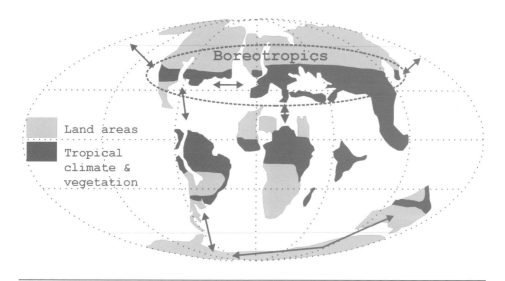

The position of the continents during the Eocene epoch (56-34 MYA), when tropical ecosystems were found at higher latitudes. Potential tropical plant migration routes are indicated. Adapted from Morley, "Interplate Dispersal Routes for Megathermal Angiosperms."

THE BOREOTROPICS

We associate particular parts of the world with distinct climatic regimes and characteristic vegetation types. The tropical belt encircling the world, for example, is largely covered with rain forest and is typified by a hot, wet environment. Regions at higher latitudes, such as northern Europe and Siberia, are dominated by temperate forests and cooler, more seasonal climates. However, these patterns have not always prevailed. During the Eocene (56-34 MYA) the world's climate was hotter than it is today, and fossils of plant groups characteristic of today's tropical regions have been found in North America and Europe, suggesting that these regions once supported floras typical of rain forests. From an examination of fossils of the clays that underlie London, for example, it is known that this region once supported a tropical flora. This northern historical tropical belt, known as the Boreotropics, might have provided an important pathway for the migration of certain plant groups, such as Malphigiaceae between North America, Europe, Africa, and Asia during the era of its existence.

Although long-distance dispersal of seed across oceans is known to occur, after the acceptance of plate tectonics scientists believed that such occurrences were generally rare, isolated events, and some questioned whether such a mechanism could explain many known plant distribution patterns. However, in recent years long-distance dispersal has increasingly been credited with contributing new additions to many of the world's floras, including the Neotropics. In particular, large numbers of common South and Central American plant groups are known to be derived from taxa originating in other continental areas, such as Africa and Europe. Some of these have been shown to have evolved very recently, at a time when no "stepping stone" routes across the world would have been available and when climatic conditions would not have allowed migration through postulated "boreotropical" pathways. Thus, long-distance dispersal is the only explanation left. Legumes, for example, are the most diverse group of plants in Belize and are represented by 80 genera and 295 species. It is now believed that the distribution pattern of this group around the world has been strongly influenced by long-distance dispersal events. Other important neotropical families whose current distribution patterns are believed to have been generated by long-distance dispersal include Melastomataceae, Annonaceae, and Rhamnaceae. Such events are not a one-way process, and plant taxa are known to have migrated both into and from the Neotropics. One example of a neotropical emigrant is the cabbage bark (*Andira inermis*), a common Belizean tree. This species is widely distributed through Central and South America but also occurs in Africa. Its arrival there is believed to have been due to emigration from neotropical stock only a few million years ago.

Although our knowledge of the geographical and evolutionary origins of plant families is far from complete, it is now clear that no single theory can adequately account for all the observed compositional elements of the neotropical flora. The splitting of Gondwana was undoubtedly critical in influencing plant distributions, but more recent migration and dispersal events are also of great importance.

Andira inermis (Fabaceae), a species widespread in Belize and throughout Central and South America. It also occurs in Africa, where its arrival is attributed to emigration from neotropical stock only a few million years ago. © Andrew McRobb.

Since the 1700s there have been many vital discoveries that have radically improved our understanding of biological patterns. One important early contributor was the British scientist Charles Lyell (1797–1875). A brilliant geologist and paleobotanist, Lyell used the fossil record to infer historical fluctuations in both the earth's climate and sea levels. By documenting the disappearance of species in the fossil record, he was also one of the first people to provide evidence for extinction. However, the two scientists most associated with clarifying the origin of species, and how biotas develop, are Charles Darwin and Alfred Russel Wallace. Both independently postulated the theory of evolution through natural selection. In essence, this theory stated that heritable characteristics conferring a competitive advantage on a population will become established and dominant over time, as the individuals that express these traits are more likely to survive and reproduce, passing them on to future generations. Both also recognized the importance of long-distance dispersal in establishing populations of species in new geographic areas. This is important, as it can result in reproductive isolation, which allows natural selection to occur independently in both populations, resulting in new adaptations, divergence, and speciation. One of Wallace's lasting contributions was the development of a map outlining the earth's biogeographic regions; he advocated many principles still followed by scientists today.

One hotly debated issue during the nineteenth century was whether long-distance dispersal or migration of taxa across hypothetical land bridges that had disappeared was responsible for the observed disjunct distribution of some species. The latter theory was supported by the renowned botanist Joseph Hooker and the geologist Charles Lyell. The essence of this debate continues today. One development that none of the great early biogeographers could have foreseen was the general acceptance of continental drift from the 1960s.

MESOAMERICAN VEGETATION THROUGH THE CENOZOIC (65 MYA–PRESENT)

Belize and other Central American countries are covered by a patchwork of tropical forest, savanna, wetland, and coastal mangrove. The exact distribution of these vegetation types is determined by a complex combination of soils, climatic regimes, and a range of other environmental factors, such as inundation by freshwater or saltwater. But how long have the vegetation patterns we see today been in existence? Has the Chiquibul always been forested naturally? What types of vegetation dominated the landscape two thousand years ago or even two million? If it has changed over time, why has this occurred?

In an attempt to analyze historical vegetation patterns, scientists have had to try to describe ancient floras based on an examination of plant fossils or by inferring species assemblages from preserved pollen. Unfortunately, it is rare for complete fossil floras to be found, and pollen deposits are best preserved in lake sediments, with the most complete sequences available only for the last 19,000 years. Furthermore, accurate identification of ancient pollen and assessment of its modern affinities can be difficult. Despite this, it is often possible to infer from these glimpses of the past which plant communities might have been historically dominant in a region. As much of Belize was lying under shallow tropical seas for most of the Jurassic and into the Pleistocene, it has no fossil records for land plants during this period, but the existence of fossils of *Cordaites*, *Neuropteris*, and *Calamites* in the Chiquibul's Santa Rosa rock (see "Granite and Limestone: From the Old to the New" earlier in this chapter) indicates that tropical swamp conditions existed during the Carboniferous era (360–290 MYA). Of course, at that time Belize did not exist in the form we know it today.

An examination of Belizean fossil remains and pollen profiles in lake sediments reveals little about vegetation patterns from the far past, although in part this reflects lack of research. So we must look to studies from other areas of Mesoamerica that have shown historical floras for the region from the Neogene period (23–1.8 MYA). These

During the Pleistocene epoch, intermittent periods of warming and cooling would likely have caused shifts in the patterns of vegetation, with areas of savanna-like ecosystem likely to have expanded during cooler, drier periods. © Sam Bridgewater.

flora are similar to those found today. A study of Costa Rican plant fossils from the Pliocene epoch (5.3–1.8 MYA), for example, has revealed the presence of ferns; tree ferns; palms; the tree genera *Symphonia*, *Alchornea*, and *Lacmella*; and the mangrove tree genus *Pelliciera*.[51] These findings suggest that rain forests and mangroves were certainly in existence at that time. However, studies of fossils from the same era from other localities reveal that more temperate floras also existed, often associated with upland regions. For example, there is fossil pollen evidence for the existence of *Juglans* (walnut), *Pinus* (pine), *Ulmus* (elm), and *Quercus* (oak) in southeast Guatemala.[52] It is believed that these and other "northern temperate genera," including *Liquidamber*, *Alnus*, *Myrica*, and *Celtis*, migrated south from North America through Central America and into South America as global temperatures dropped when the world began to approach the Pleistocene and the glacial era.

The Pleistocene epoch (1.8–0.01 MYA) was defined by intermittent cycles of cooling and warming. In the case of Central America, it is believed that at times of glacial maxima, when the temperature was coldest, countries like Belize were about 6°C colder than they are today. Pollen evidence extracted from lake sediments suggests that much of the forested areas of the Petén and Belize were more arid during these times and supported dry, open vegetation rather than forest.[53] In other countries, such as Panama, forest still persisted through all glacial phases. With every glacial maximum, lowland rain forest contracted, and montane "temperate" forest species, usually restricted to higher elevations, were able to grow at lower altitudes. At glacial minima, when conditions were hotter and wetter, rain forests expanded their range while arid savanna and dry forest ecosystems contracted.

THE EVOLUTION AND ORIGIN OF THE BELIZEAN FAUNA

Walking through the Belizean landscape, one cannot help being struck by the preponderance of animal life—from the infuriating clouds of sand fly of the coast to the growling howler monkey of the forests. Indeed, Belize can be considered a neatly packaged summation of global evolution. All primary animal classes that currently inhabit our planet are to be found here, with most showing great diversity of form. Some of these groups are relatively well documented; others remain almost scientifically unknown. The creatures of greatest aesthetic beauty are those that tend to attract our attention, with the scarlet macaw providing an example of a species that has become an object of quest for local and visiting bird-watchers. Such emotive flagship species have become figureheads for biodiversity; the conservation campaigns that highlight their individual plight provide a voice for the silent swimming, flying, crawling, and burrowing hordes that remain largely unseen or unheard deep in the forest.

Painted tree frog (*Tlalocohyla picta*). Although they first evolved around 360 MYA, amphibians have managed to navigate the pitfalls of history to become a diverse and highly successful group. © Sam Bridgewater.

Just as the main plant groups have differing evolutionary origins, so too do the primary animal lineages. Compared with the eons that mark plant and animal history, the time scale that marks the development of Belize as a distinct geographical entity in Central America is brief indeed. By the time Belize finally appeared from the ocean, all the animal classes we know today had evolved and diversified and were set to invade, colonize, and inhabit this new territory. Their own individual evolutionary stories are complicated, and much remains to be discovered. The origins of some primary classes of Belizean animals are briefly reviewed in this section. Although certain animal groups evolved before others and exhibit what are considered to be "ancestral" evolutionary traits, this does not mean that they are primitive and doomed to extinction—far from it. Frogs, for example, are amphibians and as such are dependent upon water for reproduction, but this has not stopped them from surviving for over 360 million years and diversifying greatly.

THE CAMBRIAN EXPLOSION

Although multicellular animals are known from the Ediacaran period (630–542 MYA),[54] it was during the subsequent Cambrian period (542–488 MYA) that a sudden, dramatic surge in animal evolution occurred.[55] By the end of this geological period many of the different animal phyla we know today already existed, including the sponges (Porifera), the mollusks (Mollusca), the urchins and starfish (Echinodermata), the jellyfish (Cnidaria), and the arthropods (Arthropoda).[56] Thus, by the end of the Cambrian the foundations were already established for much of today's animal life on earth. More than 80 percent of described living species are arthropods, a hugely successful group that has been safely navigating its course through 500 million years of history. The phylum Arthropoda includes crustaceans, insects, and spiders and is defined in part by the presence of segmented bodies with appendages (such as antennae, wings, and legs) and an external supporting skeleton (exoskeleton). Of the arthropods, insects are the most abundant class today, with more than one million species described and an additional 25,000 known from the fossil record.[57] It is estimated that over a billion insect species must have existed in the past; thus, only a tiny proportion of these has left a trace in the fossil record. Insect evolution began more than 400 MYA.

This first dramatic appearance of great animal diversity occurred almost 200 million years prior to the formation of Belize's earliest rocks and has been termed the Cambrian Explosion. Charles Darwin knew of its existence but was perplexed as to its cause, deeming it "inexplicable." Modern scientists have since conjured many explanations for this episode of exceptional evolutionary creativity, invoking everything from climate change to a dramatic triggering of developmental genes. However, there has been little agreement among them, and the debate rages. It has also been argued that life might have diversified significantly before the Cambrian and that the apparent explosion simply reflects our lack of knowledge of the fossil record prior to this period; recent molecular analyses seem to support this, suggesting that some of the main phyla known from the Cambrian evolved prior to it.[58] Thus, the Cambrian explosion might be more apparent than real. One of the most famous localities providing an insight into the Cambrian age is the Burgess Shale in British Columbia, its remarkable fossils popularized by the paleontologists Simon Conway Morris and Steven Jay Gould.[59]

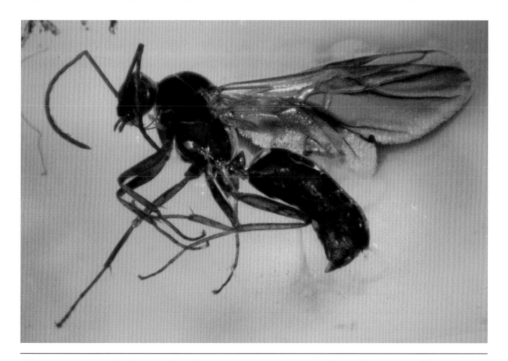

A flying ant preserved in Baltic amber. This specimen dates from the Upper Eocene period (ca. 40-34 MYA). Over 25,000 insect species are known from the fossil record. © The Natural History Museum, London.

By the time the granites were being laid down that would later form Belize's Mountain Pine Ridge and parts of the Cockscomb Basin, the vertebrates (subphylum: Vertebrata) were already well established. This group is essentially defined by the presence of a backbone containing the spinal column, with the majority also having an internal skeleton. It first appeared at the end of the Cambrian era (488 MYA).[60] The first vertebrates were most likely a kind of jawless fish, and this group would eventually evolve and diversify to become many of the familiar vertebrate groups known from Belize and around the world today. These include mammals, birds, reptiles, amphibians, and fish.

One significant evolutionary leap forward for the vertebrates was the colonization of land. The development of an internal skeleton was an important precursor to this, allowing vertebrates to withstand the force of gravity unprotected by water, but their successful invasion of land required other changes in body design, physiology, and means of reproduction. Other significant innovations, for example, included the modification of fins into legs and the development of lungs. By the Carboniferous period (359-299 MYA) the earliest amphibians had evolved, and although the number of living amphibians in the world exceeds 5,300 species today (with over 40 known from Belize),[61] the original ancestors of what would later become salamanders, toads, and frogs are now all extinct.

Morelet's tree frog (*Agalychnis moreletii*). The first amphibians are believed to have evolved by the Carboniferous period (359-299 MYA). © Paul Edgar.

The Jurassic period (200-146 MYA) is known as the age of the dinosaurs. Although famously extinct, the animal group to which they belonged—the reptiles (class: Reptilia)—still exists today. This group is well represented in Belize by crocodiles (two species), turtles, tortoises, and terrapins (fifteen species), lizards (forty-four species), and snakes (sixty-three species). The first appearance of reptiles in the fossil record is during the Carboniferous period (359-299 MYA), and one important evolutionary leap of this group was the development of the amniotic egg.[62] Prior to the evolution of reptiles, reproduction was aquatic. The fertilization of the eggs of the earliest amphibians depended on water, and even today the immature stages of life of modern amphibians—the tadpoles of frogs, for example—are aquatic. Indeed, amphibians are named after their two-phased life history. The development of the amniotic egg severed reptiles' reliance on water, as it enclosed the developing embryo within thick protective membranes while nourishing it and protecting it from the outside world. It was an evolutionary breakthrough, providing opportunities for great adaptive radiation. No longer were the vertebrates dependent on persistent bodies of water to complete their life cycles, although many continued a largely aquatic life-style. As evolution progressed, reptile form diversified, with different lineages beginning to specialize in their food requirements.

It was from the reptile lineage that birds (class: Aves) and mammals (class: Mammalia) evolved independently; mammals appeared by the start of the Jurassic period (200 MYA) and birds by the start of the Cretaceous (146 MYA). At this point in the earth's history Pangaea was fragmenting and major continents were beginning to drift apart to their current locations. The rocks that would later form Belize were accumulating lime-rich sediments under a shallow tropical sea. Both mammals and birds exhibit many important anatomical and physiological differences from reptiles, not least of which is their high metabolism and their ability to regulate their own temperature. This allowed them to continue moving, eating, and reproducing in cold

White-lipped mud turtle (*Kinosternon leucostomum*).The evolution of the amniotic egg during the Carboniferous period freed reptiles from having to rely on water for reproduction. © William Milliken.

A yellow-shouldered bat (*Sturnira lilium*). Mammals began to appear in the evolutionary record at the start of the Jurassic period (ca. 200 MYA). Photograph by Frank Greenaway. © The Natural History Museum, London.

weather. In the earliest stages of evolution mammals were small, and although two of the main infraclasses we know today diverged from one another during this period—the placentals (Eutheria) and the marsupials (Metatheria)—it was during the Paleogene (66-23 MYA) that the mammals diversified greatly to achieve many of the forms we associate with them today. The rise of mammals to become one of the dominant groups on earth today coincided with the extinction of the dinosaurs at the end of the Cretaceous period (66 MYA). Today more than five thousand species of mammals inhabit the earth, with an additional fifteen thousand estimated as having become extinct.[63]

AN INTRODUCTION TO ANIMAL CLASSIFICATION

To make sense of biodiversity and to aid understanding of evolutionary relationships, scientists classify all living organisms into groups. This discipline, called taxonomy, is of immense importance, as it provides the critical underpinnings for all other branches of biological science. One of the recognized fathers of taxonomy was Aristotle, who classified all organisms as either plants or animals. However, the foundations of the modern scientific classification system were laid by Linnaeus. Linnaeus established a system by which all organisms are grouped in nested hierarchies based on shared characteristics. At the highest level, like Artistotle before him, Linnaeus believed that all organisms could be divided into plants or animals, with these two broad groups being called kingdoms. Although modern scientists now recognize four kingdoms (see the boxed text "Kingdoms and Domains: Classifying Life on Earth" earlier in this chapter), the basic tenets of Linnaeus's system remain. Within the animal kingdom, the jaguar can serve as an example of how the nested classification system works. All animals are classified into phyla, one of which is Chordata; all chordates share the characteristic of a notochord, the embryological precursor of the vertebral column. The chordates in turn are subdivided into subphyla, including Vertebrata, all members of which—jaguar included—have backbones and spinal columns. The vertebrates can in turn be divided into ever smaller units called classes (e.g., Mammalia—those members of Vertebrata with shared characteristics, including the production of milk from mammary glands), subclasses (e.g., Theria—all those mammals that give birth to live young), infraclasses (e.g., Eutheria—those mammals that give birth to live young and have placentas), orders (e.g., Carnivora—whose members share a similar skull shape and dentition), suborder (e.g., Feliformia—all of which share a bony capsule enclosing the middle ear), family (e.g., Felidae—the cats), subfamily (e.g., Pantherinae—the large cats), genus (e.g., Panthera—lions, jaguars, leopards, and tigers), and species (e.g., *Panthera onca*—the jaguar).

The biogeographic history of animals is hugely complicated, and there is still much scientific debate as to when and where certain groups originated and how they came to inhabit the geographical locations where they are found today. Fossil evidence clearly shows us that current distribution patterns do not reflect historical ones. For example, we often think of the majority of primates (ourselves excluded) as being largely confined to the Tropics. But fossil evidence clearly indicates that during the Eocene (56–37 MYA) this group was abundant across northern temperate regions, including North America and Europe.[64] Indeed, primates may have evolved in northerly latitudes, subsequently migrating southward into the tropical countries and habitats we associate with them today. In the case of the new-world monkeys, including the howler and spider monkeys of Belize, the story is even more complicated: it is highly likely that the ancestors of this group arrived in South America from Africa rather than from North America, perhaps by a chance rafting over the Atlantic during the Oligocene (34–23 MYA).[65]

MASS MIGRATIONS: ANIMALS AND THE GREAT AMERICAN INTERCHANGE

After the supercontinent Pangaea began to fracture during the Jurassic period (200–146 MYA), the two landmasses now known to us as North and South America began to drift apart, the former as part of Laurasia and the latter comprising a section of Gondwana.[66] South America continued to form the western section of Gondwana until about 100 MYA, after which it began to break away from Africa, "drifting" toward its current position. It is known that periodic island and bridge links occurred between South America and other continental areas over the next 90 million years, and that it did not exist completely in isolation from other regions (see "Updating the Model: Evidence for Recent Evolution, Historical Migration, and Long-Distance Dispersal" earlier in this chapter). However, the extent and significance of these links are debated. Those bird species with the ability to fly long distances, of course, would have been more able to migrate over ocean and island barriers than land-dwelling species.

What is certain is that tectonic activity caused an island chain to rise in the location of present-day Central America about 10 MYA. In addition, cooling of the world's climate caused sea levels to drop as ice caps formed in northern regions. As an eventual result of these climatic and tectonic factors, a continuous land bridge formed for the first time between North and South America, with the final event being the closure of the Isthmus of Panama 3 MYA. This new terrestrial corridor enabled land organisms to migrate both northward from South America and southward from North America without having to resort to swimming or floating across wide tracts of water. The subsequent wave of biological migrations was hugely significant, resulting in a mixing and radical alteration of the faunal composition of these two previously separated American continents.[67] This "blending of biotas" is now commonly known as the Great

American Interchange, and our knowledge of it is greatest for mammals, whose fossil record is most complete. One of the pioneering pieces of research describing the interchange was published in 1940.[68] The final closure of the Isthmus of Panama also had far-reaching global effects, as the complete Central American corridor now acted as a barrier to the movement of water between the Atlantic and Pacific Oceans. This altered the patterns of the world's ocean currents and contributed to the formation of the Gulf Stream, which now warms the North Atlantic and regulates our climate.

SPLENDID ISOLATION: HOW BROAD THE DIVIDE?

Alfred Russel Wallace, the Welsh naturalist, explorer, geographer, anthropologist, and biologist who is credited with recognizing the blending of the North and South American faunas. © The Natural History Museum, London.

Although the faunas of North and South America evolved largely in isolation from each other for over 100 million years, as previously discussed for plants (see "The Gondwanan vs. Laurasian Debate" earlier in this chapter), each continent had periodic links with other geographic regions during this time. North America, for example, is believed to have been connected to Asia and, through Asia, to Europe and even Africa via the Bering Land Bridge. This link was established by ca. 75 MYA and allowed species to migrate from Siberia to Alaska and vice versa. As a result, there was a degree of similarity between the animals of all these geographically disparate continents that shared what scientists called a "Holoarctic fauna." Occasional land connections are also believed to have existed between South America, southern Africa, and Australia via Antarctica. In addition to physical land connections, both continents received occasional chance "raft" immigrants across the ocean from other continents.

Despite all these links with other continental areas, the fact remains that the faunas of South America and North America were largely different from one another at the start of the Miocene (23 MYA). Important and evolutionarily distinct components of the South American fauna, for example, included a group of marsupial mammals, anteaters, and sloths—including the extinct giant land sloth *Megatherium*—and an order of extinct herbivores known as notoungulates, which probably held the same niche of the big grazers currently found in the African savannas.

A skeleton of the giant ground sloth (*Megatherium americanum*). Now extinct, it lived in South America around 10,000 years ago. This reconstructed skeleton is on display at the Natural History Museum, London. © The Natural History Museum, London.

THE PILGRIM FATHERS

Neotropical rats and mice (sigmodontine rodents) are an extremely diverse group of mammals with about seventy-nine genera represented. Fossil evidence suggests that the ancestors of this entire group came from North America and that they were absent from South America until relatively late in the continent's evolution. Data based on an examination of the evolutionary relationships between different existing taxa of sigmodontine rodents and an estimation of their divergence times based on molecular clocks suggest that they first arrived in South America from North America 9-5 MYA, even though the first known fossils have been dated only to ca. 3.5 MYA.[69] Their estimated arrival is therefore after the formation of the first island links between the two continents (ca. 30 MYA) but before the formation of the complete land bridge (ca. 3 MYA). They are therefore believed to be one of the first groups of mammals to migrate southward across the islands that made up Central America into South America. As such, they can be considered among the pioneers of the mass movement of land organisms between the two great American continents that would later redefine the faunas of both areas during the Pliocene (5.3–1.8 MYA). Other pioneers include the raccoons, which first arrived in South America from the north about 7.5 MYA, and ground sloths, which migrated in the opposite direction from South America, arriving in the southern states of North America about 8 MYA.[70] Both these animal groups are adept swimmers. Less mobile creatures unable to swim or raft across water barriers had to wait a few million years longer until the land connection was complete before migration could occur.

EVIDENCE FOR THE GREAT AMERICAN INTERCHANGE

Much of the physical evidence for the migration of animals during the interchange comes from an examination and dating of fossil animals by paleontologists and from observations on the current distribution patterns of existing species. Despite the discovery of fossils of bats in some of Belize's caves (see the boxed text "The Chiquibul Cavern and the Great Well" earlier in this chapter), the country has a relatively poor fossil record for vertebrates. However, excellent fossil sites of this group can be found elsewhere in Central America: at El Gramal (Mexico), Patterson Site (Guatemala), Gracias (Honduras), Barrantes (Costa Rica), Arroyo del Sísmico (El Salvador), and Coca (Panama). Fossil-rich localities yielding vital information on the Great American Interchange also occur in southern California, southern Arizona, and the Buenos Aires province of Argentina.[71] Carbon dating of the sediments in which the fossils have been found allows us to determine the exact time of the interchange. For example, the first known fossil examples of peccaries in South America have been dated to 2.4 MYA. This group has a much older fossil record in North America, so it is thought that peccaries must have migrated south sometime prior to 2.4 MYA. This pattern, whereby a species previously known to occur in either North or South America suddenly occurs on the other continent around 2.5 MYA, is repeated for a range of different animal groups.

Movement of animal groups during the Great American Interchange.

THE GREAT TREKKERS: THE PARTICIPANTS OF THE INTERCHANGE

Many different animal groups from both continents were involved in the Great American Interchange. Anteaters, sloths, opossums, and armadillos, for example, which now occur in Belize, are all believed to have been originally present in South America but absent from nascent Central and North America (see table 1.1). With the formation of the land bridge, they were able to move northward. Most did not venture much farther than the Tropic of Cancer, although some genera, such as *Megalonyx* (an extinct ground sloth) and *Erethizon* (the porcupine), pushed higher into North America, with *Megalonyx* even reaching Alaska. Carbon dating of fossils of animal species found in California but believed to have originated in South America dates them no earlier than the late Pliocene (ca. 2.5–1.8 MYA). An example of such an animal was a heavily armored giant member of the armadillo group belonging to the genus *Glyptodon*. Weighing approximately as much as a small car, this slow-moving grazer became extinct during the Pleistocene (1.8 MYA–ca. 11,000 years ago), its eventual demise possibly aided by hunting pressure from humans. Examples of animal groups that were originally confined to North America and that subsequently moved southward include skunks, bears, deer, raccoons, camelids (e.g., the guanaco), cats (such as jaguars, pumas, and nonmarsupial saber-toothed cats), dogs, horses, peccaries, and tapirs. Members of many of these groups also occur in Belize today, and its present diverse fauna comprises species whose ancestors had both northern and southern origins.

Model of *Glyptodon*, now extinct. *Glyptodon* was a genus of mammals that lived between 2 MYA and 5,000 years ago. The group is believed to have originated in South America, migrating northward with the formation of the Central American land bridge. © The Natural History Museum, London.

TABLE 1.1. Some participants of the Great American Interchange and their contribution to Belize's native fauna

North American Immigrants to South America	Native to Belize	South American Immigrants to North America	Native to Belize
Bears (Ursidae)	X	Agoutis (Dasyproctidae)	✓
Camels and llamas (Camelidae)	X	Anteaters (Myrmecophagidae)	✓
Cats–puma, jaguar, etc. (Felidae)	✓	Armadillos (Dasypodidae)	✓
Deer (Cervidae)	✓	Capybaras (Hydrochoeridae)	X
Foxes (Canidae)	✓	Giant armadillos (Chlamytheriidae) EXTINCT	X
Gophers (Geomyidae)	✓	Giant ground sloths (Megatheriidae) EXTINCT	X
Horses (Equidae)	X	Glyptodonts (Glyptodontidae) EXTINCT	X
Mastodonts (Gomphotheriidae) EXTINCT	X	Ground sloths (Megalonychidae and Mylodontidae EXTINCT	X

THE ROLE OF CLIMATE: SAVANNA AND TROPICAL FOREST MIGRATIONS

Although the formation of the land bridge itself was essential for the mass two-directional flow of migrants, climate and related vegetation succession also had an essential role to play in the movement of species.[72] An examination of those migrants believed to have walked from one continent to another reveals many of them to be grazers particularly adapted to savanna ecosystems.[73] Although the vegetation history of South, Central, and North America is still poorly understood, it is believed that significant changes accompanied the cooling of the late Pliocene. At that time repeated cycles of cooling and heating associated with glacial and interglacial periods coincided with and in part were responsible for the formation of the land bridge. It is believed that this period witnessed fluctuations in the fortunes of savanna and forest vegetation, with the former expanding during glacial maxima and moist forest contracting into island-like refugia.[74] This constant flux between vegetation types is thought to have played an important part in species diversification around the globe (see "Why Are the Tropics So Diverse? The Museum and Refuge Theories" later in this chapter). It may also have been vital in facilitating the migration of mammals during the interchange, with the expansion of savanna and associated dry forest during colder, drier climatic episodes providing an increased area of favorable habitat for many of the participants.[75] Glacial minima, during which moist forest expanded, were also important for animal migrations,[76] allowing for a different suite of forest-adapted animal groups, so characteristic of present-day Belize, to colonize Central America from their prior base in northern South America. Examples of such animals include parrots, toucans, guans, and the iridescent blue morpho (*Morpho peleides*).[77] These migrations occurred around 1 MYA.

Although its geological and tectonic history is more closely related to North America than South America, the present-day fauna of Belize and, indeed, of all other Central American countries is more closely related to the biota of South America. Despite the presence of animal groups derived from the north, the overall faunal composition is considered to be Neotropical in character.

WINNERS AND LOSERS

As always in life, the Great American Interchange had its winners and losers. For some animal groups, including the opossums (who expanded northward) and deer (who expanded southward), the interchange provided excellent opportunities to increase their territories. For other groups, however, the effects were to prove ultimately disastrous. For example, prior to the formation of the land bridge, an order of hooved, grazing mammals called the notoungulates flourished in South America. These included a giant hippopotamus-size beast belonging to the genus *Toxodon* and a smaller rabbitlike creature in the genus *Pachyrukhos*. Both of these genera are now extinct, and we know of their existence only from the fossil record. It is believed that both were affected by the expanding predatory fauna from the north, although climate change and competition may also have played a role in their demise. Invading carnivores that may have preyed on the South American grazers included members of the feline family, such as the jaguar, puma, and now-extinct (nonmarsupial) saber-toothed cat.

It wasn't just some of the gentle grazers that failed to cope. Before the Great American Interchange, one of the dominant predators in South America belonged to a group of giant flightless birds with massive heads and beaks.[78] These now-extinct flesh-eating creatures were related to present-day seriemas, cranes, and rails. They are more commonly known as "terror birds," however, and reconstructions of their skeletons from fossil remnants as well as the drawing of behavioral parallels from their closest living relatives portray them as a group of deadly hunters at the pinnacle of the food chain. With the largest of the twenty-five species of terror birds believed to be almost ten feet tall and the fastest thought to be capable of running at seventy kilometers per hour, the terror birds were well-adapted killers who could outrun and catch their prey, killing them with their powerful beaks. The fossils of one genus of terror birds, *Titanis*, have been found in Florida, and it is believed that its ancestors migrated there across Central America after the formation of the Panamanian land bridge. However, ultimately the Great American Interchange heralded the start of their decline and eventual extinction as their position as the dominant carnivore was usurped by the new feline and canine predators spreading southward from North America.

About forty different genera of land mammals are believed to have migrated north across the land bridge from South America during the Great American Interchange, with about fifty migrating south from North America. The northern migrants enjoyed great success and diversified greatly, with 60 percent of them evolving once they had arrived in South America.[79] In contrast, there was comparatively little diversification by those southern migrants who arrived in North America. An analysis of the present faunal composition of South America reveals the massive impact of the interchange: eighty-five (50 percent) of the mammal genera, including most of the large mammals, are derived from members of immigrant North American families.[80] In contrast, only twenty-nine (21 percent) of the mammalian genera of North America are derived from South American immigrants. There is still debate about the reasons behind the discrepancy in evolutionary success between those groups that moved north and those that moved south, although climate-induced vegetation change, the differing impact of the respective immigrants on native ecosystems, the greater ability of the northern migrants to adapt to new habitats, the inability of southern groups to cope with the new predatory fauna, habitat competition, and the arrival of man have all been cited.[81]

THE PLEISTOCENE OVERKILL

We live in a zoologically impoverished world, from which all the hugest, and fiercest, and strangest forms have recently disappeared. . . . It is surely a marvelous fact, and one that has hardly been sufficiently dwelt upon, this sudden dying out of so many large *Mammalia.*   ALFRED RUSSEL WALLACE, *The Geographical Distribution of Animals (1876)*

At the end of the Pleistocene era about 11,000 years ago, there was a mass extinction of large grazing herbivores (the megafauna) throughout North, Central, and South America. Over fifty animal groups became extinct at this time, including the mastodonts, mammoths, gomphotheres, and giant sloths. One theory put forward to explain this event is the arrival of humans, who may have eradicated these groups through hunting, a phenomenon known as the "Pleistocene Overkill."[82] The first human inhabitants of the Americas may have arrived from the north from Asia, entering North America some 14,000 years ago via the Bering Bridge, although a countertheory exists that the first inhabitants arrived by sea. Although the arrival of humans coincides with the extinction event and there is evidence that they hunted mammoths, gomphotheres, and mastodons, it is not known to what extent other species were affected. Extinction of the megafauna was most pronounced in temperate regions of both North and South America, and climate change has been suggested as a vital causal factor.[83]

> The equatorial zone, in short, exhibits to us the result of a comparatively continuous and
> unchecked development of organic forms; while in the temperate regions there have
> been a series of periodic checks and extinctions of a more or less disastrous nature,
> necessitating the commencement of the work of development in certain lines over and
> over again. In the one, evolution has had a fair chance; in the other, it has had countless
> difficulties thrown in its way.   ALFRED RUSSEL WALLACE, *Natural Selection and Tropical*
> *Nature* (1855)

Among the many scientific hypotheses proposed to explain why rain forests are so biodiverse, two in particular have generated great debate. The first held sway for much of the twentieth century and saw the tropics as a "museum" whereby relatively stable climates through geological history—and in particular through glacial eras—resulted in low extinction rates, allowing species gradually to accumulate through time to high levels in much the same way that collections build in a museum. The Museum Theory was first suggested by the biologist Alfred Russel Wallace in the nineteenth century,[84] although it was not formally proposed for another one hundred years. It became scientifically popular in the 1960s and was based on the observation that as latitude increases, diversity decreases, and that during past glaciations, temperate and polar regions underwent severe climate changes, causing mass extinctions.[85] The theory assumed that the climate of tropical regions had remained relatively stable during these same episodes and that their floras and faunas had been unaffected.

Ceiba pentandra tree from the Chiquibul showing
a high diversity of epiphytes on its branches.
© Sam Bridgewater.

The Museum Theory was later challenged as scientific evidence accumulated suggesting that, rather than being stable over extended geological periods, tropical climates had also varied greatly during the glacial episodes of the Pleistocene.[86] This led to the development of hypotheses that argued that recent climate-driven speciation surges, rather than a gradual increase in species numbers over time in a constant environment, were responsible for the high diversity seen in the Tropics today. The most popular of these was the Refuge Theory,[87] according to which, during glacial maxima, the rain forest contracted to isolated pockets (refugia), perhaps separated from one another by a dry-adapted vegetation better able to flourish in the colder, drier conditions thought to exist at the time. It was believed that these refugia may have played an important role in biological diversification by allowing high levels of speciation in small, fragmented populations where genetic variation could be more rapidly fixed. This process of contraction into refugia and subsequent expansion when more favorable conditions returned was not a single isolated incident but occurred many times, coinciding with repeated glaciations.

The Refuge Theory was popular in the 1970s and 1980s but has since attracted vociferous criticism, especially by those studying the Neotropics. Paleoecologists, for example, have found that pollen signatures do not support theories that present-day rain forests were replaced by savanna during glacial episodes, as there is little evidence of grass from pollen cores.[88] This suggests long-term forest stability and implies that if a dry-adapted (xeric) vegetation replaced rain forest at times of glacial maxima, it was not a savanna with a well-developed grass layer. In addition, data on genetic divergence based on evolutionary trees for a number of animal groups, including birds, mammals, lizards, and frogs, indicates that speciation in tropical rain-forest animals often predates the Pleistocene, with molecular clocks indicating an earlier Miocene (23–5 MYA) or Pliocene (5–1.8 MYA) origin.[89] In other words, much speciation occurred well before the time of the postulated refugia.

The debate on the origin of diversity continues today. For example, in recent years some researchers have suggested that rain forests, rather than being replaced by savannas during glacial periods, might have been substituted instead by deciduous forests better adapted to the drier, colder conditions of the time.[90] This would account for the observed forest pollen signatures during glacial maxima but would still allow for rainforest contraction into refugia. One piece of evidence that supports this is the existence of isolated patches of seasonally dry deciduous forest scattered through South America and Mesoamerica today. Despite being separated from one another by a range of other vegetation types, the same suite of plant species repeatedly occurs in many of them. There are only two explanations for this. The first is that all these areas were once connected as a larger continuous area—perhaps forming one of the dominant vegetation types during glacial maxima. The second is that the current distribution patterns might have been caused by the long-distance dispersal of many unrelated taxa. Although it is known that long-distance dispersal has been a hugely influential factor in the distributions of disjunct species, it would appear more likely that these areas were all formerly linked. In addition, although genera are shared between many dry forest areas, the species found in many are unique, occurring there and nowhere else (endemics). The contraction of dry forest areas during times of glacial minima, when the rain forest refugia would have been expanding, might have caused some of these dry forest patches to become isolated from one another, driving speciation in the same way that species diversification is inferred for rain forest refugia.

ECOLOGICAL THEORIES EXPLAINING
PLANT DIVERSITY IN THE TROPICS

The diversity of lowland tropical forests at a local level can exceed the diversity of temperate forests at vast continental scales.[91] A great variety of studies have attempted to explain this diversity, with a broad range of scientific areas probed to provide the answers. Variously, historical factors, environmental energy, and ecological processes have all been invoked. Ecologically, the existence of high-diversity ecosystems has proved a dilemma for scientists, as a long-founded belief of ecological theory is that different species cannot coexist if they occupy the same niche and use resources in an identical manner. What mechanisms, then, enable high numbers of species to coexist in a forest when one might logically expect some to outperform and eventually exclude others? But tropical forests are not homogeneous environments. To the contrary, they are structurally diverse, and each species has its unique ecology suited to its own distinct place within that structure. As for plant species, they vary in their tolerance to light and pests, their longevity, and the size, amount, and dispersal capacity of their seed. Thus, trade-offs between the life-history traits of tropical forest plant species, no two of which are exactly alike, may facilitate their ability to coexist and promote high levels of diversity.[92] It has also been suggested that high diversity levels may be related to the frequent gaps caused by treefall, causing local heterogeneity in light, nutrient, and water conditions. This "niche differentiation" theory suggests that the range of subtly different environmental conditions created by such gaps enables many species to survive together without excluding one another. However, in experimental studies, rain forest trees showed only a limited degree of environmental specialization,[93] although gap dynamics do influence the proportion of pioneer and shade-tolerant species (see "Plant Strategies and Gap Dynamics" in chapter 5). Thus, although niche differentiation is undoubtedly important in enabling species to coexist, other mechanisms are also likely to be important. According to a related theory, larger-scale disturbances—such as those caused by hurricanes—might be significant in maintaining high levels of diversity. This hypothesis, expounded as the Intermediate Disturbance Theory,[94] states in essence that areas experiencing very high and very low frequencies of disturbance have relatively low diversity levels, with the former areas dominated by a few colonizing pioneer species with good dispersal ability and the latter dominated by a few successful late successional species. It predicts that the highest diversity levels will occur in forests with intermediate disturbance events supporting a broad range of taxa of varying degrees of ecological specialization. Pure chance is another factor that may enable even ecologically similar species to coexist.[95] The production of favorable conditions aiding the establishment and survival of understory species (such as treefall) involves random events that favor only those species that happen to be in the vicinity at the time. The next time they occur, they may favor others instead, thus serving to maintain the status quo. Thus, no single species is ever allowed to dominate. This view of the role of chance in maintaining diversity assumes that there is little competition between those understory species waiting to be "released" by some change in gap dynamics. Research indicates that this may be the case, with high predation and herbivory rates maintaining low densities of understory plants so that competitive interactions

Dense population of white poisonwood seedlings (*Sebastiana tuerckheimiana*) in the vicinity of Las Cuevas. Density-dependent mortality of seedlings may prevent this species from dominating the forest, maintaining a high level of tree diversity. © Sam Bridgewater.

between them are limited. Finally, the action of external factors such as pests may also aid the maintenance of diversity if the populations of abundant, highly competitive, and potentially excluding species are kept in check by such mechanisms.[96] This will occur, for example, if common species suffer disproportionately higher levels of pest damage and greater mortality than less abundant species; that is, the degree of mortality of a species is dependent on its density. When mortality increases with density, then positive density-dependent mortality is said to occur. This type of pest-driven population control might act on a large population of seedlings found growing near a parent tree, for example, thereby freeing up habitat for other, rarer species to exploit. Implicit in this model is that there is a degree of pest specificity, with a pest acting primarily on only one target species of plant. Essentially, this model proposes that an individual of a rare species has a greater chance of survival than an individual of a more common species. However, although pest pressure is known to be high in tropical forests and evidence of positive density dependence exists,[97] countertheories argue that the abundance of seed under the parent plant is such that only near-complete mortality of all seedlings would enable other species to survive.[98] And it is certainly true that despite high mortality, many more seedlings of the parent plant are often found growing beneath it than those of other species.

BIODIVERSITY GRADIENTS

Although not universal, there is a global trend for species richness to be highest near the equator, declining toward more temperate or polar latitudes. This phenomenon has been shown to occur in both living and fossil groups, which implies some universal governing rule. Many explanations for this biodiversity gradient have an ecological basis. One hypothesis put forward to explain the observed biodiversity gradients across latitudes suggests that high latitudes are generally more seasonal than low latitudes and that success in seasonal environments is related to broad ecological tolerance, with such species having wide latitudinal ranges. Less seasonal climates in low-latitude countries might therefore be related to lower ecological tolerance, with the result that species typically have smaller ranges, facilitating greater heterogeneity of life. Another hypothesis suggests that high levels of environmental energy might promote species richness, with the greater energy available at lower latitudes supporting greater biomass and more populations.[99] Yet another suggests that high energy levels may speed evolutionary rates through increased metabolic speeds, shorter generation times, and faster mutation rates.[100] In the case of flowering plants, it is certainly true that families in high-energy environments are more species-rich, and molecular evidence does indeed suggest that they have elevated evolutionary rates.

THE CHIQUIBUL FOREST AND BELIZE'S TERRESTRIAL ECOSYSTEMS

 **THE FIRST GLIMPSE** many visitors have of Belize is from the seat of their airplane as it begins its descent toward the urban sprawl of Belize City. This provides an ideal opportunity to see how the natural environment of the country has altered since the last visit. It is not unusual to hear passengers commenting on the appearance of new coastal developments in areas that were formerly swamp or the presence of unknown farms recently cleared from the forest. Despite these manifestations of development, the initial aerial view of the country is invariably both pleasing and reassuring: the country is still clothed in great expanses of native vegetation, and wilderness areas abound.

For the observant passenger, what is clear as the plane descends through the clouds is that no single vegetation formation dominates the land. Although forests are clearly abundant, the dark green of their canopy is consistent in neither form nor color; the forest appears to be of multiple moods and guises. In places, it breaks altogether, to be replaced by open savanna dominated by grasses, with scattered pines representing the only tree. As one descends even lower, arcing for the final runway approach, the first nonverdant colors of trees can be viewed: the vivid yellow of a flowering yemeri (*Vochysia hondurensis*), the pink of the stinking toe (*Cassia grandis*), and the white of the bri-bri (*Inga* spp.). At this lower altitude the savanna itself appears to comprise a complex mosaic of different structural forms. In some areas the pines disappear altogether and the savanna is nearly pampas-like in structure. At times it is punctuated with fingers of dense palm thickets snaking across its flat terrain; at others the pines appear to gradually build in density until one is unsure as to where the savanna ends and the forest starts. Around pools of water, yet another distinct suite of plant species appears to thrive, and the colors viewed from above contrast starkly with the savanna formations of drier areas. Occasional glimpses of the coast indicate that its fringe is covered by forest of a completely different nature from that which appears inland. This is the mangrove that represents Belize's first defense against hurricanes and plays an important role in maintaining the health of the marine ecosystem.

The Chiquibul Forest dominates Belize's central-western region. However, this ecosystem is only part of many that together make up the fabric of the country. An understanding of the wider national ecosystem landscape is important in appreciating the significance of its individual forest areas.

This chapter provides an overview of the primary ecosystems of Belize. It begins with an explanation of the system used to classify the eighty-five ecosystems believed to occur within the country. It then considers in detail the forest vegetation that occurs within the Chiquibul region and concludes with an overview of the country's other broad vegetation types. For the mangrove, savanna, and wetland ecosystems, examples of a few defining animal species are given, and particularly noteworthy ecological interactions are mentioned. However, this chapter provides only a detailed examination of the forest flora. An overview of the Chiquibul fauna is covered in chapter 4, with selected important aspects of forest ecology discussed in chapter 5.

DECIPHERING THE CODE: CLASSIFYING BELIZEAN VEGETATION AND THE CENTRAL AMERICAN ECOSYSTEMS MAP

Most of us intuitively classify our surroundings into either urban or rural areas. When traveling through the countryside, it is usually possible to further categorize our environs into those that are agricultural or natural, with the latter including such generalized habitats as "forest," "savanna," and "wetland." These broad distinctions are based

Aerial photograph of the Mountain Pine Ridge with its mosaic of habitats. The light green areas indicate populations of tiger fern (*Dicranopteris pectinata*), which readily colonizes disturbed ground and sites burned by lightning strike. Darker green areas are broadleaf scrub and woodland. Many of the pine trees in the picture have been killed by the pine beetle. © Sam Bridgewater.

largely on overall structural appearance, obvious differences in species, and knowledge of the degree of wetness of the ground. Topography also plays a prominent role in how we describe our surroundings, with lowland and montane being two important categories. However, although two areas of forest might occur in similar terrain and appear nearly identical in form at first glance, closer observation often reveals that completely different associations of species dominate them. These differences can be due to many factors, but they often reflect underlying variations in soil fertility or soil moisture. In addition, vegetation types are often in a state of flux, changing over time, with one form replacing another through a process known as succession. Thus, the science of classifying vegetation is more complex than it might first appear, as these subtleties and dynamics must be taken into account.

A visitor to Belize would not be surprised to hear that over 50 percent of the territory is covered by what is casually described as generic "jungle," forest, or rain forest. Scientists, however, have had to take a more pedantic view and have devised a rigorous and complex system of vegetation classification that takes into account all the regional forest variations. Whereas the casual observer might perceive only a few forms of forest across Belize's territory, biologists recognize over fifty! While the resulting classification system is rather unwieldy and relies on indigestible nomenclature, the resulting well-defined, precise terminology is essential in assisting land managers to conserve and manage all of Belize's biodiversity effectively.

THE EARLY VEGETATION CLASSIFICATIONS

One of the first recognized attempts at classifying vegetation in Belize is attributed to Daniel Morris, who published his *Land of British Honduras* in 1883. In this work he describes the country's three distinct types of forest, using the term "ridge" as the basis for his names. The word "ridge" is still commonly used in Belize today, but it has proved confusing to many visitors, as it denotes forest rather than a distinct topographical feature. Morris recognized "pine ridge" (forest dominated by the pine tree *Pinus caribaea*), "broken ridge" (a generic broadleaf forest), and "cohune ridge" (broadleaf forest with an abundance of the cohune palm, *Attalea cohune*). Later classifications, including those of the forester Duncan Stevenson (1928), expanded this work and described the existence of other formations, including mangroves and various types of savanna.

One of the classic botanical texts for Belize was produced by Paul Standley and Samuel Record in 1936.[1] Although dated in terms of its taxonomic classifications, this superb early treatise on the flora of the country remains an essential reference work for botanists today, providing an excellent introduction to the vegetation and land use of the country at the time. It also includes useful descriptions and keys to many of the better-known (usually woody) plant groups. This work also offers a detailed analysis of a range of vegetation types, including mangrove, three types of savanna (brackish, freshwater, and inland), pine forest, four types of high (i.e., tall) rain forest (swamp, intermediate, mountain, and advanced), and secondary rain forest. These two botanists recognized that tree assemblages vary greatly between forest types and attempted to subdivide their classifications based on the varying associations of species found within them. This use of distinct species suites as a basis for vegetation classification was adopted and refined by later ecologists, including Charles Wright.

Although other researchers subsequently provided useful descriptions of regional vegetation types, including Cyrus Lundell (1937),[2] the groundbreaking work on Belizean vegetation was produced by the British Honduras Land Survey team, led by the celebrated naturalist Charles Wright.[3] Although the aim of this project was to review the agricultural potential of the country, it did so by using natural vegetation as an indicator of agricultural suitability. The project's superb final publication, *Land in British Honduras*, was based on a profound knowledge of the country and its ecology and provides detailed descriptions of climate, soils, and the variety of vegetation cover. This work relied on a great deal of fieldwork and resulted in an excellent vegetation map for the country that still serves ecologists well today. In part, Wright's forest classifications depended on the degree to which the forests contained "lime-loving" species, with such taxa occurring in increased abundance in forest over limestone. Modern classifications have largely been based on amending and updating this original masterpiece. Wright and his co-workers classified the vegetation of Belize into eighteen main classes (see table 2.1) and identified a total of seventy-seven subtypes.

Looking across an *Eleocharis* wetland at dusk toward an area of pine ridge. © Sam Bridgewater.

TABLE 2.1. Wright et al.'s eighteen vegetation classes for Belize   79

1. Broadleaf forest rich in lime-loving species	10. High marsh forest
2. Broadleaf forest moderately rich in lime-loving species	11. Low marsh forest
3. Broadleaf forest with occasional lime-loving species	12. Herbaceous marsh and swamp
4. Broadleaf forest with few or no lime-loving species	13. High swamp forest
5. Transitional broadleaf forest rich in lime-loving species	14. Palm swamp
6. Transitional broadleaf forest poor in lime-loving species	15. Mangrove swamp
7. Transitional low broadleaf forest and shrubland	16. Littoral forest
8. Shrubland with pine	17. Littoral swamp
9. Pine forest and orchard savanna	18. Cohune palm forest

Source: Adapted from A. C. S. Wright et al., *Land in British Honduras*.

MAPPING VEGETATION: THE VALUE OF INDICATOR SPECIES

Charles Wright and his co-workers from the British Honduras Land Survey team were well aware that vegetation effectively maps underlying soils and geology as well as climate and that certain species are excellent indicators of soil fertility. For example, Belizean forests can occur both on lime-rich soil derived from limestone and upon more acidic soils from bedrock, such as granite and Santa Rosa formations (see "Granite and Limestone: From the Old to the New" in chapter 1). Although some species can occur in a wide range of soils, others tend to be largely confined to one or the other and thus can be used as indicators of soil fertility. For instance, an abundance of members of the Melastomataceae family and the presence of the trees yemeri (*Vochysia hondurensis*), banak (*Virola koschnyi*), and negrito (*Simarouba glauca*) usually show that the underlying soils are acidic, nutrient poor, and hence infertile and unsuitable for agriculture. Conversely, an abundance of breadnut (*Brosimum alicastrum*), sapodilla (*Manilkara zapota*), mahogany (*Swietenia macrophylla*), and the fishtail palm (*Chamaedorea ernesti-augustii*) often indicate that the forest occurs on more alkaline and fertile limestone substrates. Much of Belize's agriculture occurs on such soils. The cohune palm (*Attalea cohune*) is another

species that is abundant in fertile areas.

Plant species are useful indicator species of not only soil fertility but also other ecological factors, including moisture. For example, the presence of the calabash tree (*Crescentia cujete*) and the bullet tree (*Bucida buceras*)—especially in savanna areas—reveals that an area may well be frequently waterlogged; these tree species are unusual in that they are able to withstand such conditions. Likewise, if the ground layer of an ecosystem is dominated by sedges and rushes rather than grasses, this is a sign that the area is inundated, at least during certain times of the year. Climate, degree of seasonality, and altitude also play an important role in governing species distributions. Thus, the palm *Colpothrinax cookii*, magnolia (*Magnolia yoroconte*), and members of the heather family (Ericaceae) are usually found only at altitude in the cooler, moister climates of Belize's Maya Mountains, whereas the palm *Manicaria saccifera* is restricted to low-lying areas in the south, where the climate is hot and wet and the soils are frequently waterlogged. This is in stark contrast to the palm *Pseudophoenix sargentii*, which can be found only in the far north, where the climate is considerably drier and there is a much more pronounced dry season.

Since the work of Wright, other research-ers have sought to improve on Belize's veg-etation classification system. These include

A grove of calabash (*Crescentia cujete*), an indication that the area may be seasonally inundated. © Sam Bridgewater.

King's various land-use assessments as well as Iremonger and Brokaw's vegetation clas-sification of Belize, published in 1995.[4] These later classifications benefited from the use of modern technology. Whereas Wright and his team had access to only aerial photographs taken from planes, later workers were able to consult satellite images that greatly assisted with distinguishing between vegetation types. Although the terminol-ogy used in these later systems has changed from Wright's original work, the updated modifications have nevertheless relied heavily on his team's seminal work of the 1950s, and a comparison of the latest vegetation maps with Wright's original work reveals the same general patterns.

MODERN VEGETATION CLASSIFICATIONS AND THE UNESCO SYSTEM

Most biological researchers currently working in Belize use the Belize Ecosystems Map as the basis of their work. First published by Jan Meerman and Wilber Sabido in 2001 and updated in 2004,[5] this map formed part of a larger regional initiative called the Central American Ecosystems Mapping Project. This attempted to classify the ecosys-tems of Central America at a scale of 1:250,000 using a uniform methodology and ter-minology. The detailed classification system is based on that adopted by the United

Nations Educational, Scientific and Cultural Organization (UNESCO). It distinguishes different vegetation types based on a variety of criteria, the most important of which relate to physical structure (physiognomy), degree of seasonality and rainfall, leaf form (broadleaf or coniferous), altitude, topography, soils, and species composition.

Taking a pragmatic approach to classification, at its most basic level the Belize Ecosystems Map system identifies twenty generalized ecosystem classes (see table 2.2). Sixteen of these are terrestrial, and ten are types of forest. The forest types are differentiated from one another based on characters, such as whether they are dominated by broadleaf or pine species, or the presence of distinctive mangrove trees, such as *Rhizophora mangle* and *Avicennia germinans*. Altitude is another important factor, with all forests categorized as being lowland (0–500 meters in altitude), submontane (500–1,000 meters), or montane (1,000 meters and above). A further distinguishing feature relates to the level of average annual rainfall, with dry forest types experiencing less than 1,500 millimeters of rain per annum clearly identified.

The system becomes more complicated as each of the generalized ecosystem classes can be further subdivided into ecosystem types. For example, the ecosystem class "submontane broad-leaved moist forest" encompasses five distinct forest ecosystem types. One of these is called "tropical evergreen seasonal broad-leaf forest on steep karstic hills." This forest type occurs in the Chiquibul region. The name is descriptive in nature; in addition to providing details on the type of forest, it reveals information about its degree of deciduousness (i.e., although broad-leaved, the forest is evergreen and does not generally lose its leaves in the dry season), its topographic occurrence, and its underlying substrate.

The current vegetation classification for Belize can be viewed in detail online at the Biodiversity and Environmental Resource Data System of Belize website.[6]

TABLE 2.2. Meerman and Sabido's broad ecosystem classes for Belize, 2004

Open sea	Lowland pine forest
Coral reef	Submontane pine forest
Seagrass	Lowland broad-leaved dry forest
Water	Lowland broad-leaved moist forest
Sparse algae	Submontane broad-leaved moist forest
Urban	Montane broad-leaved moist forest
Agricultural uses	Lowland broad-leaved wet forest
Wetland	Submontane broad-leaved wet forest
Shrubland	Montane broad-leaved wet forest
Lowland savanna	Mangrove and littoral forest

Source: Biodiversity and Environmental Resource Data System of Belize (BERDS), "Ecosystems"; http://www.biodiversity.bz/find/ecosystem, accessed December 30, 2010.

The usual day-to-day view we enjoy of the world is from the ground level, from which our line of sight can often be limited if we are in a city or a dense forest. For stunning vistas, many of us climb mountains where, clouds permitting, we can enjoy panoramic views of the countryside below. With the advantage of height it is easier to gain perspective about one's surroundings and how individual features, landforms, and vegetation types relate to one another. The best view many of us will ever have will be from the seat of an airplane, and the stunning glimpses of Belize as one approaches by air have been referred to earlier.

Scientists have long appreciated the value of these high vantage points in gaining an insight into vegetation patterns, and a range of technologies have been developed that bring these "views from afar" to our desks in the form of remotely sensed images. The simplest of these is an aerial photograph. Dating from the late 1900s, when they were taken from balloons, aerial photos are still some of the most useful images available for ecologists and land managers today, although the balloon has long since been replaced by the airplane, rocket, or satellite.

With the arrival of the space age after World War II, the many satellites that orbit our planet provide a more distant opportunity to view the earth. The Landsat Program developed by the National Aeronautics and Space Administration (NASA) and the U.S. Geological Survey is the most famous provider of remotely sensed pictures of earth from space. Images from the Landsat Program have provided the foundation of many vegetation maps. Established in the early 1970s, Landsat images are based on sampling photo energies from various parts of the electromagnetic spectrum. Electromagnetic radiation is classified into various types according to the *frequency* of the wave. These include *radio waves, microwaves, infrared radiation, visible light, ultraviolet radiation,* and *X-rays.* The earliest of such images had relatively low resolution, but scientific advances have enabled extremely detailed images to be developed with on-the-ground resolutions of less than thirty meters. For example, the most recent manifestation of Landsat (Landsat 7) uses a sophisticated device known as an Enhanced Thematic Mapper (ETM), which covers the visible, near-infrared, shortwave, and thermal infrared bands of the electromagnetic spectrum.

In addition to satellite images, vegetation scientists can make use of radar. Although the principles behind radar imagery are complex, in essence they are based on measuring the degree of reflectance and "backscatter" of electromagnetic radiation emitted from a receiver mounted below an airplane. The degree of reflectance depends on the density and form of the reflecting object, and radar images can provide startling detail of vegetation structure.

Although all remotely sensed images are useful, they are merely tools to help us interpret vegetation patterns. The production of high-quality, functional maps depends on the skills of geographers and use of sophisticated geographical information systems (GIS), which allow manipulation of remotely sensed images to ensure that they are depicting tangible on-the-ground patterns. The putative vegetation classes produced from an office must always then be visited and checked on the ground ("ground-truthed") to verify that the vegetation types depicted are real entities associated with perceived differences in vegetation structure and species assemblages rather than artificial computer-generated constructs.

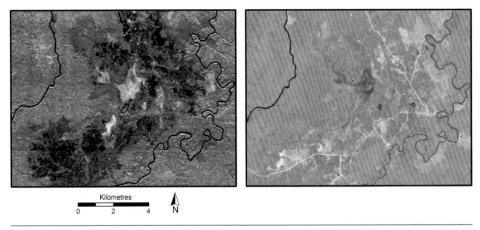

Vegetation maps of forest and savanna within the Rio Bravo Conservation and Management Area derived from radar (*left*) and SPOT (*right*) imagery. Remotely sensed images are invaluable tools for vegetation mapping. © Iain Cameron. Courtesy the Geography Department, School of Geosciences, Edinburgh University, and the Darwin Initiative project Conservation of the Lowland Savanna Ecosystem in Belize.

THE CHIQUIBUL AND THE MAYA FOREST

Scientific researchers and visitors to Las Cuevas Research Station are lured by the great expanses of biodiverse forest in which to work and roam. One of the highlights of any visit to the research station is to make the short, steep trek to the summit of a nearby hill before dawn and then to scale the observation tower that rises from its summit in time to see the sun rise over the Maya Divide. From this lofty vantage point the feeling of being in a true wilderness area is overwhelming; an uninterrupted view over the jungle canopy stretches out to all cardinal points far beyond the horizon's edge. No sounds of traffic disturb the dawn chorus, and no villages, towns, power lines, or tarmac roads yet betray human presence. Here nature still goes about its business as it has done for centuries, although it is a fallacy to believe that this forest is entirely untouched by human hand. Logging has shaped the structure of the forest by removing many of the larger, most valuable timber trees (see "Commercial Timber Extraction: Four Hundred Years of Exploitation" in chapter 3), and the ongoing unregulated extraction of forest products, such as *Chamaedorea* palm leaf (see "Xaté, Leaf of Gold" in chapter 3), as well as hunting provide cause for concern.

Few countries in Central America still retain the forest that once defined their landscapes; Belize is one of the notable exceptions. However, even in this last stronghold of the great Maya Forest, its continued existence is by no means secure. According to the Belize Ecosystems Map, approximately 60 percent (about 14,000 square kilometers) of Belize's land surface is naturally covered by some kind of broadleaf forest or shrubland.[7] The country's network of reserves is renowned for protecting 36 percent of the terrestrial and national territory.[8] Although this figure is significant, development pressures, agricultural and urban incursions, logging, and illegal forest activity con-stantly erode both the extent and ecological value of the forests that remain. At current deforestation rates (ca. 2 percent per annum) it is predicted that Belize's forest cover will decrease significantly to under 60 percent by 2020.[9] For now, though, due to its remoteness, the Chiquibul region continues to be synonymous with forest wilderness. Together, the Chiquibul Forest Reserve, the Chiquibul National Park, and the Caracol Archaeological Reserve protect over 177,000 hectares, making the Chiquibul one of the largest continuous forest expanses left in Central America.

Not least among the many environmental concerns facing our beleaguered planet is the high rate at which species are becoming extinct as a result of human activities. In recent years climate change and global warming have been added to the threats that act against the world's biota. The Red List of Threatened Species attempts to evaluate the global conservation status of all species using a standardized protocol, highlighting those most under threat. First conceived in 1963 by the International Union for Conservation of Nature and Natural Resources (IUCN), the list is updated at regular intervals, with the most recent version published online in 2010. Species considered by the Red List are classified into one of nine groups, dependent upon assessment of their status against a number of predefined criteria, including the rate of decline of the species in question, its known population size, and its geographical distribution.[10] For many species there is simply not enough information to allow any kind of assessment, and these taxa are labeled as "data deficient." Species believed to be facing an extremely high risk of extinction in the wild are classified as critically endangered. Those that are threatened, but to a lesser degree, are classified as endangered or vulnerable. A species is only classified as extinct if it is known beyond all reasonable doubt that the last individual has died. A world-famous example is provided by the dodo.

The 2010 Red List of Threatened Species assessed 55,926 species, of which 18,351 (33 percent) were considered to be endangered.[11] Globally, one in four mammals, one in eight birds, and one in three amphibians are threatened with extinction. However, only 3 percent of the world's 1.9 million described species has been assessed. Since historical scientific records began, it is known that at least 784 extinctions have occurred, but it is almost certain that many more species have disappeared from the face of the planet than this in recent times. Our limited knowledge makes it impossible to know. Although many Belizean species are covered by the IUCN Red List, assessment takes a global perspective on the species covered. Ideally, a national assessment should also be made. In 2005 a preliminary independent assessment of Belize's critically threatened terrestrial and marine species using IUCN categories was published, with a view to publishing an official Belize Red List at a later date.[12] The national "Critical List" includes 140 species: 12 amphibians, 10 reptiles, 28 mammals, 46 birds, 34 fishes/sharks, 2 corals, and 8 plants. There are some differences between the global IUCN Red List and the national list. For example, the IUCN list evaluates the roseate tern as being of "Least Concern," whereas the national list classifies it as "Vulnerable." Conversely, the silver palm (*Schippa concolor*) is considered by the IUCN as vulnerable, as it occurs only in Belize and thus its population is small globally. However, the national list classifies it as "Least Concern," as there are relatively abundant and well-conserved populations within the country. In total, 7 species are classified as Critically Endangered (e.g., *Harpia harpyja*–harpy eagle), 5 as Endangered (e.g., *Ara macao cyanoptera*–scarlet macaw), and 65 as Vulnerable (e.g., *Lontra longicaudis*–neotropical river otter).

FACING: Looking out from Las Cuevas bird tower across the Chiquibul at dawn. A rolling forest landscape stretches out to the horizon in all directions. © Alex Monro.

Of the eighty-five distinct ecosystems recorded for Belize, fifty-eight, or over half, are types of pine or broadleaf forest.[13] As a rule of thumb, forests in the north are dry, becoming increasingly wet the farther south they are found. Parts of Corozal District in northern Belize, for example, receive only 1,200 millimeters of rain per year, while in the southern parts of Toledo District 4,000 millimeters is not unusual. This dramatic difference in annual precipitation has a marked influence on the species that are found at opposite ends of the country. Some of those restricted to particular geographical localities and climatic extremes have been highlighted earlier in the chapter (see the boxed text "Mapping Vegetation: The Value of Indicator Species").

Although there are considerable floristic differences among Belize's forest areas, the forty-four broadleaf forest types classified by the Belize Ecosystems Map are prescribed by predetermined cutoff values related to altitude and topographic and climatic factors. Individual species do not respect such arbitrary designations. Forests

below 500 meters in Belize, for example, are defined as lowland, while those occurring above 500 meters (but below 1,000 meters) are defined as submontane. However, a botanist venturing across the 500-meter contour line will find it impossible to distinguish between the distinct forest types separated by this altitudinal limit, assuming the soils remain the same. An examination of species composition will find the forest types to be almost identical. Thus, it is necessary to approach the classification with a degree of flexibility. Throughout the latitudinal range of Belizean forests one is highly likely to repeatedly come across the same suite of common tree species, including mahogany (*Swietenia macrophylla*), Santa Maria (*Calophyllum brasiliense*), nargusta (*Terminalia amazonia*),

The "tourist tree," or gumbo-limbo (*Bursera simaruba*), is one of Belize's most famous trees on account of its shiny, peeling bark, used to relieve skin burn from the black poisonwood (*Metopium brownei*). The species is widespread but particularly abundant in the north. © William Milliken.

ironwood (*Dialium guianense*), and the bullet tree (*Bucida buceras*). Comparing the tree species found in two hectares of forests in Bladen Nature Reserve (south of the Maya Divide) with the tree flora of the Chiquibul region (to the north), for example, shows that 64 percent of the 140 species found in Bladen are also found in the Chiquibul. However, the abundance of these species in each site varies significantly. A direct comparison of the most common thirty trees between individual plot surveys in Bladen and the Chiquibul indicates that only five species (17 percent) are shared.[14] That said, field botanists who have learned their trade in one region of the country will find it relatively easy to relocate and work elsewhere in different designated forest types. The main species matrix is often largely the same.

So what are the main differences between Belize's primary forest types? It is beyond the scope of this book to attempt to compare and contrast in detail all forty-four types of the country's broadleaf forests. Only the flora of the Chiquibul will be discussed in detail. Over 3,400 species of vascular plants are recorded for Belize,[15] and the forest environment is the most diverse of all. Hence, a review of this nature demands a book in its own right. In addition, much remains to be discovered about the forest flora, and the data on species composition is still not available for the majority of the nation's forests. For example, by mid-2007, only 747 individual botanical collections had been made in the Cockscomb Basin Wildlife Sanctuary (CBWS), even though this area of 51,400 hectares is one of Belize's flagship protected forests.[16] These 747 collections equate to only 438 species. Considering the known high diversity of adjacent floras such as the Chiquibul, where over 7,000 botanical collections have been made, it is clear that there is an extreme paucity of knowledge on the flora of the CBWS. The same is true of many other forest areas. Thus, any kind of detailed floristic comparison is currently impossible. That said, it is possible to discuss a few generalized patterns.

The palm *Pseudophoenix sargentii* is found only in the highly seasonal forests of northern Belize. © Sam Bridgewater.

Precipitation and seasonality are extremely important ecological determinants, and the drier forests of northern Belize have their own distinct floristic character and structure. They tend to be of lower stature and of a scrubbier appearance than the wetter forests of the south. Some of their typical defining species are restricted to this region, and although they do occur farther to the north in Mexico, they are not found in southern Belize, where the climate is wetter. Examples of such species include the palm *Pseudophoenix sargentii* and *Hyperbaena winzerlingii*. Many of the dominant species that typify the northern dry forests are more climatically tolerant; however, their great abundance in the dry forests is unusual. Such species include the black poisonwood (*Metopium brownii*), gumbo-limbo (*Bursera simarouba*), warrie wood (*Caesalpinia gaumeri*), *Lysiloma latisiliquum*, and *Piscidia piscipula*. Species of *Coccoloba* (Polygonaceae—sea grape family) are also abundant in the understory. The significance of seasonality to forest ecology is discussed in chapter 4.

A BUTTRESSED KINGDOM: THE SWAMP FORESTS

One significant forest type is swamp forests, which occur under waterlogged conditions. The bullet tree (*Bucida buceras*) and ironwood (*Dialium guianense*) are often abundant in such areas, although both can also be found in dry locations. In northern Belize's swamp forests, logwood (*Haematoxylon campechianum*) is sometimes abundant, although this species has suffered past exploitation due to its value as a source of dye (see "Pirates of the Caribbean: Logwood, Baymen, and the Birth of Belize" in chapter 3). The provision tree (*Pachira aquatica*) and various species of *Inga* (pea family) provide other examples of tree species commonly associated with water. Perhaps the most visually striking tree species of swamp forests is kaway (*Pterocarpus officinalis*), its beautiful, curving, buttressed roots being a characteristic sight in such areas.

The buttressed roots of the kaway (*Pterocarpus officinalis*). © Sam Bridgewater.

As highlighted earlier in the chapter, soils are one of the primary factors determining species distributions (see the boxed text "Mapping Vegetation: The Value of Indicator Species" earlier in this chapter). This can be illustrated by a comparison of the flora of the Chiquibul Forest Reserve and what is known about the Cockscomb Basin Wildlife Reserve. The former is underlain primarily by limestone; hence the resultant soils are calcium-rich and relatively fertile. The latter is largely underlain by granites with acidic, infertile, derived soils. Species of *Sloanea*, for example, are abundant in Cockscomb but rare in limestone areas of the Chiquibul. The tendency for yemeri (*Vochysia hondurensis*) and members of the Melastomataceae to occur in more acidic areas has already been discussed. Not surprisingly, these are far more abundant in Cockscomb than the Chiquibul Forest Reserve. However, many common tree species do occur in both forest types. In addition to those generalists listed above,

A leaf of *Clidemia septuplinervia* showing the characteristic venation of the Melastomataceae. A concentration of members of this family indicates the presence of acidic, infertile soils. © Zoë Goodwin.

hog plum (*Spondias radlkoferi*), horse's balls (*Stemmadenia donnell-smithii*), white gumbo-limbo (*Dendropanax arboreus*), the cotton tree (*Ceiba pentandra*), and quamwood (*Schizolobium parahyba*) provide examples of species that can be found on both soil types.

FORESTS OF THE HIGH MAYA DIVIDE

At higher altitudes rising toward and above one thousand meters, a number of tree species occur that are absent or rarely found elsewhere. Good examples of these include *Liquidamber styraciflua*, *Hedyosmum mexicanum*, and *Magnolia yoroconte*. The Ericaceae (heather) family with its characteristic bell-shaped flowers is another group that usually prefers cooler temperate climates. Such conditions are found only at altitude, and hence such species as *Macleania insignis* and *Orthaea brachysiphon* are abundant on the chain of summits that form the Maya Mountains. Occasionally dense palm forest predominates on the Maya Divide, with *Colpothrinax cookii* restricted to these higher elevations, where it often occurs with the more generalist cabbage palm (*Euterpe precatoria*).

Montane forest at Doyle's Delight, Belize's highest mountain (1,124 meters). The abundant taller palm is *Colpothrinax cookii*, which is restricted to higher elevations in the Maya Mountains. © Sam Bridgewater.

RIDGES AND TROUGHS: FORESTS AND TOPOGRAPHY

Local topography as well as absolute elevation are known to influence species distributions. Over limestone, for example, relatively small topographical changes can dramatically alter the species composition of a forest. Due to the porous nature of limestone, water availability for plants can be poor—especially during the dry season—with drought conditions accentuated by elevation. Work conducted in the Bladen Nature Reserve has shown that a high proportion of species (61 percent) uniquely occur in these water-stressed limestone ridges (e.g., *Oxandra belizensis*).[17] These species have a tendency to be restricted to northern Mesoamerica; in the case of *O. belizensis*, the species is endemic to Belize, occurring nowhere else on the planet. Conversely, species occurring in the valley bottoms were found to be dominated by widespread neotropical generalists, such as hog plum (*Spondias radlkoferi*). Limestone forests are rare in South America and southern Mesoamerica, and these authors suggest that northern Mesoamerican species are better adapted than widespread generalists to coping with the drought conditions found on limestone ridges.

It is rare for botanists to know the names of all the many hundreds of plants they see in the forest. Usually only a few hundred scientific names of the most common or conspicuous ones are stored in the memory. More unusual or rarer species must be collected if they are to be identified at a future date. This usually requires the use of specialist literature and a herbarium (see "Herbaria: Safeguarding Our Knowledge of Plant Diversity" later in this chapter). The latter is used as the basis for comparison of unidentified specimens with others of known identity—essentially a process of playing snap. Species are classified scientifically according to structure, with great emphasis placed on their fruits and flowers. Field botanists, therefore, always prefer to collect their specimens when fertile, as this will facilitate later identification. In the absence of fruits and flowers, specimens are still often collected in a vegetative state because it is possible to name a plant accurately from just its leaves, twigs, and sometimes bark. However, for some plant groups, such as the Lauraceae (laurel family), species and even genera are vegetatively almost exactly the same, and in these cases accurate naming without fruits and flowers can be impossible.

Pressing botanical specimens at night on Doyle's Delight. Botanists usually preserve specimens for later study by pressing them between sheets of paper and either drying the press over heat or saturating the pressed paper with an alcohol solution. © Sam Bridgewater.

CONTINUED NEXT PAGE

Typically, botanists use secateurs, or long-armed pruners, to collect their specimens. For taller trees, climbing might be required with the use of foot spikes or ropes. Each plant collected is given a unique number by the collector, who then immediately presses the plant between newspaper in a portable field press. Where possible, the collector will make duplicates of each numbered specimen collected, for later distribution to the world's herbaria and plant-family specialists. In addition, duplicates must always be left in the country of origin if facilities for their storage exist. In pressing, the botanist makes sure that at least some of the leaves are turned over so that both sides can be seen. All parts of the plant contain useful characters, and the type and abundance of hairs on the leaf underside, for example, can aid classification and naming. Flowers may be pressed in the same way; if fragile, they might be placed in alcohol in a vial that is given the same number as the leaves of the specimen. Fruits can be either pressed whole if small, sliced into sections to facilitate drying, or placed complete in a separate packet bearing the number of the collection. Frequently small pieces of leaf or flower are also collected in tiny packets of silica gel for use in molecular research work. Silica gel rapidly increases the rate at which biological material dries, and the DNA of such material is easier to extract by biologists in laboratories. Finally, before moving on to the next plant, detailed notes are made of the specimen collected, including its size, the color of its flowers and fruits, the habitat in which it was found, the date, the coordinates of the location, and the names of the collectors. This information builds an identification profile of the plant that will be essential to those studying the specimen in the future. Characters such as the size and form of the leaf are not recorded, as these will persist once the plant is in a herbarium; only information that will be lost once the plant is removed from its habitat is taken.

On returning to camp or a field station at night, the botanist prepares the day's collections for processing. Ideally, collected plants should be dried slowly over heat, as this retains the color of the flowers and increases the chances that the leaves will not drop off the specimen during the drying process. One common way of doing this is to place each newspaper containing the pressed plant between pages of blotting paper, with finely corrugated aluminum sheets alternating between each specimen. The aluminum serves to conduct the heat. Once a stack of specimens, blotters, and aluminum sheets of the required size has been made, it is pressed tightly using straps and transferred to the top of a frame containing a gas or paraffin stove to dry overnight. The degree of heat applied is critical—too hot and the specimens will scorch; too cool and they won't dry. In remote locations it might not be possible to carry a stove, blotting paper, and corrugates. Instead, the pressed plants in their newspapers are made into a parcel and placed in a strong plastic bag. Alcohol of 70 percent strength is then poured over them, and the bag sealed shut. The alcohol will keep them from decaying until drying facilities become available. Although this method requires less paraphernalia to transport, the resultant collections often lose their color and the leaves frequently drop from the stems. Thus, the former method is generally preferred whenever possible.

All botanical researchers collecting plant material in Belize must first apply for a permit from the Belize Forest Department (BFD). The permit outlines exactly what studies can be conducted and the researcher's contractual obligations to Belize. All researchers must respect the laws of the country and ensure that biological material is used only in the manner stated under the terms of the permit. If there are commercial possibilities resulting from the collections, then profit-sharing agreements must be in place. For the most part, however, the latter situation does not apply, as taxonomists generally collect biological specimens for scientific study only, and they are of no commercial value. This part of the Convention on Biological Diversity was primarily intended to protect countries from unscrupulous biopirates (see the boxed text "Intellectual Property Rights" in chapter 3). Before dried plant specimens are exported, an export permit must be requested from the BFD, and the plants inspected for bugs. If they are deemed clear of infestation, a phytosanitary certificate will be issued, and they are then ready for export to the researcher's home institution.

THE SOIL OF THE CHIQUIBUL FOREST RESERVE

The diversity and structural form of the Chiquibul Forest Reserve (CFR) are influenced by both the seasonality of the climate and the soils, which are derived principally from the limestone bedrock. Much of the Chiquibul is underlain by limestone of Cretaceous age (146–66 MYA) (see "Granite and Limestone: From the Old to the New" in chapter 1), and the fine-grained clay- and silt-rich soils developed over these calcareous rocks are typically alkaline (pH 6.5–8) with significant amounts of minerals such as calcium and magnesium available for plant growth.[18] Thus, broadly speaking, they are fertile, especially when compared with the highly weathered, nutrient-depleted sandy soils of the Mountain Pine Ridge or other pine savanna and pine forest areas. However, within the CFR there are also smaller patches of nutrient-poor, coarse-textured sands whose derivation is uncertain. These support pine savanna. In addition, there are narrow bands of finer-textured riverine sediments associated with water courses, with the upper slopes of hilly areas generally having very thin soils.

One measure of soil fertility is effective cation exchange capacity, which provides an indication of the degree to which mineral ions are present, stored, and made readily available to plants. The high proportion of clay in the limestone-derived Chiquibul soils helps prevent such ions from being lost through leaching, and its cation exchange capacity is high (see table 2.3). The high proportion of clay also helps the soil store water; thus these soils are less prone to drought than generally coarse-textured savannas, which have comparatively little clay content. The clays are capable of absorbing large amounts of water and may swell and shrink during the wet and dry seasons. However, even within the Chiquibul Forest Reserve there is significant variation in soil

TABLE 2.3. Comparison of the soil properties of the Chiquibul Forest Reserve and the Mountain Pine Ridge

	Structural			Chemical		
	Sand (%)	Silt (%)	Clay	pH	CaCO$_3$	CEC
Chiquibul Forest Reserve	0	354	65	7.5	18	66
Mountain Pine Ridge	49	38	13	5	0.01	2.4

Note: Sand: 2–0.05 mm; silt: 0.05–0.002 mm; clay: <0.002 mm; pH (1:1) 0.01 M CaCl$_2$; CaCO$_3$ = inorganic carbon equivalent; CEC = cation exchange capacity (cmol(+) kg^{-1}).

Source: Adapted from Dubbin, Penn, and Hodson, "Edaphic Influences on Plant Community Adaptation."

TABLE 2.4. The main soil types of Belize

Soils of the Maya Mountains (including the Mountain Pine Ridge)	Developed from Paleozoic metamorphic and volcanic rocks with later granitic intrusions, these soils are very old, often deeply weathered, coarse-grained, generally acidic, and low in nutrient availability.
Soils of the limestone uplands and foothills	The soils derived from the weathering of Cretaceous limestone rock exhibiting karstic scenery are typically shallow and stony, although clay-rich and organic at the surface, with neutral to alkaline pH levels and plentiful calcium and magnesium, but few other nutrients. Depressions in the landscape are frequently filled with colluvia (sediments washed in from surrounding slopes).
Soils of the Toledo beds	Occurring in Toledo District, these rolling landscapes are made up of flat-bedded mudstones and siltstones with some minor but important limestones and sandstones. The soils are mostly shallow, but some deeper, reddish soils are to the south and west. They are clay-rich, well drained, and slightly acidic and have moderate levels of calcium and magnesium (from the limestone)
Pine ridge soils of the coastal plains	These soils extend across the country and are covered by pine savanna and woodland. They are probably derived from old coastal sediments and erosional deposits from the Maya Mountains; they frequently exhibit a mottled red and white clay subsoil underlying a dry, sandy topsoil. They tend to be acid with low nutrient availability (even lower than the Mountain Pine Ridge) and extreme moisture regimes. They are very susceptible to fire in the dry season.
Swamp soils	These soils are typically wet all year or for a major part of it. They are saline and covered by mangrove and mangrove associates toward the coast; inland the salinity decreases, and they are covered by freshwater swamp forest and herbaceous communities. Textures range from coarse sand to heavy clay; they are usually gray with rusty mottling (gleying), indicative of an alternating moisture regime. They are often highly organic.
Riverine alluvium	These soils are the most fertile and manageable in Belize and are most extensive in the center of the country. They are well supplied with plant nutrients. Typically they are brown, yellow, or red.

Source: Derived from Baillie et al., *Revised Classification of the Soils of Belize*.

depth, soil fertility, and water-holding capacity, depending on topography and drainage, with the soils of ridges and hilltops typically tending to be thinner (sometimes as little as five centimeters deep) and more prone to drought, and having lower levels of clay and available nutrients due to erosion than those of low-lying areas. The forest of such topographic rises tends to be more deciduous in nature.

SOIL LANDSCAPES OF BELIZE

The soils of the Chiquibul Forest Reserve are by no means unique in Belize and occur throughout the country wherever limestone occurs. Although it is beyond the scope of this book to provide in-depth information on all of Belize's soils, a summary of the main types can be seen in table 2.4. The variety of soils throughout the country is a microcosm of the soil resources throughout Central America.

FACTORS AFFECTING SOIL FORMATION

Many different factors can affect soil formation, including climate, age of the soil and its bedrock, slope and drainage, and overlying vegetation. The rainfall gradient between the north and south of Belize, for example, influences the intensity of weathering of materials and leaching. This is generally greater over the Maya Mountains and in Toledo than in the drier north. Although temperatures are relatively uniform throughout Belize, inland areas experience greater extremes—especially at altitude—and this can also increase the rate at which weathering of rocks may occur. The length of time that rocks have been exposed to weathering also affects the properties of the soil, with older surfaces of the Maya Mountains having been intensely weathered for hundreds of millions of years. As a result, few nutrients are now available.

Within any one geological formation, topography can greatly influence soil properties. There can be great differences between the soils of hilltops, slopes, and valley bottoms, for example, forming what is known as a catenary sequence. Typically, the movement of soil downslope gives rise to deeper soils at the base of a landform, often providing more favorable nutrient and moisture conditions for plant growth.[19]

Finally, as discussed earlier in this chapter (see the boxed text "Mapping Vegetation: The Value of Indicator Species"), vegetation usually maps underlying soils. However, the situation is complicated in that the individual plant species themselves can change soil properties over time. The cohune palm (*Attalea cohune*), for example, grows prolifically on deep, well-drained, fertile soils. However, this species may actually have helped to create the soils upon which it thrives through its rooting system, organic input from its discarded, prodigious sail-like fronds, and the infilling of stump voids and associated "turning over" of the soil profile.[20]

Despite having less than 0.5 percent of the world's land area, Mesoamerica is believed to support between 7 and 10 percent of all known species and 17 percent of all terrestrial species. It is considered to be the second-most important of twenty-five globally identified hotspots, when a combination of threat, species diversity, and endemism are taken into account.[21] The Maya Forest, of which the Chiquibul contributes a significant part, forms a key portion of the Mesoamerica Biological Corridor. Understanding its internal patterns of diversity is vital if its regional conservation significance is to be fully realized.

Examination of the 7,000 dried plant herbarium specimens collected from within the Chiquibul region indicates that just over 1,300 vascular plant species occur within its confines.[22] These include 320 tree species, 246 species of shrub, 452 terrestrial or epiphytic herbs (the latter being plants that grow on other plants), 182 species of vine, 20 palms, 4 cacti, 2 cycads, 107 ferns, 14 woody parasites, and 10 lycopods! This represents 40 percent of the total flora of Belize. Four of the species represented are known only to occur in Belize and nowhere else in the world. These are *Neurolaena schippii* (Rubiaceae–coffee family), *Gymnanthes belizensis* (Euphorbiaceae–spurge family), *Scutellaria lundellii* (Lamiaceae–mint family), and *Calyptranthes bartlettii* (Myrtaceae–myrtle family).

Wright's 1959 vegetation classification of the Chiquibul recognized nine classes of forest vegetation containing evergreen, deciduous, and semideciduous trees. Due to Belize's seasonal climate, a number of species, including the cotton tree (*Ceiba pentandra*) and Spanish cedar (*Cedrela odorata*), lose their leaves during the dry season as an adaptation against drought (see "The Deciduous Habit" in chapter 5). Wright's early classification took the deciduous nature of the forest into account. In recent years this classification has been extensively updated, and two complementary vegetation maps for the Chiquibul now exist.[23] A vegetation map based on the Belize Ecosystems Map is provided on p. 99. Following this map, much of the forest of the western Chiquibul is classified as tropical evergreen forest over karstic terrain, and for this region the same basic tree community dominates. As shown in table 2.5, the following major tree families are all very important: Anacardiaceae (mango family), Annonaceae (custard apple family), Apocynaceae (frangipani family), Lauraceae (laurel family), Leguminosae (pea family), Malvaceae (hibiscus family), Meliaceae (mahogany family), Moraceae (fig family), Rubiaceae (coffee family), Sapindaceae (lychee family), and Sapotaceae (chicle family). These families often dominate in tropical forests across Central and South America, and thus the Chiquibul's tree families are essentially typical in this regard.

Due to its remoteness, the eastern portion of the Chiquibul has been poorly collected. Thus little is known about the species composition of those forests overlying the acidic metamorphosed sandstones and mudstones that make up the eastern and northern flanks of the Maya Mountains. Many floristic elements will be similar to those of the more westerly limestone areas, but there will undoubtedly be differences

Species	Common Name	Species	Common Name
Anacardiaceae		Alchornea latifolia	male grape
Astronium graveolens	jobillo	Croton spp.	
Mosquitoxylum jamaicense	bastard mahogany	Sebastiana tuerckheimiana	white poisonwood
Spondias radlkoferi	hog plum	Lauraceae	
Annonaceae		Licaria capitata	laurel
Annona reticulata	wild custard apple	L. peckii	timbersweet
Cymbopetalum mayanum		Nectandra salicifolia	laurel
Xylopia frutescens	polewood	Leguminosae: Caesalpinioideae	
Apocynaceae		Dialium guianense	ironwood
Aspidosperma megalocarpon	mylady	Schizolobium parahyba	quamwood
Stemmadenia donnell-smithii	horse's balls	Leguminosae: Mimosoideae	
Aquifoliaceae		Abarema idiopoda	bastard tamarind
Ilex guianensis	birdberry	Acacia cookii	cockspur
Araliaceae		Cojoba arborea	barba jalote
Dendropanax arboreus	white gumbo-limbo	Inga punctata	
Asteraceae		Lysiloma acapulcense	bastard mahogany
Koanophyllon galeottii		Leguminosae: Papilionoideae	
Bignoniaceae		Acosmium panamense	Billy Webb
Tabebuia chrysantha	cortes	Andira inermis	cabbage bark
Boraginaceae		Dalbergia stevensonii	rosewood
Cordia alliodora	salmwood	Erythrina spp.	
Burseraceae		Gliricidia sepium	madre de cacao
Bursera simaruba	gumbo-limbo	Lonchocarpus castilloi	black cabbage bark
Protium copal	copal	Myroxylon balsamum	balsam
Celastraceae		Ormosia schipii	John Crow wood
Crossopetalum eucymosum		Platymiscium dimorphandrum	granadillo
Chrysobalanaceae		Pterocarpus rohrii	
Hirtella americana	pigeon plum	Swartzia cubensis	bastard rosewood
H. racemosa	pigeon plum	Vatairea lundellii	bitterwood
Clusiaceae		Malvaceae	
Calophyllum brasiliense	Santa Maria	Bernoullia flammea	red mapola
Combretaceae		Ceiba pentandra	ceiba, cotton tree
Bucida buceras	bullet tree	Guazuma ulmifolia	bay cedar
Terminalia amazonia	nargusta	Hampea stipitata	moho
Euphorbiaceae		Heliocarpus americanus	broadleaf moho
Acalypha diversifolia			

Species	Common Name	Species	Common Name
Luehea speciosa	moho	*Amyris belizensis*	
Trichospermum grewiifolium	red moho	*Zanthoxylum juniperinum*	prickly yellow
Meliaceae		Salicaceae	
Cedrela odorata	cedar, cedro	*Zuelania guidonia*	
Guarea grandifolia	big-leaved cedrillo	Sapindaceae	
G. tonduzii	small-leafed cedrillo	*Allophyllus* spp.	
Swietenia macrophylla	mahogany	*Cupania belizensis*	grand betty
Trichilia erythrocarpa		*Matayba apetala*	
T. havanensis		*Sapindus saponaria*	soapseed tree
T. minutiflora		Sapotaceae	
T. pallida		*Chrysophyllum mexicanum*	wild apple
Moraceae		*Manilkara zapota*	chicle
Brosimum alicastrum	breadnut	*Pouteria amygdalina*	red sillón
Castilla elastica	rubber	*P. campechiana*	mamey cerilla
Ficus spp.		*P. durlandii*	
Pseudolmedia spuria	cherry	*P. reticulata*	sapotillo
Trophis mexicana		Simaroubaceae	
T. racemosa	white ramon	*Picramnia antidesma*	
Myristacaceae		*Simarouba glauca*	negrito
Virola koschnyi	banak	Styracaceae	
Myrtaceae		*Styrax argenteus*	
Myrcia splendens		Turneraceae	
Myrcianthes fragrans		*Erblichia odorata*	conop
Pimenta dioica	allspice	Ulmaceae	
Nyctaginaceae		*Celtis iguanaea*	
Neea psychotrioides		*Ampelocera hottlei*	female bullhoof
Olacaceae		Urticaceae	
Heisteria media	cuero de sapo	*Cecropia obtusifolia*	trumpet tree
Polygonaceae		*C. peltata*	trumpet tree
Coccoloba belizensis	big-leaved grape	Verbenaceae	
Putranjivaceae		*Vitex gaumeri*	fiddlewood
Drypetes brownii	male bullhoof	Vochysiaceae	
Rhizophoraceae		*Vochysia hondurensis*	yemeri
Cassipourea guianensis	waterwood		
Rubiaceae			
Guettarda combsii	glassywood		
Simira salvadorensis			
Rutaceae			

Source: Bridgewater et al., "Preliminary checklist of the vascular plants of the Chiquibul Forest, Belize." Reproduced with permission from Cambridge University Press.

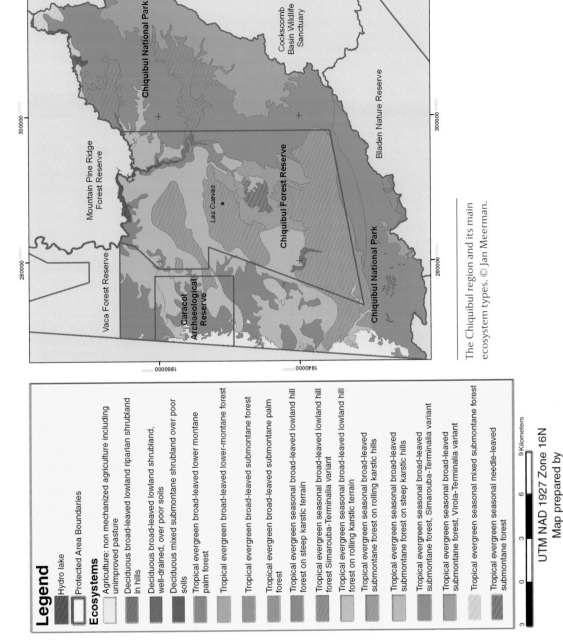

Legend

Hydro lake

Protected Area Boundaries

Ecosystems

Agriculture: non mechanized agriculture including unimproved pasture

Deciduous broad-leaved lowland riparian shrubland in hills

Deciduous broad-leaved lowland shrubland, well-drained, over poor soils

Deciduous mixed submontane shrubland over poor soils

Tropical evergreen broad-leaved lower montane palm forest

Tropical evergreen broad-leaved lower-montane forest

Tropical evergreen broad-leaved submontane forest

Tropical evergreen broad-leaved submontane palm forest

Tropical evergreen seasonal broad-leaved lowland hill forest on steep karstic terrain

Tropical evergreen seasonal broad-leaved lowland hill forest Simarouba-Terminalia variant

Tropical evergreen seasonal broad-leaved lowland hill forest on rolling karstic terrain

Tropical evergreen seasonal broad-leaved submontane forest on rolling karstic hills

Tropical evergreen seasonal broad-leaved submontane forest on steep karstic hills

Tropical evergreen seasonal broad-leaved submontane forest, Simarouba-Terminalia variant

Tropical evergreen seasonal broad-leaved submontane forest, Virola-Terminalia variant

Tropical evergreen seasonal mixed submontane forest

Tropical evergreen seasonal needle-leaved submontane forest

UTM NAD 1927 Zone 16N
Map prepared by
Jan Meerman
June 2009

0   3   6   9 Kilometers

The Chiquibul region and its main ecosystem types. © Jan Meerman.

in species. The forests of this region have been largely classified as tropical evergreen seasonal broad-leaf submontane forest, with two variants recognized: *Simarouba-Terminalia* variant and *Virola-Terminalia* variant. Tree species believed to be characteristic of these areas include *Terminalia amazonia, Vochysia hondurensis, Simarouba glauca*, and *Virola koschnyi*. These poorly described vegetation types are in need of further study. Higher-elevation forests within the Chiquibul region will be typical of those found at higher altitude and were briefly described earlier in this chapter (see "Forests of the High Maya Divide").

Although the Chiquibul is notable for its lack of rivers, a few do traverse the region. These include the Raspaculo River, the Macal River, the Chiquibul River, the Ceibo Grande River, and the Ceibo Chico River. Over one hundred species have been recorded as being particularly associated with riverine habitats within the region, and much of our knowledge of riverine ecosystems is based on floristic studies focused on the Macal River adjacent to Guacamallo Bridge and at Monkey Tail Branch.[24] Emergent trees are often scattered along the river banks, including quamwood (*Schizolobium parahyba*), ceiba (*Ceiba pentandra*), *Lonchocarpus guatemalensis*, and hog plum (*Spondias radlkoferi*). In heavily disturbed areas the grass *Tripsacum latifolium* is often dominant. The primary aquatic plant growing in fast-flowing streams is *Marathrum oxycarpum* (Podostemaceae).

Leaves, flowers, and fruit of horse's balls (*Stemmadenia donnell-smithii*), a common tree in the Chiquibul. It is a member of the Apocynaceae family, a well-represented tree and vine component of tropical forests. © Axel Poulsen.

Riverine vegetation on the Upper Raspaculo River. © William Milliken.

Within the great expanse of the Chiquibul Forest occurs an isolated patch of open pine-dominated vegetation. Called the San Pastor savanna, this area of 400 hectares is about a three-hour walk from Las Cuevas Research Station and is managed for timber production of the two pine species that occur there: *Pinus caribaea* and *Pinus tecunumanii*. This ecosystem is similar in form to the savanna areas of the Mountain Pine Ridge, which lies approximately thirty kilometers to the north (see "The Mountain Pine Ridge" later in this chapter). Significant sections of this ecosystem have been periodically burned, and although pines are abundant, the ground flora is frequently dominated by tiger fern (*Dicranopteris*

pectinata) and dumb cane (*Tripsacum latifolium*), with the latter sometimes attaining three meters in height. The soils of the San Pastor savanna are significantly different from those of the surrounding broadleaf forest in that the upper horizons have a greater proportion of sand, with the underlying soil predominantly heavy clay. This soil is less fertile than that of the forest, and it has been suggested that it represents more recently deposited erosional sediments originating from the Maya Divide to the south, although its derivation remains in doubt.[25] It is highly likely that the pine savanna of this area is maintained in its current form by fire (see "Fire and the Savanna" later in this chapter).

The tiger fern (*Dicranopteris pectinata*) can become a near-invasive species in disturbed and burned areas, such as the San Pastor savanna. © Sam Bridgewater.

Although over 300 species of trees are known from the Chiquibul, far fewer occur in any one localized area. Surveys of tree diversity conducted in hectare areas of forest close to Las Cuevas Research Station have typically revealed between 450 and 700 individual trunks over ten centimeters in diameter, representing some 50 to 80 species.[26] This is low in comparison with the tree diversity of tropical forests in South America, such as the Amazon (more than 200 tree species per hectare), and relatively poor even when compared with the tropical forests of southern Central America, which often have a diversity of around 100 tree species per hectare.[27] Low diversity is often typical of fertile soils. In addition, tree species richness tends to be highest in tropical forests that experience the greatest rainfall, declining with increasing latitude away from the equator and with increasing seasonality. Thus, in view of its location on the edge of the Tropics with an extended dry season and on fertile soils, the Chiquibul's relatively low tree diversity is to be expected.

As a general rule of thumb, tree diversity in tropical moist forests is high, but the majority of these species are actually very rare and are often represented by only one individual (or even fewer) per hectare. However, various authors working throughout the Tropics, including Belize, have recently shown that, although this might be the case, there is frequently an "oligarchy" of relatively few species that can dominate diverse forest and tree savanna communities.[28] For example, one study in the Chiquibul has shown that only ten species (out of the fifty-five recorded) account for 49 percent of the total stem area (basal area) of the forest and 72 percent of all individuals.[29] Similar studies conducted in limestone forests in the Bladen Nature Reserve, an area of unusually high species diversity, have found similar levels of structural dominance by only a few species.[30] One of these studies, for example, found that out of a total of ninety-one tree species found in one hectare, six represented 49 percent of the total basal area and eleven contributed 50 percent of the number of stems.[31]

The amargillo tree (*Vatairea lundellii*) is a member of the pea family and is a striking sight when in full flower. © Sam Bridgewater.

There have been few attempts to make comparisons between the Belizean flora and that of other territories in the region. However, the similarity of the flora of Belize's limestone areas with adjacent forests in the Petén region of Guatemala and the Yucatán Peninsula of Mexico is striking. This is not surprising, as all areas share a similar geological history and climate. An excellent study has been done investigating the floristic links of the tree flora of Bladen Nature Reserve.[32] The authors found that 60 percent of the species present were cosmopolitan in distribution, occurring from Mexico to South America, with 21 percent widely distributed within Central America, 11 percent occurring only north of 12° N latitude, and only 4 percent of more restricted northern distribution occurring in southern Mexico, Petén, and Belize. In limestone areas the percentage of species restricted to northern Central America increases with topography from valley bottom to ridge (see "Ridges and Troughs: Forests and Topography" earlier in this chapter).[33] In addition to strong floristic links between Belize and other countries in mainland northern Central America, there are similarities with the flora of the Greater Antilles and between the Yucatán region (which includes northern Belize and the Chiquibul) and karstic areas in Cuba.[34] However, about 10 percent of the Yucatán flora is believed to be endemic, occurring nowhere else in the world. The

Knowledge of the Chiquibul's flora has been built up over many decades of botanical collecting. Here a student and staff member of the Royal Botanic Garden Edinburgh use a field press to preserve specimens. © Sam Bridgewater.

palm *Pseudophoenix sargentii*, which occurs in northern Belize, is one such restricted species. Other examples that are common in the Yucatán but absent from southern Central America are provided by the black poisonwood (*Metopium brownei*) and warrie wood (*Caesalpinia gaumeri*), the former of which is recorded from the Chiquibul.

Mapping the collections from the Chiquibul reveals that they are concentrated at forty-four main locations,[35] with seventeen having more than one hundred collections. Only four sites have more than five hundred collections: the forest close to Las Cuevas Research Station, Guacamallo Bridge on the border between the Chiquibul and the Mountain Pine Ridge, Monkey Tail Branch, and Doyle's Delight, the highest peak in the Maya Divide.

HISTORY OF BOTANICAL COLLECTING IN THE CHIQUIBUL

Relatively few botanical collections were made in Belize prior to the twentieth century. Significant studies began with the efforts of Morton Peck of the Yale University School of Forestry (1905-1907) and continued with Cyrus Longworth Lundell (1928-1936), William Schipp (1929-1941), and Percival Gentle (1931-1958). These latter two early collectors are of particular note, and a number of plant genera and species have been named in their honor. These include species that occur only in Belize, four notable examples of which are the palm *Schippia concolor* (Arecaceae), the tree *Crossopetalum gentlei* (Celastraceae), the shrub *Neurolaena schippii* (Asteraceae), and the herb *Paepalanthus gentlei* (Eriocaulaceae). William Schipp was an Australian botanist who showed great entrepreneurial spirit by collecting plants throughout Belize that he advertised for sale through his *Flora of British Honduras, Price List of Seeds and Herbarium Material* (1933-1934). Many large museums and herbaria purchased his collections, and duplicates of his specimens were distributed to them. During his time in Belize, Schipp is credited with collecting over 150 species new to science, and his dried collections of these are called "types," as they provide the reference point for the original species descriptions. Many of his type specimens can be found in the herbarium of the Belize Forest Department in Belmopan. Schipp was not the only prodigious collector of this era, however. His impressive record of collecting new species was matched by Percival Gentle, a Belizean-born botanist who made almost ten thousand different collections within the country and who is still regarded as the country's most prolific collector. Unlike Schipp, Gentle collected within the Chiquibul region, although not substantially. Since Gentle, many botanists from around the world have continued to visit this forest area. The construction of Las Cuevas Research Station resulted in a significant increase in interest in the area during the 1990s, and just over seven thousand different collections have now been made within its confines. Among the most important collectors for this region are the British collectors Caroline Whitefoord and Alex Monro, both of whom work for the Natural History Museum, London, and collections made by the master's degree course of the Royal Botanic Garden Edinburgh (RBGE). What we know about the forest flora of this region is derived from an examination of these collections, which are largely found deposited in the herbaria of the Belize Forest Department; the Field Museum in Chicago; the Missouri Botanical Garden; the New York Botanical Garden; the Selby Botanical Garden in Sarasota, Florida; the Natural History Museum, London; the Royal Botanic Gardens Kew; and the Royal Botanic Garden Edinburgh.

A WALK THROUGH THE CHIQUIBUL FOREST:
A BEGINNER'S GUIDE

So what can a visitor expect to see when visiting the Chiquibul Forest for the first time? What does this immense undulating forest wilderness actually *feel* like when you are walking through it?

QUAMWOOD, NARGUSTA, AND BREADNUT: THE FOREST TREES

What surprises many people is that the Chiquibul Forest is relatively small in stature, with an average height of only twenty to thirty meters; only occasional emergent trees break through the dense interlocking canopy. In part this relates to the forest being in a state of recovery after many parts of it were flattened by Hurricane Hattie in 1961; not surprisingly, it is common for hurricane–disturbed forests worldwide to have a low canopy (see "Hurricane Ecology" in chapter 5).[36] The diminutive structure of the forest is a far cry from the tall, fifty-meter forests so typical of some parts of Amazonia, Southeast Asia, and the Congo Basin of Africa. One of the most characteristic sights when looking across the forest canopy from the observation tower is the conspicuous presence of quamwood, whose crowns are obvious from a distance either by their distinct emergent architecture or by their yellow flowers when in season. The abundance of

The flowering crowns of quamwood (*Schizolobium parahyba*) are a conspicuous sight from a vantage point above the Chiquibul canopy. This species flowers when leafless. © Sam Bridgewater.

this fast-growing species is due to its ability to colonize disturbed areas. The observation tower is an ideal place to see which tree species in the jungle are flowering. In addition to quamwood, trees with highly visible crowns during flowering include the white-flowered salmwood (*Cordia alliodora*), the red-flowered mapola (*Bernoullia flammea*), and the orange-flowered *Erblichia odorata*. The ecology of flowering is discussed in chapter 5.

Typically, there are approximately 500 tree stems with a diameter of ten centimeters or more (at breast height) per hectare in the Chiquibul, comprising a suite of between fifty and eighty species. In addition to those species listed above, around Las Cuevas Research Station itself the most dominant trees include *Pouteria reticulata* and *P. campechiana*, copal (*Protium copal*), grand betty (*Cupania belizensis*), breadnut (*Brosimum alicastrum*), chicle (*Manilkara zapota*), ironwood (*Dialium guianense*), *Trichilia erythrocarpa*, *Drypetes brownei*, horse's balls (*Stemmadenia donnell-smithii*), fiddlewood

White poisonwood (*Sebastiana tuerckheimiana*), a secondary tree species common around Las Cuevas. It is best kept at a distance because it exudes a caustic white latex when its leaves or twigs are snapped or its trunk cut. © Sam Bridgewater.

(*Vitex gaumeri*), cabbage bark (*Lonchocarpus castilloi*), hog plum (*Spondias radlkoferi*), laurel (*Nectandra salicifolia*), and white poisonwood (*Sebastiana tuerckheimiana*). The last of these has a very characteristic cylindrical trunk and dark, glossy, slender leaves with distinct drip tips. The bark and leaves, when damaged, emit copious white latex, which is highly caustic and an extreme irritant if it contacts the skin. Members of the pea family are also common constituents of the forest, including the wild tamarind (*Cojoba arborea*) and various species of *Acacia*. Due to the secondary nature of the forest, few trees have exceptional girth. In addition, past logging activities focusing on the primary timber species—especially mahogany and Spanish cedar—have further reduced the number of forest giants. Most have trunk diameters of less than ten centimeters (at breast height); few have diameters in excess of thirty centimeters. However, it is not unusual to see the remains of the giant snapped trunks scattered through the forest. Many are remnants of the tall trees that once stood before Hurricane Hattie. A significant proportion consists of the species nargusta (*Terminalia amazonia*), one of the tall forest emergents.

There is no need for a machete when strolling through the Chiquibul. The canopy overhead is largely closed, except in areas of treefall, and due to shading by the trees above, understory growth is naturally restricted and movement is thus comparatively easy. In addition to the seedlings and juveniles of the primary tree species, one of the most characteristic features of the forest understory is the abundance of palms. Of these, the spiny give-and-take palm (*Cryosophila stauracantha*) is by far the most common. Species of the palm genus *Chamaedorea* (see "Xaté, Leaf of Gold" in chapter 3) and juveniles of the bayleaf palm (*Sabal mauritiiformis*) are also common. Frequently encountered woody understory species include *Malphigia glabra*, allspice (*Pimenta dioica*), *Tabernaemontana alba*, *Hampea stipitata*, *Acalypha diversifolia*, species of *Croton*, and the large-leaved *Coccoloba belizensis*. At ground level conspicuous shrubs include *Deherainia smaragdina*, with its astonishing electric-green flowers; *Psychotria poeppigiana*, locally known as hotlips on account of its bright red bracts; species of *Calathea* and *Stromanthe* (Marantaceae), familiar to many as houseplants; the delicate purple-flowered *Ruellia matagalpae*; and the orange-fruited *Forchhammeria trifoliata*. Two prostrate species belonging to the coffee family are also common: *Coccocypselum herbaceum* and *Geophila repens*. Both have small white flowers; the former has delightful blue-purple fruits, the latter striking red. In addition, ferns make up a relatively important component of the ground flora. Occasionally, unusual species also catch the eye, including the red parasitic mushroomlike *Helosis cayennensis* (Balanophoraceae) and several species of *Dorstenia*. The latter low-growing herb belongs to the fig family and is peculiar on account of its unusual green disklike inflorescence, which resembles an inside-out fig.

IN SEARCH OF LIGHT: THE UPWARDLY MOBILE

Much of the floral diversity of the Chiquibul occurs out of sight as epiphytes high on tree trunks or as vines that seek light by growing beyond the canopy. Thus, their leaves and flowers are rarely viewed. Neotropical woody vines frequently, but not exclusively, belong to one of eight families: Apocynaceae (e.g., *Mandevilla* spp.), Combretaceae (e.g., *Combretum fruticosum*), Celastraceae (e.g., *Hippocratea volubilis*), Asteraceae (e.g., *Montanoa atriplicifolia*), Bignoniaceae (e.g., *Arrabidaea* spp.), Dioscoreaceae (*Dioscorea* spp.), Leguminosae (e.g., *Mucuna rostrata*), and Sapindaceae (e.g., *Serjania goniocarpa*). It is not uncommon for a visitor to ask the Las Cuevas staff about a tree they have seen with dense yellow flowers, only to be told that they belong to a *Combretum* vine smothering the tree in question. Although the vines remain out of view for most of their lives, their fallen flowers or fruits can sometimes be seen littering the forest floor, with the round fruits of *Strychnos panamensis* (Loganiaceae), the purple calyx of *Petrea volubilis*, and the pale lilac trumpet flowers of *Arrabidaea chica* being common finds. Vines belonging to the genera *Smilax* (Smilacaceae) and *Dioscorea* (Dioscoreaceae) are also common. The base of the stem of the latter frequently arises from a conspicuous woody tuber whose top projects from the ground surface.

The stem of the abundant give-and-take palm (*Cryosophila stauracantha*) is covered in long spines. © Sam Bridgewater.

The *Solandra grandiflora* vine flowers in the canopy and is an often-overlooked species. The only glimpse most researchers have of this beautiful plant is when the striking flowers fall to the ground. © Sam Bridgewater.

Epiphytes are plants that grow upon other plants. Although common in the Chiquibul, they are less abundant here than in the wetter forests in the south. In addition, epiphytes tend to be more abundant at higher elevation in forests with greater mist cover. Among the most conspicuous plants belonging to this broad ecological group around Las Cuevas Research Station are members of the Araceae family, with the genera *Anthurium*, *Monstera*, *Philodendron*, and *Syngonium* commonly found growing up tree trunks. The long aerial roots of members of this family are frequently seen hanging down to the forest floor from the canopy high above. Of these, *Monstera* will already be familiar to many as the "Swiss cheese" houseplant, its common name derived from its conspicuously perforated leaves. Another well-known plant group usually occurring as epiphytes is the Bromeliaceae; some of the largest—known as tank bromeliads—belong to the genus *Aechmea*. These are of great importance in the ecology of the region, as their rosette of leaves supports many diverse forms of life. Perhaps the best known epiphytes of all are orchids, of which 109 species have so far been recorded from the Chiquibul.[37] This represents 39 percent of the 279 orchid species recorded for the country. Not all orchids are epiphytes, but the majority are. These include the Belizean national flow-

Belize's national flower, the black orchid (*Prosthechea cochleata*), is an epiphyte and a relatively common sight around Las Cuevas. © Sam Bridgewater.

er, the black orchid (*Prosthechea cochleata*), which is relatively common around Las Cuevas. Other frequently seen species include *Maxillaria friedrichsthalii*, *M. uncata*, *M. variabilis*, *Nidema boothii*, and *Epidendrum rigidum*.[38] Orchidaceae is the second-most speciose plant family in Belize and represents 8 percent of all the vascular plant taxa found in the Chiquibul. A study conducted of the epiphytes occurring on fifty-two trees in the Chiquibul belonging to 16 species revealed a total of 61 orchid and 11 bromeliad species.[39] Both nargusta (*Terminalia amazonia*) and sapodilla (*Manilkara zapota*) were found to have particularly rich populations of epiphytes. Other epiphytic plant groups include Piperaceae (e.g., *Peperomia* spp.) and mosses, liverworts, and hornworts. Unfortunately, no detailed studies of these latter groups have been conducted at Las Cuevas. In general, the moss, liverwort, and hornwort flora of Belize is still poorly understood, and these groups have been greatly undercollected. A checklist of the mosses of Belize published in 1998 reported 250 species,[40] while 65 species of liverwort and hornwort have also been recorded.[41] As for vascular plants, there is a high degree of similarity between the mosses and liverworts of Belize and those of other tropical regions of the Caribbean and Central and South America. A few species are also shared with temperate North America. One site on the southern edge of the Chiquibul that has been relatively well collected for lower plants is Doyle's Delight. A single study conducted there in 1994 by a lower plant specialist revealed 30 species of liverwort and hornwort (27 of which were new to Belize), 21 genera of lichens (13 of which were new to the country), and 86 species of mosses (54 of which were new to Belize).[42] Further collecting trips throughout the country would doubtless reveal many more new records for the country.

THE WAYSIDE FLORA

One of the easiest places to see plants in flower at Las Cuevas is along the main tracks that radiate from the research station. Here trailing climbers are frequent, with *Montanoa atriplicifolia* (Asteraceae–daisy family) being among the most conspicuous when flowering. The yellow-flowered jackass bitter (*Neurolaena lobata*) of medicinal renown is another common wayside herb belonging to this diverse group. Other frequently seen climbing families include Vitaceae (e.g., *Cissus* spp.), Convolvulaceae, the morning glory family (e.g., *Ipomoea* spp.), and Sapindaceae (e.g., *Serjania* spp.). Some of the other frequently seen plants along the tracks are listed in table 2.6.

TABLE 2.6. Plants commonly seen along the Las Cuevas logging tracks

Acalypha spp. (Euphorbiaceae), 11 species	*Ludwigia octovalis* (Onagraceae)
Bauhinia spp. (Caesalpiniodeae), 3 species	*Maranta gibba* (Marantaceae)
Byttneria spp. (Malvaceae), 2 species	*Melochia* spp. (Malvaceae), 2 species
Calliandra houstoniana (Mimosoideae)	*Mimosa* spp. (Mimosoideae), 8 species
Canna indica (Cannaceae)	*Mucuna* spp. (Papilionoideae), 2 species
Costus pulverulentus (Costaceae)	*Ouratea lucens* (Ochnaceae)
Cuphea spp. (Lythraceae), 6 species	*Passiflora* spp. (Passifloraceae), 11 species
Desmodium spp. (Papilionoideae), 4 species	*Piper* spp. (Piperaceae), 14 species
Gouania lupuloides (Rhamnaceae)	*Salvia* spp. (Lamiaceae), 3 species,
Hamelia patens (Rubiaceae)	*Senna* spp. (Caesalpinioideae), 9 species
Heliconia spp. (Heliconiaceae), 4 species	*Solanum* spp. (Solanaceae)
Heteropterys spp. (Malphigiaceae), 3 species	*Spigelia humboldtiana* (Loganiaceae)
Lasiacis spp. (Poaceae), 7 species	*Stachytarpheta cayennensis* (Verbenaceae)

Montanoa atriplicifolia, a member of the daisy family, is a scrambling climber frequently seen along forest tracks. © Sam Bridgewater.

Perhaps the most striking species of all along these tracks belongs to the genus *Cecropia*. Locally known as the trumpet tree, two species are recorded for the Chiquibul. *Cecropia* is a fast-growing genus and a ready colonizer of any disturbed area, roadsides included; it can be seen lining forest tracks throughout the Neotropics. The genus is also of interest due to its association with ants (see "The Trumpet Tree's Private Army" in chapter 5). Other ecologically important species associated with disturbed areas include dumb cane (*Tripsacum latifolium*) and tiger fern (*Dicranopteris pectinata*). The former is readily seen dominating riversides, where frequent flooding disturbs the vegetation, while the latter often occurs in dense patches in the Maya Mountains in areas that have suffered from a landslide or lightning strike. This species is tolerant of fire and also dominates large expanses of the understory of the Mountain Pine Ridge.

THE FIFTH KINGDOM: FUNGI IN THE CHIQUIBUL

Fungi belong to their own biological kingdom and are considered distinct from both plants and animals, although they share certain characters with both. They are heterotrophic (nonphotosynthesizing) organisms that survive by digesting food that they absorb into their tissues. Including such groups as yeasts, slime molds, mushrooms, bracket fungi, and rusts, fungi constitute a highly diverse kingdom and show great

The trumpet tree (*Cecropia* sp.), with its characteristic leaves, is one of the most common colonizers of heavily disturbed forest areas. © Sam Bridgewater.

variety of form. Over 100,000 species have been described in the world to date,[43] although a generally accepted estimate of the total number of species in existence is 1.5 million.[44] Thus, it is believed that less than 10 percent of the planet's total number of fungal species has so far been discovered.

Fungi are of immense ecological importance. They are agents of disease and are one of the primary decomposers of organic matter. Not all fungi are "destructive," however. Many form symbiotic (mutually beneficial) associations called *mycorrhizas* with plants via their roots. Over 90 percent of plants have these associations,[45] and without them they would be far less successful in colonizing habitats. The fungi benefit from the association by having ready access to the carbohydrates produced by the plant through photosynthesis, while the plant's ability to absorb water and nutrients is increased by its interaction with the vegetative threadlike fungi. Without mycorrhizas many plant groups would be unable to survive. In addition to plants, there are many symbiotic associations between fungi and animals, one example of which is displayed by leaf-cutting ants (see "Avid Gardeners: Leaf-Cutting Ants and Their Fungal Associations" in chapter 5). They are also of great economic value to humans, providing a source of food, inoculants for cheeses, antibiotics, and agents of biological control. Yeasts, for example are fungi and act as the primary agents responsible for brewing and bread making.

An earthstar (*Geastrum saccatum*). © Sam Bridgewater.

To date there has been little research into the fungal flora of the Chiquibul. One study has sought to examine the biogeographical relationship between the fungi of North America and those of Belize,[46] with another focusing on the montane forests of Doyle's Delight.[47] The biogeographical study has found significant similarities between the mycorrhizal fungi of the Chiquibul Forest, the Mountain Pine Ridge (MPR), and the southern United States. This research has been only preliminary in scope, however, with only 59 species recorded. This clearly represents a tiny fraction of the overall fungal flora that exists. Clearly, much research remains to be done. Where focused studies have investigated the full extent of fungal diversity of tropical regions, great diversities have been found. For example, a study of the fungi of the Caribbean, published in 2001, noted 11,268 species from this broad region.[48] Because fungi are so variable in form and many are microscopic, they are problematic to research. Thus many studies focus only on "macrofungi," i.e., those that produce large, easily visible fruiting structures such as mushrooms, puffballs, and brackets, with other groups such as rusts often overlooked or ignored. A number of the macrofungi found in the Chiquibul are edible, two examples being *Lactarius indigo* and *Schizophyllum commune*. The latter is a woody decaying fungus known by the Maya as *xikin che*.

No fungi, leaves, or fruits in the Chiquibul should ever been eaten unless one is sure that they have been correctly identified and are not poisonous.

In 2004 an expedition to Doyle's Delight collected 417 fungal specimens during a ten-day period.[49] The species were found to have various geographical affinities, with about 20 percent of those identified new to science, indicating the scale of our ignorance of the local fungal flora. Some (e.g., *Hygroaster albellus*) were typical of wet montane cloud vegetation of the Caribbean region, occurring in related forests located on such islands as Puerto Rico. Others (e.g., *Marasmiellus troyanus*) also had a broad regional distribution across the Caribbean and are known primarily from lowland tropical forest. These included *Calostoma cinnabarina*, a species that has a known ectomycorrhizal association with oak (*Quercus* spp.) and that occurs as far north as North America. Surprising finds included a number of taxa belonging to the genera *Mycena*, *Arthrosporella*, and *Hygrocybe* previously unknown outside of the Amazon Basin, suggesting that the highest peaks of the Maya Mountains may represent refugia for species with previously more widespread distributions.

Cantharellus cibarius. This species of fungus is usually found associated with oak trees in areas of pine savanna such as at San Pastor in the Chiquibul or the Mountain Pine Ridge. © Alex Monro.

The cup fungus *Cookeina sulcipes* is a commonly seen species of the forest floor. It has a pantropical distribution, occurring in Asia and Africa in addition to Latin America and the Caribbean. © Sam Bridgewater.

The herbarium of the Natural History Museum, London. Over four million dried plant specimens from around the world are preserved in cabinets here and made available for study by scientists. © The Natural History Museum, London.

HERBARIA: SAFEGUARDING OUR KNOWLEDGE OF PLANT DIVERSITY

Most of the world's great botanic gardens and natural history museums are known to the public as places of recreation and learning. The Natural History Museum in London, for example, is visited by over two million visitors annually, many of whom come to see the enormous collections of fossils and animals on display. The highlight of visits to such establishments is often the reconstructions of giant dinosaur skeletons or, in the case of botanic gardens, a colorful herbaceous border or tropical greenhouse. What is less well known is that behind the scenes many of these institutions have thriving science departments dedicated to exploring and describing life on earth in its many guises. Central to this endeavor is the science of taxonomy, whereby species are described and classified. For plant taxonomists, the focus of such studies is herbaria, which house enormous collections of dried plants, mounted onto cards, precisely labeled as to their origin, and cataloged by family and geographic area. These collections are essentially libraries of the world's plant diversity, and most are stored under special environmental conditions to keep the specimens from deteriorating and to protect them from being eaten by bugs. Each of the world's herbaria is unique, and each has different numbers of collections, varying geographical foci, and historical representations. The herbarium of the Belize Forest Department, for example, focuses exclusively on the Belizean flora and has approximately ten thousand collections that serve as an excellent resource for studying the local flora. Herbaria can be much larger, however. The herbarium of London's Natural History Museum contains approximately five million specimens! Although the flora of Belize is well represented, the collections of this institution are worldwide in origin, and the earliest date back to the sixteenth century. Herbaria provide an essential reference collection for understanding global patterns of plant diversity. The specimen from which a species is first scientifically described is known as the type specimen and provides the physical reference point for that species. Without herbaria it would be impossible to make sense of plant diversity, and efforts to conserve this diversity in the future would be severely hindered.

The majority of Belize's coastline and hundreds of offshore cayes are clothed by salt-tolerant forests dominated by curious trees with bizarre rooting systems typified by the stilt roots of the red mangrove (*Rhizophora mangle*). These formations are collectively known as mangroves and cover 4.2 percent of Belize's territory.[50] Mangroves are ecologically fascinating in that they occur primarily—but not exclusively—on the margin of Belize's coast. Their component species are adapted to existing in unusually saline conditions, and the presence of this ecosystem is essential for maintaining the health and biological diversity of both the marine and terrestrial domains. Mangroves provide a vital breeding ground for fish, shrimp, and spiny lobster, for example, and serve as Belize's first land defense against hurricanes, dissipating wave energy and binding sediments together. Historically they have also been of social significance, providing a source of construction materials, fuelwood, and tannin for curing animal skins. Indeed, the name red mangrove is said to relate to its use in this way, with the tannin-rich bark turning water red when boiled. Over the last twenty years Belize's mangroves have become greatly threatened by development projects. Many of these relate to urban expansion of major population centers, including Belize City and Dangriga, as well as the development of new settlements (such as those found on the Placencia Peninsula) and the establishment of shrimp farms. Their future is also uncertain as global warming continues, with sea levels projected to rise over the next century. Mangroves will be among the first ecosystems that must face such marine encroachment. Short-term gains from development projects involving mangrove clearance may well be dwarfed by the enormous future cost to Belize as fisheries decline, biological interactions are disrupted, coastal erosion increases, and Belize's territory is left bare of protection against the first ravages of surges associated with tropical storms.

AN INTRODUCTION TO BELIZE'S MANGROVES

The word *mangrove* can be confusing, as it refers both to a distinct woody habitat—usually associated with estuary mouths, lagoons, and the intertidal zone—and to the plant species that flourish in this environment. Worldwide the mangrove habitat (also known as mangal) is primarily tropical in distribution, and much of the world's coastlines between the Tropics of Cancer and Capricorn are fringed with this distinctive vegetation type. The total area of these habitats has been estimated at 170,000 square kilometers, although globally over 35 percent has been destroyed by human activities to date.[51] Around the world, fifty-four plant species from twenty genera and sixteen families are considered to be true mangrove inhabitants. Of these, Belize has three "true" mangrove species, although others are commonly associated with the mangrove ecosystem, especially on the margins of other habitats. A floristic survey of Belize's mangroves conducted in 1992 identified over sixty vascular plant species as occurring within them or on their margins.[52]

Dominated by only three woody species, Belize's mangroves are poor in plant diversity, and a layperson could quickly become familiar with the flora. This is in stark contrast to the inland forests, where the diversity of species is such that it can take many years to become a competent field botanist.

The three classic woody mangrove species are the red mangrove (*Rhizophora mangle*), the black mangrove (*Avicennia germinans*), and the white mangrove (*Laguncularia racemosa*), with buttonwood (*Conocarpus erecta*) being one of the most common associates. Of these, the black mangrove is able to withstand the highest salinities,[53] although red mangrove often forms most readily on the seaward fringe and is the most resilient to high winds.[54] Studies have shown that the seedlings of this species are particularly adept at growing at lower tidal levels.[55] Usually either red or black mangrove dominates the vegetation, which can vary from only one meter to thirty meters in height, with white mangrove and buttonwood becoming more abundant on the landward side. Like all ecosystems, mangroves are dynamic habitats, and their distribution and the abundance of their component species are influenced by changes in sedimentation rates, disturbance such as storm damage, and response to disease.

SURVIVING THE SEA: ECOLOGICAL ADAPTATIONS OF MANGROVES

Although areas of shallow seawater can provide suitable habitats for trees and shrubs, they present severe biological constraints to any species attempting to colonize them. At the molecular level of an organism, respiration is the process whereby stored energy in the form of sugars (produced by photosynthesis in plants) is converted into energy that can be used to drive metabolic processes. Oxygen is essential for this process. Waterlogged environments such as those favored by mangroves, however, tend to have little available oxygen–they are anaerobic. Anyone who has worked in mangroves will attest that these are hot, buggy, and unpleasantly smelly places to work. The reason for the pungent fumes that bubble to the surface from the muddy substrate relates to the lack of oxygen; at low levels of oxygen, bacteria in the water and mud convert the naturally occurring chemical sulfate to sulfide, and carbon dioxide to methane. Although these gases are noxious to humans, it is the anaerobic conditions that present a conundrum to plants. They must somehow anchor themselves to the ground; to do so, however, they need to have their root systems underwater with poor access to oxygen.

STILT ROOTS AND PNEUMATOPHORES: COPING WITH OXYGEN-POOR ENVIRONMENTS

Belize's primary mangrove species have overcome the problem of an oxygen-poor environment by developing striking aerial roots of varying forms. In the case of the red mangrove, rather than branching off underground from the trunk like most trees, the roots radiate down from the stem, arcing through the air before descending into the water to take root in the mud below. These so-called stilt roots can form an impenetrable mass. It has been said, not completely in jest, that the world record for the one-hundred-meter sprint through a mangrove swamp is twenty minutes and thirty seconds![56] As much as 24 percent of the aboveground biomass of red mangrove may be in the form of these stilt roots, which are covered with special pores called *lenticels*, which allow gaseous exchange between the air and the root's internal cells. The parts of the root in the most anaerobic areas—underwater and the underlying sediment—are composed largely of a special tissue called *aerenchyma*. It contains large amounts of air space between the individual cells, allowing oxygen from the lenticels to diffuse internally through the roots to the underwater tissues, thus enabling them to respire. The stilt roots of red mangrove also have an important structural role, acting as effective guy ropes and flying buttresses that anchor the species to the unstable sediments upon which it often grows.

Although red mangrove have stilt roots, black mangrove and white mangrove have developed different solutions to the same problem. Their roots radiate from the trunk underground, like those of normal trees, and are horizontal and generally shallow. However, at regular intervals, distinct fingerlike structures rise vertically above the water into the air, up to thirty centimeters in height. These miniature root towers are called *pneumatophores*. Like stilt roots, they are covered in lenticels, are comprised largely of aerenchyma tissue, and are the basis by which the underwater root tissues are aerated.

True mangrove species such as red mangrove (*Rhizophora mangle*) with its stilt roots show various adaptations that enable them to survive in habitats inundated with seawater. © Sam Bridgewater.

Doctors warn of the dangers of a diet containing too much salt, the excessive ingestion of which is implicated in high blood pressure. In a similar way, seawater can be prejudicial to plant health due to the elevated levels of salt it contains. For plants too the problem relates to pressure. Plants need water to survive and to drive processes such as photosynthesis. The internal tissues of mangroves are not naturally as salty as those of the surrounding sea that forms the basis of their water source. In osmosis, the means by which water enters the cellular tissue of plants from the external environment, water naturally diffuses from less salty to more salty environments in an attempt to equalize concentrations. This process therefore restricts the intake of water by mangrove species. Plants attempting to colonize saltwater habitats find themselves in a situation of being inundated by the sea but unable to access the vital water they need.

Mangroves have evolved various mechanisms to cope with both the problem of water intake and elevated salt concentrations. Plants able to withstand elevated levels of salt are called *halophytes*. The negative osmotic potential is overcome in part by transpiration, the process whereby water is drawn through a plant through its xylem plumbing system, powered by the evaporation of water from its leaves. This creates negative pressure in the roots that is greater than the negative osmotic potential between the seawater and the plant's tissues. Thus, water is drawn in. Mangrove roots also have the ability to physically desalinate water, and the resultant water in their xylem is

Both the black mangrove (*Avicennia germinans*), pictured, and the white mangrove (*Laguncularia racemosa*) have pneumatophores, root sections that rise above the surface of the water to provide ready access to oxygen. © Sam Bridgewater.

as little as one tenth of the concentration of seawater.[57] In addition, their tissues can tolerate higher than normal salt concentrations. Enzymes are the chemicals that catalyze natural chemical reactions in cells. These are typically inhibited by high concentrations of salt, although mangrove enzymes are more resistant than most. Mangroves can also alter their cell chemistry to ensure that osmotic irregularities do not occur within their cells due to elevated salt concentrations. Some mangroves, black mangrove and white mangrove included, possess salt glands in their leaves and are able to secrete excess salt from their tissues by this mechanism. Careful observation of the leaves of black mangrove will often reveal them to be covered by tiny salt crystals.

REPRODUCTIVE ADAPTATIONS OF MANGROVES

Due to the environment in which they grow, mangrove species depend on water for the dispersal of their offspring. Although they share this in common with many other plant species, what is unusual is that rather than shedding seeds or fruits, some species disperse "live" seedlings with a well-developed embryo–a phenomenon known as vivipary. Thus, mangrove reproductive propagules are adapted to take root rapidly and colonize new substrates as soon as they leave the parent plant. The large elongated reproductive propagules found attached to red mangrove, for example, are not fruits, despite their fruitlike appearance. They consist of an elongated embryo attached to a fruiting structure at its base. When released, the propagules float, with dispersal aided by tidal currents. Initially they float horizontally, but over time their position shifts and they become vertical, increasing the chance that their base may lodge in the ground. Many of the propagules also sink over time, facilitating rooting in shallow water. However, they have also been known to regain buoyancy if rooting is not successful, providing a second chance at establishment elsewhere. *Rhizophora* propagules can remain viable in seawater for many months, although high rates of predation by a range of animal species both prior and subsequent to their release from the parent plant are known to occur, greatly reducing the viability of many.[58]

A newly established red mangrove (*Rhizophora mangle*). The floating reproductive propagules of this species aid its establishment in shallow saltwater. © Sam Bridgewater.

FROM DWARFS TO GIANTS: BELIZE'S DIFFERENT MANGROVE COMMUNITIES

At a national level, one of the most comprehensive surveys of Belize's mangroves occurred between 1991 and 1992, funded by the United Kingdom's Overseas Development Administration (ODA).[59] This research involved conducting topographic, floristic, hydrologic, and soil surveys covering 200 miles of coastline. It resulted in an updated national mangrove map for the country and an improved understanding of the plant biodiversity of mangroves and associated vegetation types. The national mangrove map classified mangroves by height, with the community being subdivided into those that were less than four meters in height (dwarf), between four and eight meters (medium), and over eight meters (tall). However, the Belize Ecosystems Map, based on the UNESCO system (see "Modern Vegetation Classifications and the UNESCO System" earlier in this chapter), recognizes six different primary mangrove forms. Their classification is based on where they occur (coastal/riverine fringes, topographic basins), whether they are saltwater (the majority) or freshwater, and the degree of inundation. This latter

Urban expansion in Belize City has led to the clearance of large tracts of mangrove. Here tall black mangrove is being bulldozed to make way for new housing. © Sam Bridgewater.

factor influences species composition, with red mangrove often occurring in areas of greatest inundation. As a general rule of thumb, the height of mangrove vegetation decreases with increasing salinity and with nutrient availability. Tall mangrove forests are often associated with riverine edges.

Although mangroves tend to occur in coastal regions in saltwater habitats, they can occasionally be found inland in freshwater environments, although they are not so well adapted to survive and are usually less successful than other plant groups better adapted to terrestrial, freshwater conditions. A good example of inland mangrove can be seen at Booth's River in Orange Walk District. It has been suggested that the Booth River mangroves may represent relicts from a previous geological era when the position of Belize's coastline was very different from that of today.

Although mangroves dominate the coastal fringe, other habitats occur in association with them, including forest, savanna, and wetland, the resulting coastal vegetation forming a complex mosaic. One of the most commonly associated habitats is littoral forest that occurs on more fertile, infrequently inundated soils. This forest type is highly threatened due to coastal development and is dominated by a relatively diverse range of species. Some of these are restricted to coastal regions (e.g., the palm *Thrinax radiata* and the sea grape *Coccoloba uvifera*), while others also form important components of inland forests. These include the botán palm (*Sabal mauritiiformis*), black poisonwood (*Metopium brownei*), gumbo-limbo (*Bursera simaruba*), and the coco plum (*Chrysobalanus icaco*).

BEYOND THE BITING HORDES:
THE MAGNIFICENT MANGROVE FAUNA

Although the flora of the mangrove is indeed depauperate, it is also a common assertion that few animals are to be found within this ecosystem, save for the biting insects, such as mosquitoes and sand flies. The incredible abundance of these infuriating creatures does indeed beggar belief, explaining why biologists usually prefer to focus their studies elsewhere. However, the mangrove fauna is more diverse than one might first imagine. A study conducted in Belize in 1992, for example, lists a minimum of 74 species of fish, 40 species of mammals, 178 species of birds, 30 species of reptiles, and 11 species of amphibians as occurring or likely to occur in mangroves.[60] It is necessary to add that the mangrove does not provide the primary habitat for the majority of these species. Amphibians, for example, tend not to thrive in brackish environments due to their inability to maintain their internal saltwater balance as a result of their permeable skin, although there are some notable exceptions, such as the cane toad (*Bufo marinus*). Likewise, many other animal groups visit mangroves only on an occasional or seasonal basis and are not permanent residents. Nevertheless, this ecosystem forms an important component of the broad environment from which they fashion a living.

The brown booby (*Sula leucogaster*) is often associated with mangrove vegetation. Hand-colored etching from Mark Catesby, *The Natural History of Carolina, Florida and the Bahama Islands* (1731–1743), vol. 1, plate 87. © The Natural History Museum, London.

The web of life comprises countless complex biological interactions between the world's myriad species. Where different organisms interact, with both benefiting from the association, the relationship is called symbiotic. One example of this is provided by sea sponges and red mangrove roots. The stilt roots of red mangrove may be permanently inundated by seawater. Where this occurs, they are usually colonized by a range of organisms such as shipworms, isopods (an order of marine crustacean), and sea sponges. Studies conducted in Belize on two sponge species (*Tedania ignis* and *Haliclona implexiformis*) have shown that both the sponges and the red mangroves grow more productively as a result of this association.[61] The mechanism of this positive interaction is believed to be the transfer of dissolved inorganic nitrogen in the form of ammonium from sponges to the mangrove roots via fine absorbing rootlets; in return, the sponges receive carbon from the mangrove and also a substrate on which to grow. Nitrogen, together with phosphorus, is believed to be a limiting factor restricting mangrove growth.[62] Thus, the mutualistic association with the sponges assists red mangroves to overcome this nutrient limitation. Other studies have shown that mangroves are adept at exploiting nutrient-rich conditions whenever they occur in an attempt to survive in what is generally a nutrient-poor environment. For example, their roots proliferate greatly in patches of soil containing decaying roots, enabling them to recapture the chemicals they need to survive.[63]

As with other ecosystems, few studies have been conducted on the insect inhabitants of mangroves. However, termites (e.g., *Nasutitermes* spp.) and ants (Formicidae) are well-documented mangrove inhabitants, and termitaria are striking physical manifestations of the former group. Of the thirty-four species of ant known from Belize, twenty have been recorded as occurring in this vegetation formation.[64]

The crustaceans, a broad taxonomic group that includes crabs, lobsters, and shrimps, are particularly associated with mangroves. Of these, crabs are perhaps the most obvious to the visitor. Crab species associated with Belize's mangroves include the blue land crab (*Cardisoma guanhumi*), the fiddler crab (*Uca* spp.), the large land crab (*Ucides cordatus*), the tree crab (*Aratus pisonii*), the mud crab (*Eurytium limosum*), and the root crab (*Goniopsis cruentata*). Some of these species—including the root crab and the land crab—are important herbivores feeding on mangrove vegetative parts.[65] Others, such as the mud crab, are predators and scavengers. Mangroves are essential to the well-being of many arthropods and fish, with both these groups being economically and biologically significant. The importance of mangroves has been highlighted by studies showing that shrimp and fish catches are greater in areas where there are more mangroves, and there are numerous cases when a decline in regional fishing is associated with the loss of this habitat.[66] The dense network of roots provides shelter for these animals, and organic matter contributes to local food chains. In addition, their stilt roots provide a crucial solid substrate for early developmental stages of species such as the brown shrimp (*Penaeus aztecus*) and the spiny lobster (*Panulirus guttatus*).[67]

Blue land crab (*Cardisoma guanhumi*). Copyright Hans Hillewaert. Source Wikimedia Commons.

Mangroves have a well-deserved reputation as nursery areas for many other marine animals. In terms of fish, grouper, snapper, barracuda, jewfish, bonefish, and snook provide five examples of well-known Belizean species whose ecology is strongly linked to this ecosystem.[68] Research conducted in Florida on the stomach contents of coastal species showed that 70 percent of commercially important fish in that region included mangrove detritus in their diet.[69] It is likely that similar results would be found if such studies were done in Belize.

Although many mammals, including peccaries, tapir, and even jaguars, have been recorded from mangrove areas, most only pass through en route to other habitats and rarely spend significant amounts of time within this ecosystem. That said, in other regions of the world, large terrestrial mammals are associated with mangroves. For example, the mangrove of the Ganges Delta in India is well known for being the prime habitat of the Indian tiger. In Belize one mammal is particularly associated with mangroves in the public psyche: the enigmatic sea cow, or manatee (*Trichechus manatus*). This beautiful, docile creature grazes on aquatic vegetation such as sea grass and can be seen around coastal regions where abundant mangroves occur. Bottle-nosed dolphins (*Tursiops truncatus*) have also been reported from fringing mangroves. Of the 178 bird species recorded from Belizean mangroves, the brown booby (*Sula leucogaster*), the brown pelican (*Pelecanus occidentalis*), the olivaceous cormorant (*Phalacrocorax brasilianus*), the magnificent frigate bird (*Fregata magnificens*), the tiger heron (*Tigrisoma mexicanum*), the cattle egret (*Bulbulcus ibis*), the white ibis (*Eudocimus albus*), and the Amazon kingfisher (*Chloroceryle amazona*) are among the most commonly seen.[70]

Manatee (*Trichechus manatus*) nursing her calf. Copyright Gaylen Rathburn. Source Wikimedia Commons.

Although Belize's mangroves do not have the feared reputation of Australia's equivalent habitat, which harbors the aggressive saltwater crocodile (*Crocodylus porosus*), they do nevertheless contain crocodiles, with two species recorded—the American and Morelet's crocodiles (*Crocodylus acutus* and *C. moreletii*); the former is by far the more strongly associated with this habitat. Both species are relatively docile, and reports of attacks on humans are few. When they do occur, they are usually only a defensive gesture reacting to interference with their young. Other commonly found reptile species include the beautiful, cryptically colored boa constrictor (*Boa constrictor*), the leaf-toed gecko (*Phyllodactylus insularis*), the Mayan coastal anole (*Anolis sagrei*), and turtles.[71] The first three are all faunal predators, whereas turtles are represented, among others, by the Central American river turtle (*Dermatemys mawii*), a herbivore whose diet has been shown to consist of a significant proportion of mangrove leaves.[72] Like Morelet's crocodile, this species is usually more associated with freshwater habitats.

SAVANNAS AND WETLANDS

A journey along Belize's northern, southern, or western highways can give rise to the impression that savanna, rather than forest, is Belize's dominant ecosystem. This often comes as a surprise to many travelers, who associate savannas more with the African continent. The large grazers so characteristic of African landscapes, however, have long since become extinct in Belize, as in elsewhere in Central and South America (see

"The Pleistocene Overkill" in chapter 1). This ecosystem in its many guises covers well over two million square kilometers of the Neotropics, including about 9 percent of Belize's territory.[73] This equates to about 12,000 square kilometers. Although certainly significant in extent, the dominance of this vegetation type in the Belizean landscape is more apparent than real. Forest covers over 60 percent of Belize—over four times the area of savanna—and is therefore by far the most significant ecosystem; visitors' misconceptions relate to the positioning of Belize's highways, many of which traverse great stretches of savanna.

Often having the appearance of savanna but with their own distinct ground flora and usually an absence of trees apart from a few well-adapted exceptions, wetlands are a classic habitat associated with poorly drained, waterlogged areas. Often they are small in extent, occurring as localized patches within savanna; frequently only one species appears to dominate the vegetation, although on careful observation others can usually be seen. Close to 2 percent of Belize's land is covered by this water-defined formation.[74]

Savannas and wetlands make up two of Belize's most beautiful vegetation types, and there are few sights as stirring as a view across an open pine-dotted grassland or an orange-hued *Eleocharis* sedge marsh at dusk when the landscape appears to glow. From a biologist's point of view, savannas are one of the most pleasant habitats in which to work. For botanists, most of the diversity is at ground level and therefore easily studied. This is in stark contrast to the forest, where one is largely confronted with tree trunks, and clues on the identity of the component species must be gleaned by examining bark or by using binoculars in an attempt to see the leaves and flowers thirty meters overhead. Wetlands, however, although relatively poor in plant species, present more of a problem, not least of which is the unstable nature of the unconsolidated sediments upon which they grow and the obvious presence of water. Those who have ventured into this habitat know that it is not uncommon to sink deep into the substrate underfoot and find oneself up to one's waist in foul-smelling ooze. Some forms of wetland are also dominated by sedges with vicious serrated margins on their leaves. Known locally as cutting grass, these natural blades can quickly slice open clothing and skin. Although a number of different types of cutting grass occur, one of the most frequently encountered is *Cladium jamaicense*.

BELIZE'S SAVANNA VEGETATION:
AN INTRODUCTION

If one takes a visual sweep across a large area of savanna, it quickly becomes clear that there is great variety in form, with different patches varying in their degree of openness and their defining species. Although a large number of distinct savanna types exist, for the most part they are all dominated by the same few woody species and constitute variations on a theme, with differences between them relating to local variations in soil and water availability, fire disturbance, and human management. They also often represent distinct but temporary stages in a successional regime whereby one vegetation type is naturally replaced by another through time, with the final stage called the climax community.

In Central America and on the Caribbean islands, major savanna areas occur in southern Mexico, Belize, Honduras, Nicaragua, southwest Panama, and central and eastern Cuba.[75] Many of the lowland savannas of these areas experience annual cycles of drought and flooding coinciding with the dry and wet seasons respectively. Such savannas are termed *hyperseasonal*. In Belize, savannas tend to occur on sandy deposits eroded from the Maya Mountains or old coastal sediments, and the soils derived from these are of low fertility, mild acidity, and generally coarse texture.[76] Clay can underlie the sand, and in such places the soils are poorly drained and are frequently waterlogged. Such savannas are typically of an open nature with only a few scattered trees able to withstand these conditions. On well-drained sandy soils, however, especially on low topographic rises, savannas show reduced effects of groundwater. These are termed *seasonal* savannas, and dense concentrations of pine can often be found in these areas.[77]

Despite the variety of form described above, all of Belize's savannas can be considered as generic pine-palmetto savannas, with pine (*Pinus caribaea*) and palmetto (*Acoelorraphe wrightii*) usually forming a conspicuous component of the vegetation. The Belize Ecosystems Map recognizes two distinct lowland savanna forms, classified either as short-grass savanna with needle-leaved trees or short-grass savanna with shrubs, depending on its structure.[78] This provides a broad pragmatic classification of a subtly varied ecosystem, although it underrepresents the great diversity present. However, any attempt to subdivide savannas structurally to a greater degree is a largely artificial exercise, as the different forms represent transient successional stages.

Where pine densities are especially high, such areas are usually referred to as pine ridge or even pine forest. Many of these localities are managed for their timber, and their structure has been artificially altered by human intervention, usually

The dominant defining tree in Belize's lowland savannas is the Caribbean pine (*Pinus caribaea*). This species has been managed commercially across the country for its timber.
© Sam Bridgewater.

involving the medium of fire to increase the density of the pine. Where a dense pine savanna becomes a pine ridge or pine forest is a moot point, but good examples of dense pine-dominated habitat can be found in the Mountain Pine Ridge and within the Chiquibul Forest at San Pastor. A great deal of scientific shelf space is dedicated to discussing the difference between savanna and forest. Essentially, although savannas can have a significant woody component of trees and shrub, the canopy is incomplete and a well-developed herbaceous layer dominated by grasses and sedges dominates the understory. Forests usually lack such a grassy layer due to the shade produced by a near-complete canopy. The Belize Ecosystems Map recognizes four types of lowland pine forest (usually referred to as needle-leaved forest) and three types of submontane pine forest,[79] although these are essentially very dense pine savannas.

THE PLANT DIVERSITY OF BELIZEAN SAVANNAS

Relatively few detailed floristic surveys have been conducted in Belizean savannas, and surprisingly, despite their accessibility, knowledge of their flora remains sketchy. One survey conducted in the savannas of the Rio Bravo Conservation and Management Area in northern Belize, for example, iden-

Alophia sylvestris (Iridaceae). The striking flowers of this savanna species are short lived. Like many savanna herbs, they grow from an underground bulb, which protects their tissues from fire. © Zoë Goodwin.

tified 258 species as occurring within this broad formation, which represents about 7.5 percent of the total Belizean flora.[80] Of these, 148 had an apparent preference for drier communities, with 44 found associated with wetland areas and 74 with forest margins. Of those that could be considered as "true" savanna species, 57 (22 percent) were woody, of which 15 species (only 8 percent of the total savanna flora) could be classified as trees. Other detailed savanna plant surveys have been conducted in a coastal savanna near Sapodilla Lagoon in Stann Creek District,[81] at the Monkey Bay Wildlife Sanctuary,[82] and at San Pastor in the Chiquibul.[83] It is likely that about 1,000 plant species occur in the savannas. Grasses usually form an important part of the herbaceous flora of savannas. Unfortunately, however, this plant group is often overlooked by researchers since sterile (nonflowering) grasses of different species can look remarkably similar. As a result, botanists often display a mental block when trying to identify members of this group. Represented by 74 genera and 248 species, grasses are one of Belize's most diverse plant families, and yet many plant surveys record only a fraction of the total grass diversity present. Grasses are exceeded in diversity only by the pea family (80 genera and 295 species) and the orchid family (93 genera and 279 species). The sedges (Cyperaceae), with 21 genera and 146 species, represent another speciose but poorly identified group associated with savannas and wetlands.

THE SAVANNA SPECIES SUITE

The dominant tree of all savanna areas is the Caribbean pine (*Pinus caribaea*). This species occurs widely across Central America in a variety of savanna and forest formations up to an altitude of about six hundred meters. Above this, it can be replaced by a sister species, *Pinus tecunumanii*, often mistakenly called *P. oocarpa* in Belize.[84] In some localities, including the large patch of pine savanna/forest at San Pastor in the Chiquibul, both these species can be seen growing together. The density of pine varies greatly, with different authors recording densities of between twenty and one hundred stems per hectare. However, in very dense pine savanna or pine forest it may even be greater than this. Fire is one of the predominant factors influencing pine density and is used as a management tool to increase stocking in areas considered to be of economic value.

In addition to Caribbean pine, other common important woody species of the savanna include the craboo (*Byrsonima crassifolia*) and the sandpaper tree (*Curatella americana*). Both of these species are widespread throughout the Neotropics and are regarded as indicator species of lowland Neotropical savanna.[85] Both are ecologically adaptable and can withstand occasional waterlogging.

THE PALMETTO

One of the most characteristic features of Belize's savannas is the presence of dense clumps and thickets of the palmetto palm (*Acoelorraphe wrightii*). These clumps can occur as distinct fingers stretching across large savanna areas, often following temporary watercourses. In part, the dense clumping of palmetto reflects its clonal nature, with each individual adult able to produce suckers and vegetative clones (jacks) that in turn can reach adult size.[86] Thus, a large clump of palmetto may consist of only one genetic individual. The root system of palmetto typically extends out just above the seasonal water table, but this species shows a broad degree of tolerance to different water regimes, so it can occur in both dry and marshy areas. Palmetto shows a number of adaptations that contribute to its success in the savanna. For example, its stem is protected from fire by sheathing fibrous material. Little is known about its biology, although agoutis, peccaries, and a range of bird species are involved in the dispersal of its seed. The fruits are also of medical importance due to the presence of chemicals valued for certain cancer treatments.

Other common associate woody species, especially in wetter areas, include the spindly savanna white poisonwood (*Cameraria latifolia*), the bullet tree (*Bucida buceras*), with its characteristic bifurcating branching pattern, the calabash (*Crescentia cujete*), whose gourds are often used as containers, and *Jacquinia aurantiaca*. In better-drained areas, oak (*Quercus oleoides*) can be common and is frequently associated with savanna-forest boundaries. Members of the Melastomataceae family are also abundant and indicative of nutrient-poor savanna soils, with two of the commonest species being *Miconia albicans* and *Clidemia sericea*. The exact composition of woody species of any savanna area depends on its location. For example, the dense pine savannas and forest of the Mountain Pine Ridge support *Clethra occidentalis* and *C. mexicana*, two shrub species that are absent from the savannas of northern Belize. Likewise, the endemic silver palm (*Schippia concolor*) can frequently be viewed in the pine savannas and some forest areas of Cayo and Toledo Districts in addition to the Mountain Pine Ridge, and yet it is absent in northern Belize. One plant that often catches the eye while one is traveling along a road through a savanna area is *Calliandra houstoniana*. This small, weedy shrub has beautiful delicate red inflorescences resembling pompoms. Its generic name (*Calliandra*) is derived from the Greek for "beautiful male parts," in reference to the showy flowers made conspicuous by the male sexual organs (stamens). Orchids are also common in the savanna, with two conspicuous species being the epiphytic cow-horn orchid (*Myrmecophila tibicinis*) and the terrestrial *Bletia purpurea*.

A great deal of research has been conducted across the Neotropics in an attempt to understand the factors that maintain savannas, with climate, nutrient status, and water availability all cited as critical factors. As Belizean pine savannas occur on infertile sandy soils, it has been suggested that their dominance on this substrate is due to the inability of forest species to grow in this environment. However, there are examples across Central America of broadleaf forests growing upon soils of a similar nature.[87] Although forest species can invade savannas, it can take many decades for them to become established. During this time their colonization is usually prevented by one single factor: fire.[88]

Fire maintains the structure, species composition, and diversity of savannas. If fire is excluded for extended periods, the habitat tends to become more closed as it is colonized by broadleaf trees and shrubs. The shading produced by these new recruits reduces the rich diversity of the ground flora as the savanna slowly transforms into a form of forest. If fires are relatively frequent, however, a more open habitat is maintained, with only a few fire-adapted broadleaf woody species capable of colonizing and surviving. Where forest invasion of savanna areas does occur, the first opportunistic woody colonizers have been shown to increase the fertility and humidity of their own physical microenvironment through leaf fall and shade.[89] This can reduce the chance that the area immediately around them may burn and encourage further colonization by other, nonsavanna species.[90] Thus, a positive feedback mechanism can be introduced that results in the replacement of savanna with closed forest. Usually, however, fire ensures that the savanna persists. The Caribbean pine exhibits a number of ecological adaptations that enable it to respond positively to fire. For example, its thick bark provides thermal insulation against intense heat, and the needles are resistant to a degree of scorching. Even pine seedlings less than one meter in height can survive low-intensity fires.[91] This species is also intolerant of shade and is known to germinate well on the sunlit mineral soils that result from burning.

Preventing savannas from burning can drastically alter their form and promote the establishment of forest. Too much fire, however, can have an impact on the stability of the soils and can be detrimental to even fire-adapted species such as pine. Savanna fires can occur naturally from lightning strikes, and much of the natural structural heterogeneity of savannas relates to different areas having been burned at different intensities and at varying intervals. In the Mountain Pine Ridge as many as six or seven lightning strikes are recorded per year, with approximately half of these resulting in an actual fire.[92] However, the majority of fires that occur across Belize in the dry season are caused by farming activities. A few are also caused by the careless disposal of a lighted cigarette butt from a car window. Across the world indigenous groups also periodically set fire to savannas to encourage new vegetative growth, which in turn attracts game.

FACING: The palmetto is often found in large clumps and is clonal in nature, with one individual spreading vegetatively across large areas. © Sam Bridgewater.

Fire is thus used as part of an elaborate hunting procedure. Conservation managers also use fire as a tool to maintain the structural and species diversity of the savanna areas under their protection. Of critical importance is the timing of the burn. Often a burn is conducted relatively early in the dry season to reduce the amount of above-ground biomass that might catch fire and cause a much more intense and destructive fire later. The exact interval and type of burning depend on the management objectives. For example, the Rio Bravo Conservation and Management Area in northern Belize protects 10,000 hectares of pine savanna. Part of Rio Bravo's aim is to increase the density of pine for carbon sequestration purposes while maintaining the diversity of the component species. A five- to seven-year prescriptive burning of savanna areas has been identified as the most appropriate means of achieving these dual objectives.[93]

THE MOUNTAIN PINE RIDGE AND THE IMPORTANCE OF PROVENANCE

Timber, bananas, and sugar have long been among Belize's biggest exports. A lesser-known fact is that pine seed has also been a significant traded commodity. Although it never achieved the revenue of other products, the physical effects of this trade are far-reaching and can be seen across the globe in many tropical regions. Although the Caribbean pine (*Pinus caribaea*) has a broad natural distribution across Central America, the Bahamas, and Cuba, the species has three distinct varieties, with Belize support-ing the variety known as *hondurensis*. Many countries of the world have established exotic pine plantations to supplement their native forests and to ensure a supply of timber for construction, paper production, and a range of other purposes. Due to its form and growth characteristics, Caribbean pine is one of the most favored exotic species planted, with the variety *hondurensis* comprising more than 80 percent of the world's plantations of this species.[94] The specific region where seed is collected is known as its provenance, and Belize's Mountain Pine Ridge has been the preferred provenance for much of the seed sourced for pine plantations the world over.

THE MOUNTAIN PINE RIDGE

Situated in Cayo District and covering an area of over 43,000 hectares, the Mountain Pine Ridge is one of Belize's most internationally famous regions. The beautiful stands of pine, striking caves, hidden valleys, and numerous streams and waterfalls make this area a popular tourist attraction. To arrive at Las Cuevas, one must travel through this unique ecosystem. The journey crossing the dissected granitic plateau that defines the Mountain Pine Ridge takes about an hour by car, and approximately 80 percent of the region is covered by pine forests. Although these are classified separately from pine savannas by the Belize Ecosystems Map,[95] they are considered here due to their gen-eral broad floristic similarity to the dense pine savannas of other parts of the country and the presence of a grassy herbaceous layer. In addition to many of the widespread savanna species, of particular botanical interest is the presence of the endemic silver palm (*Schippia concolor*). Polewood (*Xylopia frutescens*), with its characteristic branching, is another common associate easily seen from the road. Depending on the season, a journey through the pine ridge can be a glorious botanical experience; particularly conspicuous species include the large pink-flowered terrestrial orchid *Sobralia macrantha* and a variety of yellowed-flowered St. John's worts (hypericums), of which *Hypericum terrae-firmae* is widespread.

As in other savanna areas, the soils of the Mountain Pine Ridge are acidic, with low levels of nutrients such as phosphorus and nitrogen. They are therefore largely unsuitable for agriculture. Instead, the Mountain Pine Ridge has been managed for its timber, with fire used as one of the primary management tools to regulate regeneration of the pine that forms the primary species harvested. The high density of pine seen in the region today reflects human interference. The Mountain Pine Ridge is largely uninhabited except for a few tourist lodges, the notable exception being the Douglas da Silva Forestry Station at Augustine.

The Mountain Pine Ridge is a popular tourist attraction because of its many waterfalls. © Sam Bridgewater.

Hypericum terra-firmae is one of the many striking flowering plants of the Mountain Pine Ridge. © Sam Bridgewater.

In 2000 foresters working within the Mountain Pine Ridge noticed that patches of pine were dying. Although it is natural for all trees to die when they succumb to disease, drought, or senescence, the density and extent of deaths on this occasion were unusual and disturbing to those who first witnessed them. After further outbreaks, it soon became clear that these were the initial signs of a catastrophic infestation of a lethal cocktail of wood-boring beetles. Although the Mountain Pine Ridge has suffered the ravages of numerous fires and hurricanes in its past, this natural insect-induced disaster was the first large-scale attack of this type reported for the area. Over a two-year period, over 25,000 hectares suffered nearly 100 percent mortality of pine—about 80 percent of the pine ecosystem and about 60 percent of the entire Mountain Pine Ridge Forest Reserve.[96] Similar beetle infestations occurred in the southern coastal savannas. Five years later, and despite good natural regeneration of pines in many areas, great swathes of the pine ridge remain scarred by this episode. Tens of thousands of dead trees dating from that era continue to provide a stark reminder of how even nature's smallest beasts have the power to play havoc with the environment. The increased quantity of dead material in the ecosystem due to the beetle attack has also made the Mountain Pine Ridge more susceptible to fire.

Much of the Mountain Pine Ridge has suffered from the predations of the pine beetle (*Dendroctonus* spp.), which has killed populations of pine. © Sam Bridgewater.

In Belize two major groups of beetles are usually implicated in the death of pine trees.[97] These belong to the genera *Dendroctonus* and *Ips*. Of the former genus, five species have been identified from the Mountain Pine Ridge, one of which is the infamous southern pine beetle (*D. frontalis*). Although this species is usually cited as the primary causal agent of mass pine deaths in many Central American and American pine forests, research has indicated that in the case of the recent Mountain Pine Ridge attack, a different culprit may have been largely responsible: a yet scientifically unidentified *Dendroctonus* species.[98] This has been given the common name of the Caribbean pine beetle. However, debate continues among entomologists as to which beetle species should shoulder most of the blame.[99] In addition, five species of *Ips* are also believed to be present in the country. Although they can also attack pine trees and are found in the Mountain Pine Ridge, they usually do so only in association with *Dendroctonus*.[100] Numerous other wood-boring beetles can be found on pines, including members of the genus *Ambrosia*. These can affect wood quality, but they rarely kill trees.

The Caribbean pine beetle is tiny, typically less than four millimeters long. Its devastating effects are caused by mass infestations of a single tree. Typically, an attack will be instigated by a female boring into the bark. The pine usually responds to this minor irritation by releasing resin as a localized defense response. However, pheromones released by the female soon attract other adult beetles, and a mass onslaught ensues. The attacking beetles create chambers in the inner bark where they lay their eggs. On hatching, the larvae feed on the inner bark and sapwood, eventually pupating in chambers near the bark surface. As adults, they chew their way out through the bark in search of new trees to attack. The generation cycle for the Caribbean pine beetle is unknown, but the southern pine beetle can complete its life cycle within a month.

Various management techniques can be used to control beetle outbreaks. These include the use of artificial pheromone traps that lure beetles away from healthy trees, the felling of infected trees, and the cutting of swathes of forest around infected areas to contain the pest. However, studies have shown that the southern pine beetle can fly more than seven hundred meters before initiating a new attack, suggesting that containment lines may need to be at least this width to be effective. It is believed that the Caribbean pine beetle is capable of flying only shorter distances.

THE SAVANNA AND WETLAND FAUNA

Belize's savannas and wetlands provide habitats for a broad range of animal species. Many of these are also associated with forest areas and include peccaries, tapir, pumas, and jaguars. The biology of many of these groups will be covered in chapter 4. However, a number of species do show distinct preferences for open savanna habitats and wetland. For example, in the case of birds, the yellow-headed parrot, the jabiru stork, and the fork-tailed and vermilion flycatchers are all particularly associated with pine savanna areas, while herons, egrets, spoonbills, anhingas, rails, and ibis are common fish-eating wetland species. Among the mammals, the nine-banded armadillo can frequently be seen in the savanna, especially in forest islands; a snake with a strong predilection for this ecosystem is the neotropical rattlesnake, also known as the cascavel (*Crotalus durissus*).

THE NINE-BANDED ARMADILLO

Famed for its armored suit, its ability to dig furiously, and to jump high,[101] the nine-banded armadillo (*Dasypus novemcinctus*) enjoys an extended latitudinal range from the southern United States southward through Central and South America to northwest Argentina and Uruguay.

The vermilion flycatcher (*Pyrocephalus rubinus*) is associated with pine savanna. Hand-colored lithograph by John and Elizabeth Gould, from Charles Darwin, *The Zoology of the Voyage of the H.M.S. Beagle*, part 3, *Birds* (1841), plate 6. © The Natural History Museum, London.

Within Belize, this small mammal is a common inhabitant of broadleaf forest, pine forest, and savanna habitats, where it feeds primarily on insects. With its sharp claws it constructs underground burrows that act as refuges from predators, chambers for giving birth, and cool oases away from the elevated temperatures often found in these relatively open habitats. This species' relative lack of body hair makes thermal regulation difficult, so to escape overheating, armadillos tend to be nocturnal, frequently spending the day resting underground. Studies in northern Belize have indicated that armadillo chamber densities are high in dense pine savanna, with an average of twenty-seven separate armadillo burrows per hectare in this habitat, as compared to only six in more open savanna habitats.[102] It has been suggested that this is due in part to the fact that the well-drained soils of the denser pine areas are less likely to be flooded for extended periods during the wet season. Although burrow density can give an indication of

The nine-banded armadillo (*Dasypus novemcinctus*) is a regular inhabitant of savanna areas. The species occurs over a huge range, from Uruguay to the southern United States. This specimen is held at the Natural History Museum in London. © The Natural History Museum, London.

the size of armadillo populations, there is no direct correlation, as not all burrows are actively used and some armadillos may use more than one. In digging their burrows, armadillos unwittingly provide temporary homes for a range of other species. Snakes particularly favor these environments; neotropical rattlesnakes (*Crotalus durissus*), tropical rat snakes (*Spilotes pullatus*), and boa constrictors (*Boa constrictor*) have all been found residing in old armadillo homes.[103] Species recorded from other faunal groups include the furrowed wood turtle (*Rhinoclemmys areolata*), anoles (*Anolis* spp.,) and the basilisk lizard (*Basiliscus vittatus*).

Wherever it occurs, the nine-banded armadillo has been exploited by humans as a source of meat. It has also been used in biomedical science. Like humans, armadillos can become naturally infected by leprosy in the wild, with affected individuals known to produce antibodies against the bacterium responsible. The leprosy bacillus is difficult to grow in culture, and for this reason, medical advances in the treatment of this disease have been assisted by studies of artificially inoculated armadillos in laboratory conditions.[104] Typically leprosy attacks the nerves of the cooler parts of the body—the

The yellow-headed parrot (*Amazona oratrix*) is highly threatened due to habitat loss and poaching for the pet industry. Areas of Belizean savanna provide a relatively safe haven for this beleaguered bird. © William Milliken.

extremities, such as the hands, feet, and face. Armadillos have an unusually low body temperature, making them ideal for studying this disfiguring illness.

THE YELLOW-HEADED PARROT

One of the most celebrated animals of Belize's pine savannas is the beautiful and famously garrulous yellow-headed parrot (*Amazona oratrix*). This species is one of six known from Belize belonging to the parrot genus *Amazona*.[105] This attractive bird inhabits a range of forest and savanna habitats in Mexico, Guatemala, Belize, and Honduras.[106] Sadly, across its entire range the yellow-headed parrot is highly endangered due to large-scale loss of its natural habitat and to severe persecution through poaching—for its colorful plumage and for its excellent mimicry and speaking ability, a trait that has led to its demise at the hands of the pet industry. Population decline has been estimated at 90 percent, and as a result, this species is listed on the IUCN Red List of Threatened Species. The yellow-headed parrot is also now listed under Appendix I of CITES, which bans the trade of all wild-bred individuals (see the boxed text "Mahogany and the Convention on International Trade in Endangered Species of Wild Fauna and Flora [CITES] in chapter 3). Despite this protection, however, illegal nest-raiding continues. In Belize, populations of this bird are considered to be genetically distinct from others and are treated as a separate subspecies (*belizensis*). The majority of the populations of this subspecies occur within Belize, although they are not entirely endemic to the country. The yellow-headed parrot's favored habitat is pine savanna, although it is also associated with open broad-leaved forests. It feeds on a variety of fruits and nuts and nests in holes in tree trunks and tree branches.

Another treasured Belizean bird species whose welfare in part depends on savanna is the jabiru stork (*Jabiru mycteria*). Enjoying protection in Belize since 1973, this large fish-loving wader can grow in excess of one meter in height and live for over thirty years.[107] Although formerly only a visitor during the breeding season (November–April), the jabiru is now resident all year round. It is found associated with wetland areas, with flooded savanna being a particularly favored locality. It nests in tall, isolated trees.

THE NEOTROPICAL RATTLESNAKE (CASCAVEL)

Few sounds are as universally feared as the dry rattle emanating from the tail of the cascavel (*Crotalus durissus*). Also known as the neotropical rattlesnake, this species is widespread across the Americas and is typically found in dry habitats such as savannas and deserts. The cascavel belongs to a group of snakes called the pit vipers. All members of this group share a physical feature consisting of a pair of temperature-sensitive pits, one situated on each side of the head. As the function of these heat-detecting organs is to locate prey, they are incredibly sensitive to changes in temperature. Some pit vipers are known to be able to detect changes in temperature of one thousandth of a degree centigrade, enabling them to locate and accurately strike their prey from a considerable distance even if they are deprived of sight and hearing.[108]

Although we associate the rattle with snake aggression, it serves as a peaceful means of communication to warn us of its position. Unfortunately, this warning is often ignored. The poisonous nature of the rattlesnake is well deserved, as its venom is highly toxic and can kill if large amounts are injected and a bite remains untreated; but such fatal cases are extremely rare. Rattlesnakes are generally nonaggressive creatures who usually do their utmost to avoid unnecessary confrontations—unless it is with their intended rodent, lizard, and bird prey. However, if stepped on or interfered with, they do strike in self-defense. A high proportion of snake bites are the fault of the victim.

Snake venoms are normally classified into two groups, depending on whether they attack the victim's nerve tissues (neurotoxic) or the blood and circulatory system (hemotoxic). Venom of the tropical rattlesnake can show both these properties, and in addition to massive tissue destruction and swelling around the bitten area, a drop in blood pressure, kidney failure, and breathing problems can also occur. The venom itself is a complex mixture of enzymes and proteins that serve to incapacitate the victim and aid subsequent digestion of its intended prey. More detailed information on snake venom and its treatment is provided later in this book (see the boxed text "Snake Bites and Snake Venom" in chapter 4).

A NATURAL HISTORY OF BELIZE

Belize's wetlands account for just under 2 percent of its territory. Like savannas, they vary in form and species composition. The Belize Ecosystem Map recognizes eight distinct kinds, including *Sphagnum* shrubland, *Eleocharis* marsh, and reed swamp. Although not strictly speaking a vegetation type, areas of standing freshwater such as lakes and ponds provide a unique habitat for many plant species. The most conspicuous of these include the common water lily (*Nymphaea ampla*) and the white-flowered *Sagittaria*, which is often seen growing on the margins of these bodies of water. In shallow areas bladderworts (*Utricularia* spp.) are common, with fifteen species known from the country.

In areas of faster-flowing water, few plants are able to survive. One exception to this are members of the riverweed family (Podostemaceae), represented in Belize by two genera and six species. These mosslike plants have the ability to root against hard surfaces such as rocks, enabling them to grip firmly against the water currents around them. Although they can survive submerged, they are often exposed during the dry season, when water levels drop. This provides them with a chance to flower and reproduce.

A marsh dominated by cutting grass (*Cladium jamaicense*). © Sam Bridgewater.

One commonly observed wetland habitat in Belize is the *Eleocharis* (spike rush) marsh. Patches of this kind of damp habitat are scattered across the country, frequently occurring as localized patches within savanna. Good examples of these marshes can be found close to Hillbank and along the road between Maya Centre and Hopkins. Rarely exceeding fifty centimeters in height, this wetland type is dominated by *Eleocharis*, a genus represented within the country by seventeen species. Although generically known as spike rushes, this common name is misleading, as *Eleocharis* is in fact an unusual type of sedge and not a rush. Globally, the most famous member of this genus is the Chinese water chestnut (*E. dulcis*), whose swollen underground stems (corms) are edible and a staple of Chinese cuisine. *Eleocharis* marshes often have an orangish hue, the color of the tips of the leafless stems when infertile. Although *Eleocharis* marshes are dominated by this genus, other plants occur in association with it, including bladderworts (*Utricularia* spp.), *Xyris* spp., and the weedy, four-petaled, yellow-flowered generalist, *Ludwigia octovalis*.

A taller, denser wetland habitat is reed swamp. This can sometimes be several meters high. Typically this ecosystem is dominated by the common reed (*Phragmites australis*), cutting grass (*Cladium jamaicense*), bulrush (*Typha dominguensis*), or species of the grass genus *Scleria*. Where cutting grass predominates, entry into this system is fraught with discomfort, as the minutely toothed leaf edges are sharp. Of all Belize's wetland systems, the rarest is the lowland sphagnum peat bog, known only from a restricted area of 1,000 hectares in the Sarstoon Temash National Park in Toledo. Belize's only lowland moss-dominated habitat is believed to be unique in Central America and is thus of considerable conservation importance.

VACUUM-PACKED: BLADDERWORTS AND THE CARNIVOROUS HABIT

Although they look the picture of innocence with their tiny, refined form and beautiful flowers, bladderworts are carnivorous. Highly evolved masters of capture, they consume their prey alive to obtain the nutrients they need to survive. As such, these aquatic delights are one of the deadlier plants of wetland systems—and among the most ecologically interesting. To ensnare their victims they have an ingenious trapping mechanism based on tiny vacuum-filled flasklike bladders connected to the stem. Each of these has a sealed opening. On the outside of these bladders are bristles. If they are brushed by passing minuscule aquatic creatures such as protozoa (single-celled organisms), nematodes (roundworms), larvae, or water fleas, the seal of the bladder opening is broken and water is sucked in to fill the vacuum within, along with whatever creature triggered the mechanism. The opening then shuts, enclosing the captive, which is then slowly digested. The whole process from triggering to entombment takes only a fraction of a second. This carnivorous habit allows bladderworts to acquire an additional source of nutrients, particularly nitrogen, from the surrounding physical environment and gives them a competitive advantage over other organisms.

FROM THE ANCIENT MAYA TO THE NEW MILLENNIUM

A HISTORY OF FOREST USE IN THE CHIQUIBUL AND BELIZE

3 TO STAND AT THE SUMMIT of the tallest pyramid of the Maya city of Caracol and witness the sun setting across the forest canopy of the Chiquibul is a profoundly moving experience. At such times, it is hard to rein in the imagination, which leaps back over 1,500 years to a time when the ancient Maya lived and thrived in this now abandoned metropolis.

To arrive at Caracol, one must traverse the dusty, pine-clothed dome of the Mountain Pine Ridge before descending into the dark northern edge of the Chiquibul Forest. Reclaimed by nature after its abandonment, this immense, awe-inspiring city is testament that the fortunes of even the most powerful of civilizations can wane. Although it now lies under a forest canopy and is inhabited solely by forest creatures, the city supported an estimated 120,000 people in its heyday prior to AD 800.[1] Covering sixty-five square miles, Caracol was one of the most populous cities in the pre-Columbian world.

View from Caracol of the rolling canopy of the Chiquibul Forest. © Sam Bridgewater.

It is now known that for over two thousand years, between about 900 BC until Spanish contact, Maya civilization expanded in Belize, with few areas remaining unsettled. Within the Chiquibul, where settlements declined after about AD 1000, in addition to Caracol, the ruins of numerous smaller satellite settlements (*plazuelas*) occur hidden within the region's forests. Early expeditions into the forested region in the 1930s reported the widespread existence of human-built structures such as hill terraces at Arenal, Retiro, and Valentin.[2] Later archaeological studies in the 1990s identified evidence of Maya habitation along the Macal and Raspaculo Rivers.[3] Even today ecologists conducting their field studies excitedly report the existence of extensive but hitherto undiscovered ruins. Indeed, Las Cuevas Research Station itself is sited close to a sizable Mayan temple and causeway complex.

The Chiquibul Forest currently covers an area of around 177,000 hectares and is considered one of the natural wonders of Central America. The evidence suggests, however, that a little over one thousand years ago, vast stone and timber metropolises dominated the land. At the height of Maya civilization, the population of the Central Petén is estimated at between 3 million and 14 million people, and much of the area was an agricultural rather than a forested landscape. That the jungle and its constituent species have been able to recover since the abandonment of the enigmatic Maya settlements in this area illustrates the amazing propensity of nature to recover from catastrophic disturbance. This is a comforting thought for those who despair that development is bulldozing back the final frontiers of the world's remaining wildernesses; in Belize at least, here is one example of the wild frontier pushing back.

This chapter examines Belize's forests from a historical and human-use perspective, tracing their history of management from the ancient Maya through to the present day. It initially introduces the Maya and examines the evidence suggesting that the entire Chiquibul region was once cleared for the production of crops. It then traces the rise and decline of Belize's timber industries from the 1500s to the present day. Belize's modern history is inseparable from its forests. It was the search for timber that led the first European colonizers to settle its shores over 300 years ago, and the extraction of logwood and mahogany lay the foundations of a flourishing forest-based industry that was to drive the Belizean economy until the 1950s. It was only later that export crops such as sugar and bananas, as well as tourism, contributed more than lumber sales to the country's gross domestic product. Logging has profoundly influenced the structure of the existing forests and their ecology. The chapter concludes with a review of the current use and social and economic significance of non-timber forest products. It illustrates how their extraction has been vital for supplying local communities with many of their daily needs and describes how the harvesting of fruits, resins, and leaves has provided the basis of sizable industries.

THE MAYA LEGACY

"My name is Ozymandias, king of kings:
Look on my works, ye Mighty, and despair!"
Nothing beside remains. Round the decay
Of that colossal wreck, boundless and bare
The lone and level sands stretch far away.
PERCY SHELLY, "Ozymandias," 1819

AN ESSENTIAL MAYA CHRONOLOGY FOR THE CHIQUIBUL REGION	
pre-1500 BC	Archaic period. Development of agricultural communities throughout Mesoamerica.
1500 BC–AD 250	Preclassic period. Maya groups develop trade with neighboring cultures; city settlements established.
AD 250–750/800	Classic period. Height of Maya civilization; development of the great Maya city Caracol.
AD 750/850–1100	Terminal Classic period. Caracol abandoned.

With customary colonial arrogance, many of Belize's first European settlers initially believed they were the first significant power to discover and exploit the natural riches of Belize's interior, despite the existence of thriving Mayan towns across the region. However, as the settlers ventured inland in their feverish search for logwood and mahogany, the presence of strange, jungle-covered stone mounds and ruins would have caught their attention. They must have troubled the colonizers, just as they enthralled archaeologists hundreds of years later. They were obviously the work of a mysterious hand from the past and not directly attributable to the existing Maya they encountered.

TOWARD AN UNDERSTANDING OF ANCIENT MAYA LAND USE

The current population of the Chiquibul numbers only a few hundred, with the majority of people based either at Las Cuevas Research Station, Caracol, or the Chalillo Dam. The situation was very different around AD 600, when the region supported the extensive population of an important Central American city. The forest landscape for which the Chiquibul is now famed must have been drastically different at this time.

What we know about ancient Belizean land use can be derived from examining the past through archaeological research and paleoenvironmental studies, such as historical pollen analysis, as well as by inference from the present, informed by ethnographic studies of modern agricultural systems, linguistics, iconography, and ecology.[4] Not all of the research in this area has been conducted in the Chiquibul, although Caracol comprises a regional center of archaeological studies. To gain an insight into how the Chiquibul might have looked over one thousand years ago, evidence must be gathered from a range of different sources from across Belize and Mesoamerica.

Speculation on the plants used and cultivated by the ancient Maya is based in part on a consideration of edible or useful species known to be available to them at the time. One theory suggests that the Maya might have managed the forest vegetation around their settlements, rather than clearing it per se, with root crops such as manihot (*Manihot esculenta*), cocoyam (*Xanthosoma* spp.), and sweet potato (*Ipomoea batatas*) being the primary starchy staples grown under a forest canopy.[5] Although such species probably were an element of the Maya diet,[6] it is now doubted that they were the dominant crops, and is unlikely that the Maya subsisted primarily from cleverly maintained diverse "forest gardens," although such agriculture systems may have been used.

In an attempt to clarify the components of ancient Mayan food, researchers have consulted accounts from the Spanish Conquest.[7] This includes López de Gómara's *Primera y segunda parte de la historia general de las Indias*, first published in 1552. Additional evidence has been gleaned from ancient Maya murals and a few surviving codices. Codices are books made of bark paper (*Ficus* spp.) with pages created by accordion folds; scribes recorded subjects relating to Maya history, astronomy, religion, and agriculture. Of these, sadly, only three remain; the majority were destroyed either by the Spanish after their colonization of the region or by the dampness and heat of the tropical climate. Nevertheless, such research has suggested that a diverse range of crops were formerly cultivated, including those still dominant today: maize (*Zea mays*), beans (*Phaseolus* spp.), and squash (*Cucurbita moschata*).[8] The use of such crops is also supported by linguistic studies, which provide evidence that by about 2500 BC Maya groups were already using words for avocado (*Persea americana*), cacao (*Theobroma cacao*), maize, agave (*Agave* spp.), chili (*Capsicum* spp.), squash, cotton (*Gossypium hirsutum*), and copal (*Protium copal*).[9]

The association of well-known useful native tree species such as breadnut (*Brosimum alicastrum*) with abandoned Maya sites has been cited as evidence that such trees were protected and preferentially cultivated for their fruits and starch-rich edible seed.[10] However, such arguments have been criticized, as the conspicuous presence of this species at these sites can also be explained by ecological factors and may instead represent colonization by this well-suited species subsequent to Maya abandonment.[11] That said, it is highly likely that the ancient Maya protected and even propagated edible fruit-bearing trees such as cacao and hog plum (*Spondias radlkoferi*), and the maintenance of these and other useful trees such as guava (*Psidium guajava*), avocado (*Persea americana*), and cohune (*Orbignya cohune*) is common among the modern Maya today. One recent study in San Jose in Toledo District, for example, identified 164 different species cultivated in a small survey of Maya home gardens, although only a proportion of these were fruit-bearing.[12]

Fruit of the breadnut tree (*Brosimum alicastrum*). The large, edible, starch-rich seeds are surrounded by a thin, sweet-tasting pulp. © Sam Bridgewater.

Much archaeological research has been conducted in Belize in an attempt to clarify the main agricultural systems used by the ancient Maya and identify the primary species cultivated. For the most part, such research has involved pollen analysis of soil cores dated to the time of the Maya, with subsequent interpretation of the pollen "fingerprint" suggesting which species might have been cultivated at the time. However, this line of investigation is fraught with problems related to accurate pollen identification and the inaccuracy of the carbon dating technique. Disagreements on dates among researchers have led to differing theories on many topics, including the speed of recovery of Belize's native vegetation after the Maya collapse in certain areas.

EXAMINING POLLEN EVIDENCE

Pollen consists of tiny grains (spores) of male genetic information produced by plants during reproduction. Formed in the male flower parts (the stamens), it is transferred to the female flower part (the stigma) by pollination (see "Honey Guides, Tongue Tubes, and Love Chambers: The Pollination Ecology of the Chiquibul" in chapter 5). Pollen grains come in a wide variety of sizes and shapes, but they are usually tiny (less than one millimeter in diameter) and often roughly spherical in shape. The outer protective wall of pollen (the exine) is extremely tough and often highly sculptured. The sculpturing of pollen is characteristic for each group of plants, so by examining pollen under a microscope, researchers can sometimes determine the genus or even the species of the plant in question. The study of pollen, palynology, is an essential discipline in forensic science and archaeology. However, as many aspects of the tropical flora are not fully understood, accurate identification of pollen samples can be problematic, hindering its use in deciphering ancient Maya land use. In addition, pollen grains are often not well preserved in tropical environments, and pollen profiles can be contaminated by pollen "rain" blown in from distant areas, confusing local pollen signatures. Lake beds are often chosen to examine pollen profiles from the past, but their accurate dating is reliant on measuring sedimentation rates, which are notoriously difficult to do accurately. The actual dating of pollen cores can also prove problematic for other reasons.[13] In the case of the Yucatán Peninsula, this is due to the limestone bedrock. Dating of pollen cores is often done by radiocarbon analysis of fossilized organisms associated with the pollen core layer. Such research examines the degree of decay of an unstable form of carbon (carbon-14) in a fossil. This form of radioactive carbon occurs naturally and is absorbed by all organisms during their life. However, when they die, it ceases to be absorbed and, instead, begins to decay, with only half the original amount present after 5,568 years (its half-life). After a second period of 5,568 years, the amount is halved again, and so on. By comparing the amount of C-14 in a fossil with modern levels of C-14, it is possible to calculate the date of its death. However, in areas of limestone, lake organisms that are used to date pollen signatures can also absorb carbon from this ancient limestone bedrock, confusing the dating procedure; errors of about 2,500 years have been reported.[14]

Although there is still ongoing debate about the exact interpretation of pollen profiles from Maya times, evidence indicates a clear decline in forest species associated with the height of Maya civilization together with an associated rise in savanna, weedy, and cultivated taxa.[15] The obvious inference is that much of the region's forest was cleared and cultivated as Maya populations grew. However, climatic changes, such as prolonged periods of drought known to have occurred at about the same time, might also have caused some of the perceived changes in pollen profiles. That said, a cultural explanation is likely, and it is clear that as Maya populations increased during the Preclassic and Classic periods, significant clearance of forest for agriculture would have been required. Conversely, subsequent to the Maya collapse, in areas of Belize where settlement decreased, there is an unambiguous rise in pollen profiles of forest tree species, suggesting the widespread abandonment of agriculture, regional depopulation, and the reclamation of the area by forest. Tree genera characteristic of Belizean forest pollen profiles include breadnut (*Brosimum alicastrum*), fig (*Ficus* spp.), chicle (*Manilkara* spp.), hog plum (*Spondias radlkoferi*), and gumbo-limbo (*Bursera simaruba*), with pollen from the weedy trumpet tree (*Cecropia* spp.) suggesting forest disturbance; savanna is usually inferred from the presence of pollen belonging to craboo (*Byrsonima crassifolia*), the sandpaper tree (*Curatella americana*), oak (*Quercus* spp.), and species belonging to the shrubby Melastomataceae family.

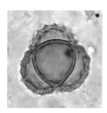

Pollen grain of *Pachira aquatic*, a tree species common along rivers in Belize. Pollen grains come in a wide variety of sizes and shapes, with their outer protective wall often highly sculptured and characteristic for the plant group. Through examination of dated pollen cores scientists are able to infer historical vegetation patterns. © Stephen Blackmore.

Trunk of prickly yellow (*Zanthoxylum* spp.), showing its characteristic spines. The presence of large amounts of the pollen of this tree in a pollen core of known date indicates the dominance of forest habitat at that place and time. © Stephen Blackmore.

Dated pollen profiles have been less successful in providing information about the intensity of agriculture and the cultivated species preferred by the ancient Maya. Significant advances in our understanding of this topic have been made by work done at San Antonio Rio Hondo and at Pulltrouser Swamp in northern Belize from deposits dated prior to AD 850.[16] Maize pollen is common from pollen cores taken from these sites, and it is clear that this species, along with squash, was widely cultivated. Indeed, from calculations based on isotope analyses of Maya skeletons, it is believed that maize was the dominant component of the ancient Maya diet.[17] Members of the plant family Solanaceae, which includes potato, tomato, tobacco, and chili peppers, would most likely have been important foodstuffs, too. It has also been suggested that cotton (*Gossypium* spp.) might well have been widely cultivated at the time, together with edible species belonging to the spinach and quinoa plant family (Chenopodiaceae). The use of these species and others is supported by the discovery of nonpollen plant remains such as mineralized seed, stem fragments, or carbonized remnants at archaeological sites.

The Maya city of Caracol in western Cayo District was rediscovered by chance in 1937 when Rosa Mai, a forest laborer looking for mahogany trees, stumbled across its ruins in a remote part of the Chiquibul Forest. It soon attracted the attentions of international archaeologists. One of the first of these was Linton Satterthwaite of the University of Pennsylvania, who drew and photographed the site's numerous carved stelae (stone markers) and altars in the early 1950s. From this and subsequent excavations, including an examination of Caracol's agricultural terraces by Paul Healey from Trent University in Peterborough, Ontario, in 1980,[18] it soon became clear that Caracol was not a small regional Mayan town but an enormous metropolis with an unusually high settlement density for the region. Intensive investigations continued with the Caracol Archaeological Project, led by Diane and Arlen Chase in the mid-1980s. During the course of this initiative, researchers increased their size estimates of the city as new discoveries were made, until the settlement was believed to be in excess of a staggering sixty-five square miles.[19]

From hieroglyphic inscriptions found at the site, it is known that Caracol was the center of one of the preeminent Maya city-states of the Classic period, with other examples including Tikal (Guatemala) and Calakmul (Mexico). Archaeologists believe that these individual political and economic centers ruled over large tracts of the region, controlling smaller "vassal" cities. The city-states themselves were either at war with one another when power struggles erupted or existing in states of fragile truce, during which trade would flourish between them. It has been postulated that the city-states coexisted in much the same way as do NATO, the European Union, and the Middle Eastern alliances of today.[20]

It is also known from hieroglyphs that Caracol defeated neighboring Tikal in AD 562, assuring its domination over a massive 4,500 square miles of territory.[21] Tikal, which is situated in the Petén region of present-day Guatemala, was one of the Maya region's most powerful cities, and its defeat resulted in a period of great prosperity for Caracol. During this time thousands of miles of stone terraces were built, together with causeways constructed to link the city with neighboring population centers, such as Naranjo, parts of which can still be seen from an examination of satellite images.

In addition to the central plaza, pyramid, and palace constructions at its epicenter, Caracol was composed of great numbers of residential units called *plazuelas*, each comprising a small plaza (square), small pyramids, tombs, and simple wood and thatch constructions. The density of these affluent habitations suggests that Caracol had an extensive middle class, and the wealth of many of its inhabitants is illustrated by the frequency with which examination of tombs has revealed teeth inlaid with jadeite or hematite, luxury items such as incense burners, and caches of malachite, obsidian, and pyrite.[22]

After AD 800 people began to abandon Caracol, and there appears to have been a breakdown in social cohesion, a phenomenon repeated in a range of other Mayan cities that were powerful during the Classic period. About AD 895 much of the central part of the city of Caracol was burned, although for the next 150 years many of the roads and agricultural fields continued to be used. But by AD 1100, the collapse was complete and the great city of Caracol had been reclaimed by the forest from which it had been originally hewn.

Neither ancient nor modern Mayan agriculture can be characterized by a single suite of cultivated crops, techniques, or cropping cycles. Instead, local environments and social circumstances have driven the evolution of a myriad of different agricultural practices, with each adapted to the needs of communities and the ecological constraints of the land. The most widely adopted modern farming technique is milpa farming (slash-and-burn), although where topography and flooding place restrictions on this system, agricultural terraces and raised fields have also been adopted.

MILPA FARMING (SLASH-AND-BURN OR SWIDDEN AGRICULTURE)

The ancient Maya almost certainly practiced a form of slash-and burn agriculture (also known as swidden or shifting cultivation), whereby a combination of crops—including maize, beans and squash—were grown together in fields claimed from forest. Typically, slash-and-burn is based on the cutting (slashing) and burning of forest areas to produce small arable fields. The ash from the burned vegetation acts as fertilizer for the established crops, which are planted at the start of the rainy season. In Belize this

The Caana (Sky Place) pyramid lies at the epicenter of Caracol. Rising to a height of 136 feet, it is the tallest of the ancient city's pyramids. The site of ritual ceremonies, it may also have been home to Caracol's rulers. © Sam Bridgewater.

type of "swidden" agriculture is known as milpa farming (*milpa* literally means "corn-field") and is still the predominant agricultural technique of the modern Maya. It is labor intensive, and even with today's modern steel axes and machetes, it can take an estimated 150 man-hours to clear and prepare a hectare of forest if a chainsaw is not available.[23] For the ancient Maya with their stone tools, it would have taken considerably longer. Typically, milpas are cultivated for one, two, or three years before being abandoned—often due to the buildup of weeds—and left to recover during an extended period of fallow while the forest reinvades and the soil is allowed to regain its fertility. The fallow period typically lasts between five and twenty years. Although milpa farming is highly effective and can be a sustainable land-use system if population levels are low, it ties up large tracts of land that must be left in a fallow state. Problems arise if the population density becomes too high. In such a scenario, shortage of land does not allow enough time for exhausted fields to recover, and insufficient forest is left surrounding the fields to allow them to regenerate ecologically during fallow periods.

A young maize plant growing in a milpa clearing hewn from the forest. © Sam Bridgewater.

It is likely that large areas of the Chiquibul may have been cleared for milpa between AD 250 and 800 and that this agricultural practice eventually became unsustainable, although this may not necessarily be responsible for the abandonment of Caracol. Across the modern world there are many examples of long-standing civilizations that continue to thrive despite environmental degradation.

AGRICULTURAL TERRACES

As archaeologists began to appreciate fully the large populations of cities such as Caracol, it became clear that milpa farming alone could not have provided the food needed by the population estimated to live within its extended confines. Milpa farming can support approximately eighty people per square kilometer, while the estimated population density of Caracol at its height was between four hundred and sixteen hundred people per square kilometer.[24] Consequently, research began to investigate whether the ancient Maya practiced more intensive farming techniques.[25]

One of the most striking ancient agricultural features to have persisted in the modern Chiquibul landscape is terraces. Such terraces are abundant in Quintana Roo and Campeche in Mexico.[26] Much of the Chiquibul region is marked by rolling limestone hills, and here, too, striking stepped stone-supported platforms are common on hillsides. These relict manifestations of Maya agriculture were examined in detail at Caracol in 1980 and were found to be uniformly and regularly built,[27] as if their construction were part of a large, centrally coordinated development scheme. The terraces found are defined as "dry field"–they were not seasonally flooded to produce water-dependent crops such as rice but were created instead to increase the available land for productive agriculture. Typically they occur on slopes with an inclination less than 50 degrees. As indicated by radiocarbon dating of preserved ceramic remnants associated with these structures, they were already in existence by AD 700, coinciding with the Late Classic period, although they may already have been in use much earlier than this. The presence in the Caracol terraces of shells of *Pachychilus*, a snail typical of flowing water, suggests that the production of these terraces was labor intensive, with fertile alluvial sediments perhaps carried in from other locations. The exact role of the Maya terraces is still debated, although their likely significance was to increase agricultural productivity by trapping soil, reducing erosion, and conserving moisture. During the heavy rains of the wet season, terraces would have slowed water runoff from slopes and in the dry season would have helped to conserve much-needed moisture. However, analysis of the soils from terraces at Caracol reveal high concentrations of clay and associated aluminum, suggesting that the intensive farming techniques of the Maya might have resulted in soil deterioration over time, a factor that would have eventually caused a decline in crop productivity.

WETLAND FIELDS

In addition to terracing, the ancient Maya probably developed a number of other sophisticated land-use practices to maximize agricultural productivity. These included the draining and hydraulic manipulation of wetland areas through the digging of canals. Such activity sometimes included the raising of soil levels, using sediments from the canals themselves, to produce fertile "wetland fields" that allowed crops to be grown all year round.[28] The development of such practices may have been a response to increasing settlement densities and a rise in demand for food. The most sophisticated modern manifestation of such techniques is the chinampas of Mexico, where intensely cropped, artificial, fertile islands are created in shallow lakes. These islands are formed by building up sediment within a wattle fence positioned in the water. Trees such as willow are used to secure the edges of the built-up islands against erosion. Devised prior to the Aztecs, chinampas were once vital in supporting the urban core of central Mexico and are still found in some regions of the country today, one example being at Xochimilco. Raised and drained fields have been shown to have been widespread in northern Belize, such as at Pulltrouser Swamp, San Antonio Rio Hondo, and Lamanai,[29] and their layout has been investigated through field excavation, with canal patterns discernible by remote radar imagery.[30] It is unlikely that these systems would have figured widely in the Chiquibul, as there are no extensive wetland areas in the region. However, related farming techniques—harnessing the fertile, moist, alluvial soils of riverbank floodplains—may well have been used on rivers such as the Raspaculo and Macal, with crops planted in damp depressions (*bajos*) during the dry season. Such techniques make use of dry-season labor and are still employed by the Kekchi Maya of southern Belize.[31]

Maximizing agricultural productivity is dependent on a reliable source of water for irrigation during the dry season or, alternatively, creation of systems that conserve water and therefore do not require irrigation. Ensuring the availability of water would have been a priority for the Maya due to the extended length of the dry season in Belize (December to May), the porous nature of the bedrock, the occurrence of droughts, and the frequently inaccessible depth of the groundwater. Any failure in water supply would have been catastrophic, and major Mayan cities were usually located close to cenotes (water-filled limestone sinkholes), permanent rivers, or lakes. Additional water conservation techniques used by the Maya included the digging of underground cisterns (chultunes) that were lined with lime cement to trap water during the wet season and the creation of artificial reservoirs and canals.[32] Studies at the Tikal archaeological site, for example, have identified at least six major artificial reservoirs that could collect approximately 900,000 cubic meters of water annually;[33] similar reservoirs were constructed at Caracol. Dams are known to have been used in the Chiquibul, and the remains of one such dam dating from the Classic period has been investigated close to Blue Hole Camp on Congrejo Creek, a tributary of the Raspaculo River.[34] Research indicates that the dam stretched for ten meters, was three meters tall and 2.5 meters thick at its base, and held approximately three hundred cubic meters of water. A small sealable spillway was found at the dam's base, allowing water flow to be regulated. Although there are agricultural terraces in the immediate area, it is believed that the function of this dam was not primarily to irrigate crops but to supply a source of fresh water to nearby communities, and perhaps even to provide a suitable environment for edible animal species such as freshwater crabs or the freshwater snail (*Pachychilus* spp.). By a strange coincidence, the vicinity of Blue Hole Camp marks the highest flooding level of the recently established and controversial Chalillo Dam. Although the environmentally destructive consequences of this modern feature are without doubt, it merely continues a tradition of water management established by the ancient Maya over one thousand years ago.

FACING: Riverine (riparian) floodplain on the Raspaculo River. Such fertile floodplains, with their buildup of river sediments, may have been utilized by the ancient Maya of the Chiquibul for growing crops during the dry season. The floodplain shown is dominated by dumb cane (*Tripsacum latifolium*).
© Sam Bridgewater.

> The city was desolate. No remnant of this race hangs around the ruins, with traditions handed down from father to son and from generation to generation. It lay before us like a shattered bark in the midst of the ocean, her mast gone, her name effaced, her crew perished, and none to tell whence she came, to whom she belonged, how long on her journey, and what caused her destruction.   JOHN STEVENS, *Incidents of Travel in Central America, Chiapas, and Yucatan, 1841*

The mysterious temples and monuments scattered throughout the forests of the Yucatán and adjacent parts of Central America have caught the human imagination since they were first brought to the attention of the outside world in the early nineteenth century. The abandonment of the great cities in Petén (Guatemala), southern Campeche (Mexico), and parts of Belize, but not in many other areas, is an enigma. A large population faced the Spaniards upon their arrival in Yucatan, and of course the Maya continue to thrive across the region to this day, including in Belize. However, five hundred years prior to the Spanish Conquest, one or more catastrophic events precipitated an internal collapse of some of their highly sophisticated city societies and associated ruling dynasties, with people moving to towns and cities around lakes.

Many independent theories attempt to explain the abandonment of great cities like Caracol by the Maya, with events such as hurricanes, earthquakes, disease, and invasion all cited as being potentially significant. The topic remains contentious to this day. It is possible that a number of interrelated factors were most likely to blame. First, the population of the areas that "crashed" might simply have grown too big, outstripping the land's ability to provide, although there is no real evidence to support this. If populations did grow, associated deforestation for agriculture and city development would have become more widespread, causing soil erosion and environmental degradation. Famine may have become increasingly commonplace as resources dwindled, although this is only conjecture, as there is no supporting evidence. Indeed, skeletal evidence of populations in the Petén at the time show no dietary problems. If there was a shortage of food, this might have been further compounded by an outbreak of crop diseases or pest attack afflicting the cultivation of the relatively few staple crops such as maize. Desperation provoked by frequent food shortages and malnutrition could, in turn, have catalyzed increased conflict between adjacent Maya city-states, with a breakdown of regional alliances and trade routes and the general populace's concomitant loss of trust in and support for the Maya rulers and priests, who were supposed to ensure the welfare of their people. There is certainly evidence of increased regional conflict at the time, although the reasons behind this are not clear. It might simply have been the result of power-seeking rulers.

A second associated factor may be climate-related. Chemical analyses of sediments from lakes in the Yucatán Peninsula have been used to reconstruct the climatic history of the region. Focusing on oxygen isotopes and gypsum precipitation, the concentrations of which are altered by changes in evaporation and precipitation, the study suggests that the Maya decline coincided with a period of prolonged drought.[35] Such a drought may have contributed to the abandonment of cities without long-term reliable water sources such as cenotes or lakes, intensifying conflict for declining water resources within and between city-states. However, even greater droughts occurred between the Preclassic and Classic periods. These didn't result in the abandonment of cities, although if the Maya were experiencing political problems and conflict at the time of the "collapse" known for the Chiquibul, the effects of drought might have been more catastrophic.

What, therefore, was the form of the Chiquibul landscape at the time of the Maya prior to their abandonment of Caracol a little before AD 1000? Was the vast, world-famous swath of forest now covering this area formerly nothing more than agricultural fields? Although we may never be certain of the form of landscape that existed then, there are many known facts that can help us to visualize how the region may have looked. We know for certain that the regional population was much larger than it is today and that agriculture was based on maize, a crop necessitating the conversion of large areas of forest to agricultural lands. We know too that the building of their vast city complexes

Temple 1, Tikal, Guatemala. The famous collapse of the lowland Maya civilization subsequent to AD 800 was site-specific. Although Caracol and other major cities in Belize were abandoned within several hundred years of the start of the decline, others, like Lamanai, continued to thrive. In addition to Caracol, neighboring Tikal in Guatemala was abandoned. © Sam Bridgewater.

such as Caracol would have required the use of great quantities of timber and palm thatch and that Maya settlements were

Artist's impression of the Las Cuevas environs at the time of the ancient Maya, ca. AD 700.
© Gwen Ritchie.

scattered throughout the Chiquibul region. Perhaps the overall picture was not dissimilar to that envisaged in the drawing above: a rolling agricultural landscape, largely cultivated in the flat lowlands but augmented by terraces on gentle slopes, with vestiges of forest retained on steeper terrain and hilltops—much like the landscape seen in Toledo District today, where Maya milpa farming continues. What is remarkable is just how quickly the forest recovered after Caracol was deserted. Indeed, by the time the first European settlers arrived in Belize a little over 500 years later, the forest had largely recovered and the trees once again dominated the land, providing the precious timber that would fuel the Belizean economy for the next 450 years.

COMMERCIAL TIMBER EXTRACTION:
FOUR HUNDRED YEARS OF EXPLOITATION

Since the 1980s we have witnessed a phenomenal growth in global environmental movements as concerns rise over the loss of our planet's last remaining wildernesses and the destructive nature of human development. Few issues, however, have attracted as much scientific and public debate or caused such worldwide emotional angst as the destruction of the world's tropical forests. An accusing finger is often pointed at foresters, who are portrayed as bogeymen wielding chain saws and felling huge swaths of forest in their quest to satisfy society's appetite for high-quality timber. Without doubt, timber extraction is an important factor leading to the permanent demise of tropical forests. But it is not the only one. The inequitable distribution of land, population growth, migration, mineral extraction, and agricultural expansion are all implicated in forest destruction, although forest industries often bear the responsibility for improving initial access to forest areas through the construction of roads.

Despite claims to the contrary, it is doubtful that many examples of ecologically sustainable tropical timber production exist in the world. However, it is lamentable that foresters are maligned for forest destruction. In many cases, it is they who have helped maintain forest cover, and the environmental alternative to forestry can be far worse. Despite having been exploited for timber extraction since the 1500s, over 50 percent of Belize is still covered by jungle. Indeed, few countries can now boast the forest cover that Belize enjoys or the high biodiversity it supports. However, although forests such as the Chiquibul may seem wild and untouched to the casual observer, these are ecosystems greatly altered by human hand. Forestry may have ecologically degraded Belize's forests, but it has also played a central role in protecting them. An understanding of the current environmental state of Belize and the Chiquibul is possible only if the history of timber extraction is first considered.

Logging operation in the Chiquibul. © Alex Monro.

Although the Spanish were the first recorded Europeans to arrive in Belize, in the early 1500s, English and Scottish pirates were the first to settle with any great permanency. By the mid-1600s, Belize and the Yucatán Peninsula provided a secure base from which they could launch attacks on Spanish vessels trading in the Caribbean. One highly valued product was the timber of a tree known as logwood, the heartwood of which yielded a dye prized by the expanding European textile industry of the time. The pirates knew that logwood fetched a high price back in Europe, and the raiding of timber-storage sites on the coast and the seizing of vessels laden with this valuable commodity provided an easy source of income.

Logwood (*Haematoxylon campechianum*) is a tree of swampy coastal forests and belongs to the pea family. Its generic name is derived from two Greek words meaning "blood" and "wood," on account of the bright red liquid emitted from its heartwood when soaked in water. The chipped heartwood was hung in sacks in dyers' vats to color wool, silk, linen, and cotton.[36] Alternatively, a solution extracted from the timber prior to dying was used directly on the cloth. A variety of hues could be obtained from logwood, including yellow, orange, red, and blue, dependent on the fixative (mordant) used.

The logwood trade was initially controlled by the Spanish, and the British governments turned a blind eye to the buccaneering activities of its nationals, with officially sanctioned pirates known as privateers. The Belizean coast provided the pirates and privateers with a safe haven, the reef-strewn shallow waters dissuading retribution from the Spanish. In 1667 the Treaty of Madrid was signed between Spain and Britain. This outlawed piracy, and many of the pirates were encouraged to legitimize their activities and establish logwood

camps in northern Belize. These pirates-turned-loggers became known as the Baymen.

Logwood production peaked in the early 1700s with the expansion of the English woolen industry. At that time a ton of logwood fetched as much as twenty-five pounds (equivalent to about two thousand pounds today),[37] with annual exports reaching eight thousand tons.[38] The Baymen did not trade directly with Europe but were dependent on the New England and Jamaican merchant ships that carried the logwood to Boston or Port Royal (Jamaica) for eventual reexport to Europe. To help supply the growing demand for the timber, African slaves were brought to Belize in the 1720s via the Antillean slave markets. Logwood prices declined in the 1750s as production exceeded demand, and the Baymen's attentions switched to mahogany.[39] By 1780 mahogany had replaced logwood as the main Belizean export. Unlike logwood, which is restricted to coastal regions, mahogany grows in the inland forests. With the change in focus, exploration of the interior of Belize began. The inaccessible Chiquibul was one of the last areas to be reached; logging began here in earnest only in the twentieth century, almost three hundred years after the first logwood tree was cut by the Baymen. To provide labor for the developing mahogany industry, many more slaves were brought to the country, and Belize's current multiethnicity is one of the legacies of the timber industry. Despite the activities of the Baymen throughout the 1700s, Spain still claimed Belizean territory as its own, although treaties signed between England and Spain in 1763 (Treaty of Paris), 1783 (Treaty of Versailles), and 1786 (Convention of London) gave English subjects an official right to cut logwood. But neither the Baymen nor the British ever fully recognized Spain's right to the territory. In 1798 the Spanish were defeated by the Baymen at the Battle of St George's Caye, and the country came increasingly under British rule. By the early 1800s it was considered a British settlement, becoming a colony in 1862. Belize finally gained its independence in 1981.

Despite the invention of synthetic aniline dyes in the 1860s and the economic dominance of mahogany, Belize still exported logwood in significant quantities until the early 1900s, with an average of twenty thousand tons traded during a secondary boom period between 1885 and 1900. During this resurgence logwood accounted for 50 percent of Belizean exports. Thereafter the industry quickly declined, and the depression of the 1930s finally sealed its fate.[40]

Flowers of the logwood tree (*Haematoxylon campechianum*). The timber of this member of the pea family can be used as a source of dye, and its presence in Belize was one of the reasons why the country was originally settled. © Sam Bridgewater.

My Lord contemptuous of his Country's Groves,
As foreign Fashions foreign Trees too loves:
"Odious! upon a Walnut-plank to dine!
No—the red-vein'd *Mohoggony* be mine!
Each Chest and Chair around my Room that stands,
Was shipp'd thro' dangerous Seas from distant Lands . . ."
THOMAS WARTON, "On Luxury," *Poems on Several Occasions,* 1748

The first European ships that reached the Caribbean in the late sixteenth century often arrived in need of reconditioning after their arduous voyages. Scouting parties were sent ashore in search of strong, flexible, rot-resistant timber suitable for making running repairs to the storm-battered ships. In this way mahogany was probably first encountered by Europeans, and news of its excellent working qualities soon spread. Walter Raleigh, for example, was reported to have patched his ships with mahogany in the West Indies in 1597. European cabinetmakers at that time were keen to experiment with new timbers, and the arrival of imported mahogany coincided with dwindling stocks of European walnut, one of the traditional stalwarts of the trade.[41] They found the beautiful color, stability, and figuring of this newly discovered timber ideal for their work, and by the middle of the eighteenth century, mahogany was the favored wood of master furniture craftsmen, including Chippendale and Hepplewhite. The demand was insatiable, and the foundations of the mahogany trade were laid.

Mahogany is the common name given to the three species of the genus *Swietenia* (Meliaceae family).[42] Comprising approximately 550 species, the family occurs worldwide, with some 125 species occurring naturally in the Neotropics. The majority of these are trees. Although mahogany is the most famous member of this group, a number of other species within the family also have significant economic value, including Spanish cedar (*Cedrela odorata*). Of the trio of mahogany species, the first is Indian (sometimes called Cuban) mahogany (*S. mahogani*), a tree native to southern Florida and the Caribbean islands. This species initially bore the brunt of the flourishing mahogany trade, and by the beginning of World War II it had become commercially extinct. More widespread is Honduran (or big-leaf) mahogany (*S. macrophylla*), a species stretching eight thousand kilometers across mainland tropical America from Mexico to southern Amazonia in Brazil. This species is now the only source of commercial mahogany. The third species, *S. humilis*, is restricted to seasonally dry forests in Pacific Central America. Due to its small and often twisted stature, it is of limited commercial value. Although three species of *Swietenia* are described, they are poorly defined biologically, and it is believed that they can hybridize freely. Yet they are maintained as distinct by taxonomists, as there is little overlap in their geographical ranges,[43] although some authors maintain that *S. humilis* is no more than a morphological variant (eco-type) of *S. macrophylla*. These three species represent "true" mahogany, although many other timber species from different parts of the world with similar timber character-istics are called by the same name.[44] These include the "African mahoganies" belong-ing to the genera *Khaya* and *Entandrophragma* (also in the family Meliaceae) as well as "Philippine mahogany" (in the family Dipterocarpaceae).

Today the United States and the United Kingdom are the biggest importers of ma-hogany in the world, and the demand for this high-quality timber is staggering. In 2000, for instance, it was estimated that an annual harvest of 57,000 mahogany trees was needed to supply the U.S. furniture trade alone.[45] However, patterns of trade are constantly changing, in part reflecting resource abundance in supplying countries. Al-though Central America was the major source of U.S. mahogany in 2000, by 2003 it was responsible for less than 10 percent of imports, the majority coming instead from South America.[46]

Mahogany (*Swietenia mahogani*). From Mark Catesby, *The Natural History of Carolina, Florida and the Bahama Islands* (1731-1743), vol. 2, plate 81. © The Natural History Museum, London.

Sectioned fruit of the big-leaf mahogany (*Swietenia macrophylla*) displaying its winged seeds. © Peter Stafford.

Swietenia macrophylla—the only mahogany species found in Belize—occurs in mixed lowland broadleaf forest. It is a relatively rare canopy emergent, occurring at low densities, and population numbers rarely exceed two individuals per hectare, although densities can be higher for immature "pre-commercial" individuals under thirty centimeters in diameter (at breast height). In part, its low abundance reflects the competitive nature of the forest environment, where most seedlings fail to survive to adulthood. In addition, the larvae of a shoot-boring moth (*Hypsipyla* spp.) attack the apical shoots of mahogany wherever it occurs at a high density—the reason that the establishment of mahogany plantations in Latin America has proven so problematic. Where the species has been grown outside of its native range and away from its natural pests, such as in the Philippines, plantations have been successful. Occurring as a tall tree in mature forest, mahogany is a light-demanding species, and moderate disturbance is ideal for its development.[47] Indeed, light hurricane damage or fire can provide ideal conditions for mahogany regeneration, with mature trees withstanding damage better than many other species. The fast-growing seedlings are also well adapted to exploit canopy gaps caused by treefall. Mahogany regenerates well in abandoned farms, and if weeds are controlled for the first few years, the seedlings can flourish in this environment. However, mahogany is vulnerable to overharvesting, which can remove the mature seed trees necessary for regeneration, and its seeds do not retain viability in the soil longer than one year.

Like many of Belize's forest trees, mahogany tends to lose its leaves during the dry season. Its small, strong-scented flowers are visited by insects such as bees and butterflies, although the exact species responsible for its pollination remain unknown.[48] Separate male and female flowers are found together on the same tree (i.e., it is monoecious), with the male flowers on each individual opening after its female flowers have already been fertilized by pollen from other individuals. This mechanism prevents self-pollination and helps maintain the genetic diversity of populations (see the boxed text "The Sex Life of Plants" in chapter 5). The fruit is a large capsule that splits during the dry season to release its winged, wind-dispersed seeds.

Although the earliest European shipments of mahogany came from Cuba, Jamaica, and Hispaniola, Belize's first settlers soon found that their adopted country also held rich reserves. By the 1770s mahogany had become the major export of the colony. The earliest laws governing mahogany extraction replicated the agreements made by the early logwood cutters, whereby a logger, upon finding a site rich in timber, would stake a claim extending a thousand paces on either side of the hut and from the water (logging usually took place close to rivers) to the water divide.[49] Later these informal but generally respected agreements were replaced by a system of land grants allocated by the superintendent of the settlement.[50]

Mahogany was first cut in accessible areas close to the coast and rivers in northern Belize, with harvesting limited to areas from which felled trees could easily be extracted. With the introduction of slaves from Jamaica around 1700 and the arrival of oxen and wagons a century later, the distances mahogany logs could be dragged before being floated downstream increased significantly. The earliest recorded logging areas were from the Belize River, with the Treaty of Versailles (1763) and the Convention of London (1786) releasing further areas for extraction. These were primarily associated with the Sibun and New Rivers. In the early 1900s logging began adjacent to the coast in the south, but it was not until the 1920s that the development of roads and tractors allowed logging in the remoter forests such as the Chiquibul.[51] In some areas of the country—the Chiquibul included—short tracts of railroad were established to facilitate the transport of logs. However, until modern times, Belize's rivers always provided the primary means of transport, with logs being chained into rafts and floated to the coast. From here, they were floated by sea to mills or loaded onto steamships.

Rafting mahogany logs down the New River, ca. 1930. © Publications of the Field Museum Botanical Series 12, 1936. Courtesy Field Museum of Natural History, Chicago.

Initially, promising logging areas were scouted by tree spotters, who estimated the quantity of wood available for harvesting and suggested suitable extraction routes. As the industry became more organized, detailed maps outlining timber volumes were produced. Early logging was done with two-man saws during the dry season, although the modern chain saw has since dramatically eased felling.

It is difficult to estimate with great accuracy mahogany exports from Belize, but it is believed that over 3.5 million cubic meters of mahogany have been cut from its forests since 1800.[52] Although demand has continued throughout its history of extraction, prices have constantly fluctuated as the world's economy has waxed and waned. Consequently, the industry has always been unstable. High export years were recorded in the 1840s, corresponding to the expansion of rail in Europe and a demand for mahogany to build railway carriages. Exports slumped during the Great Depression of the 1930s.

CONSERVING THE GENETIC DIVERSITY OF MAHOGANY

There has long been concern that the logging of mahogany could have adverse effects on its genetic diversity. Vertical growth, degree of branching, and shoot-borer resistance are all inheritable traits governed by the action of genes.[53] By preferentially removing from a population those trees which display desirable characteristics for timber, only those genetically predisposed to being of poorer form are left. This appears to have happened with S. mahogani, the only remaining populations of which are highly branched.[54]

In 2003 a paper was published in the journal Molecular Ecology assessing the genetic structure of Mesoamerican mahogany (from eight distinct populations) using a technique known as microsatellite analysis.[55] Included in the research were samples of Swietenia macrophylla taken from the Chiquibul at Las Cuevas. Although the study revealed lower genetic diversity for Mesoamerican mahogany populations than for South American counterparts, individual populations within Mesoamerica were found to be genetically distinct from one another. The authors succeeded in correlating genetic divergence with geography, and they suggested that natural barriers to breeding occur between populations and that this might explain genetic differentiation between them. For instance, the Talamanca mountain range separates populations of mahogany in Panama from others farther north in Central America. The range may therefore act as a barrier to gene flow, thus maintaining populations on either side as distinct. In addition, they surmised that genetic differences may also be explained by historical biogeography: that the glacial forest refugia postulated for the region during the last ice age (see "Why Are the Tropics So Diverse? The Museum and Refuge Theories" in chapter 1) might have been instrumental in maintaining regional, geographically isolated populations, thereby allowing them to diverge. Their findings are significant for the conservation of mahogany, as to maintain the full genetic variability of the species, populations across its range must be protected.

The onset of harvesting in the Chiquibul in the 1920s coincided with the development of a short stretch of railway in the northern part of the region from Vaca Falls south to an area known as Camp 6. Logs were harvested and transported by ox, and later by tractor, to the camp. From here they were carried by rail to Vaca Falls on the Macal River before being floated downstream to the sawmills.

Once logging in the Chiquibul became logistically feasible, forestry activities quickly spread across the region. By 1925, Retiro had been reached, and by 1955 even remote areas south of Resumadeiro had been logged.[56] The network of roads and overgrown trails in the Chiquibul today are the result of eighty years of logging activity, and many of the current place-names owe their existence to forestry. New Maria, for example, was a temporary forestry camp established in 1949. It is now the site of permanent forestry research plots. Perhaps the most famous place associated with mahogany is Millionario. Legend has it that this name reflects the great profits to be made from this species at the time. Although the area was formerly the site of a major forestry camp, there are no signs of habitation there today, except for a watchman post and equipment and resupply depot for the local mining company.

Squaring mahogany logs after felling, ca. 1930. © Publications of the Field Museum Botanical Series 12, 1936. Courtesy Field Museum of Natural History, Chicago.

In 1956 the entire Chiquibul Forest came under a single long-term license that was subsequently renewed in 1964 and again in 1977. The amounts of mahogany and cedar extracted reduced dramatically over this period, indicating that timber reserves were becoming depleted.[57] An inventory of the timber resources of the Chiquibul in 1973, for example, concluded that the remaining amount of timber of primary species such as mahogany and cedar in the area was very low, and experiments were recommended to investigate how their natural regeneration might be improved.[58] The same report recorded that large areas of the Chiquibul consisted of dense thickets only six meters in height, a reflection of the great damage caused by Hurricane Hattie twelve years previously.

In 2006 the Belize Forest Department issued a single long-term harvesting license for the Chiquibul Forest Reserve. For each of the two forest blocks identified for felling annually, a plan of operations is prepared based on a commercial stock survey and a pre-commercial inventory. Logging of hardwoods at San Pastor is being continued, although the logging of pine in areas of pine savanna is being halted to allow these areas to recover.

Planking of nargusta logs (*Terminalia amazonia*) in southern Belize (Toledo) at King's Sawmill.
© Sam Bridgewater.

The administration of all Belize's forests is the responsibility of the Belize Forest Department, which is tasked with overseeing the conservation, protection, management, and utilization of Belize's forest resources and its biodiversity. Its mandate, therefore, is broad and includes both economic and environmental concerns. The birth of the Forest Department dates back to 1886, when British colonial inspectors visiting Belize recommended the formation of a forest department to control forest management.[59] A second visit was sponsored by the Colonial Research Committee in 1921 at a time when worries were mounting about remaining mahogany stocks. As a result of the findings of this latter fact-finding trip, a conservator of forests was appointed in 1922. His role was to improve the management of existing timber reserves on crown lands, and in 1923 a Forest Trust was established. This became the Forest Department in 1935. Due to the increasing reduction in the economic importance of timber during the last century, the Forest Department has slowly seen its financial and staff resources eroded, which has made it problematic to fulfill the wide mandate given to it by the government. However, with the new perceived importance of forests and their many environmental and social benefits, it is hoped that support for the Forest Department will increase so that it can effectively regulate and administer all aspects of forest management, together with partner NGOs and local businesses.

LOGGED OUT: THE DECLINE OF BELIZE'S TIMBER INDUSTRY

> When I was a boy there was hardly, in all my acquaintance, a single reputable family which did not eat off mahogany, sit on mahogany, sleep in mahogany. Mahogany was a symbol of economic solidity and moral worth. ALDOUS HUXLEY, *Beyond the Mexique Bay*, 1934

In 1774 a mahogany tree measuring a massive 3.65 meters in diameter was reported as being felled in Belize.[60] Today it is rare to find one with a diameter in excess of fifty centimeters. The giants for which Belize was once famous have long since disappeared. Despite the continued existence of forest cover, over two hundred years of harvesting has dramatically reduced the availability of mahogany, cedar, and other large, valuable timber trees in Belize's forests. Too many trees have been extracted in too little time and with too little regard for the ecological damage caused, or the long-term consequences for the timber industry. Belize is not the sole country in this situation. An influential report published in 1992 indicated that there was not a single example of sustainable forestry to be found anywhere in the Tropics at that time.[61] There is scant evidence to suggest that much has changed during the intervening sixteen years, and the decline in Belize's mahogany stocks has been chronicled in numerous national forestry reports.[62]

Between 1922 and 1940, timber, primarily consisting of mahogany and cedar, made up 80 percent of Belize's domestic exports and was its most significant income generator. By 1980 mahogany exports had declined significantly and made up only about 20 percent of the timber produced in Belize.[63] This figure dropped further to 14 percent in 2004.[64]

An abandoned Dodge truck. Belize's forests are littered with discarded machinery and vehicles associated with the timber industry. © Alex Monro.

Unless the remaining mature mahogany trees in Belize are carefully protected to ensure that they are allowed to reproduce, and the conditions for mahogany seed germination are encouraged, it is difficult to see how this species will thrive and continue to contribute significantly to the Belizean economy in the future. Care, too, must be taken to conserve other, lesser-known timber species as they become increasingly important and sought after. Historically the forestry industry has focused on the extraction of a few primary species, but in recent years there has been diversification to include lesser-known, secondary species. These include Santa Maria (*Calophyllum brasiliense*), banak (*Virola koschynia*), granadillo (*Platymiscium yucatanum*), Billy Webb (*Acosmium panamensis*), nargusta (*Terminalia amazonia*), and sapodilla (*Manilkara* spp.). Although these species display superb working qualities, in the past they have been marginalized, as the industry is relatively traditional, relying only on a few tried and tested timbers. However, secondary hardwoods are now finally being accepted by international and local markets. At present, the primary timber harvested in Belize is the softwood pine (*Pinus caribaea*), which accounted for 27 percent of all timber produced in 2004. Much of this is used in construction.

A study in 1997 estimated that only 14 percent of Belize's total timber production could be classified as "sustained yield," suggesting that in the future there will be a shortage of even the secondary hardwoods now considered to be common.[65] However, this study looked only at timber production. If ecological considerations are taken into account, including the damage inflicted on all forests species by tree felling and log removal, then there is greater cause for concern. The ecological impact of logging can be immense.

Some perspective is needed, however, and it is unfair to point a single accusing finger at the forestry industry for the observed secondary state of much of Belize's forests. Whatever the impact of logging operations, this is small when compared with the ravages a full-blown hurricane can inflict. In recent decades Hurricanes Hattie (1961), Iris (2001), and Dean (2007) flattened massive tracts of jungle, resulting in even-aged stands of newly regenerating trees (see the boxed text "Hattie: The Mother of Hurricanes" in chapter 5). This disturbance is natural, and evidence suggests that many forest species—mahogany included—are adapted to coping with it. Indeed, they depend on disturbance to survive. Despite the absence of big mahogany trees in the Chiquibul today, the abundance of seedlings of this species found in the 1990s may be attributable to the damage caused by Hurricane Hattie in 1961,[66] providing the necessary ecological condition for this species to regenerate. Recent inventories in the La Flor area of the Chiquibul have identified extremely dense stocks of pre-commercial stems. These should reach legal harvestable diameters in a decade or more; thus, there is some cause for optimism in the future.

MAHOGANY AND THE CONVENTION ON INTERNATIONAL TRADE IN ENDANGERED SPECIES OF WILD FAUNA AND FLORA (CITES)

The Convention on International Trade in Endangered Species of Wild Fauna and Flora (CITES), ratified by signatory countries in 1973, provides a mechanism for protecting vulnerable species that are the focus of international trade. Under CITES provisions, species are listed under one of three appendices, depending on how endangered a species is perceived to be. Under Appendix I, international trade of any species listed, or any commodity derived from them, is banned. Such drastic measures are reserved for goods—such as elephant ivory and rhino horn—that derive from species threatened with extinction. Species that are not threatened with imminent extinction but are nevertheless endangered through trade are listed under Appendix II, which allows the regulated export of goods derived from them. Under Article IV of CITES, permits must be granted for exporting all species listed under Appendix II, and in-country measures, including management plans, must be in place to protect them. This appendix thus provides a mechanism by which trade can be monitored and sustainable management encouraged, hopefully preventing the need for listed species to be moved to Appendix I in the future. Should research indicate that trade in products derived from a species no longer represents a threat to its existence, the species can be delisted. In the 1990s evidence became clear that mahogany was being overexploited throughout its range in the Americas and that many of the associated logging practices were illegal, as they occurred within protected and indigenous areas. Both *Swietenia humilis* and *S. mahogani* were listed under Appendix II in 1992, with big-leaved mahogany (*S. macrophylla*) joining them in 2003. Shipments of mahogany from all signatory countries, including Belize, must now be accompanied by a CITES certificate and a supporting certificate of origin; in addition, importing countries are obliged to ensure that all shipments received have appropriate documentation.

By the 1990s it had become clear that if Belize's forestry sector was to have a future, then a radical change was needed in the way the national forests were managed. An increased emphasis on harvesting sustainability was required. Based on the best forestry information available at the time, the Forest Planning and Management Project (FPMP) was established, part of which included developing a new timber harvesting system for the Chiquibul Forest Reserve.

Traditionally, a polycyclic forest management system was used in the Chiquibul, whereby a forest was harvested at relatively frequent intervals and only the largest trees above a predetermined diameter were felled at any one time; the remainder were left for later cropping. However, in 1988, a review of the Belizean forestry industry conducted under the Tropical Forestry Action Plan (TFAP) initiative reported that such a harvesting regime was biologically inappropriate for the primary timber trees, the premise being that species such as mahogany need significant light and disturbance to regenerate. The recommendation was that Belize should change its logging practices to a monocyclic system, whereby the felling cycle of a forest is equal to the rotation length of the most important species, with all trees harvested at once. As part of this, the Chiquibul was divided into eighty blocks, each an area of 500 hectares and earmarked to be logged every forty years.[67] Under this regime two blocks (1,000 hectares) can be harvested every year.

The Chiquibul Restoration Program also outlined specific practices to aid the recovery of the forest. It was stipulated, for example, that for each logged species, at least ten trees capable of producing seed must be left within each block of 100 hectares (one square kilometer). In addition, an upper limit of eight logged trees per hectare was set to minimize ecological damage. In an attempt to safeguard the forest structure and those trees best genetically adapted to surviving, this new regime also demanded that no trees greater than one hundred centimeters in diameter should be felled, and logging is no longer allowed within twenty meters of permanent watercourses or on slopes more than twenty-five degrees and ranging for more than one hundred meters. Further obligations are placed on the license holder, such as the maintenance of firebreaks along extraction routes.

One important aim of the FPMP was to provide data on natural forest dynamics, including information on tree growth, mortality, and regeneration. As part of this research program thirty permanent one-hectare sample plots were established in forests across Belize between 1992 and 1997. Twelve of these are situated within the Chiquibul Forest Reserve. In all plots across the country, 237 tree species were identified. This represents roughly one third of the 700 tree species believed to occur nationally. Few large trees above forty centimeters in diameter were recorded as a result of both the effects of past logging and hurricane damage. A second census was done on seventeen of the original thirty plots after a three- to four-year period. Initial results indicated that although a few dominant species grow fast, the majority are very slow to increase their girth. Mahogany, for example, was shown to have relatively high growth rates while the sapodilla tree grew at only one third of its rate. This illustrates problems related to a "one size fits all" approach when assessing how to manage a forest.

In addition to the sample plots, six experimental logging plots were established to determine the long-term impact of logging on forest structure. Four of these are located within the Chiquibul Forest Reserve: at Las Cuevas, San Pastor, Grano de Oro, and New Maria.[68] Within the plots, trees were selectively felled and removed to produce a replicate model of forestry practices. Subsequent measurements three years later indicated that although there was little difference in growth rates between the logged and unlogged plots, there was a 66 percent increase in tree mortality subsequent to logging. Results from a single logged plot in the Chiquibul Forest Reserve, for example, showed that the felling of 6 trees out of the 595 recorded resulted in the deaths of an additional 46 and significant damage to 53; 490 trees (82 percent of the total) remained undamaged.

ZIRICOTE AND ROSEWOOD

With its golden yellow sapwood and warm, deep brown heartwood, ziricote (*Cordia dodecandra*) is one of the most beautiful and highly prized of Belizean timbers. A favorite of wood-carvers, this species is used in many of the beautiful polished carvings on sale in tourist shops. Widespread in seasonal forests from Honduras to Mexico, ziricote is closely related to the common forest tree salmwood (*Cordia alliodora*). In addition to its timber, ziricote produces edible fruit, and its striking orange flowers have made it popular as a street tree across the Tropics. Another species with exquisite, highly figured, valuable timber is rosewood (*Dalbergia stevensonii*). Belonging to the pea family, the dark heartwood of this genus is rich in tannins and oils. The African blackwood (*Dalbergia melanoxylon*), a closely related species native to East Africa, supplies the world demand for clarinets, oboes, and bagpipes.

Ziricote (*Cordia dodecandra*), a dry forest species. In addition to producing attractive flowers, the timber of this tree is used widely in Belize for wood carving because of its beautiful color and figure. © Sam Bridgewater.

It is now a stated policy in Belize that production from forest reserves should be under "sustainable yield practices" whereby logging does not reduce the forests' future potential to produce timber. However, such management does not necessarily ensure ecological sustainability and conservation of biodiversity. As a result, despite such initiatives as the Chiquibul Restoration Program, some ecologists and conservationists strongly object to forestry being termed "sustainable" at all. There are many who feel that Belize's forests should be allowed to recover and conserved unmolested in perpetuity as a haven for wildlife. Others, however, argue that timber harvesting gives an economic value to forests, without which they would be deemed valueless and soon converted into profit-making agricultural land.

What is clear is that any decisions regarding the future of Belize's forests should take into account their true hidden worth and not their value calculated solely on direct income generation from timber extraction. Such deeper economic analyses need to incorporate the essential environmental and social functions (ecosystem services) forests provide, even if it is difficult to place financial figures on these services. They include nutrient recycling; carbon sequestration; climate, flood, and biodiversity protection; and the nurture of social well-being. However, although it is tempting to equate logging in Belize with forest demise, agriculture and urban expansion are far more powerful and rapid agents of destruction. The challenge in forestry is to minimize the damage caused by felling and extraction activities to ensure that irreversible changes to ecosystem services and biodiversity do not occur. Although ecologists take great pains to highlight the fragility of ecosystems, nature can be surprisingly robust, a fact borne out by the continued existence of the Chiquibul despite over two thousand years of human use.

BEYOND THE TREES: THE NON-TIMBER VALUE OF FORESTS

> Like a thousand other mornings, Don Elijio and I set out early in search of plants. This day our task was to locate Billy Webb trees from which we carefully strip long slivers of bark in a way that allows the tree to regenerate easily. The bark, boiled and drunk, was an important part of Don Elijio's arsenal of plants. He used it to treat diabetes and dry coughs, and to encourage the appetite.   ROSITA ARVIGO, *Sastun: My Apprenticeship with a Maya Healer*, 1994

Until the 1980s, most debates on forest use were dominated by discussions regarding the felling of trees. In the last two decades, however, there has been a change in how forests are perceived. This shift has coincided with a realization that the social and economic values of forests are as diverse as the many species they contain. Tropical forests, in particular, can provide a bewildering range of useful products in addition to timber—such as medicines, thatch, edible fruit, wild honey, bushmeat, and dyes. As well as providing the essentials of life for forest-based communities, some of these products have significant commercial importance. The financial value of these non-timber forest products (see "Non-Timber Forest Products" later in this chapter) is increasingly considered when forests are assessed for their social and economic worth. Indeed, in some forest areas it has been suggested that their combined worth can exceed the value of timber.[69] Their extraction has been suggested as an environmentally benign commercial alternative to logging and an economic argument against the conversion of forest to agricultural or pastoral landscapes.[70]

Although non-timber forest products have been heralded as a way of managing the forest wisely and providing a source of much-needed income for local communities, there is some doubt as to how sustainable such activities really are.[71] Like timber, the extraction of these products must be carefully managed and based on a solid understanding of the biology of the species targeted. Only then can it be ensured that their extraction will not exceed the forest's ability to produce in the long term. One way of providing incentives for improved forest management of non-timber forest products is through the marketplace; the use of "eco-labels" guaranteeing buyers that the products they purchase are environmentally friendly and socially ethical is now popular (see "Eco-Labels: Harnessing the Power of the Green Market" later in this chapter). Based on certification procedures for tracking products from the consumer back to their origin, such labels play to consumer demands.

FACING: Although it was selectively logged at various intervals during the last century, the Chiquibul Forest is still intact and has a near-continuous canopy. © Sam Bridgewater.

It was once common to value forests solely for the timber they yielded. Traditional forest dwellers, however, have always taken a more enlightened view, valuing the forests for their diverse array of useful goods. Indeed, the survival of some forest-based cultures is still entirely dependent on what the forest yields. The Belize Ethnobotany Project lists in excess of one thousand plant species recorded in Belize as having a use.[72] Even for agricultural communities living in close proximity to forests, the variety of ways in which the surrounding natural resources are used is astonishing. With the increased recognition of the non-timber value of forests, the term "non-timber forest products" (NTFPs) has been coined to describe all harvested goods, except timber, of social or financial worth. This includes not only such products as fruits, nuts, mushrooms, fibers, resins, latex, bark, roots, and leaves but also bushmeat and honey.

With concern mounting worldwide as tropical forests disappear to be replaced by urban or agricultural landscapes, conservationists, scientists, politicians and economists are following the lead of communities such as the Maya and are at last beginning to appreciate the many products that forests supply. It is now understood not only that these products are essential to the livelihoods of local communities but also that their collection and marketing can be a positive instrument for sustainable development and conservation. Their sale can provide a source of local income and can even form the basis of significant international businesses.[73] A study in the rain forests of Los Tuxtlas in Mexico, for example, found that products from over 10 percent of the native flora of 860 species were traded locally, with an additional 8 percent having market potential.[74] Brazil nuts (from South America) and rattan (from Southeast Asia) provide a couple of well-known examples of NTFPs traded worldwide. The forests of Belize have also provided a number of globally traded commodities, including allspice, chicle, and xaté (see "The Chicle Industry" and "Xaté, Leaf of Gold" later in this chapter). Figures from the sale of NTFPs have been used to show that intact forests can potentially have a commercial value far higher than a consideration of their timber alone would suggest.[75] A review of twenty-four independent studies of NTFPs from around the world suggested that in 1993 the average value of NTFPs in tropical forests was worth fifty U.S. dollars per hectare per year.[76] The concept of community-managed extractive reserves has been put forward as a means of conserving forests while providing local livelihoods.[77]

However, as is clearly the case with xaté, the extraction of NTFPs is not necessarily sustainable, and overharvesting of forest products can result in ecological damage, either through harm to the species targeted or through disturbance of the wider environment. Many people are therefore skeptical about the ability of extractivism to save rain forests.[78] There is also the danger of exploitation of local communities by business interests, with the harvesting of NTFPs having the potential to be a poverty trap for those at the bottom of the market chain, which happened with rubber in Brazil. What is needed is an improved understanding of the social, economic, and cultural significance of NTFPs and the manner in which they are harvested and marketed. Scientific research has a part to play in providing critical information on the abundance and ecology of useful plants and animals and in assessing the impact of harvesting. Only through a consideration of all this information can social and economic needs be reconciled with the needs of the forest itself.

Making a house broom from the leaves of the give-and-take-palm (*Cryosophila stauracantha*), an abundant understory species. Broom making is just one of Belize's many forest crafts. © Sam Bridgewater.

The fruit of the warrie cohune (*Astrocaryum mexicanum*). The inner seed endosperm of this forest palm is edible. © Sam Bridgewater.

THE CHICLE INDUSTRY

> A minor factor which has some effect upon tapping, is a cold wind from the north, which occasionally blows during the wet months and which retards the flow of latex by causing coagulation. The natives also have a superstition, which is not borne out by fact, that the best flow of latex takes place during the days of the new moon, and they sometimes regulate their work accordingly.   H. M. HEYDER, Assistant Conservator of Forests, Empire Forestry, "Sapodilla Tapping in British Honduras," 1930

Although the identification of tropical plants can be difficult, especially in the absence of fruits or flowers, a mature sapodilla (chicle) tree can be confused with no other—not because there is anything particularly distinctive about the tree itself, but because every large sapodilla tree in Belizean forests, regardless of its remoteness, bears the scars of the chiclero. These machete slash marks are a reminder of the past glories of a once powerful regional industry.

Although the ancient Maya are believed to have chewed the sweet, sticky latex of the chicle tree (*Manilkara* spp.), it was not until the late 1880s that chicle grabbed the attention of American industrialists searching for a cheap alternative to rubber. In the course of investigating its properties, an American named Thomas Adams discovered that the latex of the chicle tree was an ideal base for chewing gum, a relatively new fashion in the United States at that time. Shortly afterward, the first flavored chewing gum, called "Yucatan," appeared on the U.S. market.[79] A number of companies, such as Wrigley's and American Chicle, soon appreciated its economic potential, and marketing proved very successful. Over the next fifty years demand for chicle and its chewing gum derivative increased, and across southern Mexico, Belize, and Guatemala chicle tappers (chicleros) scoured the forests, tapping every tree they could find in an attempt to satiate the international public's growing appetite. Regionally, such was the value of this new product that it was soon known as *oro blanco* (white gold).

Between 1930 and 1950, the peak period of chicle production, as much as 10,800 tons were exported from these countries each year,[80] and by the 1950s chewing gum had become a global phenomenon. However, a combination of declining natural yields due to overharvesting and increasing international demand led to a search for a cheaper, more secure source of gum. As a result, natural chicle was soon replaced by an industrialized synthetic substitute based on petroleum. By the 1960s, chicle production was in decline, and by the 1980s the Belizean industry had become all but dormant. However, the industry continues in a modest fashion in the Petén region, supplying manufacturers who still produce natural gum. At present fewer than two thousand tons of latex are harvested annually.[81]

It is extremely rare to find a sapodilla (chicle) tree in Belize without the scars of the chiclero's machete.
© William Milliken.

> There is a law which forbids the tapping to death of the sapodilla trees, but nobody takes much notice of it, as there is no adequate control such as the Federated Malay States have for protecting their gutta-percha trees [*Palaquium gutta*: Sapotaceae], which used to be tapped to death before a Forest Department was established.   C. HUMMEL, "Sapodilla Trees and Chicle," 1923

The chicle, or sapodilla, tree (*Manilkara* spp.) belongs to the plant family Sapotaceae. This group is characterized in part by alternate simple leaves, the presence of white sap, and often bat- or primate-dispersed fleshy fruit. The genus *Manilkara* is pantropical (i.e., it occurs in Latin America, Africa, and Asia), and there are thirty species distributed across the Neotropics. Of these, thirteen occur in Central America and the West Indies.[82] Three species are recorded from Belize: *Manilkara chicle*, *M. staminodella*, and *M. zapota*.[83] All are tall, imposing trees, have relatively small, cream-colored flowers, and are valued for their sweet, fleshy fruit (which tastes rather like treacle sponge), their hard resistant timber, and their latex. The ancient Maya used the timber of the sapodilla tree in the construction of their temples, and lintels made from this wood can still be seen, in place and in good condition, in Maya ruins such as Caracol. Although the genus is cultivated widely for its fruit, it is the tapping of its trunk for the production of chicle for which the tree is most renowned. Each of the three Belizean species of *Manilkara* recognized by scientists can be tapped for chicle, although chicleros have their own folk taxonomy that differs from that of researchers. For example, Belizean chicleros recognize three distinct varieties of chicle—*blanco* (white), *colorado* (red), and *morado* (blue)—and each is purported to have different chicle-producing properties. A 1923 article in a Belizean news-paper discusses four additional categories for chicle—female sapodilla, male sapodilla, crown sapodilla, and chicle bull,[84] although some of these names may relate to different genera. According to this particular account, female sapodilla (*Manilkara zapota*) is by far the best for chicle production. Both *M. zapota* and *M. staminodella* are abundant in forest on limestone soils and are recorded from the Chiquibul. They are almost indistinguishable from each other, the only diagnostic characters between them relating to the presence or absence of stipules (small leaflike appendages at the base of each leaf) and tiny differences in flower form. The local name for *M. stami-nodella* is "chicle bul," and the Chiquibul Forest received its name in honor of the abundance of this species within its confines.

A retired chiclero demonstrating the typical herring-bone pattern of cuts made in the sapwood of a chicle tree, 2006. © Sam Bridgewater.

Chicle tapping is a seasonal occupation occurring between September and February. This coincides with the wet season and the period when chicle trees produce the most latex. What follows is a description of past practices. Typically, a suitable tree, usually not less than twenty-five years old, is climbed by a chiclero using spurs fastened to his boots and a rope slung around the tree bole as a harness. Starting at its base, a flap of bark is cut, and underneath it is inserted a receptacle—traditionally a cloth bag water-proofed with natural rubber (*Castilla elastica*). The chiclero then ascends the tree, carving an interlocking network of downward slanting cuts around the trunk as he rises. These channels cut into the sapwood of the tree, and the latex descends along the cuts to the tree's base, where it is collected in the bag. Once the harvesting operation has been completed, the chiclero moves on to the next tree; after a period of between four and twenty-four hours, he returns to remove the full bag of latex. The amount obtained from each tree is dependent on the tree's size, the season, and the number of times it has been tapped previously. A usual yield of between 0.7 and 1.8 kilograms can

be expected, although figures as high as 14 kilograms were reported in the industry's heyday. When enough bags have been collected, the contents are poured into a cauldron. The latex is then heated over a fire and stirred constantly to reduce its water content by about 30 percent. Once the latex is deemed ready, the chiclero stretches the cooling elastic latex vigorously and then transfers it into an oblong mold. When the block (*marqueta*) of hardening latex has solidified sufficiently, the initials of the chiclero are stamped into its surface, thereby identifying its owner. Despite the industry's demand for high-quality latex, chicleros were known to adulterate the harvest from true chicle trees with the latex of "second-class" species such as sapotillo (*Pouteria reticulata*) and rubber (*Castilla elastica*) to increase their yield. Belizean chicleros often camped communally but usually worked alone, selling their chicle to contractors working on behalf of U.S. companies.

A chiclero cooking sapodilla latex to reduce the water content before the latex is molded, cooled, and turned into blocks, ca. 1930. © Publications of the Field Museum Botanical Series 12, 1936. Courtesy Field Museum of Natural History Chicago.

The tapping of a chicle tree weakens its growth, and between four and seven years are needed for recovery before it can be tapped again. Some trees, however, do not survive the process, and a mortality rate of between 5 and 15 percent has been recorded subsequent to tapping.[85] Indeed, a former assistant conservator of Belizean forests writing in 1930 noted that "a large percentage of the mature and middle-aged sapodilla now standing in the forests, is in a moribund condition due to these causes."[86] Despite this fact, there are still healthy populations of the chicle tree in forests such as the Chiquibul. Although there has been concern that the industry was not sustainable, the species involved appear to have recovered from the intensity of harvest suffered during the last century.

It is known that production in Belize was already significant by 1925, when 334,892 pounds of chicle were exported, worth a reported US$154,875. However, Belize City also functioned as a regional trading center and exported an additional 2.5 million pounds of chicle collected in Mexico and the Petén.[87] In 1930 chicle was the second-most valuable export after mahogany. The highest domestic exports were recorded in 1947, when over 1 million pounds were traded.[88]

ABOVE: After extraction from the pods, the seeds of the cacao are stripped of the white edible pulp surrounding them (*left*) and fermented, which darkens the seeds (*right*). They are then dried before being loaded into sacks and sold. © William Milliken. RIGHT: The fruit pods of cacao (*Theobroma cacao*) contain large seeds surrounded by a sweet-tasting edible pulp. Cacao was cultivated for food and drink by the ancient Maya, a tradition continued in Belize today. The seeds of cacao can be harvested, fermented, and dried and form the basis of chocolate. © Sam Bridgewater.

Modern international consumers, browsing the aisles of a supermarket or choosing timber for their homes, are confronted with a bewildering array of market products. Although the labeling of goods is improving, it is still often hard to be sure of the origins of the things we buy daily. Consumers have a choice, and as awareness of the effects of globalization increases, many are using this choice to buy products that are labeled as being of local provenance and from a fair-trade or "ecologically friendly" source.

An "eco-label" is a mark given to products certified to meet certain environmental and social standards. It is a market tool to improve the management of natural resources and promote social responsibility. In response to increased consumer demand for sustainably sourced products, the use of eco-labels has grown in a number of sectors in recent years, including food, health care, and forest products. The biggest markets for eco-labeled goods are Europe and, to a lesser extent, the United States.[89] In these countries consumers are relatively affluent and environmentally and socially concerned, so retailers recognize a potential market advantage from certified products.

All eco-labels are based on the "chain-of-custody" concept, whereby products are tracked from their origin to the marketplace, with the certifying organization monitoring the process and its label guaranteeing consumers that the products meet the standards promised. Some of the most established and accepted eco-labels relate to forest management (e.g., Forest Stewardship Council, or FSC), organic certification (e.g., Soil Association), and social responsibility (e.g., Fairtrade). Although all schemes address some aspect of sustainability, each has its own emphasis. Few fair-trade schemes, for example, have well-developed environmental standards, and organic schemes tend to focus mainly on the level of agricultural inputs rather than the social conditions of workers.

The FSC certification program was started in 1993 and represents an international partnership of foresters, environmentalists, and sociologists whose aim is to promote ecologically appropriate, socially beneficial, and economically viable forest management. By 2006, 363 managed forests, in twenty countries in the Americas alone and covering over 33 million hectares, had been awarded FSC certificates. In Belize 104,888 hectares of forest managed by the Program for Belize were certified in 1997; New River Enterprises Ltd., Orange Walk, has also managed FSC-certified forests since 2003.[90] Although the FSC initially concentrated on developing standards for the certification of well-managed timber, its scope has since broadened to include NTFPs, with the first certified NTFP product being chicle harvested from community-managed forests in Quintana Roo, Mexico, in 1999.

The global fair-trade market has also increased greatly in recent years, with sales growing 15 percent between 2008 and 2009; the estimated global retail value of fair-trade goods in 2008 was close to US$5 billion annually.[91] Most famously in Belize, the cacao grown in Toledo for the production of Green & Black's Maya Gold chocolate was the first product ever to carry a Fairtrade logo, with the producers ensured a fair price for their crop. Cacao, or cocoa (Theobroma cacao), is a small tree whose seeds are used as the basis of chocolate. The cacao used for Maya Gold is also certified as organic by the Soil Association. Another organization, the Rainforest Alliance, has likewise developed responsible standards for environmentally friendly agriculture and wild-harvested products. The Rainforest Alliance is FSC-accredited, and its Smartwood program has certified over 33 million hectares of forest in fifty-eight countries.

The cohune oil industry remains yet dormant, if I except the use for domestic and cooking purposes to which it is put among the families of mahogany and logwood cutters. Two fifths of the Colony, viz. 1.933.762 acres are it is estimated under this graceful native Prince of Wales Palm. If we allow 25 trees to the acre, a very low average, and 1,000 nuts as the annual yield per tree and accept that 100 nuts yield a quart of oil, this dormant industry, if awakened to full activity, would yield 276,537 tons of oil at a price per ton appreciably above that which obtains for coconut oil, to which it is superior.   Sir Alfred Moloney, Governor of British Honduras, quoted in Royal Gardens, Kew, *Bulletin of Miscellaneous Information*, October-November 1893

The cohune palm (*Attalea cohune*) is one of Belize's most characteristic plants, occurring in forests on fertile soils across the country. Its crown of long, spreading fronds that droop at their tips is a common sight even in pastoral areas. When forests are cleared, this species is often left, due to the fibrous nature of its trunk, which can quickly ruin a chain-saw blade. The mature cohune palm can produce as many as two thousand sizable nuts per year, and its kernels are composed of as much as 70 percent oil.[92] This oil has long been valued for domestic cooking, but entrepreneurs have also attempted to extract it on an industrial scale, though with little success to date. One of the problems is the extremely hard seed kernel's outer coat. The kernels themselves represent only 10 percent of the total nut weight, making transport of the fruit extremely expensive. Ideally, the kernels would be extracted at the site of collection. During World War I cohune nut charcoal was used in the production of gas masks. In 1929 an oil extraction industry was established in Punta Gorda by the Tropical Oil Company, which attempted to increase the abundance of cohune on 19,000 hectares of private estate.[93] At one time this business

A bunch of cohune fruits (nuts). A single cohune palm may produce as many as two thousand nuts in a single year. © Sam Bridgewater.

employed one thousand workers. However, the timing of this enterprise was unfortunate: shortly after its establishment, the Great Depression of the 1930s reduced the economic viability of the industry, and activities were halted. Prior to the outbreak of World War II, a second attempt was made to establish commercial oil production by the company Pan American Shell, and 224,070 pounds of kernel were exported in 1937.[94] This endeavor favored the use of portable nut-cracking machines placed across the country in areas of dense cohune stands, although this business soon folded. Yet sporadic harvesting continued. In 1945, for example, there are records of 1.5 million pounds of cohune nuts being harvested to produce 383,000 pounds of kernels that were exported to the United States, reportedly for the production of soap.[95]

THE MILITARY AND CONSERVATION

Perhaps one of the most curious uses of the Chiquibul Forest is as a center for jungle-craft courses and warfare training. Local Belizean guides run regular trips teaching forest survival skills to tourists, and the international TV bushcraft expert Ray Mears has also developed annual courses with local survival experts. In addition, both the Belize Defence Force and the British Army conduct training exercises within the forest, where battle skills and survival techniques are taught. The exercises run by the British Army are facilitated by the British Army Training Support Unit (BATSUB), with training areas changed regularly to reduce the impact on the forest. These exercises can be sizable events, involving as many as six hundred soldiers at any one time. The presence of the British Army provides significant financial benefits to Belize. While the army and conservationists may seem like strange bedfellows, and insensitive training can certainly have an adverse ecological impact, the relationship can also be mutually beneficial. Conservationists strengthen the army's ecological code of conduct, and the presence of Belizean and British forces acts as a deterrent against illegal activity such as hunting. The army also provides support to scientific expeditions and maintains vital communications with those working in the forest. It is not unusual to hear British Army helicopters cruising overhead on their way to exercises deep within the Chiquibul Forest, and the sound is a welcome reminder to those beneath the forest canopy that help is at hand should casualty evacuation ever be needed. The long-term conservation of forests such as the Chiquibul depends on their responsible management by a broad alliance of partners, and the Belizean and British armies have an important role in ensuring that Belize's forests are protected and managed sustainably.

XATÉ, LEAF OF GOLD

The forty-kilometer hike from the Guatemalan border to the Raspaculo River in Belize is not for the faint-hearted. The terrain of the Chiquibul is unforgiving, marked by limestone hills covered in forest and punctuated with impassable cliffs. This is a landscape as vast and wild as any remaining in Central America. Apart from a few old logging roads and unmapped forest trails, there is no easy way to make the journey. It's a desperate two-day slog, the expedition made all the harder by the restricted availability of water. Rivers are scarce, and most of the few permanent water sources reside deep inside uncharted caverns.

Despite the hardships one has to endure to traverse the region, dozens of poor farmers from Guatemala frequently make the extended trek far inside Belizean territory. Propelled by poverty, they leave their own country to face both the hardships of living in the rain forest and the knowledge that, if caught, they face heavy fines or imprisonment. What they seek is a plant known as the *cola de pescado*, or "fishtail." To them, the leaves of this elegant palm are like gold, providing a guaranteed source of hard, much-needed currency. Highly prized by the international floral industry as greenery for flower arrangements, the farmers know that if they can cut enough leaves and carry them back into Guatemala, they can earn far more than they could by working on their farms.

GIFT FROM THE GROUND

Chamaedorea is the most diverse palm genus in the Neotropics, containing between eighty and one hundred species.[96] It is a geographically widespread group of plants, occurring as an important understory component of rain forest and cloud forest from Central Mexico to Bolivia.[97] Although a few species are widespread and occur over much of this range (such as *C. pinnatifrons* and *C. tepejilote*), the majority have more restricted distributions. Particularly high numbers of *Chamaedorea* species are to be found in southern Mexico and Guatemala as well as in the mountainous regions of Costa Rica and Panama. Ten species occur in Belize alone, of which three (*C. adcendens*, *C. graminifolia*, and *C. seifrizii*) are considered to be under threat according to the IUCN Red List.[98]

There has been a great deal of interest in *Chamaedorea* palms for decades due to their considerable economic and social value. The group has many uses, including as a food source, with the palm heart of *C. woodsoniana* and the immature male inflorescences of pacaya (*C. tepejilote*) being

The leaves of the fishtail palm (*Chamaedorea ernesti-augusti*) are highly prized by the international floral industry.
© Sam Bridgewater.

particularly important.[99] However, the striking looks of some *Chamaedorea* species, their ability to grow in shade, and their resistance to wilting have attracted international interest. Their trade as houseplants and as a source of foliage for flower arrangements is a multimillion-dollar global industry.

The primary source of the material collected to supply these industries is natural forests. The two most important houseplant species are *C. seifrizii* (bamboo palm) and *C. elegans* (parlor palm), the latter being the most widely grown indoor palm in the world. Both occur wild in the forests of Belize. If your home is enlivened by a palm, it may well be a *Chamaedorea*. The regional term used for *Chamaedorea* palm leaf is xaté (pronounced "shatay"), and around twenty species are traded by the floral industry, of which three of the most important in Central America are *C. elegans* (xaté hembra), *C. ernesti-augusti* (cola de pescado, fishtail), and *C. oblongata* (xaté macho).

The majority of the world's xaté leaf originates from Central Mexico, with other important centers of harvesting located in southern Mexico and the Petén district of

northeastern Guatemala. In recent years there has been an ever-declining yield of xaté from wild populations due to long-term overharvesting. With local populations now unproductive, individual xaté collectors (*xateros*) in Guatemala have been illegally crossing into Belize to exploit a pristine resource. Belize has not traditionally utilized xaté as a non-timber forest product (see "Non-Timber Forest Products" earlier in this chapter) and thus, until recently, has enjoyed abundant and unharvested populations of this palm.

The presence of wild xaté in Belize presents an economic opportunity for Belizeans but also an environmental problem. The government is eager to establish its own industry, but there is clear evidence from other countries that doing so could endanger the natural populations of *Chamaedorea* and threaten the ecological integrity of Belize's diverse forests. The vital question is whether it is possible to establish a home-grown xaté industry that is financially lucrative while being environmentally benign.

TOP: After cutting, *xateros* load the xaté leaf into sacks that are then carried by foot or on horseback to a sorting house. These bags of illegally harvested leaves from the Chiquibul have been confiscated by the Belize Forest Department. © Sam Bridgewater. BOTTOM: After being harvested and sorted, *Chamaedorea* leaves are bundled and placed in cold storage for export. © Sam Bridgewater.

According to the World Conservation Union (IUCN), *Chamaedorea* species are among the world's most endangered palms, with around three quarters of the species threatened.[100] The biggest cause of concern for wild *Chamaedorea* populations in Central America is the destruction of their rain-forest habitat.[101] In Belize this deforestation has been largely due to clearance for development (expansion of towns and road construction) and agricultural crops such as citrus, sugarcane, and bananas. A second threat to *Chamaedorea* is the large-scale xaté exportation of seed and leaf, which began in the 1950s; increased demand over the years has resulted in overharvesting and a reduction of some *Chamaedorea* populations.[102] In general, species harvested for their leaves (e.g., *C. ernesti-augusti*) have fared better than those harvested for their seed (e.g., *C. tenella*) or stems (e.g., *C. elatior*).

THE ECONOMICS OF A GLOBAL COMMODITY

Xaté is one of Central America's most important NTFPs, with the industry worth tens of millions of U.S. dollars annually.[103] Xaté exports from the Maya Biosphere Reserve in La Selva Maya in Guatemala, for example, were worth more than US$4 million in 2000.[104] This is comparable to the economic value of timber harvest in the region, which was estimated at US$3.5-5 million in 2003.[105] In some areas, such as within the El Cielo Biosphere Reserve in Mexico, commercial harvesting of xaté leaf (in this case, of *C. radicalis*) is the principal source of income for local communities.[106]

Many communities in the Petén region of Guatemala depend on xaté, which is usually harvested in conjunction with other NTFPs, such as chicle (the latex of *Manilkara zapota*, used in some brands of chewing gum; see "The Chicle Industry" earlier in this chapter) and the culinary seasoning allspice (*Pimenta dioica*). As xaté can be harvested all year round, it provides an important and reliable income for many households. The xaté harvest in Guatemala provides approximately 6,000–10,000 seasonal and full-time jobs; processing xaté also creates employment outside of collection regions in national processing centers.

The biggest markets for xaté are the United States and Europe, although there is also demand from Japan and Russia. In addition, fresh markets are emerging in the new European Union countries such as Poland. Different species of *Chamaedorea* are preferred by different countries, although market trends vary over time. In the past Europe has favored *C. elegans* and the United States *C. oblongata*.[107] However, in recent years *C. ernesti-augusti* (fishtail palm) has become more fashionable and is now the main species exported to Europe from Guatemala.

Although there are reports that *xateros* sell their harvested xaté leaf for huge sums, the reality is that they make only a few dollars for every one hundred leaves they sell. A number of factors affect the price of a leaf, including the species, the size, the seasonal demand, the country of origin, and the export destination. In Belize the natural abundance of fishtail in the forest is low. Scientific studies show that on average there are only about two hundred individual palms per hectare in the Chiquibul.[108] Thus, for *xateros* to make a significant income, they have to roam over massive areas of forest harvesting what few leaves of value they can find. The work of a *xatero* is hard and the rewards sometimes meager. Nevertheless, they can potentially earn far more collecting xaté than from agricultural activities. Hence, the fishtail's near-mythical status in the region as the "leaf of gold." Xaté leaf requires little processing, other than refrigeration, to extend its shelf life, and the market chain is relatively simple. Typically, a *xatero* will sell his leaf to a local buyer, who then transports the leaf to a local processing plant. Here workers select only the best leaves for export, discarding over 60 percent of what a *xatero* cuts. The leaves are then bundled, stored in refrigerated units, shipped to an exporter, and sold to an international retailer; finally, they are distributed to florists. Like all exported commodities, the price of xaté rises dramatically through the market chain, and the elevated price paid by a consumer is a far cry from the relative pittance earned by *xateros*.

As the natural resource has become depleted in Mexico, Guatemala, and Belize, there has been an increasing interest in plantation-grown xaté. Xaté can be grown in high concentrations under a forest canopy, and in the long term the bulk of future xaté exports may come from managed plantation sources. Indeed, in Guatemala, 10 percent of all exports are already plantation-grown. The favorable economics of plantations makes them an attractive proposition. Whereas a natural forest may have only several hundred fishtail individuals per hectare, a plantation can have up to 60,000. Although some conservationists are in favor of plantations, others think they may be counterproductive for the forests. Those in favor believe that the wild harvesting of xaté can never be ecologically sustainable and that plantations are desirable in diverting destructive pressure away from the natural forest. Those who argue against the plantations claim that their establishment removes important economic value from natural forests, which can threaten the livelihoods of forest communities and leave the forests more vulnerable to clearance. Trial plantations of fishtail have been established by farmers working cooperatively in Belize's Cayo and Toledo Districts. The Toledo farmers intend to grow xaté leaf organically under the shade of cacao, for which they already have a guaranteed market with the chocolate manufacturer Green & Black's. They hope the xaté crops will increase the stability of their diverse agricultural activities, providing an additional small but regular income.

Chamaedorea palms are abundant throughout Belize's forests and form an integral part of the forest ecosystem. They may not have the protective thorns of the give-and-take palm (*Crysophila stauracantha*) or the statuesque size of the cohune (*Attalea cohune*), but they form a critical part of the forest's intricate web of life. Providing shade close to the ground, these palms help retain the soil moisture, and their fruits are an important food source for forest birds such as motmots and slatey tinamous. They are beautifully adapted for dispersal by birds, which are attracted to the striking coloration of the palms' dark shiny fruits, often conspicuous against the bright red fruiting structures on which they are held. The birds, in turn, are vital for dispersing the palm seeds to new areas, ensuring its long-term survival.

The genus *Chamaedorea* is dioecious, as there are separate male and female plants (see the boxed text "The Sex Life of Plants" in chapter 5). For the most part, they require high levels of shade and high humidity to survive. However, some species, such as *C. seifrizii*, which grows in the more seasonally dry forests of northern Belize, can survive in more open, arid habitats. Another Belizean species, *C. adcendens*, which is restricted to limestone outcrops in the south, has particularly leathery leaves. This may be an adaptation to surviving in more exposed habitats where desiccation can occur. The genus can grow well in lime-rich conditions, and the great expanses of limestone-derived soils in Belize are ideal for a number of species, including fishtail (*C. ernesti-augusti*).

Plants growing close to the forest floor are finely adapted to living in shade and perish when exposed to full sunlight. *Chamaedorea* palms are one such example, and this feature, in addition to their beautiful foliage, is why certain species are so highly prized around the world as houseplants. However, rapid changes in the forest canopy due to treefall can suddenly remove the critical protective shading required by those shade-loving species, and falling branches are another constant threat to survival. Chamaedoreas have thin stems for a palm and can reach sexual maturity quickly—sometimes in as little as a few years.[109] This means they can quickly exploit new shady habitats. A number of species also show a peculiar feature whereby their stems can grow horizontally for some distance (plagiotropism), rooting along the lower surface. Thus, if they are flattened by falling debris, they are often able to grow laterally away from the obstacle, take root, and then resume growing upward.

Although chamaedoreas can produce seed quickly, absolute growth rates are still relatively slow. Research done in the Chiquibul Forest at Las Cuevas has shown that an average individual fishtail palm in the forest produces only two new leaves every year.[110] This low figure mirrors results obtained by research elsewhere on other species. This kind of data is vital if we are to protect and manage in a sustainable way those species whose leaves and seeds are harvested.

Palm leaves can function as a habitat on which other species may grow, and older *Chamaedorea* leaves are frequently covered with a variety of microorganisms such as fungi, bacteria, lichens, and blue-green algae. These appear as leaf blotches called epiphylls. Although epiphylls can be harmful to the palm, reducing its ability to photosynthesize and therefore grow, they can also be beneficial. Blue-green algae, for instance, are able to fix atmospheric nitrogen that can subsequently be utilized by the palm.[111]

Fishtail seedlings (*Chamaedorea ernesti-augusti*) ready to be planted on a plantation. © Sam Bridgewater.

The attractive, conspicuous fruits of *Chamaedorea oblongata* are dispersed by birds. © Nancy Garwood.

Scientific research based at Las Cuevas has assisted the Belizean government in managing the country's *Chamaedorea* populations. Biological surveys across the country have quantified the abundance of this group of palms and highlighted their distribution. These studies have also provided vital data on how many leaves *Chamaedorea* species have naturally, how many commercially valuable leaves one can expect to find in a hectare of forest, how fast the plants grow and replenish these leaves, and how much the resource has already been degraded by illegal leaf cutting.[112] In addition, other studies have looked at the long-term impacts of leaf harvesting on the health of populations through monitored defoliation experiments and have attempted to clarify the means whereby different *Chamaedorea* species are pollinated (see the boxed text "Thrips and Palm Pollination" in chapter 5). Research on *Chamaedorea* DNA has also elucidated some of the confusing species relationships across the group's geographic range and is providing data on genetic fingerprinting, which could form the basis of an eco-labeling scheme. All this data, in addition to improving our knowledge of the natural world, is of direct relevance to conservation, providing resource managers with the necessary information on which to base their plans for sustainable management.

THE HEALING FOREST: HARNESSING THE MEDICINAL POWER OF PLANTS

> Ki Bix was only one of the many plants that Don Elijio favored in the treatment of women's ailments. Contribo vine was excellent for menstrual complaints, especially if complicated by gastric problems. . . . Most often he made a mixture containing Contribo, Copalchi, Man Vine, and Zorillo. He called this Sacca Todo, pull out everything, in reference to its marvelous eliminative powers.   ROSITA ARVIGO, *Sastun: My Apprenticeship with a Maya Healer*, 1994

Traditional cultures often rely on forests as a source of medicines. Although many Belizeans now head to the local pharmacy for their drugs, a number of Maya, Garifuna, and Creole groups continue to depend on the forest for the treatment of their ailments. Indeed, in the recent past over 75 percent of Belizeans were reported as using medicinal plants in some way.[113] Even today a wide range of medicinal plants can still be found on market stalls and supermarket shelves throughout Belize, and most Belizeans are acquainted with the stalwarts of the native medicinal trade, such as jackass bitters (*Neurolaena lobata*), Billy Webb (*Acosmium panamense*), balsam (*Myroxylon balsamum*), chicoloro (*Strychnos panamensis*), and contribo (*Aristolochia trilobata*). Although these species are some of the most noteworthy, a great many more are utilized by healers. A study conducted with Kekchi Maya healers in southern Belize, for example, showed that they use over 160 plants for medicine, the majority collected from primary or disturbed rain forest.[114] The publication of such research has done much to improve awareness of the importance of the traditional knowledge of local healers and shamans. It has also helped to foster an increased respect for those cultures whose lives have a strong connection to nature. Many traditional healers continue to work in Belize today, taking forward the tradition of Don Elijio Panti, Belize's adopted and most famous "doctor-priest."[115]

In addition to the immense social importance of wild medicines to local communities, the existence of undiscovered pharmaceuticals is often cited as a commercial reason to maintain tropical forests. A number of researchers have attempted to quantify the potential value of these medicinal products. A study published in 1995, for example, suggested that each new drug discovered from forests at the time was worth an average of US$94 million to a private drug company and US$449 million to society as a whole. The same work hazarded the guess that only one eighth of the medicines in existence had been discovered.[116] Estimates of the commercial value of potential new drugs from tropical plants vary widely from US$147 billion to US$900 billion.[117]

Although such pharmaceutical research can be of inestimable value, there is concern about how such work is conducted and who benefits from it. In particular, there has been much discussion on the ethics of working with forest communities. If commercial drugs are based on information originally provided by traditional

TOP: The chicoloro vine (*Strychnos panamensis*) is a traditional remedy for diabetes and a number of other ailments. However, its use is not recommended without the strict supervision of a qualified doctor, as the *Strychnos* genus contains many natural toxins. © Sam Bridgewater. BOTTOM: Harvesting the bark of the balsam tree (*Myroxylon balsamum*) for use as medicine. The method of bark removal depicted is extremely destructive and can kill the tree. © William Milliken.

healers, for example, how can their intellectual property rights be safeguarded and how might their own communities benefit from this work, financially or otherwise? Unfortunately, all too often the guardians of traditional forest knowledge are often seen as disposable sources of information.

A SELECTION OF COMMON HEALING PLANTS

There are far too many medicinal plants in Belize's forests to be described here, and the reader is directed to a number of excellent existing publications focusing specifically on these. One suggested starting point is Rosita Arvigo and Michael Balick's *Rainforest Remedies: One Hundred Healing Herbs of Belize*. The common names and uses of Belize's plants are also listed in *Checklist of the Vascular Plants of Belize*.[18] To provide some idea of the variety of ailments that can be treated naturally, table 3.1 lists ten plants of the Chiquibul that are used medicinally.

Removing the fluff around the meristem (heart) of the give-and-take palm (*Cryosophila stauracantha*). The resultant material is excellent for stanching wounds. © Sam Bridgewater.

TABLE 3.1.

Medicinal uses of ten common plant species found in the Chiquibul Forest

Important Note: Many plants are highly poisonous. Even those with medicinal uses can be dangerous if they are not administered correctly. In addition, the accurate identification of medicinal plants can be problematic. Trying any of the remedies listed below is not recommended; those interested in herbal cures should seek the advice of reputable traditional healers.

Scientific Name and Habit	Local Names (English, Spanish, or Maya)	Medicinal Uses
Annona reticulata (Annonaceae) Tree	wild custard apple (E); anona (S)	The crushed and pounded seeds can be applied as a poultice to treat head lice; tea made from the leaves is used to treat mouth sores and, with added sugar, provides a cough medicine.
Aristolochia trilobata (Aristolochiaceae) Vine	duck flower (E); contribo (S); flor de pato (S)	A tea made by boiling the chopped stem in water is reputedly effective against a wide range of ailments, including flu, stomach upsets, gastritis, and high blood pressure. However, the plant genus is known to contain carcinogenic compounds, and its continuous use is not recommended.
Bursera simaruba (Burseraceae) Tree	gumbo-limbo, tourist tree (E); indio desnudo (S); cha-ca (M)	A decoction of the bark boiled in water can be used as an antidote to poisonwood sap.
Cecropia peltata (Moraceae) Tree	trumpet tree (E); guaru-mo (S); cho-otz (M)	An infusion of the leaves in hot water can be drunk to treat high blood pressure and diabetes.
Chiococca alba (Rubiacae) Shrub	skunk root (E); zorillo (S); pay-che (M)	A tea made from its roots is used to treat a wide range of ailments, including colitis and stomach ulcers.
Cryosophila stauracantha (Arecaceae) Palm	give-and-take (E); escoba (S)	Light fibers from inside the leaf sheath can be used to stanch bleeding.
Guazuma ulmifolia (Malvaceae) Tree	bay cedar (E); pixoy (M)	The chopped bark is boiled in water and drunk to treat diarrhea; the edible fruits can cause constipation.
Hamelia patens (Rubiaceae) Shrub	red-headed polly (E); sanalo-todo (S); ix-canan (M)	A warm tea made from boiling the flowers, leaves, and stem in water relieves rashes, burns, and insect bites.
Mimosa pudica (Mimosaceae) Herb	twelve o'clock (E); domilón (S); xmutz (M)	Powdered dried leaves are added to food as a sedative; smoking the leaves helps alleviate muscle spasms.
Pimenta dioica (Myrtaceae) Tree	allspice (E); pimenta (S); naba-cuc (M)	The leaves and berries are boiled to make a tea to treat digestive upsets; the crushed berries can be added to fat to make a paste for the treatment of foot fungus.

The potentially high financial gains to be made from the discovery of pharmaceuticals has highlighted the importance of improving international and national legislation governing intellectual property rights. There is concern, for example, that not enough legal consideration is given to the intellectual property rights of traditional communities, which often do not benefit from modern applications derived from their cultural heritage. One widely cited example is the Maya drink *pozol*, which is produced from fermented maize. This age-old beverage is widely used against intestinal ailments. However, in 1999 an international company obtained a patent for a microorganism within *pozol* that was found to be one of the efficacious ingredients. The company undertook research known as bioprospecting, and the success of its search for medicinal compounds depended in part on traditional knowledge. However, no financial or other benefits from the discoveries were ever shared with local Maya communities. This incident has been cited as a case of what is now called biopiracy—the unauthorized use of biological resources or traditional knowledge and the inequitable sharing of benefits. Indigenous knowledge can save pharmaceutical companies time and money by helping them target their studies for new medicines. Extracts of plants used by one healer in Belize, for example, gave rise to four times as many positive results in lab tests for anti-HIV activity as specimens collected randomly.[119] In addition to exploitation of traditional knowledge, the ethics of patenting products or processes based on biodiversity and nature are hotly disputed.

There has been much criticism of the World Trade Organization's Agreement on Trade-Related Aspects of Intellectual Property Rights (TRIPS). This agreement provides for patent protection for new inventions in technology. For patents to be awarded, inventions must be proven to be new, not obvious, and useful. Traditional communal knowledge is excluded as ineligible for patenting. Inventions covered by TRIPS include new processes for the synthesis of pharmaceutical chemicals. Species cannot be patented, but isolated genes, chemicals derived from natural organisms, and modified crop varieties can. The private sector argues that its intellectual property rights should be protected through patents to encourage innovation and allow it to reap the profits that make innovation worthwhile.

The debate on intellectual property rights continues and is still far from being resolved, but the signing of the Convention on Biological Diversity (CBD) in 1992, of which Belize is a signatory, has helped to provide an initial framework for benefit-sharing agreements. Indeed, one of the central objectives of the CBD, set out in Article 1, is the "fair and equitable sharing of the benefits arising out of the utilization of genetic resources, including by appropriate access to genetic resources and by appropriate transfer of relevant technologies, taking into account all rights over those resources and to technologies, and by appropriate funding."[120] However, there continues to be conflict between Article 1 of CBD and TRIPS, and negotiations are ongoing to establish codes of conduct and workable mechanisms for benefit-sharing that are ethical as well as equitable and that recognize the intellectual property rights of all parties. Central to any resolution is the concept of prior informed consent, whereby indigenous communities and governments are fully informed about what research is being conducted, why, and what the potential results may be. The issue is further complicated by the relationship between governments and their local communities and how benefits are distributed between them. In addition, species and traditional knowledge often do not respect national boundaries.

One of the commonest products to be harvested from Belizean forests is thatch from palms. Easy to harvest, palm leaves provide a cool, light, waterproof roof—an ideal covering for houses—and have been cherished for this purpose from the ancient Maya until today. Although most modern Belizean houses no longer use thatch, many traditional Maya, Garifuna, and Creole dwellings continue to do so. Once abundant, the recent surge in demand for thatching materials, especially for tourist resorts, has resulted in a shortage of leaves and growing concerns about the sustainability of leaf-harvesting practices. This is reflected in the price for thatch leaf, which has risen sharply over the last few years. Scientific studies on the effects of leaf harvesting of palms suggest that as defoliation increases, reproductive activity decreases.[121]

In Belize the palm species most favored for thatching is known as the bayleaf, or botán, palm (*Sabal mauritiiformis*), a species common in forests across the country. Its broad, fan-shaped leaves provide superb roofing material and usually last between ten and fifteen years. Although a recent study conducted at Las Cuevas recorded only six bayleaf palms per hectare, the density of this species can vary considerably depending on the region and forest. At Rio Bravo, for example, toward the north of Belize, there are areas where this species occurs in densities above 600 individuals per hectare.[122] The genus *Sabal* is particularly characteristic of the Caribbean, Central America, and northern South America, and typically a mature bayleaf palm can be expected to have about twelve leaves. Traditionally, leaves are harvested in a period between the full and new moon, the belief being that the leaves do not last as long if they are cut outside of this period. Although the harvesting of leaves from the botán palm could be sustainable if only a few leaves were cut per palm and the plant left to recover, frequently all but one or two of the leaves are removed. In some cases the palm is even felled. Like all NTFPs, a permit is required for its extraction from national and private lands, and royalties must be paid to the Forest Department. However, much of the trade is illegal. The Chiquibul is one example of a forest area where frequent illegal harvesting of thatch occurs.

Although bayleaf is the preferred species for thatch countrywide, in the south, close to the Sarstoon-Temash National Park, leaves from the palm *Manicaria saccifera* are widely used as an alternative and are reportedly superior even to bayleaf, with thatch lasting as long as thirty years. When neither of these two species is present, thatchers resort to cohune (*Attalea cohune*), which, although functional enough, is greatly inferior, lasting only a few years before having to be replaced.

Another forest product widely used, not only in construction but also for crafts, is rope, which can be fashioned from many different species of thin, pliable lianas. However, one material particularly suited to rope making is the bark of certain tree species belonging to the Annonaceae, Malvaceae, and Ulmaceae families. Trees from these families often have bark that is exceptionally stringy and can be stripped from the trunk in long lengths, then rubbed, twisted, and sometimes plaited to provide a strong binding material. It is not uncommon to hear knowledgeable farmers talking about the moho tree, the common name often given to tree species that can provide rope. In the Chiquibul the red moho (*Trichospermum grewiifolium*) is one such species frequently used for this purpose by surrounding communities.

Making rope from the bark of red moho (*Trichospermum grewiifolium*). © Sam Bridgewater.

FOREST FOLKLORE

With Belize's many ethnic groups and the strong association of their respective cultures with nature, it is not surprising that forests appear prominently in local legend and myth. The Alux, for example, is an important character in Mayan folklore. Made from clay and small in stature, the Alux protects his master's property from wild animals, although he himself lives deep in the forest. There are many legends associated with the Alux, and hunters and chicleros have recounted finding tiny dwellings deep in the forest, believed to be his abode. Another Mayan character is the Cadejo, a long-haired canine beast with the hooves of a goat, the horns of a bull, and the tail of a puma, who, among other things, protects drunken men who are lost in the jungle. Other tales speak of La Sigua, a wicked witch whose body is entirely composed of different plants and animals, including the pods of guanacaste (*Enterolobium cyclocarpum*) for her feet. Perhaps the most famous character from Belizean folklore, however, is Tata Duende, a creature well known to Creole, Maya, and Garifuna communities. Small, old, wearing a hat, and often grasping a machete, Tata Duende represents the guardian angel of the forest, protecting all species within it. However, the most chilling tales relate to Sisimito, a hairy apelike creature who lives in the forest and feasts on human flesh.[123]

FOREST FEAST: MAKING USE OF
THE FOREST'S NATURAL LARDER

The markets of Belize are vibrant, colorful affairs where an impressive variety of fruit and vegetables is sold by Mennonite, Maya, Garifuna, Mestizo, and Creole farmers. For the most part, the produce sold is cultivated rather than wild-harvested from forests. However, at certain times of the year, a few stalls can be seen hawking strange delicacies, such as pacaya (the edible flower buds of the palm *Chamaedorea tepejilote*) and sapodilla (the fruit of the sapodilla tree, *Manilkara zapota*). These few exotic additions to the usual fare provide a glimpse of the variety of wild edible forest plants available.

One of the most well known forest foods in Belize is the breadnut, or ramón (*Brosimum alicastrum*). This large forest tree is abundant in the Chiquibul and produces round, orange fruit about the size of a large marble. The outer fruit cover is thin and sweet, revealing a large starchy seed that can be boiled and eaten like potatoes or dried and ground into flour. The cohune palm (*Attalea cohune*) is another favorite snack plant of hunters and chicleros alike. When the plant is small, the young leaves can be pulled from the ground and the tender white bases chewed. The nuts of the mature palm can also provide a tasty kernel if the impressively hard fruit can be cracked open. Oil produced from the same seed is used in cooking, and its extraction was once commercially significant in Belize (see "The Cohune Nut Industry" earlier in this chapter). For oil production the endosperm (the inner seed coat) is boiled in water and the oil

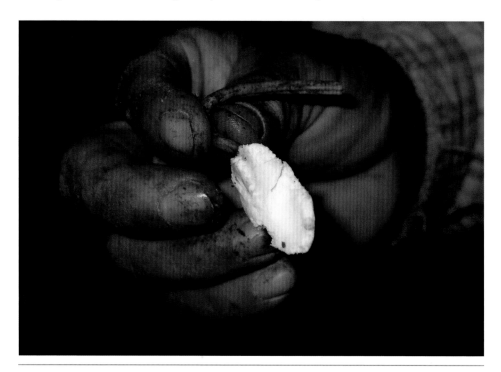

The germinating seed of the palm *Attalea cohune* can provide a tasty impromptu snack in the forest.
© Sam Bridgewater.

skimmed from the surface. A number of other palm species have seeds that can be eaten or used as a source of oil. These include *Acrocomia aculeata* and *Manicaria saccifera*.

All palm species have a tender white shoot tip (the heart), which is usually heavily protected by the leaf bases. Around the world, palm heart is widely eaten. In Belize the species from which palm heart is most commonly extracted is the mountain cabbage (*Euterpe precatoria*), and this can provide a sizable meal. The hearts of other species (e.g., the give-and-take palm, *Cryosophila stauracantha*) can be small, very bitter, and not so favored, although when roasted they may become palatable. The sustainability of extraction of palm heart for food, however, is questionable, as it results in the death of the palm. Unlike trees, palms have only a single growing tip; once this is removed, the palm cannot survive. The purple fruits of another palm species—cocano boy (*Bactris major*)—and those of the grugru palm (*Acrocomia mexicana*) and warrie cohune (*Bactris mexicana*) are also widely consumed. Other common wild foods include the fruits of the tree genus *Pouteria* (e.g., mamey cerilla—*P. campechiana*; mamey apple—*P. sapota*), the fruits of the wild custard apple (*Annona reticulata*), the hog plum (*Spondias radlkoferi*), the wild cherry (*Pseudolmedia spuria*), the roasted seeds of the provision tree (*Pachira aquatica*), the tender shoots of herbaceous spiral ginger (*Costus pulverulentus*), and the white sweet flesh surrounding the seeds of bri-bri (*Inga* spp.).

A great number of forest species are also the basis of excellent flavorings and can salvage an otherwise bland meal. Perhaps most famous of all these is the allspice tree (*Pimenta dioica*), the dried fruits of which are highly aromatic and traded internationally. Although Belize has exported allspice in the past, it does not do so today. Guatemala is now the major producer in the region, although Jamaica dominates international trade. Further spicy flavoring is provided by the fruit of the bird pepper (*Capsicum anuum*) and the broad heart-shaped leaves of the cow foot (*Pimenta auritum*), the latter providing an excellent addition to fish. In addition to food, plants can provide a source of much-needed water, especially in limestone forest areas such as the Chiquibul, where streams are few and far between. Chicleros and foresters have long put the water vine (*Pinzona coriacea*) to good use. The conspicuous thick stem of this species has reddish, flaky bark, and when the stem is cut into sections, the water within the broad xylem vessels—the internal plumbing system of plants—pours out. However, the cutting of the water vine can kill the plant and should be done only in emergencies. Another vine, *Vitis tiliifolia*, can also be used as a source of water.

A number of edible plants are poisonous to humans or other animals. For example, the heart of the give-and-take palm (*Cryosophila stauracantha*), which is bitter-tasting and barely edible to humans, is poisonous to fish, and the Maya have been known to capitalize on this property by using it for fishing. Typically, the white heart is crushed and thrown into a pool of water; the chemical saponins released from the palm heart into the water stupefy the fish, which float to the surface and are easily collected.

Drinking from the water vine (*Pinzona coriacea*). © William Milliken.

Making baskets from basket tie-tie (*Desmoncus orthacanthos*) requires great skill and is a craft for which Belize is famous. © Sam Bridgewater.

FOREST HANDICRAFTS

A number of plant species are harvested and used in the production of local crafts. On a small scale, attractive seeds are used in jewelry. The round black seeds of the soapberry (*Sapindus saponaria*) and *Canna* spp. as well as the striking brown seeds of guanacaste (*Enterolobium cyclocarpon*) provide three examples. Some of the most striking necklaces and bracelets are fashioned from the threaded seed of species belonging to the genera *Ormosia*, *Erythrina*, *Rhynchosia*, *Canavallia*, and *Abrus*. All belong to the pea family, and their seeds are shiny and variously patterned red and black, an adaptation to promote dispersal by birds. The seeds of *Mucuna*, a vine genus also belonging to the pea family, have been used for adornment all over the world. In most cases, the seeds of this genus are not traded but are carried around the planet as drift seed on ocean currents. Their striking form is a surprise to beachcombers on distant shores, who often collect their unusual find for

fashioning into brooches, amulets, and even snuff boxes (see "Seed Dispersal" in chapter 5). *Mucuna* also has another use: its hard seeds heat up rapidly when rubbed vigorously and are valued as fire starters.

One of the crafts for which Belize is renowned is basket making. The primary species used to make larger baskets is the basket-tie-tie (*Desmoncus orthacanthos*), a spiny forest vine belonging to the palm family whose stem can arc and clamber through the canopy for hundreds of meters. The stem is cut into lengths of around four to six meters and quartered. Once its spines are stripped, the sections are ideal for weaving. Smaller baskets favored for sale to tourists by the Maya in the south of Belize are woven from fibers of jipajapa (*Carludovica palmata*). This is the same species used to make Panama hats. However, this understory plant does not occur in the Chiquibul Forest.

In addition to construction materials, crafts, foods, and medicines, the forest provides a wide variety of other products, some of them surprising and not all of them legal. Incense, for example, is important in Maya medicine in addition to being used in Catholic services. One of the species most widely used for this purposes is the copal tree (*Protium copal*), which produces a white, sticky, flammable resin. In the past it was also used in the production of varnish. According to tradition, copal is best collected under the full moon, and although it can be ignited directly, it is typically placed on coals or embers and burned both as a spiritual offering and to "cleanse" illnesses.[124] Another plant product useful as incense is the bark of the balsam tree (*Myroxylon balsamum*). Together with copal, balsam bark can often be found in local markets. Due to its many uses, medicinal and otherwise, the sale of balsam bark can attract high prices—so much so that when harvesters encounter this relatively rare tree, they collect all the available bark from it, effectively "ringing" the tree. Such a practice is destructive, as it removes the cambium (a layer of tissue responsible for producing new cells) and causes the tree to die. Trees damaged in this way can be observed throughout the Chiquibul.

There is also significant domestic and international trade in ornamental plants, of which orchids and izote (*Yucca guatemalensis* and *Beaucarnea pliabilis*) are two examples. Although the trade of these species is far greater in Guatemala than in Belize, there has been widespread harvesting of izote in the Vaca Plateau, with cut stem lengths exported to West Germany for propagation. There are unsubstantiated reports of visitors to izote camps deep in the forest recording ten thousand stems of izote, each sixty to ninety centimeters in length, waiting to be sold. In the case of orchids, as indeed of all marketed NTFPs, there are informal illegal businesses supplying markets in addition to regulated, legal enterprises. Many verandas and hotels across Belize, for example, are enlivened by orchids. Although some of these have been legally obtained, many have not. Internationally, highly prized Belizean species include *Cattleya bowringiana*, *Rhyncholaelia digbyana*, *Encyclia cochleata*, *Brassavola nodosa*, *Sobralia macrantha*, and *Myrmecophila tibicinis*.

Belize's forests are not famous just for their plant products. In addition, animal life has been the focus of domestic and commercial interest. Although these species are protected by law, resources are insufficient for policing them, and illegal hunting is widespread. In particular, species such as gibnut, deer, tapir, wild pigs (peccary), great curassow, and wild turkeys are targeted for bushmeat. For some, hunting provides a thrilling pastime and the possibility of lucrative rewards for attractive skins. Jaguars, pumas, ocelots, and crocodiles have all suffered from the hunter's sport, despite the existence of CITES regulations to limit the trade of endangered species and products derived from them (see the boxed text "Mahogany and the Convention on International Trade in Endangered Species of Wild Fauna and Flora [CITES]" earlier in this

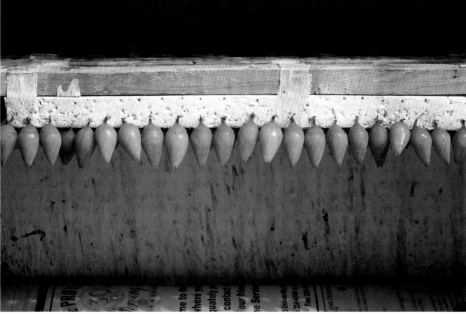

TOP: Many Belizean native orchid species, including *Cattleya bowringiana* (pictured), are harvested from the wild and traded internationally. © Brett Adams. Courtesy Belize Botanic Gardens. BOTTOM: Pupae of the blue morpho butterfly (*Morpho peleides*). A number of butterfly farms in Belize are engaged in collecting butterfly food plants, eggs, and adult butterflies from the wild. Butterfly pupae are traded internationally. © Sam Bridgewater.

chapter). However, not all animal groups are killed; some are collected alive to keep as pets, with birds of striking plumage, such as scarlet macaws and mealy parrots, bearing the brunt of such activity. In the past, when regulations governing export were less rigorous than they are today, even jaguars were captured from forests such as the Chiquibul and exported to the United States. For obvious reasons, there are few paper records pertaining to this activity. Much of the illicit export activity reportedly occurred in the 1960s and 1970s and is associated with the infamous John Little, who ran a jaguar hunting camp at Las Cuevas.

THE VALUE OF FORESTS: THE ROLE OF ECOTOURISM

About 250,000 tourists (excluding cruise-ship passengers) visit Belize every year, generating revenue in excess of US$150 million and contributing 16 percent of the country's gross domestic product. Tourism is one of Belize's most important and steadily growing industries.[125] With between one quarter and one third of all visitors spending time within protected areas during their visit, the Belize Tourist Board recognizes that the country's rich biodiversity, spectacular inland and offshore wilderness areas, and archaeological heritage are among the country's most marketable assets. In 2007, for example, just over fourteen thousand visitors were recorded for Caracol alone, while over fifty thousand visited the Mountain Pine Ridge. In part, earnings derived from the tourism industry are directly attributable to the continued presence of its forests and the perception of tourists that Belize remains one of the world's last remaining "unspoiled" countries with its fauna and flora intact. Any economic valuation of Belize's forests is therefore incomplete if this fact is not part of the equation.

THE FAUNA OF THE CHIQUIBUL

4 MUCH OF THE SCIENTIFIC WORK conducted in the Chiquibul has focused on describing its fauna, its 177,000 hectares supporting significant populations of many large mammal species that have been extirpated elsewhere regionally. The classic example is the jaguar, the largest terrestrial predator in Mesoamerica. Over four hundred jaguars are thought to reside in the forests of the Chiquibul and adjacent Maya Mountain reserves, and studies at Las Cuevas have highlighted aspects of their territorial requirements. In addition to the jaguar, other quintessentially "large" mammals roam the forests of western Belize, including pumas, ocelots, tapirs, peccaries, and spider and howler monkeys. If the smaller mammals are also considered—including bats—a total of ninety-seven species have been recorded for the Chiquibul area to date.

Birds make the other group of warm-blooded animals, and Las Cuevas has become a favored place of the more intrepid ornithologist. The principal attractions of recent years have been the harpy eagle, one of the world's most powerful raptors, and the scarlet macaw, with the Chiquibul providing one of the best sites to see this colorful bird. In addition, the environs of Las Cuevas support a broad range of specialist forest species rarely seen outside of relatively undisturbed forest habitats, including the great curassow and the crested guan.

Amphibians and reptiles are the cold-blooded counterparts of mammals and birds. They are represented in the Chiquibul by twenty-six and sixty-five species, respectively, although these numbers may rise as researchers begin to explore the more inaccessible areas of the Maya Mountains.[1] There is a great deal of scientific concern about the global decline in amphibians, and Las Cuevas has been the site of a long-term monitoring project that seeks to assess the stability of local frog populations. Of the reptiles, the poisonous snakes are those that usually interest visitors most, with the brightly colored coral snake and notorious fer-de-lance among those most frequently encountered. Other reptiles of great interest are Morelet's crocodile and the green iguana, which are associated with the Chiquibul's rivers.

This chapter gives a broad overview of the larger animal groups of the Chiquibul. Amphibians and reptiles, mammals, and birds are treated in turn, along with the regional and international context of their distribution and abundance. The ecology of each group is discussed, and detailed profiles are provided for species of particular interest: Morelet's crocodile, the green iguana, the jaguar, the tapir, the peccary, the spider monkey, the howler monkey, the harpy eagle, and the scarlet macaw. Particularly noteworthy scientific studies conducted at Las Cuevas are highlighted where these have helped to clarify issues relating to species conservation.

THE CREEPERS: AMPHIBIANS AND REPTILES

Las Cuevas staff are asked one question more frequently than any other: Are there any poisonous snakes in the Chiquibul? Being bitten by a snake and suffering an unpleasant, lingering death is a major preoccupation of many visitors. Although such concern is only natural, the fear many people have of serpents is unwarranted. The answer to their question, of course, is yes, there are some very poisonous snakes to be found in the environs of the research station—five species to be exact—but most visitors will most likely spend the days, weeks, or months of their stay without seeing a snake at all. Unless they specifically go looking for them, that is. Although snakes are believed to cause the death of 50,000-100,000 people a year worldwide,[2] snake deaths in Belize are few and far between; to provide some perspective, only one visitor to Las Cuevas in the fifteen years of its existence has ever been bitten and required medical treatment. Like most victims of venomous snakebite, the botanist lived to tell the tale.

While snakes often provoke a sense of primal alarm, in contrast, the glimpse of a brightly colored tree frog perched on a leaf brings with it a sense of wonder. Such a sight is iconic, after all, being one of the quintessential images used to portray the biological diversity of rain forests around the world. As we have become increasingly aware of the adverse impact of human activities on the planet, the need has arisen to continuously monitor the health of our most diverse ecosystems. Due to their exacting ecological requirements and their water- and gas-permeable skins, frogs are excellent biomonitors of our rain forests. If climatic conditions change or if there is too much pollution, they are among the first animals to suffer. If they begin to disappear, then there is just cause

The arboreal green vine snake (*Oxybelis fulgidus*). © Sam Bridgewater.

A Mexican burrowing toad (*Rhinophrynus dorsalis*) in a pool of water close to Las Cuevas after a heavy rain. This species escapes the droughts of the dry season by residing dormant in subterranean chambers. © Zoë Goodwin.

for alarm. Unfortunately, there has been a well-documented catastrophic decline in frog populations globally since the 1980s (see "Where Have All the Frogs Gone?" later in this chapter), and this threatened group of animals requires assistance more than ever. The Chiquibul Forest is one important region safeguarding them.

Together with crocodiles, turtles, tuataras, and lizards, snakes belong to a group of animals known as the reptiles (class Reptilia), comprising about 6,000 species worldwide. This is significantly more than the known number of mammals (about 5,000 species).[3] Classified within a different group are frogs, toads, salamanders, and caecilians—the amphibians (class Amphibia)—made up of about 4,600 species. The earliest amphibians had evolved by the start of the Carboniferous period (359 MYA), whereas the reptiles—including dinosaurs—appeared slightly later in the fossil record. Both of these groups are important elements of the ecological web. Amphibians, for example, often represent the highest proportion of vertebrate biomass in a tropical forest and are believed to be important in maintaining arthropod diversity. Both reptiles and amphibians are themselves the main prey of many other animal groups.

The branch of science that concerns itself with the study of reptiles and amphibians is called herpetology. This word is derived from the Greek *herpes*, meaning "creeping thing." And although amphibians were apparently held in low esteem by the father of taxonomy himself, Carl Linnaeus (see the boxed text "Kingdoms and Domains: Classifying Life on Earth" in chapter 1), who reportedly called them "foul and loathsome,"[4] the ancient Maya were more appreciative. Such was their respect for these coinhabitants of their land that images of these species feature prominently in their art, religion, and mythology. Indeed, the Classic and Postclassic Maya even conceived of the world as the back of a huge reptile.

USEFUL IDENTIFICATION GUIDES TO BELIZE'S AMPHIBIANS AND REPTILES

Beletsky, L. *The Ecotraveller's Wildlife Guide: Belize and Northern Guatemala.* San Diego, CA: Academic Press, 1999.

Garel, T., and S. Matola. *A Field Guide to the Snakes of Belize.* Belize City: Belize Zoo and Tropical Education Center, 1995.

Lee, J. C. *A Field Guide to the Amphibians and Reptiles of the Maya World.* Ithaca, NY: Cornell University Press, 2000.

Meyer, J. R., and C. F. Foster. *A Guide to the Frogs and Toads of Belize.* Malabar, FL: Krieger Publishing, 1996.

Stafford, P. J., and J. R. Meyer. *A Guide to the Reptiles of Belize.* San Diego, CA: Academic Press, 2000.

SOME ESSENTIALS OF AMPHIBIAN AND REPTILE BIOLOGY

Few of us ever feel energized first thing in the morning, and for some it can take several cups of coffee before the day can be faced. Even though we may consider ourselves to be poor early starters, reptiles and amphibians are slower still. Like all mammals, we can regulate our own body temperature metabolically, with the food we eat providing the necessary fuel to keep our bodies warm. In contrast, amphibians and reptiles do not have such a capability. Instead they rely on the sun's warmth to keep their body temperature high enough for them to be active. Thus, after a cold night, amphibians and reptiles are usually extremely sluggish and must bask in heat before they can even consider breakfast. This is why it is common to see anoles and other small lizards motionless on the sunny walls of the research station first thing in the morning. Colder climates, of course, present even greater difficulties for these groups to overcome, and some species must hibernate during the cold season. Extremely hot climates are also problematic; just as these animals cannot heat up by themselves, so too can cooling down be problematic. Amphibians and reptiles maintain their body temperatures through their behavior, seeking out the shade when too hot and sunbathing or absorbing heat through objects when they are cold. Because of their inability to regulate their own temperature, they are often called "cold-blooded," although the scientific term is *ecotothermic*; conversely, the warm-blooded mammals and birds are called *endothermic*.

Although being entirely dependent on the external environment for warmth has obvious drawbacks, it also has considerable advantages. Because ectotherms do not rely on metabolizing food to produce heat, they can be extremely energy-efficient, with a much higher proportion of their food intake made available for building body tissues. One reason why there are more larger mammals than reptiles and amphibians is that mammals are generally less energy-efficient. As the energy requirements of any organism tend to be higher the smaller it is, and because mammals waste energy metabolically, it makes sense for them to be bigger, thereby reducing their relative energy needs.

Spawn of Morelet's tree frog (*Agalychnis moreletii*). The females of this species lay their eggs on leaves above ponds, and the tadpoles drop into the water once they are sufficiently mature. © Sam Bridgewater.

The word *amphibian* is derived from Greek and means having a dual existence. This refers to the typical two-phase life history of this group. Reproduction usually requires water. While the larvae are typically aquatic and breathe by gills, adults are usually terrestrial or semiterrestrial and breathe by lungs and through their moist, glandular skin. However, there are many exceptions to this rule. Reptiles are less dependent on water for reproduction than amphibians due to the development in the former of a specialized amniotic egg in which the embryo is surrounded by thick protective membranes (see "The Rise of the Vertebrates" in chapter 1).

The skin of amphibians is water- and gas-permeable, so they can easily become desiccated and die. Their activity and breeding, therefore, are often related to rainfall. In addition, their behavior has evolved to ensure that water loss is reduced: they usually limit the times when they are in direct sunlight; remain in humid environments—often close to bodies of water; and, when inactive, frequently close their eyes, tuck in their legs, and press their body flat to reduce its exposed surface area. Their skin also has mucous-producing glands that help retain water. In contrast, reptiles have a thick, scaly skin that is waterproof. Thus, they are less in danger of desiccation and have been able to colonize a wider range of diverse, more arid habitats.

In Mesoamerica, the region of Central America stretching from Mexico through Panama, there are an estimated 1,800 species of reptiles and amphibians, or approximately 17 percent of the world's total.[5] In 1996 an analysis of the herpetofauna of the Yucatán, a geographic area that covers parts of southeastern Mexico, northern Belize, and the Petén region of Guatemala, revealed 182 species of amphibians and reptiles as resident—73 snakes, 48 lizards, 35 frogs and toads, 16 turtles, 6 salamanders, 2 caecilians, and 2 crocodiles.[6] Although scientists consider such diversity to be relatively depauperate when compared with other areas in Central America, 14 percent of these species are endemic to the region. Despite significant advances in our knowledge of amphibian and reptile diversity in the decade since this analysis was undertaken, there is still no certainty about how many species occur regionally. Every year new discoveries and sightings are made. One problem is that some species look very similar to one another, so claims of new records for a country are often treated with initial skepticism until they can be verified by experts. In addition, if a new species is discovered, a specimen must be collected to provide a reference type to which the new name is applied, and information about it must be published in peer-reviewed scientific journals before its existence is accepted. This process can take many years to complete. Furthermore, taxonomists are not always in agreement as to whether an apparently new form of life is sufficiently different from its nearest neighbor to deserve a distinct species epithet or whether it is simply a morphological variety of an existing species. Changes can sometimes be made to existing classification systems, resulting in amendments to generic and species names and confusing the matter further.

A recent assessment of Belize's herpatofauna indicates the presence of 165 species.[7] This represents about 90 percent of the herpetofauna of the Yucatán region, with 4 species considered national endemics: 2 snakes (*Leptophis mexicanus hoeversi* and *Tantilla hendersoni*), a gecko (*Phyllodactylus insularis*), and a frog (*Lithobates juliana*). An additional 8 Belizean species of amphibians and 23 species of reptiles are broader endemics to lowland Central American Maya forest.[8]

From the studies conducted to date, it is known that 26 amphibian species and 65 reptile species have been authentically recorded within the confines of the Chiquibul (see appendixes A and B). This represents 55 percent of the country's mainland native herpetofauna. At least another 8 species are known from broadleaf forest localities adjacent to the Chiquibul and may be expected to occur in the area. For obvious reasons, species restricted to the coast (e.g., American crocodile, *Crocodylus actus*), those confined to the habitats of the more arid north (e.g., the snail-eating thirst snake, *Dipsas brevifacies*), and those found only in the much wetter regions south of the Maya Divide (e.g., the Maya night lizard, *Lepidophyma mayae*) are not present.

A provisional checklist of the amphibians of the Chiquibul is provided in appendix A. Of the broad groups that occur, the rarest are the caecilians–limbless, burrowing terrestrial animals that look a little like giant earthworms. The eyes of these creatures are rudimentary and covered with skin or bone; thus, they are practically blind. Another unusual feature is that they have a specialized chemoreception sensory organ–the tentacle–that opens to the surface of the head through an aperture between the eyes and nostrils. The only known example of a caecilian from the Las Cuevas region is the mountain caecilian (*Gymnopis syntrema*). Although many amphibians require water for breeding, this species gives birth to live young (i.e., it is viviparous).[9] It feeds on earthworms and other soil invertebrates.

Unlike caecilians, salamanders have four legs and a distinct body and tail. The only known salamanders in the Yucatán are lungless salamanders (family Plethodontidae), which, as their name suggests, do not breathe through lungs but acquire all the oxygen they need by gaseous absorption through their skin and through the roof of the mouth, which is well supplied with blood vessels. Like the mountain caecilian, the three species of lungless salamander known from the Chiquibul do not have the free-living larval stage common to many amphibian groups. However, unlike the mountain caecilian, they lay eggs rather than giving birth to live young, with miniature adults emerging on hatching. The three species all feed on invertebrates and are often arboreal, sometimes being found in bromeliads. The largest of them is Doflein's salamander (*Bolitoglossa dofleini*), whose body can reach lengths in excess of ten centimeters.

Doflein's salamander (*Bolitoglossa dofleini*). Also known as the giant palm salamander, this is the largest of the three species of lungless salamanders known from the Chiquibul Forest. © 2002 Stephen M. Deban.

The frogs and toads of the Chiquibul are represented by a broad range of families, all of which differ from the caecilians and salamanders by being tailless in the adult phase and having elongated hind limbs specialized for hopping, jumping, or climbing. They also differ in their means of reproduction. This typically involves eggs being deposited in or close to water; the initial, larval stages of life (tadpoles) are aquatic and physically very different from the adult stage. Not least of these differences is their possession of gills (while the terrestrial adults have lungs) and a tail (which the adult lacks). The process by which a tadpole becomes an adult is called metamorphosis. Most adult anurans (order Anura) also have distinct vocal sacks that enable them to communicate with one another. Distinguishing between anuran species can be problematic, and specialists use many features to tell them apart. These include their size, the texture and color of the skin, the number of toes, the degree of foot webbing, and even the color of the iris. However, even finding frogs to identify can be difficult in the jungle undergrowth, and most herpetologists rely on calls to identify individual species.

Two particularly characteristic anuran families of the Chiquibul are the largely terrestrial rainfrogs, or stream frogs (Leptodactylidae)—one of which is reputedly named after a Mayan deity (Chac's rainfrog)—and the tree frogs (Hylidae). The latter family is very diverse in form, and many members are arboreal, possessing expanded adhesive tips to their toes that facilitate their ability to climb. The most famous members of this

group in the Chiquibul are the bright green red-eyed tree frog (*Agalychnis callidryas*) and Morelet's tree frog (*A. moreletii*), with the latter being a regional (rather than country) endemic and critically endangered (see table 4.1). Both species lay their eggs on leaves above pools; the tadpoles drop into the water below when they have sufficiently developed. One of the rarer frogs from this group is the Central American glass frog (*Hyalinobatrachium fleischmanni*), so called because the skin of the underside of its body is transparent, allowing the viscera to be seen. This species is restricted in the Chiquibul to fast-flowing streams.

In addition to the above groups, a number of other anuran families are represented. The Mexican burrowing toad

Central American glass frog (*Hyalinobatrachium fleischmanni*). © Kristine Kaiser.

TABLE 4.1. Endangered amphibians and reptiles of the Chiquibul

Species	Common Name	IUCN Category
Agalychnis moreletii	Morelet's tree frog	Critically Endangered
Bolitoglossa dofleini	Doflein's mushroom-tongued salamander	Near Threatened
Craugaster chac	Chac's rainfrog	Near Threatened
C. laticeps	Broadhead rainfrog	Near Threatened
C. sabrinus		Endangered
Crocodylus moreletii	Morelet's crocodile	Low Risk
Dermatemys mawii	American river turtle	Critically Endangered
Kinosternon acutum	Tabasco mud turtle	Near Threatened
Incilius campbelli	Campbell's rainforest toad	Near Threatened
Lithobates juliana	Maya mountain frog	Neat Threatened
Smilisca cyanosticta	Blue-spotted Mexican tree frog	Near Threatened
Syrrhophus leprus	Mottled chirping frog	Vulnerable

Source: IUCN, 2010 IUCN Red List of Threatened Species.

(*Rhinophrynus dorsalis*; family Rhinophrynidae), for example, is one of the more curious anurans to occur close to Las Cuevas. This dark, bloated species escapes the droughts of the dry season by residing dormant in subterranean chambers. Surface activity is associated with breeding and is restricted to the start of the rainy season. In addition, there are three species of toads known for the area (Bufonidae). These have poison glands in the skin and distinct poison sacs (parotid glands) on either side of the head to deter predators from attacking; hapless dogs toying with the largest member of this group–the giant toad (*Chaunus marinus*)–have been known to die if their teeth penetrate the sacs. However, even their poisonous skin does not deter a number of predators from feasting on them. These include the great black hawk (*Buteogallus urubitinga*) and the speckled racer (*Drymobius margaritiferus*).

CHARACTERISTIC REPTILE GROUPS OF THE CHIQUIBUL

The two largest reptiles of the Chiquibul region are Morelet's crocodile (*Crocodylus moreletii*, family Crocodylidae) and the green iguana (*Iguana iguana*, family Iguanidae); more detailed accounts on the ecology of both are provided later in this chapter (see "The Plight of Morelet's Crocodile" and "Bamboo Chicken"). Snakes–the most infamous of the reptile group–are believed to have arisen from lizard-like ancestors during

A cryptically colored wowla (*Boa constrictor*) coiled around a broken branch. © Paul Edgar.

the early Cretaceous period (ca. 146–100 MYA),[10] and four distinct families are represented in the Chiquibul. The largest snake with the oldest evolutionary history is the wowla, or common boa (*Boa constrictor*). Belonging to the Boidae family, this species can attain lengths in excess of two meters. Its scientific name relates to its method of killing its prey, which involves coiling around the victim and constricting it until it suffocates. Prey includes birds, bats, lizards, and small mammals, which are swallowed whole. Indeed, most snakes tend to ingest their victims intact, and many species have distensible mouths for engulfing their prey.

The majority of the snakes known from the Chiquibul are colubrids, or typical snakes belonging to a separate scientific family, Colubridae. These include the mussurana (*Clelia clelia*)–the juveniles of which are bright red and which is one of the few animals willing to prey on the fearsome fer-de-lance, or lancehead (*Bothrops asper*), as well as the frequently seen speckled racer (*Drymobius margaritiferus*). The other two primary snake families are both venomous: the pit vipers (Viperidae) and the coral snakes (Epidae). Both of these families are considered in more detail later in this chapter (see "Poisonous Snakes of the Chiquibul").

Apart from the nocturnal mud turtles (*Kinosternon acutum* and *K. leucostomum*), which are a common sight in muddy pools, and the Central American river turtle (*Dermatemys mawii*), the remaining reptiles found in the Chiquibul are predominantly lizardlike and belong to a range of families, including Eublepharidae (banded geckos), Geckonidae (geckos), Corytophanidae (basilisks, helmeted and casque-headed lizards), Phrynosomatidae (spiny lizards), Polychrotidae (anoles), Scincidae (skinks), Teiidae (race runners and whip-tailed lizards), and Xantusidae (night lizards). With experience it is usually possible to tell these different groups apart by their general "look." However, species identification can be difficult, and one of the field guides listed earlier in this chapter should be consulted.

Although Belize's Chiquibul region remains a good place to find and study amphibians, global amphibian populations are suffering a dramatic slump. Such is the scale of the reduction in their numbers that this group of animals is currently facing an extinction crisis. The plight of the world's amphibians became well publicized following the First World Congress of Herpetology, held in Canterbury, England, in 1989. At this scientific meeting many amphibian specialists realized that they had all been independently witnessing parallel declines in their focus species. Although some of the disappearances could be attributed to deforestation and habitat loss, and localized population extinctions are not infrequent in nature, what was puzzling was that amphibian populations from around the world were even crashing in undisturbed areas apparently unaffected by human interference.

In 2001 the Global Amphibian Assessment (GAA) project was launched. Its aim was to determine the scale of the decline and the causes of the threats to amphibians, with all species assessed against the categories and criteria of the IUCN Red List. Over six hundred scientists have since contributed to this project, and a number of specialist scientific groups have formed in response to the crisis. The best known of these is the IUCN Amphibian Specialist Group, which represents a merger of a number of existing entities, such as the Declining Amphibian Population Task Force (DAPTF).

CLOCKWISE, FROM LEFT: A smooth-headed helmeted basilisk (*Corytophanes cristatus*); a lesser scaly anole (*Norops uniformis*) clinging to a branch; Sumichrast's skink (*Eumeces sumichrasti*) on a palm leaf; Lundell's spiny lizard (*Sceloporus lundelli*). Photographed by Peter Stafford. © The Natural History Museum, London.

The findings of the GAA are disturbing. From the information available in 2008, it appears that one third of the world's amphibian species are threatened or extinct. One of the worst-affected regions is the Caribbean, where more than 80 percent of species are under threat. Worldwide, 38 species are known to have become extinct, with a further 120 species not found in recent years.[11] At least thirteen countries in Latin America have experienced declines or extinctions of amphibian species.[12]

THE CAUSES OF THE GLOBAL DECLINE IN AMPHIBIANS

There appears to be no single cause of the catastrophic drop in amphibian populations. Habitat destruction aside, agricultural practices have in part been blamed, with the widespread use of chemicals cited as one important contributing factor. In particular, amphibian eggs are known to be susceptible to elevated levels of environmental toxins. Amphibians may also be suffering mortality through "biomagnification" of chemical contaminant concentrations through the food chain, and their water- and gas-permeable skin makes them especially susceptible to noxious substances. One cause for concern in Belize is the widespread use of chemicals in the agricultural sector. In the south, for example, banana plantations are largely centered on the coastal plain. Unfortunately, the country's prevailing westerly winds can carry significant quantities of agrotoxins deep into the Maya Mountains, where many of Belize's rarest amphibian populations reside. Pollution has also been implicated in amphibian declines worldwide, as acid rain, petroleum, and heavy metals are contaminants known to be detrimental to amphibian development. In addition, amphibian embryos are sensitive to elevated levels of ultraviolet light caused by the thinning of the ozone level, attributed to chlorofluorocarbon pollution. Climate change has also been invoked in some regions. In particular, the increased incidence and duration of drought may adversely affect amphibian health, and stressed populations will be more susceptible to illness. The speed at which some amphibian populations have declined has also led scientists to suspect that they are suffering from a disease epidemic. For example, in recent years the chytrid frog fungus (*Batrachochytrium dendrobatidis*)—a pathogen known to cause a fatal disease in frogs and toads—has been linked to amphibian mortality in areas where declines are especially marked, such as Australia and Central America.

STUDIES OF THE ANURANS OF LAS CUEVAS AND THE CHIQUIBUL

In response to concerns about the global demise of amphibians, a working group of the DAPTF was formed in Belize in 1997, initially under the local name of the BELDAP Anuran Survey Project. This soon expanded to include neighboring regions in Mexico and Guatemala and became known as the Maya Forest Monitoring Project (MAYAMON). Using volunteer scientists and focusing on common species across the broad study area, this project has been monitoring frog and toad populations using assessments of abundance based on nocturnal calling patterns between 1900 and 2300 hours. Surveys are conducted once a month throughout the rainy season at specified locations that tend to be well-known breeding sites where anuran species are known to congregate. A permanent man-made pond associated with an old logging camp at Millionario, a site adjacent to Las Cuevas, has been a registered MAYAMON locality since 1998. Independent research at Las Cuevas has assessed the effectiveness of the MAYAMON sampling protocol and found that it is likely to detect, on average, 80 percent of species present at a pond on any given sampling night, although species that do not call for long periods of time are likely to be underrecorded. In addition, "explosive" breeders such as the Mexican burrowing toad, which reproduce mainly at the start of the rainy season, are less likely to be detected.[13]

There are at least eight ponds close to the research station, with the Macal River and the Monkey Tail Branch providing two additional river systems of amphibian significance in relative close proximity. Since the late 1990s a project allied with the MAYAMON initiative has clarified the abundance of anuran populations in the Chiquibul. This initiative is called Project Anuran.[14]

Over a four-year period Project Anuran has monitored the environmental characteristics of each of its survey sites together with the diversity, relative abundance, and calling activity of all frog species present around Las Cuevas following the MAYAMON protocol. In addition, it has conducted more focused studies on rainfrogs in the genus *Craugaster*. Anuran declines do not appear to be catastrophic in the Chiquibul region at present, but there is still insufficient evidence from these studies to ascertain their current health.

Although it is possible to assess anuran populations by sight, frogs and toads can be hard to spot, as they are often cryptically colored and hidden behind undergrowth or high in trees. Thus, one of the best means of assessing population numbers is through their calls. Fortunately, frogs and toads can often be heard at some distance, with each species having its own unique identifying call. Indeed, anyone who has stood near a pond in Belize after heavy rain will testify that the anuran chorus can be almost deafening, overloading the ears with myriad calls of different pitch and duration. Precisely due to this cacophony, however, analyzing anuran calling data and relating it to species presence and abundance can be problematic, and it takes experience to learn the calls and to be able to relate them

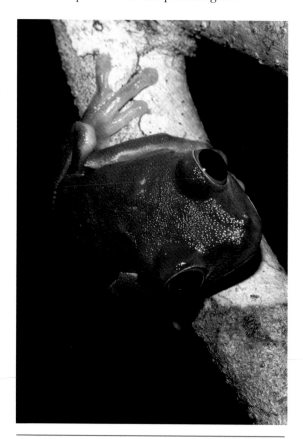

Red-eyed tree frog (*Agalychnis callidryas*). © William Milliken.

to population numbers. In addition, different species can call with different intensities at different times of the night: some call only at very specific localities within a specialized habitat and only after events such as a heavy downpour. A herpetologist visiting a pond one night might find it quiet and apparently devoid of anurans, whereas during a subsequent visit after rain the following day the frogs might be in fine voice. Typically, herpetologists record a number of criteria for each species, including the number of survey nights in which a species is heard, the number of hours it is heard calling, and the estimated number of frogs calling. Anuran calling is presumed to be associated with breeding, and thus the degree of vocalization of a species is used as a measure of reproductive activity.

The data produced by Project Anuran has helped reveal the presence of twenty-two species in the vicinity of Las Cuevas. These include the critically endangered Morelet's tree frog (*Agalychnis moreletii*) and the endemic *Lithobates juliana*. The ten most frequently observed or heard species are given in table 4.2. Many abundance and ecological differences have been found among anuran species. Initial data indicates, for example, that the mahogany tree frog, the small-headed tree frog, and the red-eyed tree frog are among the most widespread and abundant species found around the research station, although the last-mentioned is rarely seen. A number are known to be "explosive" breeders, accumulating and calling at notably high intensities only at times of intense rain. This includes the Mexican burrowing toad (*Rhinophrynus dorsalis*). Some species, like the hourglass tree frog (*Dendropsophus ebraccatus*), were found to call throughout the night. This is in marked contrast to others that call for a smaller percentage of the time, such as the painted tree frog (*Tlalocohyla picta*). There are also marked differences in peak call timing and, by inference, the peak reproductive behavior of species, with the painted tree frog, for example, frequently peaking much earlier in the evening (around 2300) than Brown's leopard frog (*Lithobates brownorum*) (around 0100). It has been suggested that the temporal partitioning of calling between species is a mechanism by which they reduce competition, with each species having a window of opportunity during which it can call with limited "noise pollution" to attract potential mates.

In addition to Project Anuran, various other expeditions have studied the herpetofauna of the Chiquibul, most notably in the upper region of the Raspaculo River in 1991, 1993, and 2000,[15] in the vicinity of the Nohoch Ch'en sinkhole in 2000,[16] and on Doyle's Delight in 2004.[17] Additional amphibian species recorded during these trips include the mountain caecilian (*Gymnopis syntrema*) and the Mexican mushroom-tongued salamander (*Bolitoglossa mexicana*). Significant insights into the region's herpetofauna also resulted from the fieldwork stages of a wildlife impact assessment for the Chalillo Dam conducted in 2001.[18]

All species try to maximize reproductive success, and the selection by females of genetically superior partners provides one means of ensuring that their offspring are given the best start in life. Studies on the genus *Agalychnis* based at Las Cuevas have shown that females of these genera tend to mate with larger-than-average males to

TABLE 4.2. Ten conspicuous anuran residents from the environs of Las Cuevas Research Station

Species	Common Name
Agalychnis callidryas	Red-eyed tree frog
Dendropsophus ebraccatus	Hourglass tree frog
D. microcephala	Small-headed tree frog
Gastrophryne elegans	Narrow-mouthed toad
Incilius valliceps	Gulf Coast toad
Lithobates brownorum	Brown's leopard frog
Rhinophrynus dorsalis	Mexican burrowing toad
Smilisca baudinii	Mexican tree frog
Tlalocohyla loquax	Mahogany tree frog
T. picta	Painted tree frog

maximize the number of offspring produced; the results suggest that mating patterns may be density-dependent and that the nature and intensity of sexual selection are potentially increased by extreme environmental conditions.[19]

STUDIES ON THE REPTILES OF LAS CUEVAS AND THE CHIQUIBUL

With the exception of expeditions to the Raspaculo River, the Nohoch Ch'en sinkhole, and the peaks of the Maya Divide; work conducted as part of the environmental impact assessment for the Chalillo Dam; and an individual taxonomic and ecological study related to Morelet's crocodile,[20] there have been few long-term scientific studies dedicated to describing the diversity and abundance of the Chiquibul's reptiles. As such, the species list provided in appendix B is quite preliminary; doubtless many more reptiles occur in the region than the sixty-five listed here.

POISONOUS SNAKES OF THE CHIQUIBUL

Although eight venomous snakes are known for Belize, only five occur in the Chiquibul (see table 4.3). These belong to two distinct families: the pit vipers (Viperidae) and the coral snakes (Elaphidae). The members of these two families are very different in form. Although venomous, these species are not immune from being hunted: the many-banded coral snake (*Micrurus diastema*), for example, is readily eaten by the similarly colored but larger nonvenomous Central American king snake (*Lampropeltis triangulum*).

At less than one meter long, the slender, secretive, terrestrial many-banded coral snake is relatively small, with its diet consisting of other snakes and lizards. It is highly conspicuous, its body displaying bright warning (aposematic) colors of alternating red, yellow, and black bands. Yet it is not the only snake species to display such colors. Several nonvenomous species, including the false coral (*Pliocercus elapoides*) and the Central American king snake (*Lampropeltis triangulum*), mimic the coloration of the coral snake to dissuade predators from attacking them.

The vipers are larger than the coral snakes; rather than displaying warning colorations, they are cryptically patterned and thus easy to tread on by mistake. They tend to be most active at night. They typically have wedge-shaped heads, rough-scaled bodies, and conspicuous "loreal" pits between their eyes and their nostrils. These pits detect infrared heat and enable them to locate warm-blooded prey such as birds and small mammals, although they also eat amphibians and other reptiles. Unlike coral snakes, pit vipers have fangs that are pivoted into position before striking from their usual resting place folded along the upper jaw. Of the vipers, the fer-de-lance, or tommygoff (*Bothrops asper*), is the largest in Belize, sometimes attaining two meters in length. Its body tends to be brown with darker triangles, the apices of which point to its backbone. The jumping pit viper (*Atropoides mexicanus*) is much feared, as it is reputed to be able to launch its body into the air when it attacks. In reality, it is capable of striking only a distance of one half of its body length. The common names of the hog-nosed viper (*Porthidium nasutum*) and eyelash palm pit viper (*Bothriechis schlegelii*) relate to their distinctive physical characteristics, the former having upturned nostrils and the latter modified scales above its eyes resembling eyelashes.

TOP: The Central American king snake (*Lampropeltis triangulum*) mimics the coral snake's coloration to discourage predators. © Paul Edgar. BOTTOM: Although small, the many-banded coral snake (*Micrurus diastema*) should be treated with respect: its bite releases a potent neurotoxin. © Paul Edgar.

Species	Common Name
Viperidae	
Atropoides mexicanus	Jumping pit viper, jumping tommygoff
Bothriechis schlegelii	Eyelash palm pit viper
Bothrops asper	Central American lancehead, fer-de-lance, tommygoff
Porthidium nastutum	Rainforest hog-nosed pit viper
Elaphidae	
Micrurus diastema	Many-banded coral snake

SNAKE BITES AND SNAKE VENOM

The function of snake venom is to incapacitate prey and initiate the process of digestion. To this end, it contains a complex mix of chemical compounds and toxins, with venom usually classified according to its primary mode of action–hemotoxic, attacking the blood and circulatory systems, or neurotoxic, acting on nerve tissue and disrupting nerve impulses. Typically a bite from a pit viper releases hemotoxic venom and is associated with tissue destruction, swelling, and blood loss; there are many reports of snakebite victims bleeding profusely internally and also from their eyes, nose, and mouth. Although localized signs from a coral snake bite can appear negligible, its strong neurotoxins are just as virulent and cause muscle paralysis and respiratory failure.

If bitten by a snake, one should seek medical assistance immediately. Fatal cases are rare, but prompt treatment will ease the symptoms and reduce the long-term effects of the venom. Although it is common for victims to attempt to treat the bite themselves by applying a tourniquet, cutting the swollen vicinity of the bite to release pressure, or even attempting to suck out the venom from the wound, such practices have not been proven to be effective. In fact, they can be extremely dangerous and exacerbate the seriousness of the situation. They should not be attempted. The treatment proposed by modern medicine is to move as little as possible, seek medical attention, and have antivenom administered through an injection or a drip by a qualified doctor. In rural locations many Belizeans will seek out local "snake doctors," who often use various plant extracts in their treatment. The efficacy of these concoctions may not be scientifically proven and they are not recommended here, despite the fact that many Belizeans swear by their effectiveness. Modern antivenom is typically derived from antibody serums produced by sheep or horses infected with venom under research conditions (the antibody serums result from the animal's immune response). As these serums can sometimes cause a severe allergic response (anaphylactic shock) in some people, they must be administered with great care. In addition, antivenoms are often specific in action, so it is important to know which species of snake caused the bite. However, taking due care while in the field and respecting the territory and space of native animals will usually ensure that a hospital visit is never required.

Lizards date back to the Carboniferous period (360-299 MYA), and the link between prehistoric times and our modern era is never more apparent than when one spies a large green iguana (*Iguana iguana*) basking upon a tree branch above a river. This magnificent creature looks uncannily like a miniature dinosaur. Calling it miniature, however, is an understatement: although the green iguana does not attain the gargantuan size of some of its ancestors, it can nevertheless attain an impressive six feet in length from snout to tail. It may look fierce, with the pointed scales adorning its back adding to its imposing stature, but it is predominantly vegetarian, feeding on leaves and fruit, although insects are also eaten by juveniles.[21] Green iguanas are ex-

Green iguanas (*Iguana iguana*) are usually found lounging in trees close to rivers. Photograph by Frank Greenaway. © The Natural History Museum, London.

cellent climbers and spend much of their life in trees, although the several dozen eggs produced annually by females are deposited in sandy holes in the ground. The green iguana is most frequently seen lounging in trees alongside rivers; when disturbed or threatened, it will make spectacular high dives into the water to make good its escape. The name of the green iguana is misleading, as individuals of this species change color as they age; juveniles are bright green, but adults are often tan or brown, usually with an orange or orange-green head. This color change is most likely related to maximizing their cryptic coloration as their habitat preferences change with age. The juveniles are more terrestrial than adults, so their bright green coloring helps them to stay hidden in undergrowth. Conversely, it is believed that the more mottled coloration of the adults is ideal for hiding in a broken tree canopy.

Despite being relatively common near rivers in the Chiquibul, the green iguana is highly threatened across its broad range from Mexico to South America. Although it has many natural enemies—such as mammals (e.g., the ocelot), birds (e.g., swallow-tailed kite), and snakes (e.g., the boa constrictor)—its current demise is largely due to human-related habitat destruction and indiscriminate hunting for food. Both the meat of the adults and their eggs are consumed. Their popularity as a source of food in Belize is such that this species is known as bamboo chicken. Unfortunately, the most highly prized individuals are females before they lay their eggs; this hunting practice is particularly harmful to the species, as it significantly reduces future population numbers.

Unlike the American crocodile (*Crocodylus actus*), which resides in the salty waters of the coast, Morelet's crocodile (*C. moreletii*) occurs primarily in freshwater habitats–lakes, rivers, swamps, and marshes. It is known only from Mexico, Guatemala, and Belize. Although this species is currently classified by IUCN as having low risk of extinction globally, it is nevertheless threatened across much of its range. In common with many of its kin, historically Morelet's crocodile has suffered the predations of commercial harvesting for its valuable skin, which is highly prized for making such items as wallets and belts. It is also hunted for meat. The plight of this species was so dire that it was believed to have been nearly extirpated from Belize by the late 1960s,[22] but it has since made a comeback. Both of Belize's native crocodile species now enjoy the protection of being listed on Appendix I of CITES (see the boxed text "Mahogany and the Convention on International Trade in Endangered Species of Wild Fauna and Flora [CITES]" in chapter 3). This bans the international trade of these species and their products from wild sources, although illicit hunting and trade continue.

Although Morelet's crocodile is best known from the northern lowlands, studies in the Chiquibul between 1991 and 2002 revealed significant populations on the Macal and Raspaculo Rivers.[23] Sightings have been made even as far upstream as Cuxta Bani. This was unexpected, as this species is rarely observed at such high altitudes (450 meters). Morelet's crocodile is known to breed with the American crocodile when these two species come into contact, but the isolated nature of the populations of Morelet's crocodile in the Chiquibul means that they are genetically pure and thus are important guardians of the species' genetic diversity.[24]

The most detailed studies on the ecology of Morelet's crocodile have been conducted in northern Belize.[25] Here nesting occurs in the wet season from June onward, with nests made on islands or on land close to water from scraped vegetation. Typically, the female lays clutches of about twenty-five eggs, and incubation takes a little over two months. In addition to nests, this species digs dens that serve as retreats for nesting females and as refuges from predators. Invertebrates (including snails) and fish provide their main source of food, although they also reportedly eat carrion and occasionally mammals, amphibians, and birds when the opportunity affords.

The Chiquibul populations of Morelet's crocodile have recently been threatened by the construction of the Chalillo Dam.

Morelet's crocodile (*C. moreletii*). © Paul Edgar.

Large stretches of the Macal and Raspaculo Rivers were flooded in 2006 as a result, including areas where this species was known to reside and nest. Although it prefers slow-moving water to fast streams, and the newly formed lake might conceivably create favorable conditions, the fluctuating water levels associated with such dams may well disrupt nesting and denning behavior. Furthermore, it is highly likely that the dam will disrupt the life cycles of the aquatic invertebrates and fish that make up part of the crocodiles' diet.[26] Careful monitoring of the existing populations of Morelet's crocodile in this area is needed in the near future. In addition to habitat loss and continued hunting, this species is threatened by pollution. For example, there is concern that the widespread use of organochlorine pesticides in northern Belize may adversely affect the long-term reproductive health of this species,[27] and mercury is another contaminant of concern.[28]

JAGUARS, CLIMBING RATS, AND JAMAICAN FRUIT-EATING BATS: THE MAMMALS OF THE CHIQUIBUL

It is a long-standing joke in the conservation field that the only animals about which the majority of the public is concerned are birds or mammals, both of which are warm-blooded like ourselves. If an animal is cute and furry or gigantic, so much the better, and thus campaigns to save such species as the orangutan, panda, and blue whale enjoy worldwide support, unlike initiatives seeking to aid the welfare of snakes, sharks, or insects. Perhaps our emotive connection with mammals is related to our common evolutionary background. Of all mammals, it is especially easy for us to emote with primates, our nearest relatives.

Although the evolutionary origin of mammals can be traced back to the Jurassic period (200–146 MYA), it was only with the demise of the dinosaurs at the end of the Cretaceous (ca. 66 MYA) that they rose to prominence to become one of the dominant groups of animals on earth (see "The Rise of the Vertebrates" in chapter 1). Today about five thousand species of mammals inhabit the planet,[29] with 152 taxa recorded for Belize.[30] Of these, nine are marine, five are endemic to the region's Maya Forest (four of these occur in the Chiquibul; see table 4.4), and two are endemic to the Yucatán Peninsula.[31] To date, ninety-seven species have been recorded for the Chiquibul Forest (see appendix C). Of all the Chiquibul mammals, by far the most diverse are the bats (order Chiroptera), represented by forty-six species; eight other mammal orders are recorded, encompassing such extremes of size as spiny pocket mice (Rodentia) and the jaguar (Carnivora). None of Belize's mammals is endemic to the country. A brief review of the events that led to the formation of Belize's fauna is given in chapter 1.

TABLE 4.4. Chiquibul mammal species endemic to the Maya Forest

Species Name	Common Name
Alouatta pigra	Mexican black howler monkey
Balantiopteryx io	Least sac-winged bat
Cryptotis mayensis	Maya small-eared shrew
Sciurus yucatanensis	Yucatán squirrel

Source: Radachowsky, *Endemism in the Maya Forest.*

USEFUL IDENTIFICATION GUIDES TO BELIZE'S MAMMALS

Beletsky, L. *The Ecotraveller's Wildlife Guide: Belize and Northern Guatemala.* San Diego, CA: Academic Press, 1999.

Emmonds, L. H. *Neotropical Rainforest Mammals: A Field Guide.* Chicago: University of Chicago Press, 1987.

AN OVERVIEW OF THE CHIQUIBUL'S MAMMAL FAMILIES

Of the ten mammalian orders occurring in the Chiquibul, the bats (Chiroptera) are by far the most diverse, with forty-six species from seven families reliably recorded for the area (appendix C). This represents about 30 percent of the total mammal species recorded for the country. Worldwide, 925 species of bat are recognized, and this group is second only to rodents (Rodentia) in diversity.[32] Bats are divided into two distinct suborders: the Megachiroptera and the Microchiroptera. Of these, the Megachiroptera (flying foxes and fruit bats) occur only in the Old World. All Belizean and Neotropical bats belong to the suborder Microchiroptera, or insect-eating bats, although their common name is a misnomer, as their diet is extremely broad—insects, fruit, flowers, fish, pollen, nectar, and even blood are all variously consumed, depending upon the species. The Microchiroptera show a number of clear anatomical traits that separate them from their Old World counterparts, but they are most famous for their extraordinary sound-based means of orientation (called echolocation). In contrast, most megachiropterans do not echolate.

The order Carnivora (carnivores) is perhaps the best known in the Chiquibul, represented by five families encompassing seventeen species: Canidae (dogs; one species), Felidae (cats; five species), Mephitidae (skunks; three species), Mustelidae (weasels; four species), and Procyonidae (raccoons; four species). Although many members of the order are indeed carnivorous, some, such as the coatimundi, are omnivorous. In addition, not all carnivores are members of Carnivora and meat-eating is not the feature that binds all members of the order together. However, many of the characters used for their classification relate to the carnivorous habit. For example, most members of this diverse order have an enlarged upper fourth premolar and first lower molar (the carnassials), which together act as efficient shears for tearing flesh. In addition, many have well-developed canines for grasping prey, and retractable claws.

The felid species are the most famous of Chiquibul's carnivores and include the region's largest predators. Of these, the jaguarundi, margay, and ocelot are relatively small, with bodies less than one meter in length and weights under 15 kilograms. In contrast, the jaguar and the puma are impressive in size, with body lengths ranging between one and two meters and weights between 30 and 160 kilograms. All the Chiquibul's cats are secretive, largely solitary species that stalk their prey and fre-

A juvenile Sowell's short-tailed bat (*Carollia sowelli*) showing the typical "noseleaf" used in echolocation by the leaf-nosed bat family (Phyllostomidae). Photograph by Frank Greenaway. © The Natural History Museum, London.

quently kill in a characteristic fashion—with a bite to the neck or head. They are rarely seen in the flesh, although their tracks and scratch marks are a relatively common sight around Las Cuevas. The cries and roars of the puma and jaguar can often be heard at night. A more detailed consideration of the jaguar is provided later in this chapter (see "The Jaguar: Master of the Forest").

The raccoon (Procyonidae) and weasel (Mustelidae) families are each represented by four species in the Chiquibul (see appendix C). The Procyonidae group is restricted to the Americas and is usually characterized by a long, distinctly banded tail and a pointed muzzle. Regionally the most conspicuous species of this group is the diurnal coatimundi, a species that has a widespread distribution from North to South America. It is frequently seen in groups (bands) of females and young. Adult males are usually excluded from these social bands except during the mating season. It is believed that this sexual partitioning reduces competition for food. In addition, the females are wary of the males, which are known to be major predators of their own young. Although single females are unable to deter predatory males by themselves, acting as a group they are more able to protect their young. If activity is detected in the canopy during a forest walk around the environs of Las Cuevas Research Station, it is highly likely to be a band of coatis. Well adapted to life in the forest canopy, they nevertheless spend much of their time foraging for arthropods and fruit on the ground, their short limbs being ideal for digging.

Two quintessential American orders of mammals are Cingulata, which includes the armadillos (family Dasypodidae), and Pilosa, the sloths and anteaters (family Myrmecophagidae). One species of armadillo is known from the Chiquibul–the nine-banded armadillo–while sloths and anteaters are represented by two species–the northern tamandua and the silky anteater. In the past all armadillos, sloths, and anteaters were classified in the order Xenarthra, which also included the now extinct giant land sloth and the glyptodont (see "The Great Trekkers: The Participants of the Interchange" in chapter 1), although their taxonomy has since been updated. Although this group diversified in South America, it famously migrated north through Central America to North America during the Great American Interchange (see "Mass Migrations: Animals and the Great American Interchange" in chapter 1).

As their name would suggest, anteaters feed primarily on ants and termites, although they will feed on other insects, such as bees, if the opportunity arises. They have no teeth and rely instead on their powerful front claws to break into social insect nests, using their extendible tongue and sticky saliva to catch their prey. Both species use their prehensile tails to grasp a branch while feeding. Although the northern tamandua can be terrestrial or arboreal and thus active by day and by night, the silky anteater (also known as the pygmy anteater) is almost exclusively arboreal and nocturnal and thus is rarely seen. During the day it rests in the canopy curled into a small ball. The ecology of the nine-banded armadillo has been covered in "The Nine-Banded Armadillo" in chapter 2.

Our closest evolutionary relatives in Belize are the monkeys (order Primates), with two species represented: the Central American spider monkey and the Mexican black howler monkey. Both occur in the Chiquibul, and the roaring of howlers (also called baboons)–especially at dusk and dawn–is one of the characteristic sounds of the forest. Although visitors may not see either species during their stay, the roars that reverberate across the forest provide a frequent reminder that we are not the only primates around. While humans are classified as primates and we have all the general physical characteristics of this order, including five-toed hands and feet and the same basic dentition, we are in a different family: Hominidae. This family is in part characterized by having a sophisticated language-based communication system and cultural development. Both the Central American spider monkey and the Mexican black howler monkey are placed in the family Atelidae and have prehensile tails, enabling them to move adeptly through the forest canopy. Because of the general interest in both these species, in-depth profiles on their ecology are provided later in this chapter (see "The Forest Swingers: The Mexican Black Howler Monkey and Central American Spider Monkey").

The order Artiodactyla is better known as the order of the even-toed ungulates on account of the plane of symmetry of the foot and the large, weight-bearing third and fourth digits. These often leave characteristic two-toed tracks. Worldwide there are over two hundred species in ten separate families, although only two occur in Neotropical

rain forest: Cervidae (deer) and Tayassui-dae (peccaries). Each is represented by two species in the Chiquibul (see appendix C). Both of the deer species–the white-tailed

The Central American spider monkey (*Ateles geoffroyi*) has effectively gained an extra arm through its grasping (prehensile) tail. © Zoë Goodwin. Courtesy The Belize Zoo.

deer and the red brocket deer–are widespread across the Neotropics, with white-tailed deer also occurring northward into North America. Although both peccaries and deer are herbivores, unlike peccaries, deer belong to a diverse group of animals known as ruminants. All ruminants have a four-chambered stomach in which the vegetable matter they have consumed is fermented. Ruminants regurgitate previously chewed and swallowed plant material (cud) stored in the first stomach chamber (the rumen) and chew it (ruminate) to ensure that the matter is thoroughly broken down before diges-tion. Of all the Chiquibul's mammals, the white-tailed deer and the brocket deer are the most widely seen, and both species forage around Las Cuevas. The two species of peccary–the collared peccary and the white-lipped peccary–are also important and conspicuous species of the Chiquibul. A more detailed treatment of their ecology is provided later in this chapter (see "The Collared Peccary and the White-Lipped Peccary").

The final two mammalian orders represented in the Chiquibul are Soricomorpha (shrews) and Perissodactyla (odd-toed ungulates). The two species of shrew belong to the family Sorocidae, while the latter group is represented in the region by a single native species, Baird's tapir. As their common name would suggest, odd-toed ungulates have an odd number of toes on each hoof, a fact clearly seen in three-toed tapir tracks. The tapir is Belize's national animal, and a more detailed consideration of its ecology is provided later in this chapter (see "The Mountain Cow").

BATS IN THE CHIQUIBUL

Although bat fossils have been dated to the early Eocene ca. 60 MYA, it is believed that they originated toward the end of the Cretaceous or beginning of the Paleocene 70–100 MYA.[33] Bats possess all the primary features that link mammals as a group but are unique in that they are winged and can fly. Unlike bird wings, which are essentially greatly modified forelimbs, bat wings are largely modified hands, a fact alluded to in the Greek name for the order to which bats belong—Chiroptera means "hand wings." Bat wings also differ from those of birds in that they are formed from an outstretched thin membrane supported by the body, limbs, and tail rather than from feathers. In addition to flight, bat wings play an important role in cooling, by nature of the rich supply of blood vessels that serve to supply the flight muscles and radiate heat. Bats are infamous for being vampires—deriving their sustenance from drinking the blood of other creatures, a trait known as sanguivory. However, it is erroneous to associate sanguivory with all bats. In fact, only 3 species of the 925 known to exist are vampires. Bat diets are incredibly diverse, and different groups specialize in eating a diverse range of foods, including insects, fruit, flowers, fish, pollen, and nectar. Dietary habits were once used by taxonomists to classify bats into distinct groups, but this approach was long ago abandoned.

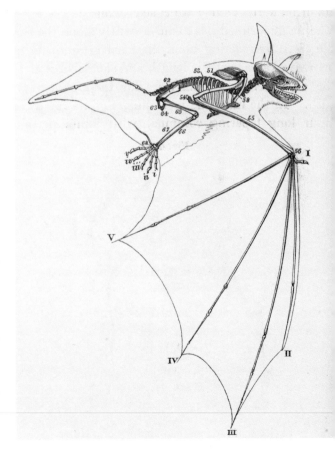

Drawing of the wing of a bat. From Richard Owen, *On the Nature of Limbs* (1849). © The Natural History Museum, London.

Bats begin to forage around dusk and are active at night, and one of the most interesting features of microchiropteran bat ecology is the means by which these animals are able to navigate to avoid obstacles and locate their prey in the dark. As humans we rely largely on visual imagery to orient ourselves, and this depends on light. Although bats can see, their ability to navigate at night is enhanced acoustically by bouncing high-frequency sounds released through their mouths or noses off their surroundings and picking up the echoes with their ears. This is called echolocation and is similar in principal to sonar. So sophisticated is this means of hearing that bats are able to gauge an object's size, shape, texture, and movement from the echoes they hear in the absence of light. Bats are not unique as mammals in using ultrasonic navigation. A number of other, unrelated groups have evolved similar systems, including the cetaceans (whales and dolphins) and even some members of the order Insectivora.

COMPILING THE CHECKLIST OF THE BATS OF THE CHIQUIBUL REGION

BY BRUCE AND CAROLYN MILLER

With its caves, its varied karst topography, and the large expanse of intact forested habitat, the greater Chiquibul—comprising the Chiquibul Forest Reserve, the Chiquibul National Park, and the Caracol Archaeological Reserve—is an important area in Mesoamerica for the conservation of bats. However, despite being key contributors to mammalian diversity in the Neotropics and frequently representing more than 55 percent of the terrestrial mammal fauna, bats are not often included in broad biodiversity surveys, and the Chiquibul has not had the intensity of bat surveys that their importance warrants. This is due to the challenges of collecting data on bats; without capture or the use of sophisticated acoustic methods that assist the researcher in characterizing bats through their calls, identification is problematic.

The historical bat records for Belize and the Chiquibul have primarily been based on the use of static fine-mesh nets to snare flying bats (mist netting) or hand-capture at cave roost sites. Although such sampling techniques provide valuable data, mist nets are biased toward the capture of species of leaf-nosed bats (Phyllostomidae) and rarely

sample species from the other families. The use of harp traps—a more sophisticated version of the mist net—and acoustic survey methods that identify bat species through their calls are increasingly commonplace in Belize and in recent years have provided data that has rapidly changed our knowledge of national species distributions.[34]

Information on the bat species present in the Chiquibul region can be gleaned from literature, museum collections, and field research.[35] There have been many taxonomic changes and revisions of Chiroptera taxa over the past ten years, and all names used in the checklist of appendix C reflect the most recent understanding of taxa.

Bat surveys at Caracol date back to two intensive mist net surveys in February and May 1990,[36] with sporadic mist netting continuing over the next five years using nets placed for intensive bird surveys.[37] In 2009 Caracol was also sampled for bats with harp traps and acoustic monitoring stations over a three-night period, further augmenting the species list. Mist net surveys were also conducted at Las Cuevas and Natural Arch during several nights in July 1992,[38] with additional surveys using harp traps and acoustic monitoring carried out at Las Cuevas in June 2001 and March–April

2008. The 2008 surveys also included netting and acoustic sampling at several cave sites outside of the Las Cuevas area and at Millionario.

The bat fauna of the Chiquibul region consists of seven families, thirty-one genera, and forty-six species—63 percent of the seventy-three known species occurring in Belize. This includes a now extinct species of bat, Dracula's vampire (*Desmodus draculae*), which is found only as a fossil. Two of the species—Thomas's sac-winged bat (*Balantiopteryx io*) and Van Gelder's bat (*Bauerus dubiaquercus*)—are of international conservation concern and recognized by IUCN as Vulnerable and Near Threatened, respectively. Currently there are several "sono-species" that represent distinct but yet unknown species based on their unique vocal signatures, and it is very likely that deep into the southern reaches of the Chiquibul new species records will be discovered for the country as well.

Sowell's short-tailed bat (*Carollia sowelli*). Illustration by John Gould, from Charles Darwin, *The Zoology of the Voyage of the H.M.S.* Beagle, part 2, *Mammalia* (1838–1839). © The Natural History Museum, London.

The tent-making bat (*Artibeus watsoni*) is famous for making its own roosting place, which it fashions by chewing a leaf so that it collapses and forms an overnight shelter. Photograph by Frank Greenaway. © The Natural History Museum, London.

THE PRIMARY BAT FAMILIES OF THE CHIQUIBUL

Of the forty-six species of bat known from the Chiquibul, the majority (twenty-two extant species) are leaf-nosed bats (Phyllostomidae). This large family is found exclusively in the New World and is extremely diverse both in form and in the types of food consumed, although the majority are insect eaters. The family name is derived from the Greek *phyllon* (leaf) and *stoma* (opening), and most family members have a leaf-shaped flap of skin above the nostrils. Rather than emitting echolocation calls through their mouths like most other bats, phyllostomids do so through their nose, using their

TABLE 4.5.

Bats of Las Cuevas Cave

Scientific Name	Common Name
Emballonuridae (Sac-Winged Bats)	
Balantiopteryx io	Thomas's sac-winged bat
Mormoopidae (Leaf-Chinned Bats)	
Pteronotus parnellii	Parnell's moustached bat
Natalidae (Funnel-Eared Bats)	
Natalus mexicanus	Mexican funnel-eared bat
Phyllostomidae (Leaf-Nosed Bats)	
Artibeus jamaicensis	Jamaican fruit-eating bat
A. phaeotis	Pygmy fruit-eating bat
A. watsoni	Tent-making bat
Carollia perspicillata	Seba's short-tailed bat
C. sowelli	Sowell's short-tailed bat
Diphylla ecaudata	Hairy-legged vampire bat
Glossophaga soricina	Common long-tongued bat
Micronycteris microtis	Common big-eared bat
Trinycteris nicefori	Niceforo's bat
Vespertilionidae (Plain-Nosed Bats)	
Myotis elegans	Elegant myotis
M. keaysi	Hairy-legged myotis

Source: Greenaway, The Bats of Las Cuevas Cave.

"nose leaves" to help focus the sounds outward. Their diversity is such that leaf-nosed bats are divided into five subfamilies. These include Glossophaginae, whose members eat fruit, nectar, and pollen, and Desmodontinae, which includes the Chiquibul's two species of vampire bat—the common vampire bat (Desmodus rotundus) and the hairy-legged vampire bat (Diphylla ecaudata). The other bat families represented are Emballonuridae (sac-winged bats), Mormoopidae (leaf-chinned bats), Natalidae (funnel-eared bats), Noctilionidae (fish-eating bats), and Verspertilionidae (plain-nosed bats), which is the largest and most widely distributed bat family in the world. Most plain-nosed bats are insectivorous, and although they can catch their prey in their mouths, some are famed for using their wings like a tennis racket, batting the insects into the tail membrane from where they are subsequently consumed. The Chiquibul's only fish-eating bat—Noctilio leporinus (commonly known as the Mexican bulldog bat)—skims over the surface of calm water and catches its prey by trailing its feet like grappling irons.[39]

BATS OF LAS CUEVAS CAVE

The cave from which Las Cuevas derives its springwater provides a cool respite from the heat of the day. Its shady entrance is guarded by clumps of tepejilote palm, and once the eyes have adjusted to the diminished light, the great size of the cavern is startling. This silent and magical underworld was once frequented by the ancient Maya. Shards of ancient ceramic pottery litter the floor, and an artificial wall seals off the corridor that leads past a fossilized riverbed and the glittering calcite stalactite and stalagmite formations of the cave's interior. These deeper recesses were sacred to the Maya, and access was restricted.

The cave's single passageway is circular, and if one follows it to its conclusion, one finally emerges in a gallery at the roof of the cavern entrance to look back at the shafts of sunlight penetrating the forest canopy. All caves are fragile environments, and many are important conservation areas. The cave at Las Cuevas is no exception, and access to its inner chambers is still controlled. Not only does it represent an important regional archaeological and geological site but it is also a prime roosting location for birds such as Ridgeway's rough-winged swallow (*Stelgidopteryx ridgwayi*). In addition, it supports substantial breeding colonies of bats, including Thomas's sac-winged bat (*Balantiopteryx io*) and elegant myotis (*Myotis elegans*);[40] the former inhabits the back regions of the cave while the latter favors areas closer to the entrance. In total, fourteen species of bat are known to roost and breed in the cave or visit it (see table 4.5).[41] Anyone venturing close by should take care not to disturb these inhabitants.

VAMPIRE BATS

Most famous as the inspiration for Bram Stoker's legend of Count Dracula, true vampire bats belong to the Desmodontinae subfamily of the leaf-nosed bats (Phyllostomidae). Only three species are known to exist: the common vampire bat (*Desmodus rotundus*), the white-winged vampire bat (*Diaemus youngi*), and the hairy-legged vampire bat (*Diphylla ecaudata*). Although all three species are recorded for Belize, only the common vampire bat and the hairy-legged vampire bat are known from the Chiquibul. Both roost in caves, and the hairy-legged vampire bat is a common inhabitant of Las Cuevas Cave.

Although similar in many aspects to other members of the family, vampire bats have a number of adaptations suited to their blood-sucking habit. These include highly modified upper incisors and canines, which assist them in wounding their prey. In addition, they have anticoagulants in their saliva to keep the blood of their victims flowing freely. Typically the common vampire bat lands close to its quarry and then crawls to it; after puncturing and opening an area of skin, it laps at the wound with a grooved tongue, which facilitates the transfer of blood into its mouth.

Although few humans in Belize are ever preyed on by vampire bats, one would be ill-advised to expose oneself to their bite, as they are common vectors of rabies. In particular, the common vampire bat presents a serious risk, as it will feed on any warm-blooded creature, although livestock are a favorite. In contrast, the hairy-legged vampire bat is believed to feed primarily on birds.[42]

The hairy-legged vampire bat (*Diphylla ecaudata*), which has been recorded from Las Cuevas Cave. Photograph by Frank Greenaway. © The Natural History Museum, London.

With its muscular, stocky body, sturdy limbs, and vicelike jaws, the jaguar is an im-mensely powerful hunter and the top predator of the Maya Forest. Weighing approxi-mately fifty-five kilograms and measuring two meters from tip to tail, it is also the larg-est member of the cat family in the Americas, albeit one of the least studied.[43] Jaguars have a widespread distribution from northern Mexico to Argentina; although they are usually associated with tropical rain forest, they can also occur in arid scrublands, pine savanna, and grasslands, where they often maintain close proximity to watercourses.

This elusive species is shrouded in regional legend and folklore. The ancient Maya held the jaguar in high esteem, and its pelt was symbolic of elite and ceremonial sta-tus.[44] Jaguar motifs are commonly observed in ancient Maya temple carvings and art; this species was believed to symbolize strength and courage and was regarded as a guardian animal spirit. Jaguar imagery was commonly associated with war and hunt-ing, and Maya warriors are often depicted wearing jaguar pelts.

Jaguars can vary widely in their coat pattern. Although the majority have dark clusters of spots (rosettes) or irregular blotches marking their light brown fur, a few are uniformly dark brown or black. Despite looking very different from their relatives, these so-called "melanistic" or black jaguars are the same species, with their difference in pigmentation being controlled by a dominant gene allele. Such jaguars are rare, however. Despite appearing dark, close observation usually reveals the jaguar's usual rosette patterning.

A jaguar sighting is considered the holy grail of the ecotourist, and there is a strong international association of this creature with Belize. This owes much to the existence of the Cockscomb Basin Wildlife Sanctuary, established in 1986 specifically to protect this species.[45] The Belize Zoo has also done much to raise the profile of the jaguar's plight. As the top predator in the region's forests, the jaguar has become an interna-tional flagship species for conservation. Considered Near Threatened by the IUCN, its current range across the Neotropics is estimated to be less than 50 percent of the area it inhabited in 1900.[46] Further deforestation decreases the availability of suitable territory for this species with each successive year that passes. In addition to habitat destruction, jaguars have suffered greatly from hunting out of fear, for the sake of sport, or because of their beautiful and valuable fur. Indeed, before Las Cuevas became a research station, it was famous in the 1970s for being the base of a legendary jaguar hunter, John Little, who set up camp near Las Cuevas Cave and hunted his quarry with dogs, usually with paying game hunters in tow. Fortunately the time of legalized jaguar hunting is over, and in 1973 the jaguar was listed on Appendix I of CITES. Although the hunting of jag-uars became illegal in Belize in 1981, illegal trade in jaguar skin continues. In addition, jaguars are still occasionally killed by farmers who view them as serial "cattle killers." Education programs that seek to improve animal husbandry and raise awareness of the importance of jaguars are going some way toward reducing jaguar-human conflict.

The jaguar (*Panthera onca*) is the top predator of the Maya Forest. © Pascal Blachier.

Few of us are ever lucky enough to see this magnificent, beautiful, solitary beast in its natural environment. The only evidence we have for its existence are tantalizing glimpses of huge paw prints left on trails in wilderness areas, scat (feces), scratch markings, and the occasional roar heard from afar. The rest must be left to our imagination. Although we may not see them, Belize is known to have relatively healthy populations of jaguars due to its enviable network of protected areas. A number of researchers have attempted to estimate the area roamed and patrolled by a jaguar (its home range), with the Chiquibul and Las Cuevas providing one geographic focus for this work.[47] These studies have variously involved the remote tracking of jaguars with radio collars or networks of camera traps triggered by motion, heat, or the interruption of beams of infrared radiation (see the boxed text "Sound and Sight: Radio Telemetry and Camera Trapping" later in this chapter). Individual jaguars can be identified by the rosette patterns on their coat, and it is possible to know how frequently an individual jaguar has been caught on any particular camera by studying the markings in the photograph. Both radio- and camera-trapping studies have yielded largely similar results, indicating that population densities are low. In the Chiquibul, for example, an average density of 7.5 adults has been estimated for one hundred square kilometers of forested territory.[48] Research conducted in the Cockscomb Basin has estimated home ranges of twenty-eight to forty square kilometers for males and ten square kilometers for females. However, range sizes may vary between seasons, with smaller areas typically occupied by females and during the wet season.[49] In addition, the individual ranges of jaguars can overlap.[50] Clearly, understanding the home range of this species for a particular area is essential when planning reserve sizes; these must be large if healthy populations of jaguars are to be adequately conserved. Although the Chiquibul and adjacent forest regions of the Maya Mountains are vast and cover an area in excess of 550,000 hectares and support an estimated population of about 400 jaguars,[51] a study in South America concluded that jaguar population sizes need to be greater than 650 individuals for the jaguars to be healthy and viable in the long term.[52] Thus, even the remote Maya Mountain region may not safeguard this species alone, and maintaining connectivity between this forest stronghold and other regional forest areas such as Gallon Jug in Belize and the Petén region of Guatemala will be critical in ensuring its survival.

Jaguars are largely nocturnal and feed on a wide range of animals, with armadillos, deer, peccaries, agoutis, and lizards all typical prey species. Studies of jaguar scat undertaken in the Cockscomb Basin indicate that, of these, armadillos represent by far the most significant component of their diet, occurring in over 50 percent of all feces investigated.[53] Elsewhere across their range they are known to have a predilection for peccaries.[54] What is certain is that their diet is versatile and the exact food favored varies from region to region according to prey availability and abundance. Even crocodiles and cattle can form a component of the jaguar's diet. However, the latter is only rarely preyed upon, and such incidences are thought to involve old, weak jaguars who find domesticated herds easier targets than their usual wild food of choice. Typically, jaguars will hunt alone by patrolling trails or lying in ambush, and once they have detected a likely meal, they will stalk the victim and attempt to position themselves as close as possible before pouncing. Like lions, tigers, and leopards, jaguars typically kill with a bite to the throat or neck; unlike their relatives, jaguars are also known to kill by biting through their prey's skull. Once killed, their quarry is dragged into dense cover before feeding begins. One might expect there to be significant competition between the jaguar and the other large regional cat, the puma. However, although studies have shown that there can be significant overlap in their ranges and times of activity, pumas are generally more adaptable in their habitat and tend to be more prevalent in drier ecosystems.[55] In addition, it is thought that competition between these species is reduced by ecological specialization, with jaguars taking larger prey than the puma and the puma showing greater diversity in its diet.

The roaring of jaguars is an effective means of communication and may function to bring them together for mating. Typically between one and four cubs (usually two) are born after a gestation of about one hundred days. The cubs are at first entirely dependent on the female for survival and suckle milk for three to six months, with meat eating beginning as they get older. After eighteen months the young frequently make their own forays into the forest and can kill independently from their mother; by two years of age they are wholly independent. Although they can live in captivity for twenty-five years, it has been estimated that in the Belizean wilds jaguars rarely live for more than eleven years.[56]

THE MOUNTAIN COW

Known locally in Belize as the mountain cow, Baird's tapir (*Tapirus bairdii*) is one of Belize's most enigmatic mammals and its adopted national animal. It represents one of only four remaining species of a genus whose fossil lineage dates back nearly 50 MYA. Of the other three species, one occurs in Malaysia and two in South America. As an odd-toed ungulate, the tapir's closest taxonomic relative is the horse family (Equidae). The local name for Baird's tapir is apt, for this gentle and largely solitary herbivore can weigh up to three hundred kilograms and attain two meters in length. Indeed, this impressive grazing creature is the largest native terrestrial mammal in the Neotropics.

Tapirs are popular creatures in Belize due to their association with the national identity, and the injured and orphaned tapirs occasionally taken into care by the Belize Zoo form one of its main attractions. The animal's popularity is also partly due to its curious extensible elongated upper lip (proboscis) and an ability to spray urine over those who invade its personal space.

Across its range from southern Mexico to northern Colombia and Ecuador, Baird's tapir is classified as Vulnerable by IUCN, although the species is considered endangered with extinction in most countries where it occurs.[57] Like many species, the tapir is threatened regionally by hunting and forest destruction. The plight of the tapir is exacerbated by its low reproductive rate, with gestation taking thirteen months and the single offspring spending about two years with the mother before becoming independent. The Chiquibul region provides one of the last strongholds in Mesoamerica for this animal, and several local studies have revealed a strong association between it and floodplain or fringing riverine forest.[58] These vegetation types provide the species with much of its diet. During an environmental impact assessment for the Chalillo Dam of the Macal and Raspaculo watersheds conducted in 2001, 76 percent of the observations of this animal occurred in such habitats.[59] The study indicated that the Raspaculo and Macal Rivers were favored sites for this secretive animal, and Baird's tapir is known to frequent, feed in, and rest in rivers and pools. Its population density is believed to be low within the Chiquibul, with density estimates ranging from only one to four individuals per twenty square kilometers. Belize is thought to support a population of many hundred to a few thousand individuals.[60]

Tapirs browse on a wide variety of leaves, shrubs, saplings, and fruit, with young shoots often preferred and early successional phases of disturbed habitats providing ideal feeding locations.[61] Grasses make up a significant proportion of the food intake

The Raspaculo and Macal Rivers are favored sites for the secretive Baird's tapir (*Tapirus bairdii*). © Humberto Wohlers. Courtesy Belize Zoo.

of Baird's tapir, and fruit from a range of tree species also provides an important dietary supplement, especially in the dry season. Fruit-producing species eaten in the Chiquibul include the breadnut (*Brosimum alicastrum*), the hog plum (*Spondias radlkoferi*), the gumbo-limbo (*Bursera simaruba*), figs (*Ficus* spp.), chicle (*Manilkara* spp.), and the guanacaste (*Enterolobium cyclocarpum*). Although a significant proportion of the ingested seed of certain species (e.g., breadnut) may be crushed by the tapir's teeth or fail to survive the many days they take to pass through its gut, of the fifty-one fruits known to be eaten by Baird's tapir, the seeds of at least thirty-nine species (76 percent) have been shown to still be viable in tapir dung.[62] Thus, this species is thought to be an important seed disperser of certain tree species, with the dung itself providing a useful growing medium for germination. It has even been suggested that tapirs are one of the few surviving natural dispersers, or potentially surrogate dispersers, of large-seeded, indehiscent fruited trees such as the guanacaste and hog plum.[63] These trees may have coevolved with members of the region's now extinct megafauna such as the mastodon, with their well-protected seed evolved to be dispersed by these now long-absent agents.[64] Tapirs can be considered one of the last representatives of the Pleistocene megafauna, and with the extinction of the original natural dispersers of certain tree species, tapirs are potentially critical to ensuring their continued survival. Tapirs usually defecate in water, and this behavior may further aid seed dispersal, with species whose seeds are able to withstand immersion (e.g., hog plum) particularly benefitting from this.

THE FOREST SWINGERS: THE MEXICAN BLACK HOWLER MONKEY AND THE CENTRAL AMERICAN SPIDER MONKEY

The Mexican black howler provides one of the characteristic sounds of not only the Chiquibul but also Belize. Although relatively small, it has a spectacular roar worthy of a beast many times its size: the sound can carry with ease across a mile of forest. For the uninitiated, it can be an unnerving experience to lie in a tent at night and hear the outrageous roars emanating from outside, but there is no need for alarm. Like its relative the Central American spider monkey, the howler monkey is vegetarian. These two New World monkeys (family Atelidae) are the only nonhuman primates found in Belize; both occur in the Chiquibul.

The Mexican black howler monkey (*Alouatta pigra*), more commonly known in Belize as the baboon, is one of the country's best-known species. This is due in part to a high-profile conservation project centered at Bermuda Landing (in Orange Walk District) focusing specifically on protecting this animal, and in part to its characteristic howl. Male howlers are able to produce their infeasibly loud call by means of a large, hollow hyoid (tongue-supporting) bone in the throat that acts as a resonating chamber. Typically baboons roar at dawn or dusk, although they can be heard throughout the day. Their calling enables competing troops to identify their territories and serves to reduce fighting between them. This species is restricted to southern Mexico, western Guatemala, and Belize and is often associated with riverine forest.

The baboon is larger than its locally residing arboreal cousin, the spider monkey, and is stockier in build; it is also an adept climber with a prehensile tail. Baboons live in smaller troops than spider monkeys—typically of between four and eight individuals, usually made up of two adults and their young. For the most part, social groups are stable, although they can be temporarily disrupted after catastrophic events such as hurricanes.[65] In contrast to spider monkeys, the juvenile male howlers leave the troop to form new communities, not the females. Although their territory varies greatly in size depending on food availability, it is usually smaller than that of the spider monkey—typically between five and six hectares; howlers travel shorter distances for foraging during the day, often only a few hundred meters.[66] Studies from the Petén region and Mexico indicate that in undisturbed forest howler monkeys' density typically ranges from thirteen to eighteen individuals per square kilometer of forest.[67] All species of howler monkey are famed for being sedentary, and they can be inactive for large periods of the day. At Monkey River, for example, it has been shown that they are inactive for 66 percent of the time and feed for 19 percent.[68] In total, 59 percent of their feeding time throughout the year is spent consuming leaves, with the remainder spent eating fruit. Although the research identified thirty-five species of

The Mexican black howler monkey (*Alouatta pigra*) is known in Belize as the baboon. The characteristic call of the male howler is the result of a large, hollow bone in the throat that acts as a resonating chamber. © Humberto Wohlers. Courtesy The Belize Zoo.

trees and vines consumed by baboons, in this specific case, over 60 percent of their diet consisted of white Maya (*Miconia argentea*), fig (*Ficus* spp.), cochito (*Myriciara floribunda*), and kaway (*Pterocarpus* spp.). Between January and March, 86 percent of their time is spent consuming leaves, whereas fruit dominates their diet between April and July due to its greater abundance. Their sedentary life-style has partially been explained by their low-quality, leaf-based diet and fermentative digestion, which require them to minimize energy. However, although widely regarded as leaf-eaters, researchers studying this species consider them better described as "as frugivorous as possible and as folivorous as necessary."[69]

The Central American spider monkey (*Ateles geoffroyi*) is a social creature, often living in communities or troops of over twenty individuals. It occurs throughout Central America from northeastern Mexico to northwestern Colombia. Although known primarily as frugivorous, this species also readily eats leaves of such trees as figs (*Ficus* spp.), breadnut (*Brosimum alicastrum*), cherry (*Pseudolmedia spuria*), and trumpet (*Cecropia* spp.) in addition to flowers, roots, decaying wood, insects, and honey. Spider monkeys are known to be important dispersers of seed; despite a lack of ecological studies in the Chiquibul, research in the neighboring Petén region of Guatemala has indicated that this species spends 57 percent of its feeding time eating fruit pulp, with 56 percent of its diet made up of the fruit, seeds, leaves, and buds of only one tree species: the breadnut.[70] However, during times of drought, there can be a greater reliance on species such as the fig. Studies on the seed of both horse's balls (*Stemmadenia donnell-smithii*) and copal (*Protium copal*)—two common species of the Chiquibul eaten by spider monkeys—have shown that they pass undamaged through the monkey's gut and readily germinate once ejected. As the home range of the spider monkey is believed to be many hundreds of hectares and they can cover as much as 5 kilometers each day, they are ideal dispersing agents. Of all species, the spider monkey deserves to be crowned king of the swingers. Unusual for a mammal, this monkey has arms that are considerably longer than its legs, enabling it to move readily between feeding trees by swinging (brachiating) hand to hand through the branches. In evolving the ability to move in this way, the spider monkey has a greatly reduced thumb, which would otherwise hinder swinging, although it has effectively gained an extra arm through its grasping (prehensile) tail, which is strong and extremely dexterous. The spider monkey is readily able to hang securely by its tail, which frees both arms for feeding. The social organization of the spider monkey is curious: although it is a social species that lives in large communities, the troop itself comprises a series of associated and changeable smaller subgroups of only a few individuals—frequently of the same sex—which forage independently of one another.[71] It is believed that in addition to increasing foraging efficiency when food is scarce, this behavior may improve territory defense and protection of young. There is also often a skewed sex ratio in spider monkey troops, with more adult females than males, due either to control before birth or to higher mortality of males when juvenile.[72] This can be particularly marked in regions where food resources are in short supply. A number of theories have been proposed to explain this phenomenon; for example, it may be a mechanism to reduce resource competition. On reaching maturity, female spider monkeys move away from the community where they were brought up to join others, while the males stay within the community where they were born.

THE COLLARED PECCARY AND
THE WHITE-LIPPED PECCARY

It always comes as a surprise to visitors that the Las Cuevas staff warn of the dangers of encountering not the predatory forest jaguar but a much smaller, predominantly vegetarian social animal: the peccary. This is sound advice. The chance of being attacked by a jaguar is almost negligible; indeed, being gored by a peccary is also extremely unlikely, but it does represent a more probable danger while visitors are walking in the forest. Peccaries belong to their own distinct family, Tayassuidae, and are even-toed ungulates (Artiodactyla) closely related to swine. This physical resemblance has earned them the name wild pig, although "warrie" is another favored term. Peccaries live in social groups, and although they do not attack humans, when startled (and particularly with young) they can panic. If one is caught in the ensuing maelstrom, their sharp teeth and powerful jaws can cause considerable damage. Usually, however, on account of a pungent smell emitted from a scent gland on their back and the loud gnashing of their teeth, one often smells and hears them long before they come into sight. In the unlikely event that one is faced with a pack of irate peccaries, the advice given is usually to climb a tree, although more often than not they will quickly pass to the side, being as eager as the onlooker to go about their business undisturbed.

Restricted to the New World, three species of peccary exist, two of which can be found in Belize: the collared peccary (*Pecari tajacu*) and the white-lipped peccary (*Tayassu pecari*). Both are widespread throughout Central and South America, although the former has a wider latitudinal distribution and is more adaptable to a broader range of open and closed natural and disturbed habitats; the latter is usually found only in closed broadleaf forest.[73] As their common names would suggest, collared and white-lipped peccaries can be distinguished from each other by the markings of their pelage: the former has a distinct white collar and the latter a white strip along the mouth and under the jaw. The third member of the family—the Chacoan peccary (*Catagonus wagneri*)—is restricted to dry forest habitats in parts of Paraguay, Bolivia, Argentina, and Brazil. All peccaries are famed for their relatively poor eyesight, although their senses of hearing and sight are well developed.

Weighing approximately twenty kilograms, the collared peccary is the more frequently seen of the Chiquibul's two species, although the larger white-lipped peccary

can occur in much larger herds—there are many accounts across its range of hundreds of animals foraging together. Typically the

The collared peccary (*Pecari tajacu*) is the more often seen of the Chiquibul's two peccary species. © Jan Ševčík.

collared peccary roams in herds of between ten and thirty individuals, although these herds may sporadically break up into smaller foraging groups. The gregarious habit gives strength in numbers and may provide collective protection from predation.[74] Social cohesion in peccaries is maintained through grunting and close physical contact between individuals, with rubbing of bodies a frequent occurrence.[75] Recognized as omnivorous, they primarily eat a broad range of plant material, including roots and tubers, and both species are known to have a predilection for fruit. If the opportunity allows, they will also feed on small animals such as amphibians and reptiles. Fruits of the families Sapotaceae (e.g., *Manilkara* spp.), Anacardiaceae (e.g., *Spondias* spp.), Fabaceae (e.g., *Enterolobium* spp.), Arecaceae (e.g., *Acrocomia* spp.), and Moraceae (e.g., *Ficus* spp.) are all known to be widely consumed. Although both species consume similar types of food, one means by which the two species might be able to coexist relates to the differing force of their bite; white-lipped peccaries are able to crack harder seed with their teeth, which gives them the ability to potentially specialize in feeding on plant species that collared peccaries are unable to use.[76] In addition, the two species have different foraging behaviors in that the collared peccary, with its narrower snout, is able to root deeper into the soil. Differences between the two species' respective herd sizes and home ranges may also play an important role; white-lipped peccaries occur in bigger herds and typically roam farther, sometimes as far as ten kilometers per day.[77]

The smaller home ranges of the collared peccary may allow them to quickly consume fallen fruit as soon as it is available, whereas the larger herds of white-lipped peccaries are more likely to capitalize on species with clumped distributions. Although no research has been conducted on the feeding habits of peccaries in the Chiquibul, such as Baird's tapir, they are considered to be important as both predators and dispersers of seed, with a proportion of those consumed passing through the gut unharmed. Given their wide home ranges, both species deposit seeds a significant distance from the parent plant and play a significant ecological role in maintaining forest diversity. They also have similar gestation periods of about five months, resulting in a usual litter of two. This contrasts starkly with the true pigs of the Old World (family Suidae), which have larger litters.

MAMMALS AND RESEARCH IN THE CHIQUIBUL

In addition to general inventories of regional mammal diversity and abundance, much of the research work conducted at Las Cuevas has focused on clarifying the population status and home ranges of the larger cats, most notably the jaguar and the ocelot. Despite their importance as predators, relatively little is known about their behavior and ecology due to their elusive nature and nocturnal habits.[78] One critical piece of information required for their effective conservation is the amount of space needed to maintain a healthy population. Favored means of obtaining such data are through the use of radio collars and telemetry, camera trapping, and global positioning systems. The first two techniques have been used extensively in the Chiquibul (see boxed text).

SOUND AND SIGHT: RADIO TELEMETRY AND CAMERA TRAPPING

Because the felids of Central and South America are rarely seen, information on their ecology traditionally has relied on studying their tracks, scratch marks left on trees, and feces (scat). In recent years, however, technology has advanced sufficiently to enable more sophisticated techniques to be added to the ecologist's armory. The first of these is called telemetry and relies on capturing the cat under study and fitting it with a radio collar. Its movement can then be tracked remotely from hilltop locations using antennae that can discern the direction of the cat's radio collar from the recorder. If three or more antennae are used simultaneously from widely spaced points, it is possible to get an accurate fix on the position of the cat at that moment. Although this system works well once operational, the process is intrusive—the animal must first be caught and tranquilized before the radio collar can be fitted—as well as potentially dangerous, both to the animal, which may be injured in the trap, and to the researcher who must fit the collar. In addition, it is highly labor intensive to monitor the animal at frequent intervals thereafter. Recent years have seen an increased use of camera traps triggered by heat or motion through the interruption of beams of infrared radiation. Individual jaguars can be identified by the unique rosette patterns on their coat that are consistent throughout their life.

CONTINUED NEXT PAGE

By analyzing information on the geographic range and spread of the camera trap grid, along with photographic data on the number of times individuals are caught on film by specific cameras, researchers can estimate jaguar population sizes and density. However, the statistical models used to make such calculations assume a closed population with no births, deaths, immigration, or emigration. Of critical importance for achieving reliable estimates of home range when conducting such studies is the placement of the cameras at intervals that are appropriate for the expected home range of the species in question and the habitat studied. For example, it has been shown that a grid of twenty cameras at grid intervals of 1.5 kilometers in an area of 50 square kilometers is appropriate for ocelots in rain forest in Central America.

In a study of jaguars conducted in the Chiquibul in 2002,[79] a grid of eighteen remotely triggered camera trapping stations was established across the forest region covering an area of 165 square kilometers. This research was conducted over a two-month period at the start of the dry season (January–February). Seven individual jaguars were photographed during this work, of which four were male, one was female, and two were of undetermined sex. Through complex statistical calculations the data suggests that there are between seven and nine jaguars per one hundred square kilometers of forest, although the researchers believe that this may be an underestimate. Either way, when compared with other locations across the Neotropics where comparable studies have been done, the Chiquibul appears to have

a relatively high population density of this threatened species. Considering the great size of the Chiquibul, which covers an area of 177,000 hectares, and the known extirpation of jaguars across their historic range, it is clearly an extremely important area for preserving this flagship species. Felids with large space requirements, such as jaguars, are good focal species for conservation, as the effective protection of their habitat will also protect the many other species that reside within their range. Indeed, although the study described above focused primarily on jaguars, the camera traps were also effective in recording a number of other regional animal species (see table 4.6), of which the Virginia opossum, common opossum, and white-lipped peccary were the most frequently caught. However, the analysis of population data for these species is problematic because of the difficulty in identifying distinct individuals from photographs. The long-term health of the existing jaguar population of the Chiquibul will ultimately depend on the maintenance of the population densities of its prey species, such as armadillos, deer, and peccaries. One cause for concern is illegal hunting of these species for bushmeat, much of it related to illegal *Chamaedorea* (xaté) leaf harvesting (see "Xaté, Leaf of Gold" in chapter 3); there is concern that if such activities are not checked, the Chiquibul's biodiversity could be degraded. Although a tropical forest may be huge in extent, have a complete forest canopy, and thus look to be the picture of biological health from a helicopter, it can be largely devoid of its larger animal species, known as the "empty forest syndrome."

TABLE 4.6. Common animal species recorded by camera traps in the Chiquibul

Carnivores	Herbivores	Birds	Other
Jaguar	Brocket deer	Ocellated turkey	Armadillo
Puma	White-tailed deer	Chacalaca	Common opossum
Ocelot	Collared peccary	Tinamou	Virginia opossum
Margay	White-lipped peccary	Curassow	Tamandua
Tayra	Depp's squirrel	Guan	
Striped hog-nosed skunk	Paca		
Coati	Agouti		
Gray fox	Mouse		

Source: Kelly, "Jaguar Monitoring in the Chiquibul Forest," p. 28.

Every jaguar has a distinctive pattern of rosettes (spots) on its coat, enabling researchers to identify individuals through camera trapping. © Stephen Blackmore.

In-depth research on the ocelot (*Leopardus pardalis*) has been conducted at Las Cuevas. About the size of dog and weighing ten to fifteen kilograms, this beautiful species is much smaller than the jaguar, although like its larger relative, it has beautifully patterned fur that attracted the attention of the fur trade in the past, especially from the 1950s to the 1980s.[80] The ocelot is widespread across the Americas from southern North America into Argentina, but due to hunting and habitat loss it is now rare and endangered in many areas. Whereas it has been observed in a range of ecosystems, including mangrove and savanna, its preferred habitat is rain forest. In the wild, ocelots are believed to live for about ten years, with the majority of individuals attaining adult size and breeding only after two years. On average, a litter of one or two cubs is produced annually, and the female takes sole responsibility for their care. Lactation can last up to nine months, although cubs will leave the den and accompany their mother after eight weeks. Of the estimated five offspring produced by a female ocelot during her lifetime, only two will survive to reach reproductive age.[81]

Ocelots are solitary creatures with excellent sight, preying on a wide range of mammals, lizards, and ground birds. Opossums are particularly favored prey in Belize.[82] Although significant competition for food might be expected with other felids of similar size, such as the margay, it is believed that conflict is minimized through ecological separation. For example, food competition with the arboreal margay is reduced, as the ocelot is predominantly terrestrial, despite being an adept climber. Differences in activity times also enable coexistence; the jaguarundi, for example, is active during the day, while the ocelot is nocturnal.

Research on ocelots conducted at Las Cuevas in 2003 and 2004 using radio telemetry and camera trapping techniques has provided useful density estimates of this species for the Chiquibul as well as insights into its home range.[83] Data obtained from the study of six ocelots collected over one year suggests that, on average, home ranges are twenty to thirty square kilometers, depending on the statistical approach taken when assessing the data, with territories increasing in size during the dry season, when water is less available. Although ocelots are known to be territorial, this research showed that overlap occurs between territories. A combined consideration of camera trapping and telemetry data indicates that in the Chiquibul there are about twelve ocelots per one hundred kilometers of forest, giving a regional population of

An ocelot (*Leopardus pardalis*) resting in grass. Photograph by Peter Stafford. © The Natural History Museum, London.

about two hundred individuals. Ocelot activity was found to be greatest at night between 7 p.m. and 4 a.m. However, the results summarized above are broad averages derived from a complex dataset. The sizes of individual home ranges were found to vary greatly between individuals, and camera trapping and telemetry can yield conflicting data. Nevertheless, this research has shed light on the ecology of this rarely seen species and laid an excellent foundation for future regional studies. It has also assessed the relative merits of two important techniques used in cat studies, highlighting the danger of camera trapping studies in potentially overestimating target animal densities.

SMALL-MAMMAL DENSITY, SOIL FERTILITY, AND THE COMMON OPOSSUM

Although impressively diverse mammals inhabit the Chiquibul (see appendix C), a study investigating the abundance of the region's smaller mammals—under 1.5 kilograms in weight—has shown that population densities are low.[84] Conducted between 1999 and 2001, this research used various sizes of mesh traps, baited with banana in grid networks in twelve different locations, to sample small mammals around the broad environs of Las Cuevas. Trapping was done at night at the onset of the dry and rainy seasons. During the course of the study, over 10,000 trap nights were undertaken, with a success rate of 1.3 percent. This resulted in the capture of only ninety-six individuals of thirteen species during the entire study. The three most common species weighing less than two hundred grams were the Mexican mouse opossum (*Marmosa mexicana*), Desmarest's spiny pocket mouse (*Heteromys desmarestianus*), and the big-eared climbing rat (*Ototylomys phyllotis*). These accounted for 68 percent of all mammals captured. Thus, the small-mammal community appears to be dominated by only a few species. In the larger traps the common opossum (*Didelphis marsupialis*) was by far the most abundant mammal caught, weighing in excess of two hundred grams. However, all traps in the study were placed on the ground; thus, species that are known to feed predominantly in the canopy, such as the gray four-eyed opossum (*Philander opossum*), may have been underrepresented.

The research also found that trap success was greatest in areas of high leaf litter and that trap success and mammal densities were highest at the onset of the dry season, although more females were found to be breeding at the onset of the wet season. These results are to be expected, as mammals time their reproductive activity to coincide with the months when there is the greatest abundance of fruit and seed—often the start of the wet season; population densities are highest as the wet season comes to a close and before food resources start to decline.

Although the diversity of mammals found in this study was comparable with the findings of similar studies conducted in other forest areas across the Neotropics, the density of small mammals was shown to be extremely low, with only six individuals estimated per hectare. Studies conducted in the forests of Bladen and Cockscomb, for example, have shown small mammal densities to be at least three times higher. The authors of the study cited above suggest a number of factors that might explain the low density of small mammals at Las Cuevas. One theory proposed is that the low small-mammal densities recorded are due to the relatively high density of the common opossum, which made up 55 percent of all small mammals trapped. The common opossum is a generalist feeder and might outcompete the other species present. In addition, they are omnivores and are known to prey on other small mammals. Finally, the local high densities of larger predatory mammals such as the ocelot and jaguar might maintain small-mammal densities at a low level.

COMPARING THE MAMMAL DIVERSITY OF THE CHIQUIBUL, BLADEN, AND COCKSCOMB

The region known in Belize as the Maya Mountains encompasses a single sweeping expanse of forest of more than 550,000 hectares. It comprises many of Belize's major conservation areas, including the Chiquibul National Park, the Chiquibul Forest Reserve, the Caracol Archaeological Reserve, Cockscomb Basin Wildlife Sanctuary, Bladen Nature Reserve, and the Columbia River Forest Reserve. Although the forest is largely unbroken between these areas, local variations in climate, geology, and altitude produce subtle variations from one site to another in the assemblage and density of the species defining each area.

In an attempt to assess how the diversity and abundance of mammals varies across the Maya Mountains, mammal data obtained from observations and trapping studies has been compared between the different forest reserves of the Maya Mountain forest.[85] Bats were not included in the analysis. In total, fifty-one species of mammals were recorded at all four sites, of which the Chiquibul Forest Reserve had the largest diversity, with forty-two species (82 percent of the total). The data revealed a low percentage of mammal species (fifteen) at all four sites (29 percent), with eleven species (22 percent) noted at one site only. Although the high mammal diversity of the Chiquibul Forest Reserve can in part be explained by the fact that more intensive studies on mammal diversity have been conducted around Las Cuevas than at the other localities and thus sampling error may account for some of the differences observed, nevertheless, this study has highlighted the fact that mammal diversity in Belize cannot be assumed to be the same in contiguous but geographically separate areas. It is common for conservation data to be collected at one localized site of about twenty-five square kilometers and the findings then extrapolated and taken as representative of a protected area or region. This may not be true.

SCARLET MACAWS, SAPSUCKERS, AND SOLITAIRES: THE BIRDS OF THE CHIQUIBUL

With a recorded avifauna of about six hundred species,[86] representing 6.5 percent of the world's total,[87] Belize is an increasingly popular locality for international holiday or-nithologists. At the jungle lodges there is invariably an early-morning clamor to watch exotic-looking collared aracaris (*Pteroglossus torquatus*) as they feed on fruit left out on tables at dawn, while during the day minibuses are often parked at the side of the road to allow a group of birders to scan the undergrowth for elusive species under the tute-lage of a local guide.

Although many of Belize's birds are widespread, some have relatively narrow geo-graphic ranges; nineteen are restricted to the region's lowland Maya Forest area, with twelve known to be endemic to the Yucatán Peninsula. Three of these—the ocellat-ed turkey (*Meleagris ocellata*), the Yucatán poorwill (*Nyctiphrynus yucatanicus*), and the Carolina wren (*Thryothorus ludovicianus*)—are recorded from the Chiquibul.[88]

Belize and the Chiquibul have birds to suit all tastes. For those impressed by predators, the region has one of the largest, most powerful raptors on earth in the rare harpy eagle (*Harpia harpyja*); the Chiquibul represents a forest area where this species has been seen wild in recent times. The Chiquibul is the national stronghold of the scarlet macaw (*Ara macao*), one of the most graceful, beautiful, enigmatic birds. In its twenty-two species of hummingbird, Belize has some of the smallest and most industrious birds, with over half the coun-try's species recorded around the environs of Las Cuevas. The magic of ornithology is that one does not necessarily have to ven-ture to wilderness areas for bird sightings, but if the effort is made, it can be richly re-warding. Belize's great forest expanses such as the Chiquibul provide superb birding opportunities—especially for sightings of forest specialist bird families such as the

Emerald toucanet (*Aulacorhynchus prasinus*). Hand-colored lithograph by John Gould and Henry Constantine Richter, from John Gould, *A Monograph of the Ramphastidae, or Family of Toucans*, 2nd ed. (1854), plate 47. © The Natural History Museum, London.

curassows (Cracidae), trogons (Trogonidae), and manakins (Pipridae). In addition, the Chiquibul and elevated sections of the adjacent Maya Mountain Massif provide the only sites within the country where one is likely to see such species as the stripe-tailed hummingbird (*Eupherusa eximia*), the spotted woodcreeper (*Xiphorhynchus erythropygius*), the slaty antwren (*Myrmotherula schisticolor*), the violet saberwing (*Campylopterus hemileucurus*), the keel-billed motmot (*Electron carinatum*), the rufous-capped warbler (*Basileuterus rufifrons*), and the shining honeycreeper (*Cyanerpes lucidus*). A few species, including the scaly-throated foliage-gleaner (*Anabacerthia variegaticeps*) and the tawny-throated leaftosser (*Sclerurus mexicanus*), are recorded only from Belize's highest mountain peaks and are seldom seen. Almost a dozen of the Chiquibul's bird species are considered to be endangered globally (see table 4.7).

Many visitors to Las Cuevas arrive at dusk, and their first bird sighting is usually the common pauraque (*Nyctidromus albicollis*) darting dangerously low above the track in front of the Land Rover's headlights. The "p'weeoo" call of this species may also be the first sound they hear as they lie in their beds as dawn approaches, although the

Yellow-bellied sapsucker (*Sphyrapicus varius*). Hand-colored aquatint colored, engraved, and printed by R. Havell and Son, from John James Audubon, *Birds of America*, Double Elephant folio (1831–1834), plate 190. © The Natural History Museum, London.

Keel-billed toucan (*Ramphastos sulfuratus*). Hand-colored lithograph by John Gould and Henry Constantine Richter, from John Gould, *A Monograph of the Ramphastidae, or Family of Toucans*, 2nd ed. (1854), plate 3. © The Natural History Museum, London.

pauraque's eerie cry is soon drowned out by the cacophony of other, louder species such as chacalacas and mealy parrots. The dawn chorus at Las Cuevas can be deafening, and few visitors are able to sleep through it. The best time to see birds at the station, as elsewhere in the country, is at dusk or dawn, and observant birders wandering the local network of trails of Las Cuevas at these times can compile an impressive species list. A favored birding site is the research station's veranda, where, coffee in hand and from the comfort of a chair, one can see many of the region's most characteristic birds gracing the clearing and surrounding trees: crested guans, curassows, ocellated turkeys, toucans, and Montezuma oropendolas. A checklist of 293 bird species reliably recorded for the Chiquibul region to date is provided in appendix D, although this list should be considered provisional.

USEFUL IDENTIFICATION GUIDES TO BELIZE'S BIRDS

Jones, H. L. *Birds of Belize.* Austin: University of Texas Press, 2003.

Howell, S, N. G., and S. Webb. *A Guide to the Birds of Mexico and Northern Central America.* New York: Oxford University Press, 1995.

Beletsky, L. *The Ecotraveller's Wildlife Guide. Belize and Northern Guatemala.* San Diego, CA: Academic Press, 1999.

TABLE 4.7. Endangered bird species of the Chiquibul

Species Name	Common Name	IUCN Status	NLCS Status
Ara macao cyanoptera	Scarlet macaw		Endangered
Crax rubra	Great curassow	Near Threatened	Vulnerable
Dendroica cerulean	Cerulean warbler	Vulnerable	Vulnerable
Electron carinatum	Keel-billed motmot	Vulnerable	Vulnerable
Falco deiroleucus	Orange-breasted falcon		Vulnerable
Harpia harpyia	Harpy eagle	Near Threatened	Critical
Harpyhalieatus solitarius	Solitary eagle	Near Threatened	Critical
Meleagris ocellata	Ocellated turkey	Near Threatened	Vulnerable
Morphnus guianensis	Crested eagle	Near Threatened	Critical
Penelope pupurascens	Crested guan		Vulnerable
Sarcoramphus papa	King vulture		Vulnerable

Source: IUCN, *2010 IUCN Red List of Threatened Species*; Meerman, *National List of Critical Species*; Meerman, *Protected Areas System Assessment.*

Like any other group of animals, birds seek to live in regions that optimize their survival and breeding success. Unlike most other animals, however, most birds have the power of flight and are thus well equipped to travel great distances quickly, if necessary, to ensure that they always have access to the resources they need. The drivers of bird migration are the changing seasons. A temperate area that may be ideal for a bird to breed during the summer, for example, might prove too cold and have insufficient food resources to maintain it through winter. Thus, the species in question may migrate south to an area with a warmer climate and more abundant food. Such an annual movement is classic for many of Belize's migrants: summer is passed breeding in the United States, Canada, or Alaska while the winter months are spent in Belize and other regions of Central or South America.

Annually, an estimated five billion birds from five hundred species leave their breeding grounds in North America to spend the winter farther south;[89] the majority reach Central America, and a few, such as the scarlet tanager (*Piranga olivacea*), travel as far as South America, a distance of about six thousand miles. The numbers of migrant birds are so great at certain times of the year that early radar operators were able to detect them, calling these unknown echoes "angels." Of the 574 species of bird reliably recorded from Belize, 30 percent are present only at certain times of the year.[90] A little over 50 percent of the bird species seen are exclusively tropical; of those associated with temperate regions, 80 percent are migratory, residing in Belize only during winter. Indeed, for some species, Belize represents nothing more than a temporary pit stop en route to other destinations farther north or south. For example, the beautiful scarlet tanager can be seen in Belize's forests for short periods of time between mid-September and mid-October and again from late March to early May as it travels between its breeding grounds in North America and western South America. The red-eyed vireo (*Vireo olivaceous*) is another transient species that never resides in Belize for long. There have been a number of independent mist net and point count studies that have helped to clarify the proportions of the Chiquibul's resident and migrant bird populations.[91] With data collected between January and April over a number of years, this work suggests that about 25 percent of the avifauna sampled at these times consists of migrants. In coastal ecosystems and the freshwater habitats in eastern Belize, the proportion can be considerably higher.

Even within Belize, species that are permanently resident are known to migrate locally as food availability changes, and a species may vary greatly in abundance at different times of the year. For example, the scarlet macaw is characteristically associated with the Chiquibul region northwest of the Maya Divide. However, between January and April it can be found east of the Maya Mountains in areas such as Cockscomb and Bladen. For true migrants, annual movements are controlled by biological clocks,

The red-eyed vireo (*Vireo olivaceus*), a transient. Hand-colored aquatint colored, engraved, and printed by R. Havell and Son, from John James Audubon, *Birds of America*, Double Elephant folio (1831–1834), plate 150. © The Natural History Museum, London.

with some species arriving in the country at almost exactly the same time each year. The black-and-white warbler (*Mniotilta varia*) is a species known from the Chiquibul's broadleaf forest. It always arrives from its breeding grounds in the United States in the third week of July.[92]

The routes taken by migrants vary depending upon the species, although many tend to follow coastlines as "leading lines." The yellow-bellied sapsucker, for example, is a migrant species of broadleaf forest recorded from the Chiquibul. It nests in Alaska, Canada, and North America but can be found in Belize from mid-October to late April after having migrated through mainland Mexico. This species is a solitary nocturnal migrant and is unusual in that it feeds off sugar-rich sap that it obtains from drilling small parallel holes in trees. Many warblers, tanagers, vireos, and even some hummingbirds, such as the ruby-throated hummingbird (*Archilochus colubris*), are known to undertake the hazardous journey directly across the Gulf of Mexico, a nonstop journey of about 500 miles, which, flying at between 20 and 30 mph—the average flight speed of passerine (song) birds—can take up to eighteen hours.[93] Some species fly as high as 4,500 meters to make use of favorable winds.[94] The migratory flights over the Gulf of Mexico are one of the world's great natural phenomena. Occasionally migrants are caught up in inclement weather such as cold fronts, and such events can prove catastrophic. Many species are not able to make the crossing against a headwind, and crews on fishing boats and oil rigs have reported being invaded by exhausted birds seeking refuge in this situation. Many more, however, will not find the shelter they seek and will ditch into the Gulf and die. To fuel this journey, migratory species must accumulate fat reserves that can equal up to 50 percent of their weight, 45 percent more than the fat found on nonmigratory birds.[95]

Perhaps the most significant group of Belizean migrants is the Parulidae family (the wood warblers). This exclusively New World group comprises 116 species, of

The magnolia warbler (*Dendroica magnolia*), a winter migrant to the Chiquibul. Hand-colored engraving by George Edwards, 1758. Original artwork held by the Natural History Museum. © The Natural History Museum, London.

which 46 are known from Belize and 23 from the Chiquibul. All but 6 of these insect-eating species breed in North America, with many migrating directly across the Gulf of Mexico.[96] One of Belize's rarest species is the cerulean warbler (*Dendroica cerulea*), a spring and summer transient of higher elevations in the Maya Mountains as it travels between North America and western South America. Indeed, the Chiquibul and the Maya Mountain region may be important stopover points or provide navigational features for this route.[97]

LOGGING AND THE FOREST BIRD COMMUNITY

Many forest animals are sensitive to habitat disturbance, and widespread or even selective logging of a forest can have an extremely damaging impact on the local fauna. As part of the Forest Planning and Management Project, which sought to improve the yields of timber from Belize's forest reserves (see "Forest Renewal: The Chiquibul Restoration Program" in chapter 3), bird studies were conducted in the Chiquibul during February and March in 1995 (before logging) and 1996 (after logging) to assess whether timber felling affects the number and abundance of species known to prefer undisturbed forest habitats.[98] The study focused on four 18-hectare forest plots; half of each area was selectively logged at an intensity of six trees removed per hectare. Data for this study was collected using a number of complementary techniques, such as dawn bird censuses, with all birds seen or heard within a fifty-meter radius recorded; mist netting during daylight hours; and behavioral observations.

During the course of this research, 139 bird species were recorded, of which 25 percent were migrants. Although there were a number of small changes in the abundance and diversity of resident and migrant species among the four plots and between the logged and unlogged halves of each plot, many were not statistically significant. However, clear changes did occur at the species and bird family levels. For example, after logging, eighteen species were not detected in forest areas where they had previously been recorded. They represented some of the region's quintessential forest species, including the collared forest-falcon (*Micrastur semitorquatus*), the crested guan (*Penelope purpurascens*), the great curassow (*Crax rubra*), the nightingale wren (*Microcerculus philomela*), and the slaty-breasted tinamou (*Crypturellus boucardi*). However, the authors of the research took care to point out that these species were rare to begin with. The curassows (Cracidae) declined in all areas over the course of the study, and, in general, other specialist forest families such as the trogons (Trogonidae) and manakins (Pipridae) declined in numbers in logged areas, while families of habitat generalists such as the thrushes (Turdidae), mockingbirds and thrashers (Mimidae), and seedeaters and sparrows (Emberizidae) showed an increase in abundance. When the data was analyzed by dietary guild, it was found that large omnivores and frugivores declined in logged areas, while small insectivores increased. As the scale of the study was relatively small, many of the effects of logging may have been buffered by the large expanse of surrounding forest. In addition, due to its long history of disturbance by hurricanes and logging, one might expect the Chiquibul's avifauna to be adapted to such impacts and thus be relatively resilient. Nevertheless, this research has highlighted the need to monitor bird populations when logging occurs at the level of the landscape.

Violaceous trogon (*Trogon violaceus*). Hand-colored lithograph by John and Elizabeth Gould, from John Gould, *A Monograph of the Trogonidae, or Family of Trogons* (1838), plate 18. © The Natural History Museum, London.

The birds of the Chiquibul are diverse in number and form, and each species is uniquely adapted to survive and succeed in its chosen habitat. Although the broadleaf forest that dominates the region comprises, broadly speaking, a single generic ecosystem, a multitude of ecological niches and habitats exist within it. All have been successfully exploited by bird species. Some, such as the slaty-breasted tinamou (*Crypturellus boucardi*), are ground dwellers, while others, like the red-throated ant-tanager (*Habia fuscicauda*) and the keel-billed toucan (*Ramphastos sulfuratus*), largely inhabit the forest understory, subcanopy, or canopy regions. Others, including the Amazon kingfisher (*Chloroceryle amazona*), are associated with riverine habitats, while flycatchers like the great kiskadee (*Pitangus sulphuratus*) are most often seen in disturbed forest clearings. Species vary in their height and mode of travel—the slaty-tailed trogon (*Trogon massena*), for example, flies through the canopy, whereas the scarlet macaw (*Ara macao*) flies above it. Most species must constantly flap their wings to stay airborne, although a few have the ability to glide and soar on thermals (e.g., the turkey vulture, *Cathartes aura*). The region's bird species have also evolved to eat the wide variety of forest foods available, and specialist seed-, fruit-, flower-, nectar-, insect-, reptile-, and mammal-eating

Black-crowned night heron (*Nycticorax nycticorax*). Hand-colored aquatint colored, engraved, and printed by R. Havell and Son, from John James Audubon, *Birds of America*, Double Elephant folio (1831–1834), plate 236. © The Natural History Museum, London.

taxa exist. Usually, the form of a species provides a clue as to its diet. Seed eaters such as the scarlet macaw or white-collared seedeater (*Sporophila torqueola*), for example, tend to have thick, heavy bills, while the hooked bills of hawks, kites, and eagles are designed to catch, rip, and consume prey.

Although much is known generally about the bird species commonly found in the Chiquibul, the exact habitat preferences of many remain uncertain. A number of studies have been conducted close to Las Cuevas with a view toward understanding the habitat associations of the local avifauna. A mist-netting study conducted in forest and forest-edge habitats toward the end of the 2005 dry season showed that, of a sample of forty-six species, twenty-three taxa (50 percent) had an apparent preference for the forest interior and sixteen for the forest edge, with seven occurring equally in both.[99] Birds typical of forest-edge areas tended to be small seed-eating species belonging to such taxonomic groups as the seedeater and sparrow family (Emberizidae), while typical forest species such as the red-throated ant-tanager tended to be larger birds with more omnivorous diets.

THE SCARLET MACAW: THE ENVIRONMENTALIST'S CALL TO ARMS

Humans have always been fascinated by parrots and their bright plumage, and few are as attractively colored as the scarlet macaw (*Ara macao*). A sighting of this species is regarded as a near-religious experience by some, and those who have witnessed the breathtaking sight of a group of these large, long-tailed, majestic birds flapping just above the jungle canopy can understand why. Typically the scarlet macaw is seen in pairs, although groups of between four and six are also common; flocks in excess of twenty individuals can occur, and such congregations may be particularly associated with the end of the breeding season. Although they are unmistakable once seen, more often than not it is their loud "rrahk" cry that initially signals their presence overhead. The scarlet macaw has recently reached iconic status in Belize because of its adoption as a flagship conservation symbol. Throughout the high-profile campaign to prevent construction of the controversial Chalillo Dam, for example, the plight of the scarlet macaw in particular attracted the media, and its image was used by environmentalists as a call to arms.

The parrot family (Psittacidae) contains 352 species, of which 150 are native to the New World;[100] 10 species occur in Belize,[101] of which 6 are known from the Chiquibul (see table 4.8). Parrots come in a great range of shapes and sizes, but the majority are recognizable by their rounded bills and downturned upper mandible. Due to the combined predations of habitat destruction and the pet trade, parrots around the world are under threat, with 123 species (35 percent of the total) listed by IUCN as Endangered or Near Threatened. Belize's yellow-headed parrot (*Amazona oratrix*) is considered endangered globally,[102] while nationally the scarlet macaw is designated in the same category by local conservation organizations.[103] A victim of the predations of the pet industry, the scarlet macaw is listed in Appendix I of CITES, and its trade is banned. The population size of this species in Belize is unknown, largely on account of the remoteness of the terrain it inhabits. However, what is certain is that the population is low, with no researchers giving estimates greater than 250 individuals; some local experts believe its true numbers to be half this figure.[104] The entirety of the Maya Forest region of Central America is thought to support only 1,000 individuals.

The scarlet macaw can be found from southern Mexico to Amazonia, and Belize supports populations of the northern subspecies *Ara macao cyanoptera*. This subspecies, which occurs north of Costa Rica, is larger, has a bigger bill, and has more blue on its wing than its southern counterpart. Originally found in many parts of Belize, such as in the vicinity of the Hummingbird Highway, southern Stann Creek, and the Mountain Pine Ridge, habitat loss in the last few decades has forced the scarlet macaw to retreat largely to the Chiquibul region to make its last stand against human encroachment. This species typically nests in the natural cavities of large trees, such as quamwood (*Schizolobium parahyba*), near rivers and floodplains, and there are fears that the recently constructed Chalillo Dam threatens the scarlet macaw's stronghold in the country. This dam has recently flooded an estimated 20 percent of the macaw's critical wet-season habitat, affecting two of the bird's three primary breeding grounds—the Macal and Raspaculo Rivers.[105] (The Monkey Tail Branch is the third, as yet untouched habitat.) The association of macaws with riverine areas is particularly pronounced during the dry season. Although other scarlet macaw populations are known to exist regionally, the nearest occur in the Petén region of Guatemala and are isolated from those in Belize. Thus, the populations that occur in the Chiquibul are extremely vulnerable to extinction.

The scarlet macaw (*Ara macao*) is one of Belize's flagship conservation species. The Chiquibul provides one of its last safe havens in Central America. © Humberto Wohlers. Courtesy The Belize Zoo.

TABLE 4.8. Parrots of the Chiquibul

Common Name	Species Name
Amazona farinosa	Mealy parrot
A. autumnalis	Red-lored parrot
Ara macao	Scarlet macaw
Aratinga nana	Olive-throated parakeet
Pionopsitta haematotis	Brown-hooded parrot
Pionus senilis	White-crowned parrot

The scarlet macaw primarily feeds on seeds and unripe fruit in the forest canopy, and many of the region's tree species make up its diet: the hog plum (*Spondias radlkoferi*), quamwood, cedar (*Cedrela odorata*), the trumpet tree (*Cecropia* spp.), and prickly yellow (*Zanthoxylum* spp.).

CURASSOWS, GUANS, AND CHACALACAS

The loud, reverberating morning chorus of the chacalaca—especially raucous before a thunderstorm—is the forest's natural wake-up call and one that heralds the start of the day at Las Cuevas. The plain chacalaca (*Ortalis vetula*), whose common name is derived from its call, is a common species in Belize and is related to the crested guan (*Penelope purpurascens*) and the great curassow (*Crax rubra*), both of which are considerably rarer. These three species all belong to the highly vocal Cracidae family, a characteristic component of the Neotropical and Chiquibul avifauna. The fifty cracid species are confined to the New World, and only the three species listed above occur in Belize.[106]

Cracids are characterized by elongated bodies and tails, small heads, and well-developed hind toes that enable them to grasp branches.[107] This last feature is important, as cracids are primarily arboreal, forest-dwelling birds, and the great curassow and crested guan rarely make sustained flights. When they choose to do so, they tend to flap their wings a few times before gliding with their long tails, which provide balance. Although both are considered arboreal species, the great curassow is more terrestrial than the crested guan and can be seen feeding on the ground; however, like its relative, it still nests, roosts, sings, and often feeds in trees. Of the three species that occur in the Chiquibul, the plain chacalaca is the smallest and least showy. Although neither the crested guan nor great curassow has striking plumage, both have very colorful adornments. Male crested guans have an unfeathered blue face and red throat wattle. Both sexes of the great curassow have distinctive curly crests, the male also marked by a bright yellow knob on its bill.

Both the crested guan and great curassow are highly threatened regionally due to hunting and habitat loss. The Chiquibul provides a relatively safe haven for these species, but even here hunting associated with *xatero* activity (see "Xaté, Leaf of Gold" in chapter 3) is a cause for concern. Both species occur from Mexico to northern South America, with about 80 percent of their diet consisting of fruit and seed; important dietary components are dog's balls (*Thevetia ahouai*), breadnut (*Brosimum alicastrum*), figs (*Ficus* spp.), chicle (*Manilkara* spp.), and cherry (*Pouteria* spp.).[108]

The great curassow (*Crax rubra*) belongs to the highly vocal Cracidae family. © Humberto Wohlers. Courtesy The Belize Zoo.

One of the recent conservation successes in Belize has been the reintroduction of small numbers of harpy eagles (*Harpia harpyja*) to augment diminishing natural population numbers. Although reintroductions in recent years have focused on the Rio Bravo Conservation and Management Area (RBCMA) in Orange Walk, this high-profile national wild release conservation program began at Las Cuevas Research Station, with the first introductions, facilitated by the Peregrine Fund, occurring in 2003. Harpy eagles were not extinct in Belize prior to this date but were extremely rare, verifiable sightings being few and far between. Globally the Harpy Eagle is considered Near Threatened by IUCN, but nationally this species is considered Critically Endangered.[109] Prior to reintroduction, one of the few areas where sightings of this species periodically occurred was the Chiquibul.

The Harpy Eagle is the largest eagle in the Americas: it has a wingspan of nearly two meters and weighs up to nine kilograms. With powerful talons that have been compared in size to the claws of a grizzly bear, it is also one of the most powerful raptors in the world. In addition to its impressive size, this species is visually

The harpy eagle (*Harpia harpyja*) is the largest eagle in the Americas. There were only scattered sightings of the species before 2003, when it was reintroduced to the Chiquibul. © William Milliken.

striking on account of its black breast band, neck ruff, and crest feathers. Its natural range is from southern Mexico to northern Argentina, but due to habitat fragmentation and hunting, it is threatened across its range and has been extirpated in many areas. It lives primarily in lowland forest and hunts a range of arboreal creatures such as sloths, monkeys, kinkajous, opossums, coatis, and reptiles. Typically harpy eagles nest in tall emergent trees and lay two eggs, although usually only one hatches. The breeding period is long, and three years may pass between successive breeding attempts. Adults are believed to live for between thirty and fifty years.

Belize's harpy eagle reintroduction program is supported by a captive breeding program based at the Neotropical Raptor Center in Panama.[110] Young eagles are hatched in Panama and initially kept in brooders, where they are hand-fed. After one month they are moved to an imprinting chamber, where they imprint on an adult of their species before being transferred to a flight chamber, where they fledge; contact with people is kept to a minimum throughout the program so that the eagles will not become habituated to human presence. Four young eagles were transferred to Belize and Las Cuevas on March 20, 2003. After being temporarily confined in a hack box to keep them safe while they adapted to their new surroundings, the birds were released into the wild after three weeks (April 12). Throughout the first few months, when the eagles had not begun to hunt for themselves, they were fed rats, initially at the hack site itself and then later at particular habitual feed trees as the eagles began to feel more at home in the forest and roamed farther away from the hack box. The first documented wild kill by one of the birds was a kinkajou in December 2003, eight months after their initial release. Of the four harpy eagles released at Las Cuevas, all survived the first year, although one later died in July 2004. Between 10 and 30 percent of eaglets might be expected to survive naturally to adulthood. The three survivors were subsequently relocated to the Rio Bravo Conservation and Management Area in August 2004. Currently, wild local populations of this beleaguered species in the Maya forests of Belize, Guatemala, and Mexico have been bolstered by thirteen captive-bred birds. However, it will be many years before the impact of the reintroduction program will be known. As yet, there is little information on the breeding success of captive-bred individuals in Belize.

RHYTHM AND RECOVERY

ECOLOGICAL ASSOCIATIONS, SEASONALITY, HURRICANES, AND FOREST DYNAMICS

5 THE "WEB OF LIFE" is an evocative term that often finds its way into the popular press as the scientific community continues to confirm and describe the many mutual dependencies of the species with which we inhabit our planet. It serves to illustrate both the complex way in which all life is connected and the fragility of these linkages. The latter issue is increasingly seen as significant as we become aware of the detrimental impact our activities have on the planet. Like it or not, we have a critical role in determining the future and health of our planet's web of life. Through processes such as deforestation, species extinction, pollution, and climate change, we are slowly severing the natural cords upon which are our own existence may ultimately hang.

The web of life of a tropical forest is hugely complex and a daunting area of study for an ecologist. Although the broad concepts of many ecological associations are known—such as the dependence of many forest plants on different animal groups for their pollination—more often than not, the precise nature of the linkages remains obscure. We might know that mahogany flowers are frequently visited by bees and butterflies; however, not all the visiting insects will be pollinators, and the species or group of species responsible for ensuring reproductive success are unknown. Focused, detailed research over many years often reveals that the degree of association is highly specific, as typified by the common understory palm genus *Chamaedorea*, whose species are entirely dependent for reproduction on the pollination prowess of a single tiny species of thrip (see "Thrips and Palm Pollination" later in this chapter). In a similar manner, successful dispersal of the fruits of pollination is usually dependent on external help, often from animals.

This chapter begins by providing an overview of a few selected ecological associations of the Chiquibul Forest. It assesses the pollination syndromes and dispersal mechanisms critical in maintaining the lifelines of the major plant groups; it then looks at ants as another example of ecological mutualism through their feeding association with fungal gardens and their role in defending certain tree species, including *Cecropia* and *Acacia*, from unwanted pest attacks.

Due in part to its seasonal climate, the Chiquibul Forest exhibits strong biological rhythms, with distinct peaks in flowering and fruiting during the year and with many species of trees losing their leaves during the dry season in response to water stress. The geographic location of Belize within the Caribbean hurricane belt also means that the

Chiquibul region is periodically affected by catastrophic winds and rain, such as Hurricane Hattie, the last significant hurricane to hit, in 1961. The structure and diversity of the forest around Las Cuevas owe much to the impacts of these intermittent storms, and this ecosystem is in a state of recovery from past perturbations. However, the forest ecosystem is a resilient one, and through dynamic processes of resprouting, tree recruitment, and ecological succession, highly disturbed open forest can eventually return to its former closed state.

The second half of the chapter discusses the important ecological factors determining the Chiquibul's biological seasonality before concluding with an overview of hurricane ecology and a discussion of forest dynamics and the process of ecological succession.

HONEY GUIDES, TONGUE TUBES, AND LOVE CHAMBERS: THE POLLINATION ECOLOGY OF THE CHIQUIBUL

The most visually striking feature of a plant is often its flowers, and the variety of structure, color, size, and scent of flowers to be found within the Chiquibul and other tropical forests provides an endless source of fascination to visitors. Flowers have evolved in

order to facilitate the pollination process, and the amazing diversity of their form reflects the many pollination mechanisms in existence. Some flowers are tiny, colorless, and petalless and require the use of a hand lens for inspection; many members of the Euphorbiaceae (spurge) family, for example, have evolved flowers of this type. Other species have developed floral structures at the other extreme, such as the orange, gaudy giants of *Erblichia* (Turneraceae), which are conspicuous from several hundred meters.

Hummingbird-pollinated flower of the forest tree *Erblichia odorata* (Turneraceae). The genus has an interesting distribution pattern: one species is known from the Neotropics and four from Madagascar. © Sam Bridgewater.

One of the best means to investigate the manner in which plants and animals interact is through a close examination of pollination, a process of vital ecological importance and one of the defining natural processes shaping life on earth.

Pollination is the process by which pollen grains containing male genetic information produced by the male sexual parts of a flower (stamens) are transferred to the female sexual parts (carpels) of the same flower or other flowers. The carpels contain the ovule with its female genetic information. The process of pollination is vital for the reproduction of gymnosperms and flowering plants. Without pollination, ovules cannot be fertilized, seed cannot develop, and the great majority of plants cannot reproduce and diversify. Fruit development is also usually dependent on the pollination process, the fruits themselves acting as the cornerstone of local ecological systems by providing food for many different kinds of life and the means by which plant seeds are dispersed away from the adult.

For pollination to occur, an independent agent is usually needed to carry the pollen from where it is produced (the anthers of the stamens) to where it is required (the stigma of the carpels) by the same or another flower. The transporting agent may be an environmental vector, such as wind or water (*abiotic* pollination), or it may be an animal (*biotic* pollination). Plant-animal pollination mutualisms are believed to date back into the Cretaceous era (146–65 MYA), when insects began to acquire food from previously wind-pollinated flowers, and the plant species upon which they fed enjoyed elevated reproductive success as a result. Ever since those initial interactions, plants and animals have continued striving to survive and maintain their lineage. In so doing, some have coevolved and developed extremely sophisticated, mutually beneficial pollination relationships.

Recent decades have seen the decline of increasing numbers of pollination vectors, causing great concern. Insects are particularly important in this regard. The recent sharp drop in bee populations, for example, in the United States and elsewhere due to the introduction of parasitic mites, the increased use of pesticides, and climate change, is well documented.[1] The demise of these essential pollination vectors may herald the start of the disappearance of plant species that depend upon them to reproduce and those animal species dependent on the fruits produced as a result. Indeed, our own well-being is entirely dependent on pollination, as the crops critical for our survival are largely reliant upon natural pollination. It has been estimated, for example, that over 30 percent of human food is derived from bee-pollinated crops; thus, we should be deeply concerned about bee population declines.[2] Economic assessments conducted in the United States have already shown that the decline in populations of honeybees (*Apis* spp.) is costing the agricultural sector many billions of dollars annually.[3] More important than money, clearly, is the fact that if crucial pollinators are removed, the very foundations of our existence may be taken away.

Hermaphroditic flower
of *Symphonia globulifera*.
© Alex Rodríguez.

THE SEX LIFE OF PLANTS

Flowers occur in an array of different guises, not only in their color and broad form but also in their sexuality. The majority of rain-forest trees (ca. 65 percent) are hermaphrodites,[4] with each individual flower containing both male and female sexual organs. There are many examples of such species from the Chiquibul, including the chewstick tree (*Symphonia globulifera*). Less common are tree species such as cedar (*Cedrela odorata*), which have separate male and female flowers on the same individual (monoecy). Some species, like *Alchornea latifolia*, even have separate male and female flowers on entirely different individuals—i.e., each individual is either male or female (dioecy). Globally, about 6 percent of angiosperm species are dioecious,[5] although about 25 percent of rain-forest trees are believed to have this sexual system.[6] In dioecious species, as each individual of a species is either male or female, pollen transfer must occur between different individuals (outcrossing). For monoecious and hermaphrodite species, one might expect self-pollination to occur.

However, studies on tropical trees suggest that the majority are obligate outcrossers.[7] Outcrossing is generally advantageous, as it facilitates genetic mixing during reproduction and maintains genetic diversity. There are various means by which monoecious and hermaphroditic species ensure that they do not pollinate themselves. Some monoecious species, for example, develop their male and female flowers at different times. Others have different flower forms expressed by different individuals to ensure that pollen from the stamens of the flower of one individual cannot be physically transferred by the pollinator to another flower on the same individual. In addition, many have developed self-incompatibility mechanisms so that even if pollen transfer does occur between different-sexed flowers on the same plant, the development process of the seed is halted. The existence of such isolating mechanisms can also serve to restrict gene flow between closely related species, ensuring that they are maintained as distinct, even though they may occur in close geographic proximity.

Although every plant species is unique in its means of pollination, plants can usually be grouped into one of a few general groups depending on the form of the flower. Thus, the flowers of wind-pollinated species share certain characteristics, as do those pollinated by moths, flies, or hummingbirds. These shared characteristics are called pollination syndromes. Although not all species have flowers that can easily be placed into a syndrome, the attempt to categorize plants in this way has nevertheless provided a useful means for gaining insight into their floral ecology.

WIND POLLINATION

The gases of the atmosphere are in constant motion, striving to maintain equal pressure around the globe. Wind currents are the physical manifestation of air flowing from areas of high to low pressure, and they provide the means by which pressure differences are stabilized. This movement of air represents a free and useful vector by which pollen can be carried from one flower to another; not surprisingly, many plant species have evolved floral structures to make good use of it. Although some global wind currents are largely predictable, local wind currents are not always reliable in their daily occurrence, their strength, or their direction. Thus, wind pollination (anemophily) is often viewed as being inefficient, unpredictable, and inferior to animal-based pollination; clearly, a capricious vector is not ideal if the future of your species depends upon the success of the pollination process. It was once thought that anemophily was a primitive trait in flowering plants. However, it is now believed that in some plant groups, wind pollination mechanisms have evolved out of insect pollination.[8] About 18 percent of all flowering plants are wind-pollinated; among tropical trees this type of pollination is rare, with only 2.5 percent of species estimated to be anemophilous.[9] But despite its famed inefficiency, anemophily has clearly brought with it great evolutionary success. Indeed, in areas of low species diversity, newly colonized habitats, and regions with short growing seasons or adverse climates, anemophily may be superior to other pollination forms.

Typically, wind-pollinated flowers tend to be unisexual, small, and inconspicuous, as there is no need for colors, elaborate structures, and rewards. The wind is immune to attractants and requires no thanks. These flowers tend to produce large amounts of pollen, increasing the odds that at least a few grains will successfully alight at their intended destination. Their stigmas are large and feathery to increase the chance that they can catch pollen from the wind currents that swirl around; in addition, the stamens are often exerted from the flower. In deciduous species, flowering often occurs before the leaves appear to make more efficient use of the wind, or the flowers are held well away from the leaf mass.

Sometimes it can be problematic to discern whether a species is wind-pollinated. It is not uncommon for flowers that appear to fit the anemophilous syndrome to be frequented by small generalist insects such as eusocial (colonial) bees; some even produce nectar for visiting insects. However, these visitors may be pollen scavengers and not necessarily involved in transferring pollen from one flower to another. Visiting insects can perform other functions in addition to pollination. For example, nectar might be produced to attract predatory wasps that protect the flowers and leaves from herbivores.

Within the Chiquibul, examples of typically anemophilous plant families include Moraceae (e.g., *Trophis racemosa*), Euphorbiaceae (e.g., *Alchornea* spp. and *Acalypha* spp.), Chloranthaceae (e.g., *Hedyosmum* sp.), and Urticaceae (e.g., *Myriocarpa longipes* and *Pilea* spp.).[10] In the case of the closely related families Urticaceae and Moraceae, wind-pollination can be assisted by explosive pollen release, and the flower frequently matures within the bud with the stamens bent under pressure toward the center. When the flowers open, they do so explosively as the elastic stamens spring out, releasing stored energy and firing their pollen load into the air. This explosive release might be due to an environmental cue related to temperature, humidity, or disturbance, but the phenomenon is poorly researched. In the white mulberry, one Chinese member of the Moraceae (fig) family, the speed of this process has been shown to be in excess of half the speed of sound, making it the fastest known movement in the plant kingdom![11] Despite the small proportion of anemophilous tropical trees across their range, a study conducted in deciduous forest in Mexico has indicated that wind pollination may be common in the dioecious trees of the region. In the study cited, 42 percent of all dioecious species were found to be anemophilous.[12]

In addition to many flowering plants, all conifers—including *Pinus caribaea*—are wind-pollinated. Although conifers do not produce flowers, they produce both male and female cones, the former containing pollen sacs and the latter ovules. Cycads were also once thought to be primarily anemophilous, although it is now believed that insects are their primary pollen vectors. Ferns, mosses, and fungi do not produce pollen and thus cannot be considered to be anemophilous. However, their reproductive cycle often depends completely or in part upon the dispersal of their spores by the wind.

WATER POLLINATION

The second pollination syndrome related to environmental rather than biological factors is hydrophily, or water pollination. Hydrophilous pollination involves the use of water as a vector, but this does not necessarily mean that the pollen itself comes into contact with water.[13] Instead, it might be transported dry across the water's surface or protected by floating flowers or anthers. Relatively speaking, the hydrophilous syndrome is rare, and there are few examples of it from the Chiquibul. One might reasonably expect this syndrome to evolve in aquatic species, a likely candidate being the conspicuous river weed *Marathrum oxycarpum* (Podostemaceae), which spends its life largely submerged, clinging to rocks in fast-flowing rivers. However, this renowned aquatic family is usually pollinated by wind or insects, with flowering often occurring

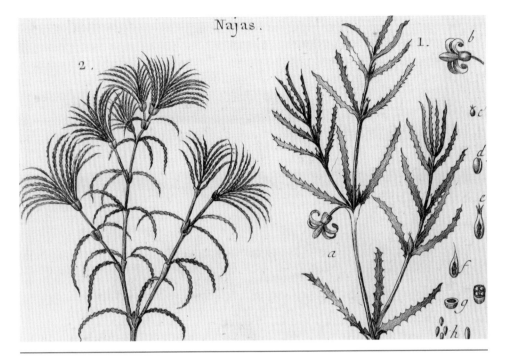

The genus *Najas*, represented by *N. wrightiana* in the Chiquibul, is water-pollinated. From Jean Baptiste Lamarck, *Encyclopédie méthodique. Nouvelle édition enrichie de remarques, dédiée à la sérénissime République de Venise* (1784), plate 799.

during the dry season, when water levels have dropped and the plant is exposed.[14] An aquatic species in which water pollination is known to occur is *Najas wrightiana* (Najadaceae), which has been recorded in the Macal River. The exact means by which hydrophily occurs in this species remains uncertain, but it is believed to be submarine. It has been suggested that the stamens split from the mature male flowers of the submerged plant and rise to the surface, where they open, releasing their pollen load. The pollen then sinks and alights on the stigmas of the submerged female flowers.[15]

ANIMAL MATCHMAKERS: BIOTIC POLLINATION

Animals are the primary pollination vectors for the majority of flowering plants. For tropical trees worldwide it has been estimated that over 95 percent of species are pollinated by a huge range of living creatures as diverse in form as tiny microscopic wasps to flying foxes.[16] Plants are unable to find their own mates by themselves, so animals do this for them, essentially acting as sexual matchmakers. This mutually beneficial (symbiotic) relationship is an example of coevolution. For the animals, a visit to a flower can bring a reward of pollen, nectar, or oil that provides a source of food or fragrance, the latter often useful in attracting the opposite sex. The production of these materials by the plant requires energy and represents a considerable investment. Of all these products, nectar is the most important.[17] The light hum heard close to heavily flowering trees is the noise of insects intently foraging largely for nectar. The insects are unaware that in the course of their wild-harvesting activities, they are transferring pollen from one flower to another, thereby facilitating the pollination process. Although animal pollination is directed, more predictable, and less wasteful than wind pollination, there is still no guarantee that the pollinator will always successfully transfer pollen from one flower to another. Even with animal pollination, only an estimated 1 percent of the pollen finally reaches the appropriate stigma.[18]

INSECT POLLINATION

Insects are by far the most important and widespread pollination vectors: over 67 percent of flowering plants are believed to be dependent upon them,[19] and this percentage rises to 90 percent in tropical forests.[20] Although the technical term for this pollination mechanism is *entomophily*, a number of pollination syndrome subtypes are known, depending on the group of insects involved. Among the most ecologically significant of these is specialized pollination by bees (mellitophily), butterflies (psycophily), beetles (cantharophily), flies (myophily), and carrion and dung flies (sapromyophily). However, many plant species are insect generalists with little or no physical specialization and make their nectar and pollen available to a wide variety of visitors of different shapes and forms. Examples of species from the Chiquibul with such generalist flowers include the gumbo-limbo (*Bursera simaruba*) and the white gumbo-limbo (*Dendropanax arboreus*).[21]

Immature flowers of *Guatteria diospyroides*. At anthesis the three petals arc up to form a pollination chamber. © Alex Rodríguez.

BEETLE POLLINATION

Beetle pollination (cantharophily) has a long evolutionary record dating back over 100 MYA and is believed to be derived from generalist and wind-pollinator ancestors.[22] Examples of plant families represented in the Chiquibul that are commonly (but not exclusively) beetle-pollinated include Magnoliaceae, Annonaceae, and Lauraceae. However, it is thought that beetle pollination is generally rare in Mesoamerican lowland canopy trees, the syndrome being more common among subcanopy trees, of which about 10 percent are pollinated in this way.[23] The typical flowers of the Annonaceae (custard apple) family, for example, provide a good example of specialized adaptation to beetle pollination.[24] As the three-parted yellow, green, or reddish fleshy flowers initially develop, the central part containing the densely packed stamens is exposed. When the flower reaches its fully mature stage (anthesis), the petals arc over the stamens to form an enclosed pollination chamber where strong odors are produced. The odor attracts beetles, and the primary function of the pollination chamber is to retain its pollinators, which often remain for several days until the petals drop.

In addition to the three families cited above, beetle pollination is common in the Cyclanthaceae, Myristacaceae, Araceae, and Arecaceae (palm) families.[25] In the case of Araceae species, the tiny flowers are clustered into a spiky structure called a spadix, which is frequently surrounded by a large leaflike structure called a spathe. Many members of this family (e.g., *Philodendron* spp.) are known to be thermogenic (heat-producing), with their spadix producing intense heat (30°-45°C), at least during the first night of flowering.[26] This heating has been associated with the production of scent thought to attract insects to the flowers. Various insect groups are known to frequent Araceae flowers, although beetles and flies are predominant.

THRIPS AND PALM POLLINATION

Due to their small and inconspicuous flowers, palms were once believed to be wind-pollinated. Recent research, however, indicates that most are insect-pollinated. One detailed piece of research conducted at Las Cuevas and focusing on the understory palm genus *Chamaedorea* (see also "Xaté: Leaf of Gold" in chapter 3) has provided important information on the complex nature of palm pollination systems.[27] For many decades there was confusion over whether this genus was wind- or insect-pollinated. The production of copious dry pollen, for example, is common of wind-pollinated plants, while the production of a fragrance as an attractant is indicative that animals are the primary vectors. Species may even use both agents: with insect-induced wind pollination, visiting insects are not the pollinating agent, but their activity is required within the relatively closed flowers to facilitate the release of pollen into the air.[28] Research at Las Cuevas focusing on four *Chamaedorea* species—*C. ernesti-augusti, C. neurochlamys, C. oblongata,* and *C. tepejilote*—found that many different groups of insects visit the flowers, including ants and bees. However, for all four species studied, only one species of thrip appeared to be the actual pollinator—*Brooksithrips chamaedoreae.*[29] Thrips belong to the order Thysanoptera and are tiny insects with fringed wings. Traditionally they have been overlooked as pollinators because they were thought to lack the features of efficient plant pollinators, such as specialized structures (like the pollen sacs of bees) to carry pollen. Thrips are also poor fliers, spending much of their life in the flowers they visit. It is now known that they are pollinators of many species from a diverse range of families, including Annonaceae, Euphorbiaceae, Monimiaceae, and Cycadaceae. In the case of the cyads, which are known to be among the most primitive of seed plants (see "The Gymnosperms" in chapter 1), research into the origin of cycads and their thrip, beetle, and weevil insect pollinators suggests that thrips might be among the oldest pollinators of plants, having originated after cyads but before beetles and weevils.[30]

CONTINUED NEXT PAGE

The thrips visiting *Chamaedorea* flowers are provided with many rewards: a source of nectar, pollen, and petals on which to feed; a venue for mating; and a place for laying eggs. In addition to the natural scent produced by the flowers themselves, the visiting thrips release pheromones to attract potential mates. As a result, large numbers of thrips can be found on *Chamaedorea* inflorescences. The relationship between *Brooksithrips chamae-doreae* and the species of *Chamaedorea* it pollinates is one of dependent mutualism. Male

Chamaedorea flowers are necessary for the successful completion of the thrip's life cycle from egg to larva to pupa and then adult.

Chamaedorea is not the only common genus of plant in the Chiquibul that is thrip-pollinated. The common tree *Castilla elastica* is also known to be pollinated in this manner. Studies in Panama have shown that 85 percent of the floral inhabitants of 285 plant species were thrips; thus, these diminutive, overlooked insects are potentially more important pollinators than once thought.[31]

Male inflorescence of the fishtail palm (*Chamaedorea ernesti-augusti*), a species pollinated by thrips. The three male sexual parts (stamens) of each individual flower are conspicuous. The central structure of each flower is the pistillode, a sterile vestigial female organ. © Holly Porter Morgan.

FLY POLLINATION

One of the more curious pollination systems to be found within the Chiquibul is shown by the seven species of vine belonging to the genus *Aristolochia* (Dutchman's pipe or birthwort). The strange, inflated, pipe-shaped flowers of this genus typically produce a rank smell on the day the flowers open, the scent attracting flies that usually feed on carrion, feces, or fungi. These flies belong to a variety of different families, although those in the Phoridae (scuttle or coffin flies) family are particularly noteworthy visitors.[32] These enter the flower neck, deceived into thinking they are alighting on their preferred food; once they enter, their exit is delayed, as many *Aristolochia* species, such as *Aristolochia pilosa*,[33] have evolved a trap-and-release mechanism to assist the pollination process. Specialized hairs keep the visitors from escaping. Some of those entrapped may carry pollen from previous visits to other *Aristolochia* flowers and, while entombed in the inflated flower base (utricle), will pollinate the stigma, which always matures before the stamens. The visitors remain trapped until the second day, when the stamens have subsequently matured, at which time they are further dusted with pollen, ready for the pollination process to start again. To this end, the unwitting pollinators are released once the stamens have shed their pollen and the hairs, hitherto preventing escape, have wilted. Not all species of Dutchman's pipe employ a trap-and-release mechanism. There is evidence that some, including *Aristolochia maxima*, attract their pollinators not by deceit but by providing a convivial environment for them to breed and lay their eggs in, with the wilted and falling flowers providing a source of nourishment for the developing larvae.[34] Fruit flies (*Drosophila* spp.) have been recorded as being important in this regard. The provision of a suitable breeding site appears to be sufficient to maintain the flies within the flower while the stigmas are pollinated and the stamens mature; thus, deceit is unnecessary. A common plant of the Chiquibul understory believed to be fly-pollinated is the shrub *Deherainia smaragdina*. This species produces large, unusual bright green flowers.

Flower of the fly-pollinated shrub *Deherainia smaragdina*. © Sam Bridgewater.

The flowers of *Aristolochia grandiflora* attract pollinating flies. © Alex Monro.

Psycophily, or butterfly pollination, is often characterized by flat flowers with nectar well hidden within narrow floral tubes or spurs. The shape of the structure provides a stable landing platform for the delicate visitors that access the hidden nectar by inserting their long, slender, retractable proboscis into the flowers. Typically, psycophilous flowers are vivid in color, with red and orange being common. Members of the sunflower (Asteraceae) family frequently show this syndrome, and in tropical regions butterflies represent nearly 75 percent of all visitors to this important and diverse group, although social bees are also significant pollinators.[35] Many members of the Asteraceae family are also able to reproduce asexually and require no pollinating agents. In psycophilous flowers nectar production is generally small, compelling the butterflies to visit many flowers, thereby facilitating cross-pollination. In addition, the nectar is frequently rich in amino acids; this is ideal for butterflies that, unlike bees, are typically unable to obtain their protein from pollen, depending entirely upon nectar for their sustenance instead. However, butterflies in one important group—the *Heliconius* genus—are exceptions to this rule and are known to supplement their nectar diet with pollen.[36]

In addition to butterflies, moths pollinate flowers (phalaenophily). One notable example of this is the small shrub *Augusta rivalis*, which is common alongside the rivers of the Chiquibul region. It belongs to the Rubiaceae (coffee) family, many members of which are moth-pollinated. Plants pollinated in this way typically grow in the understory or subcanopy and have flowers that are white and strongly scented and that frequently open at twilight or during the night, when their intended vectors are most active. *Augusta rivalis* is no exception to this general rule. Its flowers, which usually have a thin petal (corolla) tube that is six to nine centimeters long, are known to be pollinated by large night-flying hawkmoths (Sphingidae) that track up and down the rivers at night, feeding off the nectar at the base of the floral tubes.[37] Hawkmoths are fast-flying insects and typically hover while they feed, expending large amounts of energy in flight.[38] Thus, they need copious supplies of energy-rich food. Not surprisingly, hawkmoth-pollinated flowers tend to have large reserves of nectar.[39]

Smallanthus uvedalius. The flower form of the Asteraceae (sunflower) family, with its stable landing platform, is typical of butterfly-pollinated flowers, although not all psycophilous flowers have this shape and not all members of Asteraceae are psycophilous. © Sam Bridgewater.

BY **JOHN S. ASHER**, Division of Invertebrate Zoology, American Museum of Natural History, and **STEVEN K. JAVOREK**, Agriculture and Agri-Food Canada, Atlantic Food and Horticulture Research Centre

As key pollinators of an incredible diversity of flowering plants, bees play a vital role in maintaining the structure and functioning of the Chiquibul ecosystem.

Published data on the bees of Belize is very limited, with a mere thirty species recorded from the country.[40] Until the turn of the millennium the bee fauna of the Chiquibul Forest was virtually undocumented, although some material exists in collections, such as specimens from Millionario dated from 1973 in the American Museum of Natural History.

Data on the bee fauna was compiled following study of approximately 1,500 specimens collected on fourteen trips to the Chiquibul between 2003 and 2009 through a cumulative sampling effort of approximately 500 man-hours. Sampling was conducted in different seasons as follows: April and May (2003-2009: 320 man-hours), February (2005-2007: 100 man-hours), November and December (2004, 2007: 50 man-hours), and October (2006: 30 man-hours). Most of the collecting was done in the vicinity of the Las Cuevas Research Station (16°43'58" N, 88°59'9" W) extending northwest to Millionario and east to the Monkey Tail Branch. Other collecting locations included Natural Arch (16°36'36" N, 89°01'19" W) and the junction of Millionario-Caracol Roads (16°50'41" N, 89°2'37" W) north to the Guacamayo Bridge (16°51'55" N, 89°2'17" W). The majority of bees were collected by net as they foraged on flowers or gathered minerals and nesting resources (mud, resin, and leaf material). Chemical baits (cineole, methyl salicylate, vanillin, eugenol, skatole, and limonene oxide) were used to attract male orchid bees (tribe Euglossini). Orchid bee-baiting stations were located

Euglossa variabilis visiting the orchid *Coryanthes speciosa*. Males visit orchids to collect scents that they use to attract females. © Steven Javorek.

CONTINUED FROM PREVIOUS PAGE

in the forest under generally closed canopy conditions along trail systems (fifty Hectare Plot, Bird Tower, and Monkey Tail Branch trails) originating at the Las Cuevas Research Station.

The bees of the Chiquibul Forest are represented by five families, fifty-nine genera, and 130 species (including morphospecies). The bee fauna is typical of Central America, with the most species-rich family being Apidae (thirty-seven genera, 80 species), comprising 61 percent of the bee fauna. Halictidae: Halictinae (twelve genera) and Megachilidae: Megachilinae (four genera) are also well represented, comprising 20 percent and 14 percent of bee species, respectively. Combined, the families Andrenidae (three genera, 3 species) and Colletidae (three genera, 3 species), previously undocumented from Belize, made up only a minor component of the bee fauna (5 percent). Eusocial bees, which include the stingless bees (tribe Meliponini) and the introduced honeybee (tribe Apini), comprise 16 percent of the bee fauna. The remaining 84 percent of species are noneusocial, including strictly solitary and communal or otherwise primitively social species. Adult female bees provision nests with pollen and nectar and, in the case of the apine tribes Tapinotaspidini, Tetrapediini, and Centridini, plant oils. Oil bees were represented by five genera and 16 species and comprised 12 percent of the bee fauna.

Bees were found nesting in a variety of substrates: preexisting cavities or sheltered areas where nests were constructed out of mud, resin, and/or wax; tunnels excavated by the bees in soil; and preexisting holes in wood or in the ground. Cleptoparasitic bees (bees that utilize the provisions of other bee species) made up 10 percent of the bee fauna (nine genera, 13 species).

Species identification of bees from the Chiquibul Forest proved difficult due to insufficient taxonomic literature and reliably determined reference material. Comparisons to material in the American Museum of Natural History and other collections from Panama, Guatemala, Mexico, and elsewhere often resulted in no match with the Belizean specimens or multiple apparent matches, suggesting the existence of new species, new synonymies, unresolved cryptic species complexes, or possibly misdetermined reference material. A great deal of revisionary study will be required before species determinations can be made with confidence across the entire fauna. The diverse genera *Megachile*, *Augochlora*, and *Lasioglossum* are in particular need of study, but numerous problems exist even within "well-known" taxa such as the Meliponini tribe.[41] The description of the bee fauna of the Chiquibul remains incomplete, as each trip continues to yield additional genus and species records.

BEE POLLINATION

Globally, bees are one of the most important pollination vectors, and mellitophily is critical to the successful reproduction of many tropical forest plant species.[42] For example, a study conducted at La Selva in Costa Rica indicated that over 40 percent of all the tree species were pollinated by bees,[43] of which large bees such as carpenter bees (*Xylocopa* spp.) were particularly common pollinators of canopy species. Most bees visiting flowers do so to harvest pollen that is used as the primary food for their brood. To aid this extractivism, they have specialized brushes, hairs (scopae), or pollen baskets (corbicula) on their hind legs to assist with carrying. Nectar may also be mixed with pollen to facilitate its transport. However, some types of bees may be attracted to flowers for the other products they provide, including oils and perfumes. All members of the Malphigiaceae plant family, for example, have a pair of conspicuous oil-producing glands (elaiophores) on each of the sepals of their flowers, and related structures are known in about 3 percent of all angiosperm families.[44] Some species—including *Mouriri myrtilloides* from the Chiquibul—even have oil glands on their anthers, although less than 2 percent of all the known bee species collect oil.[45] Many members of the Centridini tribe of the Apidae family have specialized hairs on their legs that serve as blades to cut into the oil glands; the bees use the oil primarily as a foodstuff for their brood and as a waterproof lining for their brood cells.

Important plant families of the Chiquibul known to be commonly pollinated by bees include Burseraceae, Bignoniaceae, Clusiaceae, Leguminosae, Sapotaceae, and Orchidaceae.[46] Studies have shown that many different types of bees can visit the same species of flower. For example, in a study of one of the common trees of the Chiquibul, the white cabbage bark (*Andira inermis*), flowers of a single individual were visited by over seventy bee species;[47] yet not all will be active pollinators. Of all plants, orchids are perhaps the most famously associated with bees, and their unusual association with one kind of bee in particular—the euglossine—has been the focus of much research (see "Orchids and Euglossine Bees" later in this chapter). Approximately 60 percent of all orchids are pollinated by bees, 10 percent of which are euglossines,[48] although moths, butterflies, ants, birds, and flies can also be pollen vectors. Typically, flowers pollinated by bees have some kind of stable platform, as bees must generally land in order to forage; many orchids have just such a structure.

With 109 species, orchids are the second-most diverse group of plants in the Chiquibul after the pea family (Leguminosae) and show a great variety of form.[49] Many are epiphytes and are characterized by pseudo bulbs that are organs for food and water storage. Orchids are famed for their beautiful, brightly colored, intricately designed flowers and their highly evolved and specialized pollination mechanisms. Orchids have three petals, one of which (the labellum) is usually highly modified and ornate and which may contain a nectary or spur. One unique feature is the structure of their sexual parts, the majority having a single stamen borne on a structure called a column (also known as a gynostemium). In essence, the column represents a fusion of all the male and female sexual parts. The anthers containing the pollen are usually located inside a depression on the column, and their exact position varies greatly and is of vital importance in the pollination process, determining which species of insect—from the many that may visit the flowers—are the pollinators. In many orchids the pollen itself is massed into structures called pollinia, the bases of which often taper to a stalk. Pollinia are known only in two plant families—Orchidaceae and Apocynaceae (in those members that were formerly in the Asclepiadaceae family)—and the evolution of this adaptation has likely played an important role in promoting the diversification of these groups.[50] Pollinia are typically deposited with incredible precision on the heads or bodies of an orchid's specific pollinator, and the flowers are formed so that only the stigmas of flowers of other individuals of the same species will pick up the pollen package should an insect carrying pollinia visit. Although many bee species may visit an orchid flower, only those that are of the right shape and size will accurately pick up the pollinia from one flower and deposit them in the correct place on another of the same species. Sometimes trigger mechanisms are involved in placing the pollinia.

The golden shower orchid (*Oncidium sphacelatum*), a common native orchid of the Chiquibul region, is pollinated by the oil-collecting bee *Centris nitida.* © Brett Adams. Courtesy The Belize Botanic Garden.

ORCHIDS AND EUGLOSSINE BEES

One of the most spectacular pollination mutualisms occurs between many species of neotropical orchids and euglossine bees (orchid bees) belonging to the Euglossini tribe. Five genera and 190 species are known from the tribe, with many of these being beautifully iridescent.[51] Examples of orchid genera present in the Chiquibul typically pollinated by euglossine bees include *Stanhopea, Dichaea, Chysis, Cycnoches, Galeottia, Gongora, Lycaste, Sobralia,* and *Vanilla.*

Euglossine bees are predominantly solitary, and both male and female bees visit and pollinate a range of flowers as they search for nectar, pollen, and resins. Nonorchid plant species from the Chiquibul pollinated by euglossines include the wayside shrub *Thevetia ahouai,* the vine *Arrabidaea chica,* and the tree *Andira inermis.* Evidence exists that in some cases the bees follow regular feeding routes (traplining). Unlike the female bees, the males visit flowers specifically to collect perfumes, which they harvest and store with specially modified legs. These fragrances are the main attractant and reward. Unlike other insect-pollinated flowers, nectar is not usually provided. In the case of orchids, the association between orchid and male bee can be highly specific, with one species of orchid being pollinated by only one species of bee.[52] In some associations the specificity of the attracting odor produced by the flower is believed to restrict the number of pollinating bee species. In others, flower size, shape, and color are important. However, evidence exists that in many associations the male bees are not dependent on any one orchid host and that an orchid may be visited by many different species of bee, although due to incompatibility between the structure of the flower and the visiting bee species, not all are pollinators.[53]

When one is examining plants at close quarters to watch bees hovering and landing on a range of flowers as they forage for pollen or perfume, occasionally a bee will make an especially loud but usually short-lived buzz, not dissimilar to a driver revving the engine at a traffic light. This noise is produced when the muscles of the bee's thorax are activated in a shivering mode while the wings remain disengaged, and it often occurs when bees alight on flowers where the anthers open by pores rather than slits, as in the genus *Solanum*, which belongs to the tomato family and is represented by sixteen species in the Chiquibul.[54] Other examples include *Mouriri myrtilloides* (Melastomataceae family) and the large, yellow-flowered *Cochlospermum vitifolium*.[55] The latter species is typical of disturbed habitats and is known to be primarily buzz-pollinated by carpenter (*Xylocopa* spp.) and *Centris* bees. The buzzing—also known as sonication—causes the anthers to vibrate, thereby facilitating the release of the pollen through pores. Many bee taxa are involved in buzz pollination, although honeybees (*Apis* spp.) do not display this behavior.

The beautiful, metallic-colored euglossine bees (*Euglossa* spp.) are believed to pollinate approximately 10 percent of orchids. © Steve Javorek.

The genus *Cochlospermum*, common across the Neotropics, is indicative of disturbed habitats and is known to be buzz-pollinated. © Jim Ratter.

CATERING TO ALL TASTES: FLOWER COLOR AND FRAGRANCE AS POLLINATOR ATTRACTANTS

Just as we wear fashionable clothes of diverse hues and perfume or aftershave to attract the opposite sex, so have flowers evolved a wide range of scents and colors to communicate with, and attract, their pollinators. The relative importance of color and scent varies greatly, depending upon the specific pollinating group. Hawkmoths, for instance, are known to rely primarily on scent to find flowers from a distance, using sight only at closer ranges; beetles, carrion flies, and euglossine bees are also known to be guided primarily by fragrance. In contrast, butterflies are believed to use long-distance visual clues to locate their nectar sources. Unlike humans, insects do not have noses. Instead they detect scent through their antennae; for some groups these are highly sophisticated organs that give insects the capability of "stereo olfaction" and enable them to navigate accurately by the sense of smell.[56]

Many chemicals are involved in the production of flower scents—such as terpenoids, aromatics, and sulfur-containing compounds. Floral scents are often specific to certain pollination syndromes. The production of carvone oxide, for example, is unique to flowers that are pollinated by male euglossine bees, such as those produced by some orchids, whereas sulfur compounds are particularly common in bat-pollinated flowers.[57] A good example of the evolutionary sophistication of floral scent is provided by the variety of orchid taxa that produce fragrances mimicking the sex pheromones of female bees of certain species. These orchids are pollinated when the aroused males of the same species attempt to copulate with them.

Flower colors are the result of plant pigments called flavonoids, which are divided into two main classes: anthocyanins (purple, blue, and most reds) and anthoxanthins (pale ivory to yellow). It is difficult for us to judge visually how flower color appears to animals, as the eyes of different taxonomic groups can be receptive to light from different parts of the spectrum. Some groups of insects and birds can see ultraviolet light, a capability that we do not have. The pigments of flowers that appear white to us absorb light in the ultraviolet region of the spectrum; they can appear blue-green to ultraviolet-sensitive insects such as bees.[58] Areas of pigment that absorb ultraviolet light are frequently found at the center of many bee-and butterfly-pollinated flowers, often accompanied by thin lines of similar pigment radiating toward the flower's center. These are nectar or honey guides and are highly visible to the intended pollinator, as they stand out against the other surrounding pigments.[59] Their function is to assist the visitor in locating the center of the flower, in the way that runway lights at night guide an airplane home. There has been much debate as to whether flower signals have driven the evolution of bee vision.[60] Although this may be the case, it is believed that insects in general were already well adapted to distinguish between different flower colors—especially ultraviolet, blue, and green—more than 500 MYA.[61] This is about 400 million years before the extensive radiation of the angiosperms; thus, insect-pollinated flowers probably evolved to capitalize on preexisting insect vision. In addition to insects, other animal groups have distinct color preferences, although there are no hard and fast rules. Colors in the human visual system cannot be used to accurately classify flowers into pollination syndromes.[62] That said, bat-pollinated flowers tend to be dull-colored, and bats are generally believed to be color blind.[63] However, strong visual contrasts are thought to help them locate their favored flowers. For this reason, bat-pollinated flowers are often held away from the plant that produces them. In contrast, birds such as hummingbirds tend to have a preference for red flowers.[64] For hummingbirds this is a learned association between color and reward, as hummingbirds can be trained to visit flowers of other colors. Most bees, however, lack sensitivity to red, and thus bee-pollinated flowers tend to be a color other than red.[65]

Nectar chemistry also differs among pollination syndromes. The nectar of bee-pollinated plants usually has a higher concentration of sugars than those pollinated by birds.[66] Even within a pollination syndrome, the types of sugars in the nectar may vary, depending upon the exact pollinator. The nectar of hummingbird-pollinated flowers, for example, is rich in sucrose, while flowers pollinated by perching birds are typically dominated by hexoses.[67]

FIG WASPS

The fig genus *Ficus* is highly diverse, comprising about seven hundred species worldwide.[68] Over twenty different species of figs are known from Belize,[69] eight of which have been recorded from the Chiquibul.[70] A fig flower (synconium) is a curious structure. Most flowering plants have their flowers on display to facilitate the pollination process, but the small flowers of figs are amassed into an inflorescence that is hidden from view by being turned in on itself and presented in the form of a hollow fig; the structure can be thought of as being similar to a small ball with a mass of flowers lining the inside of its hollow cavity and with a single tiny entrance at its apex. Fig wasps are the only pollinators of these flowers, and the association between figs and fig wasps is one of classic obligate mutualism. Fig wasp is the broad name given to tiny wasps that breed exclusively in the enclosed inflorescences of figs. Beautifully colored and often with a distinctive metallic sheen, they belong to the Agaonidae family.

Figs and fig wasps are entirely reliant on each other to complete their reproductive cycle. This interdependence is highly specialized. Although it was originally thought that each fig species was pollinated by only one species of fig wasp, it is now known that the one-to-one rule does not always hold true and several may be involved.[71] However, studies of the widespread fig species *Ficus pertusa*, which is known from Belize and is pollinated by the fig wasp *Blastophagus sylvestrii*, have shown that 99 percent of the wasps arriving at this

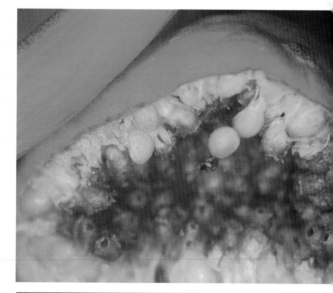

Cross section of a single synconium of the fig *Ficus citrifolia*.
© Daniel Solano.

fig are of this species, indicating that host specificity is extremely high.[72] The fig–fig wasp association has developed over millions of years, with each species of an association evolving reciprocal adaptations. One such adaptation is the length of the wasp's ovipositor, the structure through which it lays its eggs. This exactly matches the length of the style and ovary of the host fig in which its eggs are laid.

Figs can be either monoecious or dioecious (see the boxed text "The Sex Life of Plants" earlier in this chapter). Among monoecious species, male and female flowers occur on the same fig. The typical fig wasp's life cycle and associated pollination sequence described here are for these mixed-sex flowers. The female fig wasp locates the figs in which she breeds by tracking chemical signals produced by the developing flowers. Such volatile chemicals might be attractive only to the intended species of fig wasp.[73] Although the fig appears completely enclosed, there is a minute opening to its interior called the ostiole. It is through this narrow passage that the fig wasp must crawl to gain entry to the fig flowers that she needs to complete her breeding cycle. Even for fig wasps, which are tiny and flattened in form, it is a tight squeeze to negotiate the ostiole; progress is aided by backward-pointing teeth on the female's mandibles, lower head, or legs. Once inside the fig, she locates the ovaries of some of the many small female flowers lining the fig cavity. She attempts to lay her eggs close to the ovule via an ovipositor, a process that is not always successful because the female flowers are of two types: those whose style and ovary lengths are compatible with the length of the female's ovipositor and those whose are not.[74] These two types of female flowers ensure that not all of the fig's ovaries will be injected with eggs and that some will develop into seed. During the attempts of the female fig wasp to lay her eggs, she dusts the stigmas of other flowers with pollen borne from the original fig where she hatched. In monoecious figs, it is impossible for male flowers to pollinate female flowers within the same fig, as the male flowers develop later. This ensures cross-pollination between different genetic individuals. Ovaries in which eggs have been deposited are transformed into tiny galls, and it is within these that the next generation of fig wasp larvae develop, feeding on the ovaries. Each wasp offspring therefore develops at the cost of a seed. Once the female wasp has laid her eggs, she generally dies, trapped within the fig, although some have been known to escape and visit other figs.[75] Once mature, all the individuals of the next generation of wasps emerge from their galls into the cavity at the same time. Both males and females are present. The male's life span is short, however. His role is to breed with the female and then chew an exit through the developing fruit through which she can exit. Once this is done, he has served his function and dies. Before leaving, the female of some species (e.g., *Blastophaga* spp.) collects pollen into special pollen pockets; in others (e.g., *Tetraopus* spp.) her body becomes passively dusted with pollen.[76] Active collection of pollen occurs for about two thirds of all the fig wasp species. Once this pollen load is delivered to the next fig flower, the cycle is complete. The fig in which she developed continues to mature, becoming sweet and fleshy and providing a source of food for many forest animals. For this mutualistic association to continue, it is essential that the flowers of different fig trees within the same population mature at different times so that a tree with developing flowers of the right age is always available for the recently emerged female fig wasp to locate.

MAMMAL POLLINATION

Frugiverous (fruit-eating), vegetarian, and omnivorous (diet-generalist) mammals—humans included—are eager consumers of the fruits of the pollination process. Indeed, all mammals are directly or indirectly entirely dependent on the products of pollination for their survival. What is less well known is that some mammals are also involved in the pollination process. Although there is evidence that mammals such as the woolly opossum (*Caluromys derbianus*) and rodents can be involved in pollination,[77] such incidents appear to be rare. However, what is certain is that bats are important pollen vectors for a broad range of plant groups, and an estimated 0.7–1 percent of the angiosperm flora of the Neotropics is believed to be pollinated in this way.[78]

Bat pollination (*cheiropterophily*) occurs throughout the Tropics. In the Neotropics it is performed by members of the leaf-nosed bat family (Phyllostomidae). Of the leaf-nosed bats, the subfamily Glossophaginae has evolved the highest degree of specialization for feeding from flowers, and nectar-feeding bats typically have long, hair-tipped tongues that enable them to collect the nectar found deep within a flower. The nightly energy expenditure of bats is high. For their size they are among the biggest energy users of all mammals.[79] Thus, they need large amounts of fuel, and bat-pollinated flowers typically have abundant nectar to ensure that their pollinating vector does not run out of energy. Although the production of copious nectar is costly to the plant, the investment is worthwhile, as bats can be effective pollinators by transferring pollen over large distances. Typically, a glossophagine bat hovers while feeding, only spending a short period of time—often less than one second—before moving on to the next flower. Because bats must continually feed to maintain their energy reserves, it is important that they can easily find the flowers upon which they feed. Although the sense of scent is vitally important and bats are able to see, they famously orient themselves by echolation, and it has been proven that certain flowers with a high echo reflectance are particularly good at helping bats to locate them. It has been shown that some species belonging to the genus *Mucuna*—a vine member of the pea family, five species of which are known to occur in Belize—have an upper petal (vexillum) that is particularly effective at being detected by bats.[80]

One important tree species from the Chiquibul believed to be bat-pollinated is the ceiba (*Ceiba pentandra*), the sacred tree of the Maya. Across the Neotropics, a variety of bat species have been recorded as frequent visitors to the large, night-opening white flowers of this widely distributed species, and ceiba pollen has been recorded from bat fur. Studies in Brazil indicate that the spear-nosed bats *Phyllostomus hastatus* and

Flower of the provision tree (*Pachira aquatica*), a bat-pollinated species. © Axel Poulson.

P. discolor are important pollinators; both these species occur in Belize. However, a variety of other nectar-feeding long-tongued bats also occur within the country's confines, including the common long-tongued bat (*Glossophaga soricina*) and the brown long-tongued bat (*G. commissarisi*). The ceiba is known to be a prodigious nectar producer, making it an attractive pit stop for nectar-feeding bats; at least ten liters of nectar are produced by a single tree during one night.[81] Although the ceiba is believed to be primarily bat-pollinated, many other groups of animals visit its flowers during the day, including birds, which may also be involved in pollination.[82] However, it has been shown that nectar production begins at dusk,[83] and bat-pollination would thus seem to be the favored mechanism. Another member of the ceiba family (Malvaceae *sensu lato*) known to be bat-pollinated is the provision tree (*Pachira aquatica*), which is commonly found growing along the banks of Belize's rivers.

BIRD POLLINATION

The classic bird-pollinated flower tends to be bright, with red, orange, and yellow among the most favored colors. Usually such flowers are also tubular in form and fairly rigid, and their stamens are positioned to deposit pollen on the bill and head of the visiting bird.[84] One of the most important bird groups that act as pollinators in Central

America are hummingbirds, which hover as they probe for nectar at the base of flowers with their long, curved bills. Hummingbird pollination is greatest at lower structural levels in the forest and is relatively rare for canopy trees. There are numerous examples of bird pollination (*ornithophily*) in the Chiquibul, including the common wayside shrubs *Hamelia patens*, *Psychotria elata*, *Russelia sarmentosa*, *Justicia aurea*, *Helicteres guazumaefolia*, *Odontonema callistachyum*, *Costus pulverulentus*, and *Heliconia* spp. The *Heliconia* genus (wild plantain) is represented in the Chiquibul by four species. These understory plants are particularly abundant at forest margins, along riverbanks, and in disturbed areas. Their bright inflorescences—yellow flowers and bright orange or red bracts—are famously pollinated by hummingbirds. In addition, many bromeliads (e.g., *Tillandsia multicaulis*) are known to be hummingbird-pollinated,[85] as are many species of *Erythrina*, a tree belonging to the pea family. Although some hummingbird species are known to be territorial, others follow regular feeding routes between flowers (traplining) in different *Heliconia* populations.[86] Birds do not have a well-developed sense of smell, so bird-pollinated flowers usually have only a faint odor, if one is present at all. Although their olfactory powers may be poor, they have more complex color vision than humans; whereas we have the ability to see three primary colors (red, yellow, blue), with all other colors formed from a combination of these, diurnal birds have a visual system characterized by four or five pigments as well as receptors containing oil droplets that can filter and refine wavelength perception.[87] In addition, like bees, birds have an ability to see ultraviolet light. There is a known correspondence between the length of hummingbird bills and the length of the tubular flowers they pollinate.[88] Although short-tubed flowers allow access to nectar by both long- and short-billed birds, long-tubed flowers tend to exclude short-billed pollinators. Some short-billed hummingbirds are known to cheat long-tubed flower species by piercing the floral tube at its base with their bill. Although it has been suggested by some

Costus pulverulentus (Costaceae) is hummingbird-pollinated. © William Milliken.

authors that the nectar of hummingbird-pollinated flowers has a high sugar content to satisfy the high energy needs of their pollen vectors, their nectar is generally dilute, containing only about 16–28 percent sugar.[89] For many insect-pollinated flowers, sugar concentrations of nectar are far higher.[90] It is not necessarily advantageous for a plant population to satisfy the appetites of its visitors completely, as this will reduce the chance that the pollinators will visit flowers from many individuals and from many populations, a situation ideal for effective cross-pollination. In addition, if sugar concentrations are too high, the resultant nectar would be highly viscous. Such a thick solution might inhibit rapid ingestion by hummingbirds that depend to an extent on passive capillarity, the spontaneous movement of liquids up narrow tubes.

Although they are the most frequently seen, hummingbirds are not the only birds to pollinate flowers; many other groups are also known to be nectar-feeding, including vireos, warblers, tanagers, finches, orioles, blackbirds, and honeycreepers.[91] Some of the species in these groups also act as pollinators. One well-researched plant species common in the Chiquibul is the vine *Combretum fruticosum*. The yellow-red "bottle brush" flowers of this species are often highly visible in the canopy of the forest and can be readily seen from the veranda of the research station when in season. A study of this species, conducted in Mexico, recorded thirty-one bird species feeding on its nectar.[92] Of these, twenty-one were captured with pollen on their bodies, suggesting that they might be pollinators. They included various orioles, warblers, and buntings. The provision of a convenient perching platform appears to be common in such cases; this is rare in species that are pollinated only by hummingbirds.

The vine *Combretum fruticosum* is very likely to be bird-pollinated. © Sam Bridgewater.

One of the largest trees of the Chiquibul is the mapola (*Bernoullia flammea*), and the striking red flowers of this forest giant can be seen from the observation tower during the dry season. Its floral display is particularly striking because it flowers when leafless. Unlike hummingbird-pollinated flowers, the flowers of the mapola face inward, making it difficult for hovering visitors to access their nectar.[93] Research conducted in Mexico has shown that perching birds such as the melodious blackbird (*Dives dives*), the great-tailed grackle (*Quiscalus mexicanus*), and the orchard oriole (*Icterus spurius*) are frequent visitors to mapola flowers and are highly likely to be among the pollinators.[94] All of these species are common in Belize, the last being a migrant that visits Belize between August and April. Although many species of *Erythrina* are hummingbird-pollinated, a few are known to be pollinated by nonhovering birds.[95] In these species the inflorescence is held horizontally, with the flower relatively open to allow easy access to the nectar within the flower.

SEED DISPERSAL

The Cornish Coast of southern England juts out into the Atlantic Ocean, pointing almost directly to the Caribbean many thousands of miles to the west. Beachcombing is a favored pastime in the region, and occasionally a collector walking along the high tide mark will be rewarded with an unusual prize released by the sea: a bean. But not just any bean. A bean unknown from the European flora: an *Entada*. It started its life upon a vine in the tropical forests of Central America, was washed down rivers into the Caribbean Sea, floated across thousands of miles of ocean carried by the North Atlantic Drift, and was washed up in a cove, ending its life as a treasured keepsake in a curiosity cabinet. The scenario above is no flight of fancy. Every year thousands of tropical seeds end up on European shores, and their appearance is so common that they have been given specific names by the locals who find them. The sea bean (*Mucuna* spp.) and Mary's nut (*Entada* spp.) represent just two examples of Belizean genera showing exceptional dispersal powers.[96] Some have even been shown to still retain the capacity to germinate, despite spending many months or even years at sea.

Although plants do not have the ability to move, their fruit and seed can be transported away from the parent so that the species can exploit new habitats. Although such long-distance transport as described above may not be the norm, dispersal mechanisms are nevertheless critical for plant survival and involve a wide variety of vectors. Some are self-propelled by explosive release mechanisms, while others hitch rides with wind, water, or animals.

Mary's nut (*Entada gigas* seed), washed up on a Scottish shore. Drift seeds from Central America can travel many thousands of miles across the Atlantic, washing up on foreign shores months or even years after having been dispersed. © Sam Bridgewater.

Without effective dispersal mechanisms, all seed would fall en masse close to the parent tree. Even though there are clear advantages to occupying a site whose soil conditions successfully allowed the parent plant to reach maturity, such a situation can also be problematic, as the seedlings would be in direct competition with one another for limited nutrients and light. If they are from a light-demanding species, they will also be at a distinct disadvantage growing in the canopy shade of their parent. In addition, having a high density of seed and seedlings in one location makes them more susceptible to pest predation. Such density-dependent mortality provides a selective advantage for plants to disperse their seed widely and may be one of the major mechanisms by which species diversity in tropical forests is maintained (see "Ecological Theories Explaining Plant Diversity in the Tropics" in chapter 1).

What is clear is that the dispersal of seed is of great importance in maintaining forest structure and diversity. If a species shows a good dispersal ability, it will have a higher chance of exploiting new establishment opportunities, such as forest gaps, should any become available. Dispersal ability also has genetic consequences—those species whose seed can disperse far from the parent plant have an increased likelihood of outbreeding, which can confer increased fitness and an evolutionary advantage.[97] Because of these factors, one might therefore expect the majority of individuals of a species to be widely spaced. However, clumping of individuals of a single species is frequently found in tropical forests, as shown by a study from Bladen Nature Reserve, to the south of the Chiquibul and the Maya Divide.[98]

The two primary seed dispersal mechanisms in the Chiquibul are animals and wind.

ANIMAL SEED DISPERSAL

Between 62 and 93 percent of all tropical trees produce fleshy fruit eaten by a broad variety of vertebrates,[99] and about 90 percent of tropical arboreal animals consume fruit.[100] This suggests that frugivores and omnivores—primarily mammals and birds but to a lesser extent fish and reptiles—are of great importance in the dispersal of seed and the maintenance and structure of tropical forests.[101] Indeed, the global rise to dominance of flowering plants during the Cretaceous era (146–66 MYA) has been attributed in part to their successful coevolution with mammals and birds, with increased dispersal capacity being a vital contributing factor. This assumes, of course, that not all seeds are destroyed while they are handled, are eaten, or pass through the gut of the feeding animal. Such predation is indeed highly significant and is an important force in structuring forest communities. Although most of the fruit produced by the parent tree may fall mostly below it and a high proportion of the seed ingested by animals may be destroyed, the strategy of animal dispersal will nevertheless be worthwhile even if only a small percentage of seeds are effectively dispersed to sites where their chance for survival might be higher.[102] Animal dispersal is more likely than wind dispersal to be directed, with the distribution of scattered seed and fruit related to animal behavior. For example, it has been suggested that tropical birds often feed within canopy gaps, thus skewing the release of seeds of those plant species distributed by them toward this habitat.[103]

Two primates are found in the Chiquibul Forest: the Mexican black howler monkey (*Alouatta pigra*) and the Central American spider money (*Ateles geoffroyi*). Both are significant consumers of fruit, able to ingest and transport much larger seeds, such as those of the hog plum (*Spondias radlkoferi*), than can be carried by the majority of birds. The ecology and food preferences of both species are explored elsewhere (see "The Forest Swingers: The Mexican Black Howler Monkey and the Central American Spider Monkey" in chapter 4). Spider monkeys in particular are highly frugivorous and are known to ingest a large variety of plant fruit, with most seeds passing through their gut undamaged. They also roam over large home ranges—often hundreds of hectares—making them ideal dispersers.[104] A study conducted in Amazonia, for example, has shown that, on average, an individual spider monkey defecates daily over 500 seeds larger than 1 millimeter in diameter and over 100 seeds larger than 3 millimeters in diameter.[105] In this study, the vast majority of the seed dispersed was more than 100 meters from the feeding tree, the average distance being about 450 meters. The perceived importance of primates in dispersal is such that there is great concern about forests where hunting is rife and the massive impact it may have on forest diversity and structure. The hunting associated with the *Chamaedorea* leaf industry in the Chiquibul (see "Xaté, Leaf of Gold" in chapter 3), for example, is certainly cause for concern.

Primates are far from being the only arboreal mammals to disperse seed. Squirrels, kinkajous, coatimundis, and many bats, including the Jamaican fruit-eating bat, are also highly frugivorous and contribute to seed dispersal. Seeds of species of *Solanum*, *Piper*, *Ficus*, and *Cecropia*, for example, are all known to be dispersed in part by this last group of animals.[106]

Terrestrial mammals are also of great significance as both secondary dispersers and predators of fruit and seed once they have reached the ground. Although much of the seed found by such animals is destroyed when eaten, a proportion is often

The Mexican black howler monkey (*Alouatta pigra*) is a significant consumer of fruit and an important agent in dispersing the seed of trees such as the hog plum (*Spondias radlkoferi*). © Zoë Goodwin.

removed and buried (cached) for later consumption but then never retrieved. Although seed-eating large rodents (granivores) such as the paca and agouti are certainly significant, a study in Belize has indicated that smaller rodents may also be important dispersers through caching.[107] Desmarest's spiny pocket mouse is a burrowing rodent, and this species has been shown to be significant in transporting and burying female bullhoof (*Ampelocera hottlei*) and warrie cohune (*Astrocaryum mexicanum*) fruit. Dispersal is rarely far from the parent plant and may still suffer from density-dependent mortality, but the burial of the seed of these species by small rodents may nonetheless enhance germination prospects. Tapirs, peccaries, and deer are also implicated in seed dispersal, despite destroying a high proportion of the seeds they consume. Their dietary preferences and the role that tapir may play in ensuring the long-term existence of large-seeded trees, most of whose original dispersers have become extinct, were discussed earlier (see "The Mountain Cow" in chapter 4).

A high percentage of the birds at Las Cuevas are frugivores, and parrots, toucans, trogons, pigeons, tinamous, finches, manikins, tanagers, sparrow, blackbirds, thrushes, the crested guan, and the great curassow are among those groups whose diet consists of a high proportion of fruit and seed. Like bats, birds are highly motile and range over large distances, making them ideal seed dispersers. However, much of the seed consumed by some of these groups (e.g., parrots) is destroyed when eaten. Bird-dispersed fruit of understory plants are typically small, fleshy, and showy, because either the fruit

The red arillate seeds of *Compsoneura sprucei* (Myristacaceae) are attractive to birds. © Sam Bridgewater.

is brightly colored or it is conspicuous due the contrast between its dark color and that of the bright fruiting structure on which it is borne. For example, the understory palm genus *Chamaedorea* has black fruits that grow on a bright orange fruiting structure, and the fruits of *Heliconia* are conspicuous against the plant's brightly colored bracts. In contrast, the fruits of bird-dispersed canopy trees are usually not fleshy but open at maturity to reveal seeds with bright, palatable, bird-attracting attachments (arils). Examples of such genera include *Inga*, *Guarea*, *Compsoneura*, and *Virola*. Some plant species have even evolved imitation arils; the resulting seed is termed "mimetic." Such adaptations are believed to deceive birds into feeding off them with no fleshy reward given in return, as with John Crow bead (*Ormosia schipii*). Yet birds that eat mimetic seeds may gain some advantage even without a food reward; according to one hypothesis, hard seeds of genera such as *Ormosia* may act as grit in the gut and aid with the grinding and digestion of other seed species.[108]

Even insects such as ants and dung beetles are known to act as secondary dispersers of seed.[109] Dung beetles locate fresh herbivore and frugivore dung, transport it short distances, and bury it, a process that can aid seed germination. The seed of ant-dispersed species typically have fat-rich appendages (called elaiosomes) to attract their disperser, which collects and transports the seed to the nest, where the elaisome is consumed and the seed discarded unharmed. The ant nest may provide ideal opportunities for germination.

WIND DISPERSAL

Although animal dispersal of seed is the dominant syndrome of tropical forests, wind assistance (anemochory) is also of considerable significance, especially in more seasonally dry areas, where about 30 percent of canopy tree species may be dispersed in this way.[110] Indeed, many of the Chiquibul's most characteristic trees are wind-dispersed, including mahogany (*Swietenia macrophylla*), cedar (*Cedrela odorata*), quamwood (*Schizolobium parahyba*), nargusta (*Terminalia amazonia*), jobillo (*Astronium graveolans*), and the ceiba (*Ceiba pentandra*). The fruits of wind-dispersed species may themselves be adapted for wind dispersal; for example, they may have attachments like wings (e.g., nargusta in the Combretaceae family), a habit also common in the pea (Fabaceae) and soapberry (Sapindaceae) families, or they may open with the released seed, adapted to be carried by the wind. The white, feather-light kapok fibers surrounding the seed of the ceiba tree provide one such example. Frequently, wind-dispersal mechanisms are timed to coincide with the dry season.[111] Indeed, in some cases (e.g., quamwood), dispersal depends on the drying of the fruit pod to explosively launch the seed and its attachment into the air when under tension.

Wind-dispersed seeds are frequently of characteristic form. All tend to show adaptations that slow their rate of descent by making them float or gyrate as they fall, thereby maximizing the probability they will move horizontally under the influence of wind.

The winged fruits of the vine *Serjania lundellii* are wind-dispersed. © David Harris.

Some groups of plants (e.g., Orchidaceae) typically produce tiny dustlike seed that are light and thus easily transported. Others, such as mahogany and cedar, have propeller-type protuberances that aid their dispersal through gyration, although not all members of the mahogany family (Meliaceae) show this dispersal form. Other species have light, papery wings of various forms, a trait common in the mayflower family (Bignoniaceae), or they have seeds with fine hairs to increase aerial buoyancy (e.g., Bombacaceae). There is no need for the fruits or seeds of wind-dispersed species to be brightly colored or to contain a high proportion of sweet, edible pulp, which are typical traits of animal-dispersed species. Wind dispersal is uncommon among understory shrubs.

KEYSTONE SPECIES

Although all species are in some way interdependent if an ecological web is examined closely enough, some appear to play a pivotal role in the ecology and maintenance of diversity. These are called keystone species because their well-being is essential for the survival of many other forms of life. It has been argued that such species should receive special conservation status, as their extinction would precipitate a wave of further extinctions of those species that depended upon them.[112] However, the concept of keystone species has been much criticized, and some researchers believe that there is insufficient evidence to suggest that, except for a few proven cases from coral reef research,[113] only a few specific species provide the cornerstone of ecological webs. They also argue that it may be counterproductive for conservation initiatives to single out putative keystone species for special protection until there is a better understanding of the relative importance of all links in an ecosystem.

The fruiting and flowering of plants in tropical forests is not constant throughout the year, and there can be times when food resources are in short supply for frugivores. In particular, there tends to be a general dearth of fruit resources toward the end of the wet season and at the beginning of the dry season. Certain groups of plants in tropical forests are known to provide valuable fruits that sustain many species of animal during these times of scarcity. In Belize this role may be provided by fig trees (*Ficus* spp.), of which twenty-two species occur in the country. Figs are fast-growing and, although generally rare in the forest in terms of population numbers, are among the most diverse tree genera of the Chiquibul. They are especially prevalent in disturbed areas around river margins. Figs are often portrayed as keystone species due to their notoriously copious production of fruit, the fruit's palatability, and the large numbers of animal species that are known to eat them.[114] For example, toucans, guans, tanagers, orioles, agoutis, peccaries, kinkajou, coatis, spider and howler monkeys, and fruit-eating bats are all known to be generalist feeders of figs. Some species, such as the common Jamaican fruit-eating bat (*Artibeus jamaicensis*), are even known to be specialist fig consumers, with fig species particularly adapted to bat dispersal producing dull green, sweet-smelling fruit (e.g., *Ficus colubrinii*).[115] Those that attract birds in addition to other generalist frugivores tend to have smaller, brightly colored fruit (often red) and are not scented (e.g., *Ficus insipida*). Figs are not the only trees to produce valuable fruit resources. Many others, including the sapodilla (*Manilkara* spp.), the hog plum (*Spondia radlkoferi*), the cherry (*Pseudalmedia spuria*), and a wide range of palms (including *Chamaedorea* spp.) also produce copious amounts of palatable fruits. However, what sets figs apart from these species are their fruiting times. All individuals of hog plum and sapodilla tend to flower and fruit at roughly the same time (synchronously) in the periods February–March and July–August respectively, thus producing a short-lived glut of food, followed by a long period of famine until the next fruiting episode the following year. Fig species are very different in that the individuals of a single species of a population tend to flower at different times (asynchronously), so there is usually fig fruit available somewhere in the forest.[116] It is for this reason that they are considered keystone species, providing a source of year-round food and sustaining frugivores over lean periods of the year when other tree taxa are not fruiting. In part, the asynchronous flowering and fruiting behavior of individuals of each fig species has been attributed to their unusual, highly specific association with their pollinating wasps (see "Fig Wasps" earlier in this chapter). The wasps have a relatively short life cycle, so the fig species need a constant source of flowers throughout the year to ensure that their populations are maintained. However, all the flowers produced by any one individual mature at the same time. This is thought to have evolved to force the agaonid wasps to depart from the tree in which they developed in search of other flowering trees, thus promoting outcrossing.

BIOLOGICAL RHYTHMS AND SEASONAL CHANGES

Built on top of a hill, the observation tower of Las Cuevas rises to a height of seven hundred meters and provides exceptional views across the forest canopy. Such vistas are usually the sole preserve of the thermal-soaring turkey vultures or the scarlet macaws as they track to their roosting and feeding sites. If one makes weekly ascents of the tower, it soon becomes clear that every day the surveyed panorama is subtly different from that of the preceding week. This is due to distinct sequences in the biological rhythms of the forest's component species as they flower and fruit or shed their leaves. Visitors to Las Cuevas in February, for example, are likely to witness one of the most spectacular canopy displays of all as the quamwood tree (*Schizolobium parahyba*) comes into flower. This species is common throughout the Chiquibul, and its dense yellow flowers are clearly visible scattered throughout the canopy as all individuals of the

Canopy view of flowering red moho (*Trichospermum grewiifolium*), along with a close-up of the flowers and leaves. © Sam Bridgewater.

species flower synchronously in a glorious display. Throughout the year, such sequences continue, and there is rarely a month when no canopy tree is in flower, although there are distinct flowering "peaks" that tend to coincide with the dry season. As the dry season progresses, a number of species also lose their leaves, and as the deciduous habit is displayed, the canopy varies in color as leaves of individual trees senesce before falling. The deciduous nature of Belize's different forest types is an important criterion used in their classification (see "Modern Vegetation Classifications and the UNESCO System" in chapter 2), and Belize's markedly seasonal climate is one of the most important factors influencing its ecology.

Phenology is the scientific discipline dedicated to investigating the patterns and causes of regular, natural phenomena such as leaf loss and flowering. In recent years interest in phenology has risen dramatically, as climate change causes alterations in these patterns. There are concerns that shifts in flowering and associated fruiting times might upset the natural balance between these and other species whose life cycles are inextricably linked.

THE DECIDUOUS HABIT

Autumn in temperate regions is famous for the associated beautiful color changes undergone by the leaves of the deciduous forest trees. This event occurs when the days become shorter and colder, being a precursor to winter leaf fall. The most famous manifestation of this annually occurring phenomenon is "the fall" of the maple and oak forests of New England, which has become an important ecological tourist attraction. The changes in leaf color are due to changes in the leaves' pigmentation: a reduction in the production of the usually dominant photosynthetic green pigment (chlorophyll), increased visibility of carotenoids (yellow, browns, and orange pigments), and increased production of red and purple pigments (anthocyanins).

Although the event is less publicized, some plant species of tropical forests also lose their leaves en masse at certain times of the year, a phenomenon often associated with periods of drought. Water is necessary for plants to photosynthesize, but there is constant loss of this resource through evaporation from leaves. This loss creates a water pressure difference between the foliage and the roots, causing water to be drawn from the roots through the plant's internal plumbing system (xylem). The process is not problematic when water is readily available from the soil—as it is during the wet season—but it can be harmful to the plant if there is no water to replenish what is being lost. One manifestation of this stress is the creation of "air embolisms" within the xylem. Belize has a pronounced dry season between February and June that is particularly marked in the north. Many plant species in Belize, including a number of trees in the Chiquibul, avoid water stress by shedding their leaves during these periods of water stress. However, the forests in the north tend to be far more deciduous. Although not all species shed their leaves entirely, there is generally a visibly pronounced difference in canopy cover between seasons. Particularly noteworthy deciduous species of the Chiquibul include the quamwood (*Schizolobium parahyba*), the cedar (*Cedrela odorata*), and the bay cedar (*Guazuma ulmifolia*); many more shed their leaves entirely or in part. The cue for leaf fall is still poorly understood. Changes in day length, temperature, and evaporation rates associated with the onset of the dry season have all been cited as potential triggers, but the onset of water stress is thought to be the most important.[117] Variations in the rooting patterns of species, in the inherent resistance of their leaves to drought, and in leaf construction and maintenance costs also influence the manifestation of the deciduous or evergreen habit and the relative timing of leaf fall.[118]

There have been few detailed studies on the deciduous nature of Belize's trees, with the notable exception of one study conducted toward the end of the dry season in Shipstern Nature Reserve on the northern coast.[119] This research focused on ten deciduous species, including the gumbo-limbo (*Bursera simaruba*), black poisonwood (*Metopium brownei*), *Lysiloma latisiliiquum*, and the breadnut (*Brosimum alicastrum*). Data from this work revealed that the majority of the trees studied produced new flushes of leaves toward the end of the dry season (April), shortly before the main onset of the rains. This seems surprising at first glance, as mass production of new leaves is costly to the trees and water availability is a prerequisite for leaf expansion. If sufficient water is unavailable, any new leaf flushes are likely to be lost. However, this might not present a problem to species with an ability to store water in their trunks (e.g., gumbo-limbo), or those which are deep-rooted or have ready access to hidden supplies of groundwater. Thus, conditions of drought may be more apparent than real, and although important, the incidence of rain is not necessarily the only determining factor. Studies have shown that trees of dry forests tend to deploy a greater percentage of their roots deeper in the soil than their counterparts in wet forests, and this is likely a mechanism for increasing their access to water. It is believed that the early leafing of deciduous tropical species is favored by trees to make maximum use of the higher levels of sunlight available during the dry season.[120] It is also a means to avoid predation by herbivores, which are at their least abundant at this time.

FLOWERING SYNCHRONY

For species whose individuals are unable to pollinate themselves, some degree of flowering synchronization between different individuals is paramount for their survival. It has been proposed that the evolutionary "driver" of flowering synchrony is the increased chance of outcrossing and the associated genetic variability it provides.[121] Mass flowering may also increase the potential attractiveness of a plant species to its pollinators and increase their foraging efficiency.[122] The number of individuals available to inter-breed at the same time within a population clearly influences the number of potential offspring produced and the degree of genetic mixing. This in turn can influence the rate at which a species evolves. In addition to the exact time that flowering begins, its longevity is important. Exact synchronization of flowering is especially important for species whose individuals have very short-lived flowers, lasting only a night or a day. If flowering of an individual of such a species deviates from other individuals by just twenty-four hours, there may be no chance for reproduction that year. Not all species flower synchronously, of course; figs provide a good example of a group of plants whose coevolutionary success with fig wasps depends on asynchronous flowering (see "Fig Wasps" earlier in this chapter).

Synchronous flowering of many individuals of quamwood (*Schizolobium parahyba*) is apparent in this view of the Chiquibul Forest canopy. © Sam Bridgewater.

Just as water availability is critical for leaf production, so too is it essential for flowering to occur, and flowering may vary within a species in areas of high or low groundwater availability. Flowering peaks during the dry season is a common occurrence across the Tropics, and there is a clear link between sunlight levels (which are highest in the dry season due to reduced cloud cover) and flower and fruit production.[123] Among the many theories that have been put forward to explain this phenomenon, one suggests that the dry season provides optimal conditions for reproductive success.[124] According to this theory, leafless flowering improves the visibility of flowers to pollinators, while the weather of the dry season provides ideal conditions for important pollinating insect groups, such as bees. Conversely, populations of harmful herbivorous insects that might eat flowers are known to be particularly low during this season. However, clarifying the factors that trigger flowering is complicated, as many months might separate the actual development of flower buds and final flowering, which suggests that different cues might be triggering the two events.[125] In addition, although many species flower only once a year, some—including the cedar (*Cedrela odorata*)—may flower several times, especially in both August and December, with both events coinciding with different stages of the rainy season.

It is thought that flowering during the dry season might be advantageous if it results in fruit that develops in time for their seeds to be shed at the start of the rainy season, providing improved chances for seedling success. The mode of seed dispersal is also a factor influencing the time at which fruits mature. It has been argued, for example, that wind-dispersal of seeds is most efficient during the dry season, when leaves are often absent.[126] Fruit development times for trees in the Caribbean vary widely among species, although between three and six months is typical of the time required.[127] Flowering while leafless may also ensure that leaf production can occur promptly at the onset of the wet season, with no competition for resources needed for flower production.[128] Rapid leaf production at this time is vital, as it ensures that species can grow quickly and compete for limited forest light. The flowering period varies from species to species and can last for many weeks. Across its geographical range, for example, salmwood (*Cordia alliodora*) typically flowers for between six and eight weeks.[129]

The sight of giant buttresses stretching out from the bases of trees excites the curiosity of first-time visitors to tropical forests. Such features are rare in their temperate counterparts. Buttresses are absent in some species and small in others, or they can be huge, stretching many meters up the trunk of a tree and curving away into the jungle. Tree taxa of the Chiquibul that typically show strong buttressing include the ceiba (*Ceiba pentandra*), swamp karay (*Petrocarpus officinalis*), nargusta (*Terminalia amazonia*), and mahogany (*Swietenia macrophylla*). Many old forestry photos show scaffolds that loggers have erected around the base of giant trunks of mahogany trees so they could be cut, the buttresses making felling at ground level impossible.

As a general rule, most of the soil nutrients required by tropical forest trees are located in the upper soil close to the surface. Thus, trees tend to concentrate their root growth laterally to maximize their ability to absorb what resources are available; deep tap roots are often rare. The lateral roots can, however, develop associated "sinker roots" that descend deeper into the soil. Shallow rooting makes trees unstable and buttresses provide structural strengthening. This is especially important in areas where wind, tree lean, and asymmetrical crowns provide significant forces acting to uproot them. Often tree crowns grow asymmetrically away from their neighbors and into forest gaps, and it has been shown that such asymmetry can cause great instability.[130] Buttresses provide a means of countering the canopy torque experienced by the roots and base of the trunk, and significant correlations exist between the existence and direction of buttresses on a trunk and the direction of destabilizing forces.[131] As one might expect, there is a tendency for large buttresses to occur on a trunk in a direction opposite to the force, in much the same way as a guy rope acts to secure a tent against the wind. Although it is commonly believed that buttresses act primarily as tension supports,[132] it is more likely that they act structurally in both tension- and compression-bracing capacities, transferring forces smoothly from sinker roots to the trunk.[133] Studies conducted in Malaysia have shown that, for some species, the "rooting strength" of buttressed trees is almost double that of unbuttressed ones, with the buttresses contributing 60 percent of a tree's anchorage.[134]

The triggers of buttressing are still poorly understood. It is not uncommon, for example, to see individuals of the same species and similar size growing in almost the same location but with very different buttress characteristics. One explanation for this difference might be that buttress development is triggered by forces acting on a tree at an early stage of its life.[135] The buttresses developed in response may then remain long after the stresses that initially caused them have disappeared. In the case of the swamp karay, it has been proposed that buttresses act to spread the weight of the tree over a larger area of the unconsolidated muddy sediments that commonly characterize the swamps in which it grows.[136] In such cases, the buttresses are thought to prevent soil collapse in much the same way as snowshoes prevent the wearer from sinking into a drift.

Flying above the constant undulating canopy of the Chiquibul, one can easily get the mistaken impression that the forest is immutable. Seasonal color variations in the canopy aside, the canopy always looks roughly the same. This is because a single aerial snapshot does not provide the necessary focus or time scale to perceive the near constant alterations that occur to the forest structure and its component species. Tropical forests are dynamic systems, with individual species constantly germinating, growing, and eventually dying, to be replaced in turn by new recruits (forest turnover). Tropical forests are as dependent on tree death as on tree recruitment for maintaining their long-term health, structure, and diversity. In an attempt to clarify how forest turnover takes place and the speed at which it occurs, a network of permanent sample plots based on standardized methodologies has been established across the Tropics.[137] The plots indicate that tree mortality rates are often on the order of 1 or 2 percent per year, with recruitment rates broadly matching this, although the mortality rates of seedlings and saplings are far higher as they struggle to establish themselves.[138] Permanent forest plots have also been established at Las Cuevas by the Belize Forest Department,[139] but insufficient time has passed between censuses to permit reliable estimates on mortality to be made. Although forests have historically been viewed as steady-state systems, it has recently been suggested that turnover rates of tropical forests are increasing due to the effects of global warming and the rise in atmospheric CO_2 levels.[140] Essentially this theory suggests that, as elevated CO_2 levels raise photosynthetic rates, a "fast forward" growth-and-death button has been pressed. But critics of this hypothesis point out that even if higher CO_2 levels do exist, growth rates and related mortality rates may be influenced by other factors, such as nutrient availability, and that the available data is not sufficiently robust to support the theory.[141] Studies on the CO_2 flux of Amazonian forests indicate that these ecosystems are currently net absorbers of carbon, sequestering an estimated 0.6 billion tons (gigatons) per year,[142] although this current phase of apparent forest growth may be due to a number of factors in addition to climate change, such as recovery from past disturbance or even recovery after logging events.[143]

Change comes in many forms and occurs at many scales. It can manifest itself as the drop of a single branch in the forest canopy or the fall of a tree. Both events can cause significant local alterations to the environment, such as an increased amount of light reaching the forest floor. At the extreme of the disturbance scale is the flattening of large expanses of forest through hurricanes and other catastrophic events. The process of change associated with disturbance—such as that caused by treefall—is called gap dynamics, and much research has been conducted on how forests recover from such perturbations.[144] Essentially, all forests are mosaics of intermingling forest patches in different stages of recovery from disturbance.

When one drives in on the final stretch of dirt track toward Las Cuevas, it is apparent that certain species seem to dominate the more open disturbed areas: the trumpet tree (*Cecropia* spp.), *Heliconia* spp., *Piper* spp., and the shrub *Trema micrantha*. Plant species vary widely in their optimum growing conditions; some need high levels of light for their seeds to germinate and their seedlings to thrive. Others can do so only in deep shade. Many show intermediate characteristics between these extremes.

Species that are able to germinate, grow quickly, and reproduce on disturbed areas with high levels of light are often called pioneers, or "light-demanders." Light is essential for their success, and they are unable to germinate and grow in shade.[145] Thus, they cannot regenerate under a full forest canopy and require disturbance events to provide the necessary elevated levels of light they require. These so-called pioneers typically form the first stage of a long ecological succession that eventually results in a disturbed forest patch reverting to its mature form. An alternative name given to pioneers is "early secondary species" because they dominate the initial secondary growth phase of a disturbed forest area. Classically, the first phase of succession is dominated by herbs, shrubs, and climbers, with pioneering trees such as *Cecropia* replacing them in turn. Typically, pioneer trees grow quickly to make maximum use of the light gap while it lasts, produce soft wood, and reproduce quickly, as their life expectancy can be limited. Their abundant, small, often wind-blown seeds tend to have good dispersal ability and can remain dormant in the soil for relatively long periods of time. These traits enable them to disperse to distant, newly formed gaps before they die or to remain dormant in the soil until a gap appears. Although many pioneer tree species such as *Cecropia* have a short life span (ten to thirty years),[146] others may survive in the forest for much longer periods even though they may not regenerate in the absence of further gaps. Common long-lived pioneers associated with the Chiquibul are the bay cedar (*Guazuma ulmifolia*), hog plum (*Spondia radlkoferi*), the cotton tree (*Ceiba pentandra*), salmwood (*Cordia alliodora*), quamwood (*Schizolobium parahyba*), and gumbo-limbo (*Bursera simaruba*). Even classic timber species such as mahogany (*Swietenia macrophylla*) and cedar (*Cedrela odorata*) can be considered long-lived pioneers. All of these species may survive up to one hundred years or more. Not surprisingly, due to regular hurricane disturbances, a high proportion of the canopy tree species of Belize's forests belong to this group.

As the suite of light-demanding pioneer species establish themselves in a forest gap, they change their own local environment by creating shade on the forest floor. With the increase in shade produced by their own canopies, the seeds and seedlings of the pioneer species are less able to germinate and grow. This prepares the way for another guild of species to follow them: the "shade-demanding" or "climax" tree species, which are experts at capitalizing on such conditions. In contrast to pioneers, they tend to produce fewer, larger seeds that can survive for relatively long periods until they can establish themselves in the dark conditions of the forest understory. As they can germinate

A fast-growing trumpet tree (*Cecropia* sp.) capitalizes on a forest gap. © Sam Bridgewater.

in shade and their seedlings can survive under the forest canopy, climax species are not dependent directly on exploiting the occasional gaps that occur through random disturbance events, such as treefall. Thus, they do not need to disperse as far. Climax species (sometimes also called "late successional" species) typically grow slowly, produce dense wood, and can live for many hundreds of years. Classic examples of such taxa in the Chiquibul are rosewood (*Dalbergia stevensonii*) and chicle (*Manilkara* spp.). Although the seedlings of climax species are shade-tolerant, if there is too much shade they may not grow much, if at all, surviving in a state of suspended animation. Such seedling or sapling "banks" may remain in a dormant condition for many years, waiting until a change in the canopy above provides sufficient light to release them, at which point they continue to grow.

Forest succession is a gradual process, and it is usually possible to find long-lived pioneers and true climax species growing together. However, the longer an area of forest remains undisturbed, the greater the dominance of climax species, in general. Of course, ecological succession rarely occurs according to classic textbook descriptions, and a study at Las Cuevas has shown that many tree species growing in the same place at the same time have characteristics of both pioneer and climax taxa.[147] Yet the concept of pioneer and climatic species, while an artificial construct, is useful for understanding the ecology of gap dynamics.

HURRICANES AND THE IDENTITY OF BELIZEAN FORESTS

Most of Belize's visitors spend at least some time relaxing on the cays, and snorkeling or diving on the famous 185-mile-long coral atoll is considered an essential travel experience. Although warm tropical waters are necessary for the development of coral reefs and their associated biodiversity, farther out to sea they can occasionally precipitate the birth of one of the world's most fearsome and destructive natural events: the hurricane.

Reputedly named after the Maya god of wind and storm, Hurikan, hurricanes are the ultimate storm system, characterized by an area of exceptionally low pressure, high wind, and torrential rain.

In the Tropics, delimited as a zone around the globe by the Tropics of Cancer (23.5° N) and Capricorn (23.5° S), the heat of the sun routinely evaporates water at the ocean surface. As the water vapor rises, it cools and condenses, releasing latent energy as heat. It is this energy that supplies a hurricane with its fuel. Under certain specialized climatic conditions a nascent storm can build as a result of this evaporation-condensation process; the heat generated can increase wind levels, causing the atmospheric pressure to drop. This is turn facilitates greater evaporation of water from the sea's surface, further condensation, further energy production, and the creation of a positive-feedback system. In essence, a hurricane is a self-sustaining, super-sized power station, and as long as it resides over a warm mass of water, it can continually build in strength.

As they move across the ocean's surface steered by atmospheric winds, the storm clouds associated with a hurricane weather system begin to rotate. This is due to the Coriolis effect of the earth spinning on its axis. In the northern hemisphere the direction is anticlockwise. Once mature, hurricanes can be many hundreds of miles wide and usually have a single eye at their center, giving them their famous cyclopean appearance when viewed by satellite. The eye represents an area of sinking air and is associated with low winds. But the gales associated with the eye wall are of incredible strength, reaching speeds in excess of 150 miles per hour (see table 5.1). The low-pressure system and wind effects can cause an enormous rise in sea level and unusually high tides (storm surge) inland, swamping low-lying areas. In addition, heavy rainfall can cause flooding when such systems reach land. The majority of hurricane deaths are due to drowning.

The power of hurricanes is such that they are among the most destructive natural events known, with the energy produced every hour far exceeding that released from the explosion of a large nuclear bomb. Not surprisingly, when such storms reach land,

TABLE 5.1.

Classification of tropical cyclones

Beaufort Scale	10-Minute Sustained Winds (Knots)	Cyclone Type
0-6	<28	Tropical Depression
7	28-29	
	30-33	
8-9	34-47	Tropical Storm
10	48-55	
11	56-63	
12	64-72	Hurricane (Category 1)
	73-85	Hurricane (Category 2)
	86-89	Major Hurricane (Category 3)
	90-99	
	100-106	Major Hurricane (Category 4)
	107-114	
	115-119	
	> 120	Major Hurricane (Category 5)

they can have a catastrophic effect, not only on human habitation but also on native vegetation: mature trees can be twisted and snapped with ease, and large-scale forests can be all but flattened. Anyone who has attempted to work in the eastern region of the Columbia River Forest Reserve in Belize after Hurricane Iris (2001) is well aware of how widespread treefall and abundant associated growth of secondary vegetation such as vines can make passage impossible.

However, it would be wrong to regard hurricanes only as destructive forces. They are also regenerating ecological agents and are an essential part of the region's cycle of life. Belize is a mosaic of vegetation forms, many of which are in various stages of recovery from hurricane disturbance. The richness in habitat form and species diversity found in the country can in part be attributed to these periodic storms. Disturbance is thought to play an important role in maintaining ecosystem function and diversity by preventing competitive exclusion. Indeed, forest habitats in recovery from disturbance may be among the most diverse systems on earth, a theory known as the Intermediate Disturbance Hypothesis (see "Ecological Theories Explaining Plant Diversity in the Tropics" in chapter 1).[148] According to this theory, without disturbance, unhindered succession of species eventually leads to dominance of the ecosystem by only a few highly competitive species. Hurricanes are therefore part of the natural order that maintains Belize's biodiversity in a healthy condition.

Belize City after Hurricane Hattie struck on October 31, 1961. © Belize Archives and Records Service.

Belize is no stranger to hurricanes, and there is an annual sense of trepidation as the hurricane season approaches (June-November). Although hurricanes are not a regular event, a significant number of these catastrophic storms hit Belize each century, and almost everyone in the country has a tale of hunkering down in a storm shelter while a marauding wind screams outside. According to a study of the effects of hurricanes on Belize's forests, thirty-two hurricanes struck the country between 1785 and 1978.[149] The Caribbean region as a whole is affected by an average of four or five hurricanes every year.[150] In recent years, Belize has been hit by Hurricane Dean (2007) and Hurricane Iris (2001). The former crashed into the Yucatán Peninsula close to Corozal, flattening large swathes of forest in the north; the latter swept in across Toledo District in southern Belize, destroying those unfortunate villages lying in its path and razing substantial tracts of pine savanna and forest, including parts of the Columbia River Forest Reserve. Although both these storms were terrible events, the storm that will forever remain in the collective Belizean psyche, and the one with the greatest impact on the Chiquibul region, is Hurricane Hattie.

Born in the Atlantic off the coast of Panama on October 25, 1961, Hurricane Hattie tracked northward in its infancy, increasing in strength and ferocity as it took initial aim on Cuba. The accurate tracking of hurricanes is a dark art. Whenever one appears in the Caribbean, meteorologists frantically attempt to predict its whimsical course, not always with success. At such times, the populations of those countries within range are on tenterhooks, hoping that the storm will not focus its devastating eye upon them. Unfortunately for Belize, on this occasion, as Hattie passed to the west of Honduras, it swung east on October 30, making landfall at midnight on Halloween, October 31. At this stage Hattie was classified as a category 4 hurricane, with average winds of 160 mph, gusts of 200 mph, and a storm surge four meters above the tidal average. Turneffe, Caye Caulker, and other low-lying cays were completely submerged by a tidal wave as the hurricane passed, with 50 percent of Belize City also destroyed by flooding and ferocious winds. It was due to the ravages of Hurricane Hattie on Belize's old coastal capital that a new one, Belmopan, was subsequently established in the comparative safety of Belize's interior. With Belize City largely destroyed, a temporary town was also established to house refugees. The eponymous Hattieville was originally intended for temporary shelter but still exists as a thriving center of population today.

Hurricanes are unable to maintain their power away from the sea, and as Hattie passed westward over mainland Belize and the Maya Mountains, it lost strength, although it was still powerful enough to flatten great areas of forest, including parts of the Chiquibul. In total, over 33 percent of Belize's total forest area was heavily affected by this event.[151] Even today, the twisted and snapped trunks of tree species such as nargusta (*Terminalia amazonia*) are a common sight around Las Cuevas, providing a reminder of the power of that Halloween storm. Since that time the forest has been slowly recovering from the hurricane's impact.

Although Hurricane Hattie continued to lose power as it passed into Guatemala, it survived for an additional seven days as a tropical storm, waxing and waning in strength. With each successive phase the storm was given a new name. Existing as a tropical storm in the Pacific west of Guatemala, it was called Simone, and Inga was the final name as it breathed its last farther to the north and east in the Bay of Campeche.

Due to the catastrophic effects of episodic hurricanes, Belize's forests rarely develop fully to reach ecological maturity (i.e., a "climax community") but are maintained in a state of constant change and succession, with plant and animal communities heavily influenced by disturbance. Although it is clear that hurricanes can cause the widespread uprooting and snapping of trees, branch breakage, and defoliation, their impacts on species' population dynamics are poorly understood. Such information needs to come from long-term studies of hurricane-impacted forests. Although some data exists from Belize, detailed investigations in the region have been conducted primarily in other Caribbean countries: Jamaica, Puerto Rico, Honduras, and Nicaragua.

THE EFFECTS OF WIND DAMAGE ON FOREST TREES

To understand the ecological effects of a hurricane, knowledge of the storm's intensity is of critical importance.[152] Data on generic hurricane wind speed is often available both as average wind speeds and as maximum wind gusts, with severe gusts generally causing more damage than steady winds. As gusts tend to be localized, however, and are often far removed from the nearest meteorological station, they can be difficult to quantify for a specific forest area. In addition, as a hurricane passes, the wind direction can change completely in a short period of time, causing extra stresses on trees. This effect is likely to be amplified if the wind comes from a direction not usually experienced, as trees may be preconditioned to withstand only the stresses of normal prevailing winds. A wide range of other factors also influence the damage caused by a hurricane, such as the amount of rainfall and the length of time a storm builds. If it gradually strengthens, trees will most likely lose their leaves; without them, they are less likely to be severely damaged by the later, more violent winds associated with a hurricane's eye wall.

Although there have been many studies worldwide of the impact of catastrophic wind on forest, there has been no standardized system for quantifying the extent of damage apart from one or more of the following: trunk snapping, trunk uprooting, trunk leaning (i.e., stem damage), canopy and branch damage, and tree death.[153] After Hurricane Hattie, it was reported that a thirty-mile-wide strip of Belizean forest around the eye wall was severely damaged; 60 percent of all trees were blown down, and those remaining consisted of trunks with little or no crown.[154] In the most severely affected areas—between Mullins River and Stann Creek—a 90 percent windthrow of trees was reported. However, the degree of tree death can be hard to ascertain from initial storm damage; even if a tree has been uprooted, in broad-leaved forests a high percentage often resprout later. For example, work conducted in Nicaragua in broadleaf forests impacted by Hurricane Joan in 1988 showed that only 27 percent of trees remained standing after the storm; yet three months later 77 percent of all standing, uprooted, and snapped trees had resprouted.[155] Conversely, trees that might initially appear to have survived more or less intact may later decline in fitness and die, perhaps due to increased susceptibility to attack by fungi and other pathogens. Studies conducted in Puerto Rican forests before and after Hurricane Hugo in 1993 showed that about 7 percent of trees had died a year after the storm, compared with normal background mortality levels of between 2 and 5 percent per annum.[156] But after two to three years, mortality rates declined, and the researchers suggested that these lower levels of post-hurricane tree mortality were due to the storm's removal of trees predisposed to die, including those that were already old. There is also a difference between the responses of pine and broadleaf forests. Research on pine formations in Jamaica after Hurricane Gilbert revealed that although 75 percent of the stems of rain-forest trees were uprooted or broken, compared with only 44 percent of the stems of pine-forest trees, tree mortality in the pine forest was far greater (58 percent) than in the rain forest (13 percent).[157]

Forest in Toledo District showing the impact of hurricane and fire. © Sam Bridgewater.

Although forest damage can be widespread, it is unusual for a forest to be blown over in its entirety. All areas may suffer some degree of damage, but areas where complete blowdown occurs can often be small; different researchers describe areas ranging from less than one hectare to many thousand as typical.[158] Critical factors influencing the degree of damage include the evenness of the canopy and the existence of preexisting treefall gaps, which can increase turbulent airflow. Topography and soils can also influence the degree of storm damage. In the Cockscomb Basin, for example, it has been reported that the oldest undisturbed forest prior to Hurricane Hattie is located in protected lee valleys high on the Maya Divide, while areas on windward slopes and ridges are typically more secondary and disturbed in nature. However, although this may appear to be logical, it is not always true. The species that make up

View across the Chiquibul from the high Maya Divide. Topography can influence the degree of hurricane damage, with lee valleys being relatively protected from high winds and offering a degree of protection to the forests that lie within. © Sam Bridgewater.

ridgetop forests may be naturally adapted to withstanding winds, with a streamlined canopy reducing hurricane damage; leeward slopes may actually experience increased turbulence as the hurricane winds pass over associated ridges. Any factor that restricts root growth, such as shallow soils and high water tables, will increase susceptibility to wind damage. Soil erosion is also often associated with hurricanes, with the reduction in forest canopy reducing soil protection. An investigation of the source of floodwaters in parts of Belize in 1962 traced their origin to mountain areas denuded of forest by Hurricane Hattie the preceding year,[159] although such areas can be quickly colonized by bracken and tiger fern, affording the soil some degree of protection. Areas affected by hurricanes are also more susceptible to fires.

There can be considerable differences in the damage experienced by different tree species, depending on their size, architecture, bole (trunk) diameter, wood density, and rooting pattern. It is not always the largest trees that are most heavily damaged. Tall trees with a small canopy and flexible stems could be expected to be more resistant to damage than trees of a similar size with full crowns and inflexible trunks. Smaller trees could be expected to enjoy a greater degree of protection, although they would be more prone to damage by the falling of the larger trees around them. It is difficult to generalize and predict exactly how a given species of a certain size occurring in a known location will react, and different researchers working in different locations have often found conflicting evidence as to how species are affected.[160] A complex series of factors is clearly at work. Thus, although a tree with strong wood density could be expected not to break, it may be prone to uprooting if it has a shallow root system and an expansive crown. It is generally agreed that the shorter canopies of the frequently disturbed rain forests in the Caribbean region, compared with their counterparts in mainland South America, are the consequence of severe storms, which predominantly affect taller trees.[161] In addition, differences in susceptibility may exist between pioneer and late successional species; the former have a tendency toward fast growth and weak wood, making them potentially more susceptible to hurricane damage. This was one of the findings of a 2002 study on the effects of Hurricane Iris on howler monkey diets in forest located at Monkey River.[162] The results of this study suggest a clear difference in resistance of forest trees; species such as *Cecropia peltata*, *Stemmadenia donnell-smithii*, *Inga edulis*, and *Ficus* spp. all experienced high mortality. In contrast, *Pterocarpus belizensis*, *Guazuma ulmifolia*, and *Spondias radlkoferi* suffered lower death rates. In addition, this study indicated that tree species may differ in the type of damage sustained. For example, among hurricane-damaged individuals *Miconia argenta* was identified as a species particularly prone to uprooting (63 percent), whereas *Inga edulis* suffered primarily from snapped trunks (82 percent). Forestry studies after Hurricane Hattie revealed that, as a species, mahogany was fairly resistant to hurricane damage.[163] Differences among hardwood species in their resistance to hurricane damage are summarized in table 5.2.

TABLE 5.2.

Resistance of forest hardwoods of Stann Creek District to damage from Hurricane Hattie

CLASS ONE: Species suffering from heavy damage (tree uprooted, trunk snapped, over 50% of crown missing, complete defoliation)	
Santa maria	Calophyllum brasiliense
Negrito	Simarouba glauca
Yemeri	Vochysia hondurensis
Waika chewstick	Symphonia globulifera
CLASS TWO: Species suffering from moderate damage (tree standing with less than 50% crown missing, complete defoliation)	
Mahogany	Swietenia macrophylla
Carbon	Tetragastris sp.
Nargusta	Terminalia amazonia
Gumbo-limbo	Bursera simaruba
Prickly yellow	Zanthoxylum spp.
CLASS THREE: Species suffering from light damage (tree intact with only part of crown missing)	
Billy Webb	Acosmium panamense
Cortes	Tabebuia chrysantha
Quamwood	Schizolobium parahyba
Banak	Virola koschnyi

Source: Adapted from Friesner, *Hurricanes and the Forests of Belize.*

RESILIENCE AND REGENERATION

Hurricanes have a dramatic impact on Caribbean forests. But although their structure is heavily altered, these ecosystems are known to be resilient, recovering quickly after disturbance. It is difficult to generalize about the exact route whereby a forest may recover from such catastrophic damage; this will depend on the severity of disturbance, the size of the resulting canopy gaps, the type of forest, and the topography. If gaps are small, the area may be quickly shaded over as trees at the gap edge extend their canopy outwards. Larger gaps may experience colonization by pioneering shrubs (either from seed dispersed into the area or from a dormant seed bank in the soil), the rapid growth and "release" of preexisting seedlings and saplings, and the resprouting of fallen larger trees. Research indicates that the resprouting of damaged trees is one of the primary means of hurricane regeneration, suggesting that the primary species of hurricane-impacted forests can maintain their presence rather than being replaced by new pioneer taxa seeking to exploit the new canopy gaps.[164] This opposes classic successional theory, which suggests that colonizing secondary species such as *Cecropia* are likely to increase in abundance in heavily disturbed forest (see "Plant Strategies and Gap Dynamics" earlier in this chapter). Such a secondary successional pattern is common after forests are cleared by slash-and-burn agriculture. Other factors are also important. Fire, for example, can greatly influence recovery—and can be of more lasting significance than the initial wind damage itself. Post-hurricane burns associated with an increase in available fuel at ground level have been cited as increasing the recruitment of mahogany into forests in the Yucatán.[165]

Typically after a hurricane, the forest canopy is massively reduced, with increased amounts of leaf litter and detritus, elevated levels of light, and an increase in temperature at ground level. This results in short-lived elevated levels of nutrients in the soil. Initially, substantial regrowth of damaged and fallen species occurs, together with some establishment and growth of colonizing pioneers and light-demanding species. However, this successional process can be less pronounced after hurricanes than after disturbances such as regular localized treefall and slash-and-burn agriculture.[166] Initial regeneration can be startling, and the biomass of herbs and seedlings can be many times higher than that usually found under an undisturbed forest canopy.[167] In addition, tree densities and species diversity levels can be significantly higher when compared with those prior to perturbation.[168] However, over a period of many decades, whichever pioneers have managed to become established are eventually replaced by shade-tolerant species and the forest slowly returns to normal. One of the striking features of the Chiquibul is the abundance of various genera of understory palms, of which *Cryosophila stauracantha* and species of *Chamaedorea* are among the most significant. Palms have been shown

Leaf of *Sabal mauritiiformis*. The high density of palms in the Chiquibul may relate, in part, to their ability to survive the high winds associated with hurricanes. © Sam Bridgewater.

to have a high degree of survivorship in hurricane-damaged forests, and it has been suggested that their abundance in the region can be partly attributed to this episodic natural disturbance.[169]

Although the resprouting of preexisting trees is important in regeneration, the establishment of pioneers can still be significant. Five years after Hurricane Iris had damaged the forests around Machaca Hill Lodge in southern Belize, an ecosystem assessment revealed an abundance of fast-growing early and late successional species, including quamwood (*Schizolobium parahyba*), *Acalypha diversifolia*, and *Trema micrantha*. Observations of forest regeneration in the region shortly after the hurricane also mention the abundance of the wild papaya (*Carica papaya*).[170] A similar assessment conducted in the Columbia River Forest Reserve in 2004, three years after the hurricane, revealed that 50 percent of the dominant tree individuals represented only four pioneer genera, including *Heliocarpus*, *Cordia*, *Cecropia*, and *Cestrum*.[171] Common forest trees that were hurricane survivors included *Pouteria durlandii*, the cotton tree (*Ceiba pentandra*), ironwood (*Dialium guianense*), breadnut (*Brosimum alicastrum*), the bayleaf palm (*Sabal mauritiiformis*), and bastard mahogany (*Mosquitoxylum jamaicense*). In this same

Fruits of a broadleaf moho (*Heliocarpus americanus*). This species can be found in abundance in early successional forest recovering from hurricanes. © Sam Bridgewater.

study the authors expressed concern about the low level of mahogany regeneration. After a hurricane it can be common for the surviving mahogany trees to be released from competition, setting seed heavily and resulting in abundant regeneration shortly afterward, and in the Chiquibul abundant mahogany seedlings were recorded after Hurricane Hattie.[172] In the Columbia River Forest Reserve study, the authors suggest that the low levels of mahogany witnessed were due to a combination of factors: past heavy extraction of seed trees for timber, the high mortality of mahogany trees due to the hurricane, and poor seed production rates.

PREPARING FOR A HURRICANE

For those that have never experienced a hurricane and who have a daredevil streak, it might be tempting to stay close to the action and witness one of the world's greatest meteorological events firsthand. Such foolhardiness, however, could well end in tragedy. Although concrete buildings may appear to provide adequate protection and one is likely to be safe in such constructions far inland, no residential buildings are guaranteed 100 percent secure from the incredible pressure vortices associated with categories 4 and 5 hurricanes. In addition, storm surges and tidal waves close to the coast and wind-blown debris, torrential rain, flash floods, mudslides, and treefall inland can kill or maim in moments. Even far into the interior, in areas such as the Chiquibul, treefall associated with high winds can make access and retreat impossible for extended periods of time. Thus, it is advisable to evacuate such areas if a hurricane is expected. For visitors to Las Cuevas, the nearest hurricane shelter is located at Augustine in Mountain Pine Ridge.

In Belize a series of hurricane warnings are now issued if a tropical storm or hurricane approaches. As it develops or moves into a quadrant south of latitude 21° N and between longitude 80° W and 83° W, a hurricane alert is announced and all residents in the cays are advised to leave to the mainland. Should the storm or hurricane continue to approach and move into the quadrant south of a line delimited by latitude 20° N and between longitude 83° W and 85° W, a hurricane watch takes effect. At this stage, the international airport may be closed, and it is advisable for residents of coastal areas to move to higher ground in the interior. Once south of latitude 20° N and west of longitude 85°, the hurricane is deemed likely to strike the coast within twenty-four hours, and a hurricane warning is issued. The phases of hurricane advisories are depicted by flags: a single red flag for a hurricane alert; a single red flag with a black circle for a hurricane watch; and two red flags, each with a black circle at their center, for a hurricane warning. A green flag means the hurricane (or tropical storm) no longer poses a threat.

Numerous official hurricane shelters are scattered throughout Belize, and during the hurricane season visitors should always make sure they are fully informed about the weather and are familiar with their nearest secure hurricane shelter. Local radio and TV stations provide the best source of information. For more detailed information on safety, Belize's National Emergency Management Organisation (NEMO) should be consulted.

ANTS AND ECOLOGICAL MUTUALISM

The mutually beneficial (symbiotic) associations that exist between the roots of plants and mycorrizal fungi are well publicized, but plants are not alone in capitalizing on the unique biological features of fungi. One of the characteristic sights of the Neotropical jungle floor is the network of the tiny congested motorways of leaf-cutter ants. If these highways are traced back to their source, an example of an extraordinary obligatory fungus-animal relationship can be found.

AVID GARDENERS: LEAF-CUTTING ANTS AND THEIR FUNGAL ASSOCIATIONS

Just as humans carefully tend their home plots to grow vegetables and fruit, an estimated two hundred species of gardening ant of the Attini tribe cultivate fungi upon which to feed.[173] These associations are believed to be ancient, dating back to 50 MYA.[174] In the New World the genera *Atta* and *Acromyrmex* belong to this tribe and jointly comprise the infamous leaf-cutting ants, a Belizean example of which is *Atta cephalotes*. The role of leaf-cutting ants in forest ecology is a source of ceaseless fascination to biologists. Studies in Panama, for example, have suggested that as much as 80 percent of leaf damage in rain forests might be attributable to leaf-cutters, and it is also known that they can also be significant collectors of flowers and fruits.[175] They are thus highly significant grazers of Neotropical vegetation. Their

The forest floor of the Chiquibul is crossed by a network of leaf-cutter ant motorways, with millions of these industrious social insects carrying cut leaves and flowers back to their nest. © Sam Bridgewater.

activity undoubtedly influences the ecological dynamics of tropical forests and may be important in maintaining diversity. In addition, they are also responsible for increasing the organic content of the soil through their fungal gardens. Unfortunately, their prolific grazing ability means that they are also significant economic pests with the ability to ravage cultivated crops.

Like most animals, ants are unable to digest cellulose and lignin, the main structural compounds of plants. Whereas herbivorous grazing mammals have overcome this problem by supporting large populations of cellulose-digesting bacteria in their guts, Attini ants have opted for an alternative approach. This is to effectively subcontract part of their digestion to external fungi. The ants provide warm, moist growing conditions for the fungi, supplying them with a constant food source in the form of plant material—leaves, flowers, and fruits. In return, the ants feed off protein- and sugar-rich structures (gongylidia) produced by the fungus colony. The colonial-living leaf-cutter ants vary in form, with some specialized to scout, some to cut, and others to carefully tend the fungal gardens back at home.

Leaf-cutter colonies are usually established by winged females that depart well-established preexisting colonies carrying a small amount of cultivated fungus in their mouths.[176] Once a favorable site is located, the fungus is cultivated, and as it grows the female starts to lay her eggs on it to form a new worker population. Over months and years the colony expands and may eventually comprise thousands of subterranean chambers and access entrances with several hundred discreet fungal gardens supporting hundreds of thousands or even millions of ants.[177] A single colony may last as long as a decade.[178]

Evidence suggests that although *Atta* colonies sample the majority of the plant species in close proximity, they are selective about the species they harvest intensely, preferring to focus their attentions on less than 25 percent of those available.[179] Those species selected may change seasonally as flowers or new leaves are produced, and selection relates to optimizing the nutrition of the cultivated fungus while reducing the concentration of potentially harmful plant chemicals, such as tannins or aluminum.[180] Research also indicates that leaf-cutters prefer to cut a selected but nevertheless diverse range of plants rather than focusing on one or two locally abundant species.[181] Each colony forages in a radius of up to several hundred meters from its center, with smaller colonies exploiting smaller territories. Activity can occur at all times of the day or night; within a particular period of a few weeks or months, one or the other is favored, but a colony can quickly switch from a diurnal to nocturnal existence. The speed of movement of the ants has been calculated at about one meter per minute, although ants heavily laden with plant materials or forced to negotiate vertical tree trunks move more slowly.[182] Unlike the major highways of human cities, the ants travel in both directions on the same trail; despite heavy congestion, gridlock never results from major crashes, cargo drops, or incidents of road rage. Although collisions do occur, only brief pauses in traffic flow occur.

Leaf-cutting ant (*Atta cephalotes*). This soldier has sharp mandibles that can easily slice through skin.
© Alex Wild.

Pivoting around their hind legs, which fasten them to a leaf or flower, leaf-cutter ants have sizable pincerlike mandibles to help them slice up plant material. To aid this process, the ants produce high-frequency vibrations from a modified gaster (part of the posterior portion of the body) that are transmitted to the leaf or flower through their bodies and mandibles.[183] This serves to stiffen the material of interest and makes it easier to cut. It may take as many as fifty bites to collect a single piece of leaf.

Unfortunately, there is relatively little information on the species of fungi that leaf-cutters cultivate because the fungi produce fruiting bodies in the ant colonies relatively infrequently, and such structures are critical for identification. They are known to belong primarily to the broad fungal group Basidiomycotima (the club fungi), with the Lepiotaceae family being particularly important.[184]

Farmers are often distressed by weeds and diseases that can quickly destroy the fruits of their labors. Ant farmers must also be on their guard and meticulously tend and weed their fungal colonies to keep them healthy and free from foreign fungal invaders. One type of fungus is especially important in this regard. Belonging to the genus *Escovopsis*, it specializes in feeding on the ants' fungal gardens and is known only from this peculiar habitat.[185] However, the ants are believed to be able to combat *Escovopsis* infection by carrying *Streptomyces* bacteria on their bodies.[186] This produces a fungicide that is toxic to the unwanted intruder.

The careful cultivation of fungal gardens by Attini ants is not the only example of ants possessing a highly evolved horticultural ability. Various ant genera–including *Azteca*, *Camponotus*, *Solenopsis*, and *Crematogaster*–are also known to create ant gardens by planting the seeds of epiphytes on their nests. Common plant genera cultivated in this way include *Peperomia* (Urticaceae), *Epiphyllum* (Cactaceae), and *Anthurium* (Araceae). Ant gardens are particularly common in forest areas where light levels are high, such as along riverbanks. There has been some dispute over the exact benefits and means of evolution of this association and whether the seeds of ant gardens are planted by the ants or they simply colonize this habitat independent of ant interaction.[187] What is uncertain is whether this is a case of coevolution or of both parties simply being preadapted to benefit from each other. Benefits to the plants include an ideal growing medium provided by the ant nest material and protection from herbivory. Ant nests are created from a nutrient-rich substance known as carton, a mixture of plant material, vertebrate feces, and ant secretions. Benefits to the ants might include a source of food from seed attachments such as arils or through nectaries, structural strengthening to their nests through plant roots, protection of the nest from heavy rain, and protection from fungal attack by chemicals produced by the ant-garden plants.[188]

Few studies exist on ant gardens in Belize. Those that have been conducted have focused on *Azteca* gardens on orange plantations. In one study a survey of 255 trees containing ant gardens revealed 31 epiphytes associated with them. Of these, *Aechmea tillandsioides* (Bromeliaceae), *Codonanthe macradenia* (Gesneriaceae), and *Epidendrum imatophyllum* (Orchidaceae) were among the most common, of which the last is reported to occur in this unusual habitat.[189]

THE TRUMPET TREE'S PRIVATE ARMY

With experience comes knowledge, and fledgling botanists quickly learn which plant species must be treated with respect. These include the black and white poisonwoods with their highly toxic sap (*Metopium brownei* and *Sebastiana tuerckheimiana*) and the spiny give-and-take palm (*Cryosophila stauracantha*). Some plants, however, are to be given a wide berth due to the animals that fiercely protect them, with ants being particularly adept herbivore police. Examples in the Neotropics include the genera *Triplaris*, *Acacia* (see "House of Thorns: Coevolution between Acacia and Ants" later in this chapter), *Cordia*, and *Cecropia*. Plants that live in close association with ants are called myrmecophiles (which means "ant-loving").

The genus *Cecropia* is represented by two species in Belize and is known as the trumpet tree. With its light gray, horizontally ridged trunk, open branching pattern, and lobed leaves that resemble large baseball gloves, *Cecropia* is a characteristic sight along roadsides. It is a fast-growing pioneer species that is quick to exploit disturbed areas. The tree also enjoys certain fame for the medicinal properties of its leaves, which are reputed to be efficacious when smoked in curing lung conditions and in treating ganja (marijuana) addiction.

The association between *Cecropia* and its inhabiting ants belonging to the genus *Azteca* is one of mutualism. The resident biting ants defend the tree from herbivory and overgrowth by vines. In return, the tree provides shelter for the ants within its hollow trunk (hence the common name trumpet tree) and with food in the form of glycogen-rich structures called Müllerian bodies. These are found on hairy pads (trichilia) on the leaf petioles. The production of these food sources is costly to the tree, but the vigilant defense activities of the *Azteca* ants make the investment worthwhile.[190] The ants may also obtain additional food by feeding on honeydew produced by homopterans (sucking insects), which they tend within the tree's trunk.[191] Not all *Cecropia* trees are inhabited by *Azteca* ants, although studies have shown that the majority occurring in natural conditions in lowland Central America do have this association. On many of the Caribbean islands and in urban environments distant from the natural forest, *Azteca* ants may be largely absent, with other ant groups—such as the crazy ant (*Paratrechina longicornis*), a tramp ant—sometimes being resident. This species, which receives its common name from its jerky, spirited movement, is also believed to capitalize off homopteran honeydew in the *Cecropia* trunk. Although *Azteca* ants are thought to defend *Cecropias*,

The hollow stem of a *Cecropia* (trumpet tree) is divided into chambers to house fierce *Azteca alfari* ants. Here the ants raise their brood and tend to mealybugs. © Alex Wild.

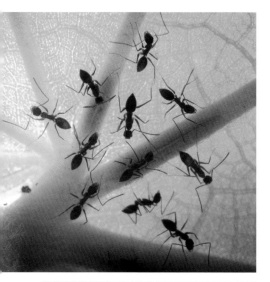

Crazy ants (*Paratrechina longicornis*) drinking from nectaries on the underside of a leaf. Many plants attract ants with nectaries, and in return, the ants help remove the plant's herbivorous pests. © Alex Wild.

they can sometimes coexist with other species such as the crazy ant, although such associations may be only temporary. They may not always be able to defend their terrain against other insects, especially in unnatural environments, or that they may not recognize certain intruders as a threat to themselves or their host.[192] Some researchers have gone so far as to question whether the *Cecropia-Azteca* relationship is always mutual. For example, work in Brazil suggests that *Azteca* ants do not always defend the *Cecropia* trees from harmful leaf miners or clear climbers from the trunk.[193] In addition, transplanted *Cecropia* trees are able to grow in the absence of their tiny friends, so defense by *Aztecas* does not always appear to be essential to their survival. However, it has been suggested that in these cases the trees thrive only because either they are growing away from natural forest, in vine-poor areas, or their usual herbivores and competitors are absent.[194] Despite these apparent exceptions, significant evidence supports the theory that ants are important in ensuring the survival of Cecropia trees.

HOUSE OF THORNS: COEVOLUTION BETWEEN ACACIA AND ANTS

There are believed to be about fifty species of *Acacia* in the Neotropics.[195] This group of feathery-leaved shrubs and trees belongs to the pea family and is represented by ten species in Belize, of which four occur in the Chiquibul. Although most acacias have prickles, thirteen species are notable for having strikingly swollen, hollow spines that are inhabited primarily by aggressive ants belonging to the genus *Pseudomyrmex* (e.g., *P. ferrugineus*). These are the famous ant-acacias that for over a century have provided a much-cited example of ecological mutualism. The five different ant-acacias recorded for Belize are *A. collinsii, A. cornigera, A. globulifera, A. gentlei,* and *A. cookii,* of which the latter two occur in the Chiquibul. These species are typical of disturbed habitats, and their local name is cockspur or bull's-horn acacia in reference to their conspicuous spines.

The ant genus *Pseudomyrmex* comprises about two hundred species, all of which generally form colonies in dead twigs and branches. Only ten species have developed specialized associations with ant-acacias.[196] Similar to the *Azteca-Cecropia* symbiosis,

ant-acacias and their residents have developed a mutualistic arrangement. The ant is dependent upon the acacia for food and shelter, while the acacia relies upon the ants for protection from insect attack and

Pseudomyrmex spinicola. In exchange for protection, swollen-thorn acacia trees provide *Pseudomyrmex* ants with food and shelter. Here an ant harvests a protein-rich food body that will be fed to the ant larvae. © Alex Wild.

from vines and other neighboring plants that might smother it.[197] The food resources provided by the acacia are protein-rich Beltian bodies—small orange-yellow waxy structures modified from the tips of the leaflets—as well as nectar from glands on the leaves, which provides an additional source of sugar. The Beltian bodies are primarily fed to the ant larvae. The relationship is obligate in that both partners are wholly reliant on each other for survival, although some additional foraging away from the acacia is known to take place in some *Pseudomyrmex* species, and thus a degree of infidelity occurs.[198]

The symbiosis typically begins when a queen ant locates an unoccupied cockspur and bores into one of the hollow thorns, within which she lays her eggs. As the colony grows, all the thorns on a plant will become inhabited, with worker ants relentlessly patrolling both the plant itself and an area of ground around it. Typically, 25 percent of the workers in a colony will be routinely patrolling their territory at any given time, with this percentage increasing if a threat to their colony or host acacia is perceived. Any plants or insects that encroach upon their territory are driven off through aggressive biting or are weeded out. Those species of *Pseudomyrmex* that inhabit acacia thorns have developed a number of ecological traits that distinguish them from other species in the genus. For example, acacia-ant colonies are typically active twenty-four hours a day, while other *Pseudomyrmex* colonies are diurnal. This reflects the absolute importance to the acacia-dependent colonies of protecting the plant upon which they rely. Hence, the occupied acacia is provided with optimal growing conditions. It has been shown that, without assistance from its tenants, an ant-acacia is poor at defending itself from insect attack and, being intolerant of shade, is easily overcome and killed by competing plants.[199] Unlike other species within the genus, ant-acacias have developed a range of ecological attributes to promote a successful association with their ants. This includes rapid sprouting of leaves after fire and the maintenance of their leaves for extended periods of the dry season. Both these characteristics are to ensure that the ant colony is rarely without food, although *Pseudomyrmex* colonies are known to be tolerant of starvation for up to five weeks.[200] Should the tree be abandoned, it would be ill equipped to survive under natural conditions. The presence of the *Pseudomyrmex* ants might be thought to be detrimental to the reproductive success of ant-acacias by discouraging pollination and seed dispersal vectors from visiting. However, it has been shown that, for some species, certain parts of the plant are patrolled more infrequently and these tend to flower more abundantly. Thus, not all parts of the plant are always fiercely protected.[201] This might be due to fewer Beltian bodies being produced by the leaves of the older branches that support the flowers. In addition, research indicates that the mature flowers of some ant-acacia species may produce a chemical repellent that deters the ants from visiting. Ant-acacias also typically flower at the end of the dry season, when the ant colonies are weakest and the stingless *Trigona* and small carpenter *Ceratina* bees that form an important pollinator group are not easily dissuaded from their hunt for flower nectar.[202] Ant-acacias are also unusual in the genus in that they are bird-dispersed; although visiting birds are attacked as they eat the fruits, the ants do not seem to deter them. Indeed, birds such as orioles (*Icterus* spp.) are known to enjoy feasting off acacia ants in addition to the fruits; the great kiskadee (*Pitangus sulphuratus*) and other birds are even known to nest in ant acacias.[203] In such cases, the birds may preferentially choose ant-acacias because of the extra protection afforded by the ants against egg predators. However, the birds and nestlings themselves must be resilient against ant attack.

APPENDIX A

Provisional Amphibian Species Checklist of the Chiquibul

Scientific Name	Common Name
Order Gymnophiona (Caecilians)	
Caecilidae (Caecilians)	
Gymnopis syntrema	Mountain caecilian
Order Caudata (Salamanders)	
Plethodontidae (Lungless Salamanders)	
Bolitoglossa dofleini	Doflein's mushroom-tongued salamander
B. mexicana	Mexican mushroom-tongued salamander
B. rufescens	Northern banana salamander
Oedipina elongata*	Central American worm salamander
Order Anura (Frogs and Toads)	
Bufonidae (Toads)	
Chaunus marinus	Giant toad
Incilius campbelli	Campbell's rainforest toad
I. valliceps	Gulf Coast toad
Leptodactylidae (Rainfrogs and Stream Frogs)	
Craugaster alfredii	Alfredo's rainfrog
C. chac	Chac's rainfrog
C. laticeps	Broad-headed rainfrog
C. sabrinus	Maya stream frog
Syrrhopus leprus*	Mottled chirping frog
Hylidae (Tree Frogs)	
Agalychnis callidryas	Red-eyed tree frog
A. moreletii	Morelet's tree frog
Dendropsophus ebraccatus	Hourglass tree frog
D. microcephalus	Small-headed tree frog
Hyalinobatrachium fleischmanni	Central American glass frog
Tlalocohyla loquax	Mahogany tree frog
T. picta	Painted tree frog

Scientific Name	Common Name
Scinax staufferi	Stauffer's tree frog
Smilisca baudini	Mexican tree frog
S. cyanosticta	Blue-spotted tree frog
Gastrophryne elegans	Elegant narrow-mouthed toad
Rhinophrynidae (Burrowing Toads)	
Rhinophrynus dorsalis	Mexican burrowing toad
Ranidae (True Frogs)	
Lithobates brownorum	Brown's leopard frog
L. juliana	Maya mountain frog
L. vaillanti	Green forest frog

Note: This checklist was kindly contributed by Peter Stafford, Natural History Museum, London.

*Species known from localities adjacent to the Chiquibul Forest (exclusive of Mountain Pine Ridge) and of probable occurrence in the area.

Scientific Name	Common Name
Order Crocodilia (Crocodiles)	
Crocodylidae (Crocodiles)	
Crocodylus moreletii	Morelet's crocodile
Order Testudines (Turtles and Tortoises)	
Dermatemydidae (Central American River Turtles)	
Dermatemys mawii	Central American river turtle
Kinostemidae (Mud Turtles and Musk Turtles)	
Kinosternon acutum	Tabasco mud turtle
K. leucostomum	White-lipped mud turtle
Suborder Sauria (True Lizards)	
Eublepharidae (Banded Geckos)	
Coleonyx elegans	Yucatán banded gecko
Geckonidae (Geckos)	
Hemidactylus frenatus	Common house gecko
Sphaerodactylus glaucus	Smooth-scaled dwarf gecko
S. millepunctatus	Spotted gecko
Thecadactylus rapicauda	Turnip-tailed gecko
Corytophanidae (Basilisks, Helmeted Lizards, and Casque-headed Lizards)	
Basiliscus basiliscus	Striped basilisk
Corytophanes cristatus	Smooth-headed helmeted basilisk
C. hernandezii	Hernandez's helmeted basilisk
Laemanctus longipes	Eastern casque-headed iguana
Iguanidae (Iguanas)	
Iguana iguana	Green iguana
Phrynosomatidae (Spiny Lizards)	
Sceloporus lundelli	Lundell's spiny lizard
S. teapensis	Rose-bellied spiny lizard
Polychrotidae (Anoles)	

Scientific Name	Common Name
Anolis biporcatus	Central American green anole
A. capito	Big-headed anole
A. lemurinus	Ghost anole
A. rodriguezii	Slender anole
A. sericeus*	Silky anole
A. tropidonotus	Greater scaly anole
A. uniformis	Lesser scaly anole
Scincidae (Skinks)	
Mabuya unimarginata	Central American mabuya
Plestiodon sumichrasti	Sumichrast's skink
Sphenomorphus cherriei	Brown forest skink
Teiidae (Racerunners and Whiptails)	
Ameiva festiva	Middle American ameiva
A. undulata*	Rainbow ameiva
Xantusidae (Night Lizards)	
Lepidophyma flavimaculatum	Yellow-spotted night lizard
Anguidae (Alligator Lizards)	
Diploglossus rozellae	Galliwasp
Suborder Serpentes (Snakes)	
Boidae (Boas)	
Boa constrictor	Common boa
Colubridae (Typical Snakes)	
Adelphicos quadrivirgatus	Middle American earth snake
Amastridium sapperi	Rusty-headed snake
Clelia clelia	Mussurana
Coniophanes fissidens	White-lipped spotbelly snake
C. imperialis	Black-striped snake
C. schmidti	Schmidt's black-striped snake
Dendrophidion nuchale	Red-tailed forest racer
Drymarchon melanurus*	Black-tailed cribo
Drymobius margaritiferus	Speckled racer
Imantodes cenchoa	Blunt-headed tree snake
Lampropeltis triangulum	Central American king snake

Scientific Name	Common Name
Leptodeira septentrionalis	Spotted cat-eyed snake
Leptophis ahaetulla	Green parrot snake
L. mexicanus	Mexican parrot snake
Mastogodryas melanolomus	Dryad snake
*Ninia diademata**	Ring-necked coffee snake
N. sebae	Red coffee snake
Oxybelis aeneus	Brown vine snake
O. fulgidus	Green vine snake
Oxyrhopus petola	Red-banded snake
Pliocercus elapoides	False coral snake
Pseudoelaphe flavirufa	Tropical rat snake
Pseustes poecilonotus	Brown tree snake
Rhadinaea anachoreta	Peten brown snake
*Scaphiodontophis annulatus**	Guatemalan neck-banded snake
*Senticolis triaspis**	Neotropical rat snake
Sibon dimidiata	Slender snailsucker
S. nebulata	Speckled snailsucker
S. sartorii	Sartorius's snailsucker
Spilotes pullatus	Tiger rat snake
Stenorrhina degenhardtii	Degenhardt's scorpion-eating snake
Tantilla hendersoni	Peten centipede eater
T. schistosa	Red-earth centipede eater
Tantillita lintoni	Linton's dwarf short-tailed snake
Xenodon rabdocephalus	False lancehead
Elapidae (Coral Snakes)	
Micrurus diastema	Many-banded coral snake
Viperidae (Pit Vipers)	
Atropoides mexicanus	Jumping pit viper
Bothriechis schlegelii	Eyelash palm pit viper
Bothrops asper	Central American lancehead; fer-de-lance; tommygoff
Porthidium nasutum	Rainforest hog-nosed pit viper

*Species known from localities adjacent to the Chiquibul Forest (exclusive of Mountain Pine Ridge) and of probable occurrence in the area.

Scientific Name	Common Name
Order Artiodactyla (Even-Toed Ungulates)	
Cervidae (Deer)	
Mazama americana	Red brocket deer
Odocoileus virginianus	White-tailed deer
Tayassuidae (Peccaries)	
Pecari tajacu	Collared peccary
Tayassu pecari	White-lipped peccary
Order Carnivora (Carnivores)	
Canidae (Dogs)	
Urocyon cinereoargenteus	Gray fox
Felidae (Cats)	
Leopardus pardalis	Ocelot
L. wiedii	Margay
Panthera onca	Jaguar
Puma concolor	Puma
P. yagouaroundi	Jaguarundi
Mephitidae (Skunks)	
Conepatus leuconotus	Hog-nosed skunk
C. semistriatus	Striped hog-nosed skunk
Spilogale angustifrons	Southern spotted skunk, polecat
Mustelidae (Weasels)	
Eira barbara	Tayra, bushdog
Mustela frenata	Long-tailed weasel
Galictis vittata	Grison, bushdog
Lutra longicaudis	Neotropical otter
Procyonidae (Raccoons)	
Bassariscus sumichrasti	Ringtail, cacomistle
Nasua narica	Coatimundi

Scientific Name	Common Name
Potos flavus	Kinkajou
Procyon lotor	Raccoon
Order Chiroptera (Bats)	
Emballonuridae (Sac-Winged Bats)	
Balantiopteryx io	Thomas's sac-winged bat
Diclidurus albus	Northern ghost bat
Peropteryx kappleri (P)	Greater dog-like bat
P. macrotis	Lesser dog-like bat
Rhynchonycteris naso	Proboscis bat
Saccopteryx bilineata	Greater white-lined bat
Molossidae (Free-Tailed Bats)	
Cynomops mexicanus	Mexican dog-faced bat
Molossus molossus (P)	Velvety free-tailed bat
M. rufus	Black mastiff bat
M. sinaloae	Sinaloan mastiff bat
N. laticaudatus	Broad-eared bat
Mormoopidae (Leaf-Chinned Bats)	
Mormoops megalophylla	Ghost-faced bat
Pteronotus davyi	Davy's naked-backed bat
P. parnellii	Parnell's moustached bat
Natalidae (Funnel-Eared Bats)	
Natalus mexicanus	Mexican funnel-eared bat
Noctilionidae (Fish-Eating Bats)	
Noctilio leporinus	Mexican bulldog bat
Phyllostomidae (Leaf-Nosed Bats)	
Artibeus intermedius	Intermediate fruit-eating bat
A. jamaicensis	Jamaican fruit-eating bat
A. lituratus	Great fruit-eating bat
A. phaeotis	Pygmy fruit-eating bat
A. toltecus	Toltec fruit-eating bat
A. watsoni	Tent-making bat
Carollia perspicillata	Seba's short-tailed bat
C. sowelli	Sowell's short-tailed bat

Scientific Name	Common Name
Centurio senex	Wrinkle-faced bat
Desmodus draculae (fossil records only)	Giant vampire bat
D. rotundus	Common vampire bat
Diphylla ecaudata	Hairy-legged vampire bat
Glossophaga commissarisi	Commissari's long-tongued bat
Glossophaga soricina	Common long-tongued bat
Lonchorhina aurita	Tome's sword-nosed bat
Micronycteris microtis	Common big-eared bat
Mimon cozumelae	Cozumelan golden bat
Sturnira lilium	Yellow-shouldered bat
Tonatia saurophila	Stripe-headed round-eared bat
Trachops cirrhosus	Fringe-lipped bat
Trinycteris nicefori	Niceforo's bat
Vampyressa thyone	Northern yellow-eared bat
Vampyrum spectrum	False vampire bat
Vespertilionidae (Plain-Nosed Bats)	
Bauerus dubiaquercus	Van Gelder's bat
Eptesicus furinalis	Argentine brown bat
Lasiurus ega	Southern yellow bat
L. intermedius	Northern yellow bat
Myotis elegans	Elegant myotis
M. keaysi	Hairy-legged myotis
Rhogeessa aeneus	Yucatan yellow bat
Order Didelphimorphia (Opossums and Allies)	
Didelphidae (Opossums)	
Caluromys derbianus	Central American woolly opossum
Chironectes minimus	Water opossum
Didelphis marsupialis	Common opossum
D. virginiana	Virginia opossum
Marmosa mexicana	Mexican mouse opossum
M. robinsoni	Robinson's mouse opossum
Micoureus alstoni	Woolly mouse opossum
Philander opossum	Gray four-eyed opossum

Scientific Name	Common Name
Order Soricomorpha (Shrews)	
Soricidae (Shrews)	
Cryptotis mayensis	Maya small-eared shrew
C. parva	Least shrew
Order Perissodactyla (Odd-Toed Ungulates)	
Tapiridae (Tapirs)	
Tapirus bairdii	Baird's tapir
Order Primates (Apes and Monkeys)	
Atelidae (New World Monkeys)	
Alouatta pigra	Mexican black howler monkey
Ateles geoffroyi	Central American spider monkey
Order Rodentia (Rodents)	
Cuniculidae (Pacas)	
Cuniculus paca	Paca, gibnut
Dasyproctidae (Agoutis)	
Dasyprocta punctata	Central American agouti
Erethizontidae (Porcupines)	
Sphiggurus mexicanus	Mexican porcupine
Geomyidae (Gophers)	
Orthogeomys hispidus	Hispid pocket gopher
Heteromyidae (Spiny Pocket Mice)	
Heteromys desmarestianus	Desmarest's spiny pocket mouse
Muridae (Rats and Mice)	
Mus musculus	House mouse
Cricetidae (Voles, New World Rats, and Mice)	
Ototylomys phyllotis	Big-eared climbing rat
Oryzomys couesi	Marsh rice rat
Reithrodontomys gracilis	Slender harvest mouse
Sigmodon hispidus	Hispid cotton rat
Tylomys nudicaudus	Peter's climbing rat
Sciuridae (Squirrels)	
Sciurus deppei	Depp's squirrel
S. varigatoides	Variegated squirrel

Scientific Name	Common Name
S. yucatanensis	Yucatan squirrel
Order Cingulata (Armadillos)	
Dasypodidae (Armadillos)	
Dasypus novemcinctus	Nine-banded armadillo
Order Pilosa (Sloths and Anteaters)	
Myrmecophagidae (Anteaters)	
Tamandua mexicana	Northern tamandua
Cyclopes didactylus	Silky anteater

Note: The bat sections of the checklist were kindly contributed by Bruce and Carolyn Miller.

P = Probable but not confirmed.

Provisional Bird Species Checklist of the Chiquibul

Scientific Name	Common Name	Temporal Pattern
Order Apodiformes (Hummingbirds and Swifts)		
Apodidae (Swifts)		
Chaetura vauxi	Vaux's swift	R
Panyptila cayennensis	Lesser swallow-tailed swift	R
Streptoprocne zonaris	White-collared swift	R
Trochilidae (Hummingbirds)		
Amazilia candida	White-bellied emerald	R
A. cyanocephala	Azure-crowned hummingbird	R
A. tzacatl	Rufous-tailed hummingbird	R
Campylopterus curvipennis	Wedge-tailed sabrewing	R
C. hemileucurus	Violet sabrewing	R
Eupherusa eximia	Stripe-tailed hummingbird	R
Florisuga mellivora	White-necked jacobin	R
Heliothryx barroti	Purple-crowned fairy	R
Lophornis helenae	Black-crested coquette	R
Phaeochroa cuvieri	Scaly-breasted hummingbird	R
Phaethornis longirostris	Long-billed hermit	R
P. striigularis	Stripe-throated hermit	R
Order Caprimulgiformes (Nightbirds)		
Caprimulgidae (Nighthawks and Nightjars)		
Chordeiles acutipennis	Lesser nighthawk	WV
C. minor	Common nighthawk	SR
Nyctidromus albicollis	Common pauraque	R
Nyctiphrynus yucatanicus	Yucatan poorwill	R
Nyctibiidae (Pootoos)		
Nyctibius jamaicensis	Northern pootoo	R
Order Charadriiformes (Shorebirds and Relatives)		

Scientific Name	Common Name	Temporal Pattern
Scolopacidae (Sandpipers and Allies)		
Actitis macularia	Spotted sandpiper	WV
Order Ciconiiformes (Storks, Herons, and Relatives)		
Ardeidae (Herons, Egrets, and Bitterns)		
Agami agami	Agami heron	R
Ardea herodias	Great blue heron	WV
Bubulcus ibis	Cattle egret	WV
Butorides virescens	Green heron	WV
Egretta caerulea	Little blue heron	WV
E. thula	Snowy egret	WV
E. tricolor	Tri-colored heron	WV
Nycticorax nycticorax	Black-crowned night heron	WV
Nyctanassa violacea	Yellow-crowned night heron	R
Ciconiidae (Storks)		
Mycteria americana	Wood stork	R
Order Columbiformes (Pigeons and Doves)		
Columbidae (Pigeons and Doves)		
Columba nigrirostris	Short-billed pigeon	R
C. speciosa	Scaled pigeon	R
Columbina minuta	Plain-breasted ground dove	R
Claravis pretiosa	Blue ground dove	R
Geotrygon montana	Ruddy quail-dove	R
Leptotila cassini	Gray-chested dove	R
L. rufaxilla	Gray-fronted dove	R
Order Coraciiformes (Kingfishers and Allies)		
Alcedinidae (Kingfishers)		
Ceryle torquata	Ringed kingfisher	R
Chloroceryle aenea	American pygmy kingfisher	R
C. amazona	Amazon kingfisher	R
C. americana	Green kingfisher	R
Motmotidae (Motmots)		
Electron carinatum	Keel-billed motmot	R
Hylomanes momotula	Tody motmot	R

Scientific Name	Common Name	Temporal Pattern
Momotus motmota	Blue-crowned motmot	R
Order Cuculiformes (Cuckoos and Relatives)		
Cuculidae (Cuckoos and Allies)		
Coccyzus erythropthalmus	Black-billed cuckoo	M
Crotophaga sulcirostris	Groove-billed ani	R
Piaya cayana	Squirrel cuckoo	R
Order Falconiformes (Falcons and Allies)		
Accipitridae (Kites, Eagles, Hawks, and Allies)		
Asturina nitida	Gray hawk	R
Buteo brachyurus	Short-tailed hawk	R
B. magnirostris	Roadside hawk	R
Buteogallus anthracinus	Common black hawk	R
B. urubitinga	Great black hawk	R
Chondrohierax uncinatus	Hook-billed kite	R
Elanoides forficatus	Swallow-tailed kite	SR
Harpagos bidentatus	Double-toothed kite	R
Harpia harpyja	Harpy eagle	R
Harpyhaliaetus solitarius	Solitary eagle	R
Ictinia plumbea	Plumbeous kite	SR
Leptodon cayanensis	Gray-headed kite	R
Leucopternis albicollis	White hawk	R
Rostrhamus sociabilis	Snail kite	R
Spizaetus ornatus	Ornate hawk-eagle	R
S. tyrannus	Black hawk-eagle	R
Spizastur melanoleucus	Black-and-white hawk-eagle	R
Cathartidae (American Vultures)		
Cathartes aura	Turkey vulture	R
Coragyps atratus	Black vulture	R
Sarcoramphus papa	King vulture	R
Falconidae (Caracaras and Falcons)		
Falco deiroleucus	Orange-breasted falcon	R
F. rufigularis	Bat falcon	R

Scientific Name	Common Name	Temporal Pattern
Herpetotheres cachinnans	Laughing falcon	R
Micrastur ruficollis	Barred forest-falcon	R
M. semitorquatus	Collared forest-falcon	R
Order Galbuliformes (Jacamars and Puffbirds)		
Bucconidae (Puffbirds)		
Malacoptila panamensis	White-whiskered puffbird	R
Notharchus macrorhynchos	White-necked puffbird	R
Galbulidae (Jacamars)		
Galbula ruficauda	Rufous-tailed jacamar	R
Order Galliformes (Chickenlike Birds)		
Cracidae (Curassows and Guans)		
Crax rubra	Great curassow	R
Ortalis vetula	Plain chacalaca	R
Penelope purpurascens	Crested guan	R
Odontophoridae (New World Quail)		
Dactylortyx thoracicus	Singing quail	R
Odontophorus guttatus	Spotted wood-quail	R
Phasianidae (Turkeys and Quail)		
Meleagris ocellata	Ocellated turkey	R
Order Gruiformes (Coots, Cranes, and Rails)		
Heliornithidae (Sungrebes)		
Heliornis fulica	Sungrebe	R
Rallidae (Coots, Rails, and Relatives)		
Aramides cajanea	Gray-necked wood-rail	R
Laterallus ruber	Ruddy crake	R
Order Passeriformes (Perching Birds)		
Cardinalidae (Saltators, Grosbeaks, and Buntings)		
Caryothraustes poliogaster	Black-faced grosbeak	R
Cyanocompsa cyanoides	Blue-black grosbeak	R
C. parellina	Blue bunting	R
Passerina cyanea	Indigo bunting	WV
Pheucticus ludovicianus	Rose-breasted grosbeak	WV

Scientific Name	Common Name	Temporal Pattern
Saltator coerulescens	Grayish saltator	R
S. maximus	Buff-throated saltator	R
S. atriceps	Black-headed saltator	R
Coerebidae (Bananaquit)		
Coereba flaveola	Bananaquit	R
Corvidae (Jays)		
Cyanocorax morio	Brown jay	R
C. yncus	Green jay	R
Dendrocolaptidae (Woodcreepers)		
Dendrocincla anabatina	Tawny-winged woodcreeper	R
D. homochroa	Ruddy woodcreeper	R
Dendrocolaptes sanctithomae	Northern barred woodcreeper	R
Glyphorynchus spirurus	Wedge-billed woodcreeper	R
Lepidocolaptes souleyetii	Streak-headed woodcreeper	R
Sittasomus griseicapillus	Olivaceous woodcreeper	R
Xiphocolaptes promeropirhynchus	Strong-billed woodcreeper	R
Xiphorhynchus erythropygius	Spotted woodcreeper	R
X. flavigaster	Ivory-billed woodcreeper	R
Emberizidae (Seedeaters and Sparrows)		
Amaurospiza concolor	Blue seedeater	R
Arremon aurantiirostris	Orange-billed sparrow	R
Arremonops chloronotus	Green-backed sparrow	R
Oryzoborus funereus	Thick-billed seed-finch	R
Sporophila americana	Variable seedeater	R
S. torqueola	White-collared seedeater	R
Tiaris olivacea	Yellow-faced grassquit	R
Volatinia jacarina	Blue-black grassquit	R
Formicariidae (Antthrushes)		
Formicarius analis	Black-faced antthrush	R
Furnariidae (Ovenbirds)		
Anabacerthia variegaticeps	Scaly-throated foliage-gleaner	R
Automolus ochrolaemus	Buff-throated foliage-gleaner	R
Sclerurus guatamalensis	Scaly-throated leaftosser	R

Scientific Name	Common Name	Temporal Pattern
S. mexicanus	Tawny-throated leaftosser	R
Synallaxis erythrothorax	Rufous-breasted spinetail	R
Xenops minutus	Plain xenops	R
Hirundinidae (Swallows)		
Hirundo rustica	Barn swallow	T
Progne subis	Purple martin	T
Stelgidopteryx serripennis	Northern rough-winged swallow	R
S. ridgwayi	Ridgway's rough-winged swallow	R
Tachycineta sp.	Swallow	
Icteridae (Blackbirds and Allies)		
Amblycercus holosericeus	Yellow-billed cacique	R
Dives dives	Melodious blackbird	R
Icterus prosthemelas	Black-cowled oriole	R
I. galbula	Northern oriole	WV
I. mesomelas	Yellow-tailed oriole	R
Psarocolius montezuma	Montezuma oropendola	R
Quiscalus mexicanus	Great-tailed grackle	R
Mimidae (Mockingbirds and Thrashers)		
Dumetella carolinensis	Gray catbird	WV
Parulidae (Wood Warblers)		
Basileuterus culicivorus	Golden-crowned warbler	R
B. rufifrons	Rufous-capped warbler	R
Dendroica caerulescens	Black-throated blue warbler	WV
D. castanea	Bay-breasted warbler	T
D. dominica	Yellow-throated warbler	WV
D. fusca	Blackburnian warbler	T
D. graciae	Grace's warbler	R
D. magnolia	Magnolia warbler	WV
D. pensylvanica	Chestnut-sided warbler	WV
D. petechia	Yellow warbler	WV
D. virens	Black-throated green warbler	WV
Geothlypis trichas	Common yellowthroat	WV
Granatellus sallaei	Gray-throated chat	R

Scientific Name	Common Name	Temporal Pattern
Helmitheros vermivorus	Worm-eating warbler	WV
Icteria virens	Yellow-breasted chat	WV
Mniotilta varia	Black-and-white warbler	WV
Oporornis formosus	Kentucky warbler	T
O. philadelphia	Mourning warbler	T
Protonotaria citrea	Prothonotary warbler	T
Seiurus aurocapilla	Ovenbird	WV
S. motacilla	Louisiana waterthrush	WV
S. noveboracensis	Northern waterthrush	WV
Setophaga ruticilla	American redstart	WV
Vermivora chrysoptera	Golden-winged warbler	WV
V. peregrina	Tennessee warbler	WV
V. pinus	Blue-winged warbler	WV
Wilsonia canadensis	Canada warbler	T
W. citrina	Hooded warbler	WV
W. pusilla	Wilson's warbler	WV
Pipridae (Manakins)		
Manacus candei	White-collared manakin	R
Pipra mentalis	Red-capped manakin	R
Sylviidae (Gnatcatchers)		
Polioptila caerulea	Blue-gray gnatcatcher	R
P. plumbea	Tropical gnatcatcher	R
Ramphocaenus melanurus	Long-billed gnatwren	R
Thamnophilidae (Antbirds)		
Cercomacra tyrannina	Dusky antbird	R
Dysithamnus mentalis	Plain antvireo	R
Microrhopias quixensis	Dot-winged antwren	R
Myrmotherula schisticolor	Slaty antwren	R
Taraba major	Great antshrike	R
Thamnistes anabatinus	Russet antshrike	R
Thamnophilus doliatus	Barred antshrike	R
Thraupidae (Tanagers)		
Chlorophanes spiza	Green honeycreeper	R

Scientific Name	Common Name	Temporal Pattern
Chlorospingus ophthalmicus	Common bush tanager	R
Cyanerpes cyaneus	Red-legged honeycreeper	R
C. lucidus	Shining honeycreeper	R
Eucometis penicillata	Gray-headed tanager	R
Euphonia affinis	Scrub euphonia	R
E. elegantissima	Blue-hooded euphonia, elegant euphonia	R
E. gouldi	Olive-backed euphonia	R
E. hirundinacea	Yellow-throated euphonia	R
Habia rubica	Red-crowned ant-tanager	R
H. fuscicauda	Red-throated ant-tanager	R
Lanio aurantius	Black-throated shrike-tanager	R
Piranga rubra	Summer tanager	WV
P. leucoptera	White-winged tanager	R
Ramphocelus sanguinolentus	Crimson-collared tanager	R
R. passerinii	Scarlet-rumped tanager	R
Tangara larvata	Golden-masked tanager	R
Thraupis episcopus	Blue-gray tanager	R
T. abbas	Yellow-winged tanager	R
Troglodytidae (Wrens)		
Campylorhynchus zonatus	Band-backed wren	R
Henicorhina leucosticta	White-breasted wood-wren	R
Microcerculus philomela	Nightingale wren	R
Troglodytes aedon	House wren	R
Thryothorus ludovicianus	Carolina wren	R
T. maculipectus	Spot-breasted wren	R
Uropsila leucogastra	White-bellied wren	R
Turdidae (Thrushes)		
Catharus minimus	Gray-cheeked thrush	T
C. ustulatus	Swainson's thrush	T
Hylocichla mustelina	Wood thrush	WV
Myadestes unicolor	Slate-colored solitaire	R
Turdus assimilis	White-throated robin	R
T. grayi	Clay-colored robin	R

Scientific Name	Common Name	Temporal Pattern
Tyrannidae (Tyrant Flycatchers)		
Attila spadiceus	Bright-rumped attila	R
Contopus cinereus	Tropical pewee	R
C. cooperi	Olive-sided flycatcher	T
C. virens	Eastern wood-pewee	T
Elaenia flavogaster	Yellow-bellied elaenia	R
Empidonax alnorum	Alder flycatcher	T
E. flaviventris	Yellow-bellied flycatcher	WV
E. minimus	Least flycatcher	WV
E. traillii	Willow flycatcher	T
E. virescens	Acadian flycatcher	T
Gymnocichla nudiceps	Bare-crowned antbird	R
Legatus leucophaius	Piratic flycatcher	SR
Leptopogon amaurocephalus	Sepia-capped flycatcher	R
Lipaugus unirufus	Rufous piha	R
Megarhynchus pitangua	Boat-billed flycatcher	R
Mionectes oleagineus	Ochre-bellied flycatcher	R
Myiarchus crinitus	Great-crested flycatcher	T
M. tuberculifer	Dusky-capped flycatcher	R
M. tyrannulus	Brown-crested flycatcher	SR
Myiobius sulphureipygius	Sulphur-rumped flycatcher	R
Myiodynastes luteiventris	Sulphur-bellied flycatcher	SR
M. maculatus	Streaked flycatcher	SR
Myiopagis viridicata	Greenish elaenia	R
Myiozetetes similis	Social flycatcher	R
Oncostoma cinereigulare	Northern bentbill	R
Onychorhynchus coronatus	Royal flycatcher	R
Ornithion semiflavum	Yellow-bellied tyrannulet	R
Pachyramphus aglaiae	Rose-throated becard	R
P. cinnamomeus	Cinnamon becard	R
P. polychopterus	White-winged becard	R
Poecilotriccus sylvia	Slate-headed tody-flycatcher	R
Pitangus sulphuratus	Great kisadee	R

Scientific Name	Common Name	Temporal Pattern
Platyrinchus cancrominus	Stub-tailed spadebill	R
Rhynchocyclus brevirostris	Eye-ringed flatbill	R
Rhytipterna holerythra	Rufous mourner	R
Sayornis nigricans	Black phoebe	R
Schiffornis turdinus	Thrush-like schiffornis	R
Terenotriccus erythrurus	Ruddy-tailed flycatcher	R
Tityra inquisitor	Black-crowned tityra	R
T. semifasciata	Masked tityra	R
Tolmomyias sulphurescens	Yellow-olive flycatcher	R
Tyrannus couchii	Couch's kingbird	R
T. melancholicus	Tropical kingbird	R
T. tyrannus	Eastern kingbird	M
Vireonidae (Vireos)		
Hylophilus decurtatus	Lesser greenlet	R
H. ochraceiceps	Tawny-crowned greenlet	R
Vireo flavifrons	Yellow-throated vireo	WV
V. flavoviridis	Yellow-green vireo	SR
V. griseus	White-eyed vireo	T
V. olivaceus	Red-eyed vireo	T
V. philadelphicus	Philadelphia vireo	WV
Vireolanius pulchellus	Green shrike-vireo	R
Order Pelecaniformes (Pelicans and Relatives)		
Anhingidae (Darters)		
Anhinga anhinga	Anhinga	R
Pelecanidae		
Pelecanus occidentalis	Brown pelican	R
Phalacrocoracidae (Cormorants)		
Phalacrocorax brasilianus	Neotropical cormorant	R
Order Piciformes (Woodpeckers and Relatives)		
Picidae (Woodpeckers)		
Campephilus guatamalensis	Pale-billed woodpecker	R
Celeus castaneus	Chestnut-colored woodpecker	R

Scientific Name	Common Name	Temporal Pattern
Dryocopus lineatus	Lineated woodpecker	R
Melanerpes aurifrons	Golden-fronted woodpecker	R
M. pucherani	Black-cheeked woodpecker	R
Piculus rubiginosus	Golden-olive woodpecker	R
Sphyrapicus varius	Yellow-bellied sapsucker	WV
Veniliornis fumigatus	Smoky-brown woodpecker	R
Ramphastidae (Toucans)		
Aulacorhynchus prasinus	Emerald toucanet	R
Pteroglossus torquatus	Collared aracari	R
Ramphastos sulfuratus	Keel-billed toucan	R
Order Podicipediformes (Grebes)		
Podicipedidae (Grebes)		
Tachybaptus dominicus	Least grebe	R
Order Psittaformes (Parrots)		
Psittacidae (Parrots)		
Amazona albifrons	White-fronted parrot	R
A. autumnalis	Red-lored parrot	R
A. farinosa	Mealy parrot	R
Ara macao	Scarlet macaw	R
Aratinga nana	Olive-throated parakeet	R
Pionopsitta haematotis	Brown-hooded parrot	R
Pionus senilis	White-crowned parrot	R
Order Strigiformes (Owls)		
Strigidae (Typical Owls)		
Ciccaba nigrolineata	Black-and-white owl	R
C. virgata	Mottled owl	R
Glaucidium brasilianum	Ferruginous pygmy owl	R
G. griseiceps	Central American pygmy owl	R
Otus guatemalae	Vermiculated screech owl	R
Pulsatrix perspicillata	Spectacled owl	R
Order Tinamiformes (Tinamous)		
Tinamidae (Tinamous)		
Crypturellus boucardi	Slaty-breasted tinamou	R

Scientific Name	Common Name	Temporal Pattern
C. cinnamomeus	Thicket tinamou	R
C. soui	Little tinamou	R
Tinamus major	Great tinamou	R
Order Trogoniformes (Trogons)		
Trogonidae (Trogons)		
Trogon collaris	Collared trogon	R
T. massena	Slaty-tailed trogon	R
T. melanocephalus	Black-headed trogon	R
T. violaceus	Violaceous trogon	R

R = resident; WV = winter visitor; SR = summer resident; T = transient.
Of the 294 species listed, 48 are visitors (16 percent).

CHAPTER 1

1. Gradstein, Ogg, and Smith, eds., *Geologic Time Scale.*
2. McLoughlin, "Breakup History of Gondwana."
3. Anwar, "Rare Earth and Trace Element Approach."
4. Bateson and Hall, *Geology of the Maya Mountains.*
5. Schafhauser et al., "Lower Cretaceous Pelagic Limestones."
6. Anwar, "Rare Earth and Trace Element Approach."
7. Ibid.
8. Schafhauser et al., "Lower Cretaceous Pelagic Limestones."
9. Day, "Conservation of Karst."
10. T. E. Miller, "Geologic and Hydrologic Controls."
11. Sapper, "Über Gebirgsbau und Boden."
12. Ower, "Geology of British Honduras."
13. Dixon, *Geology of Southern British Honduras.*
14. Bateson and Hall, *Geology of the Maya Mountains.*
15. T. E. Miller, "Geologic and Hydrologic Controls."
16. Czaplewski, Krejca, and Miller, "Late Quaternary Bats."
17. T. E. Miller, "Geologic and Hydrologic Controls."
18. T. E. Miller, "Inside Chiquibul."
19. Czaplewski, Krejca, and Miller, "Late Quaternary Bats."
20. T. E. Miller, "Inside Chiquibul."
21. Rogers, Sutton, and Stafford, *Report of the New Millennium Expedition.*
22. King et al., *Land Resource Assessment.*
23. Bateson and Hall, *Geology of the Maya Mountains.*
24. Balick, Nee, and Atha, *Checklist of the Vascular Plants.*
25. Ibid.
26. Bridgewater et al., "Preliminary Checklist."
27. Balick, Nee, and Atha, *Checklist of the Vascular Plants.*
28. Bridgewater et al., "Preliminary Checklist."
29. Kenrick and Davis, *Fossil Plants.*
30. Dixon, *Geology of Southern British Honduras.*
31. Crane, "Phylogentic Analysis of Seed Plants."
32. Wikström, Savolainen, and Chase, "Evolution of the Angiosperms."
33. De Bodt, Maere, and van de Peer, *Genome Duplication.*
34. Ibid.
35. Wikström, Savolainen, and Chase, "Evolution of the Angiosperms."
36. Magallon, Crane, and Herendeen, "Phylogenetic Pattern."
37. Wikström, Savolainen, and Chase, "Evolution of the Angiosperms."
38. Crane and Scott, "Angiosperm Diversification."
39. Wikström, Savolainen, and Chase, "Evolution of the Angiosperms."
40. Thomas, "Conservation."
41. Flora Mesoamericana, "About Flora Mesoamericana."
42. Biodiversity and Environmental Data Resource System of Belize, "Welcome."
43. M. W. Chase et al., "Phylogenetics of Seed Plants."
44. Angiosperm Phylogeny Group, "Update."
45. Balick, Nee, and Atha, *Checklist of the Vascular Plants.*
46. Raven and Axelrod, "Angiosperm Biogeography"; Gentry, "Neotropical Floristic Diversity."
47. Gentry, "Neotropical Floristic Diversity."
48. R. T. Pennington and Dick, "Role of Immigrants."

49. Davis et al., "Laurasian Migration."
50. Zerega et al., "Biogeography."
51. Graham and Dilcher, "Studies."
52. Ibid.
53. Colinvaux, "History of Forests."
54. Schopf, *Major Events.*
55. Fortey, "Cambrian Explosion."
56. Cracraft and Donoghue, *Assembling the Tree.*
57. Ibid.
58. Fortey, "Cambrian Explosion."
59. Gould, *Wonderful Life*; Morris, *Crucible of Creation.*
60. Schopf, *Major Events.*
61. Cracraft and Donoghue, *Assembling the Tree.*
62. Schopf, *Major Events.*
63. Cracraft and Donoghue, *Assembling the Tree.*
64. Tavaré et al., "Using the Fossil Record."
65. Fleagle and Kay, "Platyrrhines."
66. McLoughlin, "Breakup History of Gondwana."
67. Simpson, "History of the Fauna"; Webb, "Ecogeography."
68. Simpson, "Mammals and Land Bridges."
69. Engel et al., "Molecular Systematics."
70. Marshall, "Land Mammals."
71. Webb, "Great American Faunal Interchange."
72. Webb, "Ecogeography."
73. De Vivo and Carmignotto, "Holocene Vegetation."
74. R. T. Pennington, Prado, and Pendry, "Neotropical Seasonally Dry Forests."
75. Marshall, "Land Mammals."
76. Webb and Rancy, "Late Cenozoic Evolution."
77. Webb, "Great American Faunal Interchange."
78. Marshall, "Terror Birds."
79. Marshall, "Land Mammals."
80. Marshall et al., "Mammalian Evolution."
81. Webb, "Ecogeography"; Marshall, "Land Mammals"; de Vivo and Carmignotto, "Holocene Vegetation."
82. Martin, "Discovery of America."
83. Beck, "Discerning the Cause."
84. Wallace, *Natural Selection.*
85. Dobzhansky, "Evolution in the Tropics"; Fischer, "Latitudinal Variations."
86. Van der Hammon, "Pleistocene Changes."
87. Haffer, "Speciation."
88. Colinvaux et al., "Paradigm to Be Discarded."
89. Moritz, "Diversification of Rainforest Faunas."
90. R. T. Pennington, Prado, and Pendry, "Neotropical Seasonally Dry Forests."
91. S. J. Wright, "Plant Diversity."
92. Tillman, "Competition."
93. Brown and Whitmore, "Dipterocarp Seedlings."
94. Connell, "Diversity."
95. Hubbell and Foster, "Biology, Chance, and History."
96. Janzen, "Herbivores."
97. Harms et al., "Pervasive Density-Dependent Recruitment."
98. Hubbell, "Seed Predation."
99. D. H. Wright, "Species-Energy Theory."
100. Rhode, "Latitudinal Gradients."

CHAPTER 2

1. Standley and Record, *Forests and Flora.*
2. Lundell, *Vegetation of the Peten.*
3. A. C. S. Wright et al., *Land in British Honduras.*
4. King et al., *Land Resource Survey of Toledo*; King et al., *Land Resource Survey of Stann Creek*; King et al., *Land Resource Assessment*; Iremonger and Brokaw, "Vegetation Classification for Belize."
5. Meerman and Sabido, *Central American Ecosystems Map.*
6. Biodiversity and Environmental Resource Data System of Belize, "Welcome."
7. Meerman and Sabido, *Central American Ecosystems Map.*
8. Belize Forest Department / Food and Agricultural Organisation, *Latin American Forestry Sector.*
9. A. A. Young, "Belize's Ecosystems."
10. IUCN, *2001 IUCN Red List Categories and Criteria, version 3.1.*
11. IUCN, *2010 IUCN Red List of Threatened Species*, "Summary Statistics."
12. Meerman, *National List of Critical Species.*
13. Meerman and Sabido, *Central American Ecosystems Map.*

14. Bird, *Sustaining the Yield*; Brewer and Webb, "Seasonal Evergreen Forest."

15. Balick, Nee, and Atha, *Checklist of the Vascular Plants.*

16. Akers, "Preliminary Checklist."

17. Brewer et al., "Relationships of Phytogeography."

18. Dubbin, Penn, and Hodson, "Edaphic Influences."

19. Furley and Newey, "Variations in Plant Communities."

20. Furley, " Significance of the Cohune Palm."

21. Conservation International, *Ecosystem Profile.*

22. Bridgewater et al., "Preliminary Checklist."

23. Meerman and Sabido, *Central American Ecosystems Map*; Penn, Sutton, and Monro, "Vegetation of the Greater Maya Mountains."

24. Urban, Bridgewater, and Harris, "Macal River"; Bridgewater et al., "Preliminary Checklist."

25. Hicks, "Describing the Plant Diversity."

26. Queensborough, "Floristics and Phytogeography"; Bird, *Sustaining the Yield.*

27. Gentry, "Changes in Plant Community Diversity."

28. Queensborough, "Floristics and Phytogeography"; Pitman et al., "Dominance and Distribution"; Bridgewater, Ratter, and Ribeiro, "Biogeographic Patterns."

29. Queensborough, *Floristics and Phytogeography.*

30. Brewer and Webb, "Seasonal Evergreen Forest"; Brewer et al., "Relationships of Phytogeography."

31. Brewer and Webb, "Seasonal Evergreen Forest."

32. Ibid.

33. Brewer et al., "Relationships of Phytogeography."

34. Chiappy-Jones et al., "Floristic Affinities."

35. Bridgewater et al., "Preliminary Checklist."

36. De Gouvenain and Silander, "Tropical Storm Regimes."

37. Bridgewater et al., "Preliminary Checklist."

38. Jebb and Sayers, *Survey of the Epiphytes.*

39. Ibid.

40. Townsend, "Checklist of the Mosses."

41. Whittemore and Allen, "Liverworts and Hornworts."

42. Matola, *Expedition to Doyle's Delight.*

43. Kendrick, *Fifth Kingdom.*

44. Hawksworth, "Magnitude of Fungal Diversity."

45. Kendrick, *Fifth Kingdom.*

46. Kropp, *Historical Biogeography of Fungi.*

47. Meerman and Matola, *Doyle's Delight.*

48. Minter, Rodríguez Hernández, and Mena Portales, *Fungi of the Caribbean.*

49. Ibid.

50. Meerman and Sabido, *Central American Ecosystems Map.*

51. Valiela, Bowen, and York, "Mangrove Forests."

52. Furley and Ratter, *Mangrove Distribution.*

53. Zisman, *Mangroves in Belize.*

54. Hogarth, *Biology of Mangroves.*

55. Ellison and Farnsworth, "Seedling Survivorship."

56. Hogarth, *Biology of Mangroves.*

57. Ibid.

58. Farnsworth and Ellison, "Global Patterns."

59. Furley and Ratter, *Mangrove Distribution.*

60. Zisman, *Mangroves in Belize.*

61. Ellison, Farnsworth, and Twilley, "Facultative Mutualism."

62. Feller, "Effects of Nutrient Enrichment."

63. McKee, "Root Proliferation."

64. McKeon and Feller, "Supratidal Fauna."

65. McKee, "Mangrove Species Distribution."

66. Zisman, *Mangroves in Belize.*

67. Ibid.

68. Sedberry and Carter, "Fish Community."

69. Zisman, *Mangroves in Belize.*

70. Ibid.

71. McKeon and Feller, "Supratidal Fauna."

72. Moll, "Food and Feeding Behavior."

73. Meerman and Sabido, *Central American Ecosystems Map*; Mistry, *World Savannas.*

74. Meerman and Sabido, *Central American Ecosystems Map.*

75. Huber, "Neotropical Savannas."

76. Furley et al., "Savannas of the Rio Bravo."

77. Furley, "Further Observations."

78. Meerman and Sabido, *Central American Ecosystems Map.*

79. Ibid.

80. Bridgewater et al., "Vegetation Classification."
81. Farruggia, *Floristic Description*.
82. Laughlin, "Flora of the Pine Savanna at Monkey Bay."
83. Hicks, "Describing the Plant Diversity."
84. Farjon and Styles, Pinus (*Pinaceae*).
85. Huber, "Neotropical Savannas."
86. Milne, "Biogeographical and Ecological Study of *Acoelorraphe wrightii*."
87. B. W. Taylor, "Outline of the Vegetation of Nicaragua."
88. Kellman, "Synergistic Relationships."
89. Kellman and Miyanishi, "Forest Seedling Establishment"; Kellman, "Soil Enrichment."
90. Kellman, "Synergistic Relationships."
91. Myers, O'Brien, and Morrison, *Fire Management*.
92. Kellman, "Synergistic Relationships."
93. Nature Conservancy, *Ecological Role and Management of Fire*.
94. Anoruo and Berlyn, "Caribbean Pine."
95. Meerman and Sabido, *Central American Ecosystems Map*.
96. Billings et al., "Bark Beetle Outbreaks."
97. Midtgaard and Thunes, *Pine Bark Beetles*.
98. Ibid.
99. Haack, Eckelmann, and Green, "Southern Pine Beetle Outbreak."
100. Midtgaard and Thunes, *Pine Bark Beetles*.
101. Gilbert, "'Little Armored Thing.'"
102. Platt, Rainwater, and Brewer, "Aspects of the Burrowing Ecology."
103. Ibid.
104. Kirchheimer and Storrs, "Attempts to Establish the Armadillo."
105. Jones, *Birds of Belize*.
106. BirdLife International, "*Amazona oratrix*."
107. McKinley and Francl, "*Jabiru mycteria*."
108. Stafford, *Snakes*.

CHAPTER 3

1. A. F. Chase and Chase, "Mighty Maya Nation."
2. Lundell, "1936 Michigan-Carnegie Botanical Expedition."
3. Belize Electrical Company, *Macal River*.

4. Turner and Miksicek, "Economic Plant Species."
5. Wiseman, "Agriculture and Historical Ecology."
6. Pohl and Miksicek, "Cultivation Techniques."
7. Pohl, "Ethnohistorical Perspective."
8. Turner and Miksicek, "Economic Plant Species"; Pohl, "Ethnohistorical Perspective."
9. Turner and Miksicek, "Economic Plant Species."
10. Lundell, "Plants Probably Utilized."
11. Lambert and Arnason, "Ramón and Maya Ruins."
12. Levasseur and Olivier, "Farming System."
13. Vaughan, Deevey, and Garrett-Jones, "Pollen Stratigraphy."
14. Ibid.
15. Ibid.; Wiseman, "Agriculture and Vegetation Dynamics."
16. Bloom, Pohl, and Stein, "Analysis of Sedimentation"; Wiseman, "Analysis of Pollen."
17. Tykot, Van der Mere, and Hammond, "Stable Isotope Analysis."
18. Healey et al., "Caracol, Belize."
19. A. F. Chase and Chase, "Mighty Maya Nation."
20. Appenzeller, "Clashing Maya Superpowers."
21. A. F. Chase and Chase, "Mighty Maya Nation."
22. Ibid.
23. Wilk, "Dry Season Agriculture."
24. Healey et al., "Caracol, Belize."
25. Healey, "Ancient Maya Dam."
26. Turner, "Prehistoric Intensive Agriculture."
27. Healey et al., "Caracol, Belize."
28. Pohl, "Ethnohistorical Perspective"; Turner, "Prehistoric Intensive Agriculture"; Matheny, "Maya Lowland Hydraulic Systems."
29. Turner and Harrison, "Prehistoric Raised Field Agriculture"; Wiseman, "Analysis of Pollen"; Bloom, Pohl, and Stein, "Analysis of Sedimentation"; Lambert, Siemens, and Arnason, "Ancient Maya Drained Field Agriculture."
30. Matheny, "Maya Lowland Hydraulic Systems"; Adams, Brown, and Culbert, "Radar Mapping."

31. Wilk, "Dry Season Agriculture."
32. Turner and Harrison, "Prehistoric Raised Field Agriculture."
33. Scarborough and Gallopin, "Water Storage Adaption."
34. Healey, "Ancient Maya Dam."
35. Hodell et al., "Solar Forcing."
36. Bancroft, *Experimenting Researches.*
37. Twigger, "*Inflation.*"
38. Camille, "Historical Geography of the Belizean Logwood Trade."
39. Ibid.
40. Ibid.
41. T. D. Pennington, "Mahogany."
42. T. D. Pennington, *Meliaceae.*
43. Ibid.
44. T. D. Pennington, "Mahogany."
45. Robbins, *Mahogany Matters.*
46. Blundell and Rodan, "Mahogany and CITES."
47. Snook, "Catastrophic Disturbance."
48. T. D. Pennington, "Mahogany."
49. Weaver and Sabido, *Mahogany in Belize.*
50. Ibid.
51. Ibid.
52. T. D. Pennington, "Mahogany."
53. Roth Novick et al., "Genetic Structure."
54. T. D. Pennington, *Meliaceae.*
55. Roth Novick et al., "Genetic Structure."
56. M. S. Johnson and Chaffey, *Inventory of the Chiquibul.*
57. Bird, *Sustaining the Yield.*
58. M. S. Johnson and Chaffey, *Inventory of the Chiquibul.*
59. Weaver and Sabido, *Mahogany in Belize.*
60. Ibid.
61. Poore et al., *No Timber without Trees.*
62. Weaver and Sabido, *Mahogany in Belize*; Bird, *Sustaining the Yield*; M. S. Johnson and Chaffey, *Inventory of the Chiquibul.*
63. Weaver and Sabido, *Mahogany in Belize.*
64. Central Statistics Office, *Abstract of Statistics.*
65. Bird, *Sustaining the Yield.*
66. Ibid.
67. Ibid.
68. Ibid.
69. Peters, Gentry, and Mendelsohn, "Valuation of an Amazonian Rainforest."
70. Godoy and Bawa, "Economic Value and Sustainable Harvest."
71. Bridgewater et al., "*Chamaedorea* (Xaté)"; Godoy and Bawa, " Economic Value and Sustainable Harvest"; Hall and Bawa, "Methods."
72. Balick, Nee, and Atha, *Checklist of the Vascular Plants.*
73. Peters, Gentry, and Mendelsohn, "Valuation of an Amazonian Rainforest."
74. Ibarra-Manríquez et al., "Useful Plants."
75. Mendelsohn and Balick, "Value of Undiscovered Pharmaceuticals."
76. Godoy, Lubowski, and Markandya, "Method for the Economic Valuation."
77. Browder, "Limits of Extractivism."
78. Ibid.
79. Schwartz, "Some Notes on the Folklore."
80. Shanley et al., *Tapping the Green Market.*
81. Ibid.
82. T. D. Pennington, *Sapotaceae.*
83. Balick, Nee, and Atha, *Checklist of the Vascular Plants.*
84. Hummel, "Sapodilla Trees and Chicle."
85. Lundell, "Chicle Exploration."
86. Heyder, "Sapodilla Tapping," p. 109.
87. Ibid.
88. Heinzman and Reining, "Commercial Non-Timber Forest Products."
89. Shanley et al., *Tapping the Green Market.*
90. Forest Stewardship Council, "FSC Certificate Database."
91. Fairtrade Labelling Organizations International, "About Fairtrade."
92. Goodban, *Cohune Palm.*
93. Ibid.
94. Heinzman and Reining, "Commercial Non-Timber Forest Products."
95. Goodban, *Cohune Palm.*
96. Hodel, Chamaedorea *Palms.*
97. Henderson, Galeano, and Bernal, *Field Guide to the Palms.*
98. Walter and Gillett, 1997 *IUCN Red List.*
99. Oyama, "Conservation and Exploitation."
100. Walter and Gillett, 1997 *IUCN Red List.*
101. Oyama, "Conservation and Exploitation."
102. Endress, Gorchov, and Peterson, "Harvest of the Palm."
103. Commission for Environmental Cooperation, *In Search of a Sustainable Palm Market.*
104. Alianza para un Mundo Justo, "*Growing Together.*"

105. Chemonics International, *Community Forest Management*.
106. Jimenez Perez et al., *Manejo de palmilla*.
107. Castillo Mont, "Palms of Guatemala."
108. Bridgewater et al., "*Chamaedorea* (Xaté)."
109. Henderson, Galeano, and Bernal, *Field Guide to the Palms*.
110. Wicks, "Preliminary Fishtail Xaté."
111. Bentley, "Nitrogen Fixation."
112. Bridgewater et al., "*Chamaedorea* (Xaté)."
113. Balick, Arvigo, and Romero, "Development of an Ethnomedical Forest Reserve."
114. Amiguet et al., "Consensus Ethnobotany."
115. Arvigo, *Sastun*.
116. Mendelsohn and Balick, "Value of Undiscovered Pharmaceuticals."
117. Ibid.
118. Balick, Nee, and Atha, *Checklist of the Vascular Plants*.
119. Cox and Balick, "Ethnobotanical Approach."
120. Convention on Biological Diversity, Article 1.
121. O'Brien and Kinnaird, "Impact of Harvest"; Flores and Ashton, "Harvesting Impact."
122. O'Hara, "Potential Effects of Leaf Harvesting."
123. Folklore Book Fund Committee, *Characters and Caricatures*.
124. Arvigo and Epstein, *Rainforest Home Remedies*.
125. Belize Tourism Board, *Travel and Tourism Statistics, 2008*.

CHAPTER 4

1. Stafford, *Annotated Inventory*.
2. Stafford, *Snakes*.
3. Pough et al., *Herpetology*.
4. Ibid.
5. Campbell, "Distribution Patterns."
6. Lee, *Amphibians and Reptiles*.
7. Stafford et al., "Distribution and Conservation."
8. Radachowsky, *Endemism in the Maya Forest*.
9. Lee, *Amphibians and Reptiles*.
10. Stafford, *Snakes*.
11. IUCN, *2010 IUCN Red List of Threatened Species: Amphibians*.

12. B. E. Young et al., "Population Declines."
13. Kaiser, "Evaluation."
14. Fitzherbert et al., "Project Anuran."
15. Rogers, Sutton, and Stafford, *Report of the Joint Services Scientific Expedition*; Rogers, *Main Report*.
16. Rogers, *Main Report*.
17. Meerman and Matola, *Doyle's Delight*.
18. Minty, *Preliminary Report*.
19. Briggs, "Mating Patterns."
20. Stafford et al., "Morelet's Crocodile."
21. Hirth, "Some Aspects"; R. W. Henderson, "Aspects of the Ecology."
22. Stafford et al., "Morelet's Crocodile."
23. Ibid.
24. Platt, "Ecology and Status of Morelet's Crocodile"; Dever, "Examination of Genetic Structure."
25. Platt, "Ecology and Status of Morelet's Crocodile."
26. Stafford et al., "Morelet's Crocodile."
27. Wu et al., "Organochlorine Contaminants."
28. Rainwater et al., "Mercury in Morelet's Crocodile Eggs."
29. Cracraft and Donoghue, *Assembling the Tree of Life*.
30. Meerman, *Compilation of Information on Biodiversity*.
31. Radachowsky, *Endemism in the Maya Forest*.
32. Hill and Smith, *Bats*.
33. Ibid.
34. B. W. Miller, "Community Ecology of the Non-Phyllostomid Bats."
35. B. W. Miller, "Risk Assessment."
36. Howell, "Bats of Caracol."
37. B. W. Miller and Miller, *Biodiversity Reconnaissance*; B. W. Miller and Miller, personal communication.
38. B. W. Miller and Miller, *Biodiversity Reconnaissance*.
39. Hill and Smith, *Bats*.
40. Greenaway, *Bats of Las Cuevas Cave*.
41. Ibid.
42. Hill and Smith, *Bats*.
43. Kelly, "Jaguar Monitoring."
44. Sharer, *Ancient Maya*.
45. Rabinowitz, *Jaguar*.
46. Silver et al. "Use of Camera Traps."
47. Ibid.

48. Ibid.
49. Sunquist and Sunquist, *Wild Cats.*
50. Rabinowitz and Nottingham, "Ecology and Behaviour of the Jaguar."
51. Meerman, *National Protected Area.*
52. Eizirik et al., "Análisis de la viabilidad."
53. Rabinowitz and Nottingham, "Ecology and Behaviour of the Jaguar."
54. Sunquist and Sunquist, *Wild Cats.*
55. Noss et al., "Pumas y jaguares."
56. Rabinowitz, "Jaguar Predation."
57. Brooks, Bodmer, and Matola, *Tapirs.*
58. Minty, *Preliminary Report.*
59. Ibid.
60. Brooks, Bodmer, and Matola, *Tapirs.*
61. Minty, *Preliminary Report*; Brooks, Bodmer, and Matola, *Tapirs.*
62. Brooks, Bodmer, and Matola, *Tapirs.*
63. Fragoso and Huffman, "Seed Dispersal."
64. Janzen and Martin, "Neotropical Anachronisms."
65. Pavelka et al., "Population Reduction."
66. Horwich and Lyon, *Belizean Rain Forest.*
67. Estrada et al., "Survey."
68. Pavelka and Knopff, "Diet and Activity."
69. Ibid., p. 105.
70. Cant, "Feeding Ecology."
71. Muskin and Fischgrund, "Seed Dispersal."
72. Chapman et al., "Post-Weaning Resource Competition."
73. Sowls, *Peccaries.*
74. Byers and Bekoff, " Social, Spacing, and Cooperative Behavior."
75. Ibid.
76. Kiltie, "Bite Force."
77. Mayer and Wetzel, *Tayassu pecari.*
78. Kelly, "Jaguar Monitoring."
79. Ibid.
80. Murray and Gardner, *Leopardus pardalis.*
81. Dillon, *Ocelot Density.*
82. Murray and Gardner, *Leopardus pardalis.*
83. Dillon, *Ocelot Density.*
84. Kelly and Caro, "Low Density of Small Mammals."
85. Caro et al., "Inventorying Mammals."
86. Jones, *Birds of Belize.*
87. Del Hoyo, Elliott, and Sargatal, *Handbook.*
88. Radachowsky, *Endemism in the Maya Forest.*
89. Elphick, *Atlas of Bird Migration.*

90. Jones, *Birds of Belize.*
91. Arcadia University, *Biodiversity and Landscape Structure*; Mallory, *Impacts of Silvicultural Trials.*
92. Jones, *Birds of Belize.*
93. Elphick, *Atlas of Bird Migration*; Moore, "Neotropical Migrants."
94. Gauthreaux, "Neotropical Migrants."
95. Able, "How Birds Migrate."
96. Elphick, *Atlas of Bird Migration.*
97. Arcadia University, *Biodiversity and Landscape Structure.*
98. Mallory, *Impacts of Silvicultural Trials.*
99. Arcadia University, *Biodiversity and Landscape Structure.*
100. Forshaw, *Parrots of the World.*
101. Jones, *Birds of Belize.*
102. IUCN, *2010 IUCN Red List of Threatened Species.*
103. Meerman, *Protected Areas System Assessment.*
104. Minty, *Preliminary Report.*
105. Ibid.
106. Jones, *Birds of Belize.*
107. Delacour and Amadon, *Curassows.*
108. Ibid.
109. IUCN, *2010 IUCN Red List of Threatened Species*; Meerman, *Protected Areas System Assessment.*
110. Curti, "Harpy Eagle Restoration."

CHAPTER 5

1. Allen-Wardell et al., "Potential Consequences of Pollinator Declines."
2. Kearns and Inouye, "Pollinators."
3. Allen-Wardell et al., "Potential Consequences of Pollinator Declines."
4. Bawa, Perry, and Beach, "Reproductive Biology."
5. Renner and Won, "Repeated Evolution of Dioecy."
6. Renner and Feil, "Pollinators"; Bawa, Perry, and Beach, "Reproductive Biology."
7. Bawa, Perry, and Beach, "Reproductive Biology.".
8. Cox, "Abiotic Pollination."
9. Bush, "Neotropical Plant Reproductive Strategies."
10. Renner and Feil, "Pollinators."

11. P. E. Taylor et al., "High-Speed Pollen Release."
12. Bullock, "Wind Pollination."
13. Cox, "Hydrophilous Pollination."
14. Philbrick and Novelo, "New World Podostemaceae."
15. Cox, "Hydrophilous Pollination."
16. Bawa, "Plant-Pollinator Interactions."
17. McDade and Weeks, "Nectar."
18. Hardy, "Pollen Dispersal."
19. Kearns and Inouye, "Pollinators."
20. Bush, "Neotropical Plant Reproductive Strategies."
21. Bawa et al., " Reproductive Biology: Pollination Systems."
22. Gottsberger, "Pollination and Evolution"; Bernhardt, "Convergent Evolution."
23. Bernhardt, "Convergent Evolution."
24. Gottsberger, "Pollination and Evolution."
25. Bawa, "Plant-Pollinator Interactions."
26. Gibernau et al., "Beetle Pollination."
27. Porter Morgan, "Thrips."
28. Listabarth, "Insect-Induced Wind Pollination."
29. Porter Morgan, "Thrips."
30. Terry, "Thrips."
31. Sakai, "Thrips Pollination."
32. Sakai, *Aristolochia.*
33. Wolda and Sabrosky, "Insect Visitors."
34. Sakai, *Aristolochia.*
35. Mani and Saravanan, *Pollination Ecology.*
36. Mendoza-Cuenca and Macías-Ordóñez, "Foraging Polymorphism."
37. Linhart and Mendenhall, "Pollen Dispersal."
38. Oliveira, Gibbs, and Barbosa, "Moth Pollination."
39. Ibid.
40. Moure, Urban, and Melo, *Catalogue of Bees.*
41. Camargo and Pedro, *Meliponini lepeletier.*
42. Bawa, "Plant-Pollinator Interactions."
43. Bawa et al., "Reproductive Biology: Pollination Systems."
44. Buchmann, "Ecology of Oil Flowers."
45. Ibid.
46. Bawa, "Plant-Pollinator Interactions."
47. Ibid.
48. Arditti, *Fundamentals of Orchid Biology.*
49. Bridgewater et al., "Preliminary Checklist."
50. S. D. Johnson and Edwards, "Structure and Function of Orchid Pollinaria."
51. Cameron, "Phenology and Biology."
52. Dressler, "Pollination by Euglossine Bees."
53. Bawa, "Plant-Pollinator Interactions"; Ackerman, "Specificity and Mutual Dependency."
54. Thorp, "Collection of Pollen."
55. Snow and Roubik, "Pollen Deposition."
56. Weiss, "Vision and Learning."
57. Ibid.; Winter and von Helversen, "Bats as Pollinators."
58. Weiss, "Vision and Learning."
59. Altshuler, "Flower Color."
60. Chittka et al., "Adaptation, Constraint, and Chance."
61. Ibid.
62. Altshuler, "Flower Color."
63. Allen-Wardell et al., " Potential Consequences of Pollinator Declines."
64. Altshuler, "Flower Color."
65. Ibid.
66. Baker, "Sugar Concentrations."
67. Gryj, Martínez del Rio, and Baker, "Avian Pollination."
68. Jousselin, Raspus, and Kjellberg, "Convergence and Coevolution."
69. Balick, Nee, and Atha, *Checklist of the Vascular Plants.*
70. Bridgewater et al., "Preliminary Checklist."
71. Jousselin, Raspus, and Kjellberg, "Convergence and Coevolution."
72. Bronstein, "Maintenance of Species-Specificity."
73. Ibid.
74. Weiblen, "Phylogenetic Relationships."
75. Gibernau et al., "Consequences of Protecting Flowers."
76. Ramírez, "Fig Wasps."
77. Steiner, "Nectarivory."
78. Winter and von Helversen, "Bats as Pollinators."
79. Ibid.
80. Ibid.
81. Griebel, Gibbs, and Queiroz, "Flowering Phenology."
82. Toledo, "Pollination of Some Rain Forest Plants."
83. Griebel, Gibbs, and Queiroz, "Flowering Phenology."

84. Rengifo, Cornejo, and Akirov, "One Size Fits All."
85. Bawa et al., "Reproductive Biology: Pollination Systems"; Ordano and Ornelas, "Cost of Nectar Replenishment."
86. Styles, "Ecology."
87. Altshuler, "Flower Color."
88. Rengifo, Cornejo, and Akirov, "One Size Fits All."
89. McDade and Weeks, "Nectar."
90. Baker, "Sugar Concentrations."
91. Toledo, "Pollination of Some Rain Forest Plants."
92. Gryj, Martínez del Rio, and Baker, "Avian Pollination."
93. Toledo, "Pollination of Some Rain Forest Plants."
94. Ibid.
95. Bawa, "Plant-Pollinator Interactions."
96. Nelson, *Sea Beans and Nickar Nuts.*
97. Augspurger, "Morphology and Dispersal Potential."
98. Brewer and Webb, "Seasonal Evergreen Forest."
99. Jordano, "Fruits and Frugivory."
100. Howe and Westley, *Ecological Relationships.*
101. Janzen, "Herbivores."
102. Clark, Poulsen, and Parker, "Role of Arboreal Seed Dispersal Groups."
103. Levy, "Tropical Wet Forest Treefall Gaps."
104. Link and Di Fiore, "Seed Dispersal."
105. Ibid.
106. Medellin and Gaona, "Dispersal by Bats and Birds."
107. Brewer and Rejmánek, "Small Rodents."
108. Foster and Delay, "Dispersal of Mimetic Seeds."
109. Vander-Wall, Kuhn, and Beck, "Seed Removal."
110. Howe and Smallwood, "Ecology of Seed Dispersal."
111. Frankie, Baker, and Opler, "Comparative Phenological Studies."
112. Scott Mills, Soulé, and Doak, "Keystone-Species Concept."
113. Paine, "Trophic Complexity."
114. Janzen, "How To Be a Fig."
115. Kalko, Herre, and Handley, "Relation of Fig Fruit Characteristics."
116. Janzen, "How To Be a Fig"; Herre, "Overview of Studies."
117. S. J. Wright and Cornejo, "Seasonal Drought"; Borchert, "Soil and Stem Water Storage."
118. Sobrado, "Cost-Benefit Relationships."
119. Sayer and Newbery, "Role of Tree Size."
120. Zimmerman et al., "Flowering and Fruiting Phenologies."
121. Janzen, "Synchronization of Sexual Reproduction."
122. Ibid.; van Shaik, Terborgh, and Wright, "Phenology of Tropical Forests."
123. Zimmerman et al., "Flowering and Fruiting Phenologies."
124. Janzen, "Synchronization of Sexual Reproduction."
125. Borchert, "Phenology and Control of Flowering."
126. Newstrom et al., "Diversity of Long-Term Flowering Patterns."
127. Zimmerman et al., "Flowering and Fruiting Phenologies."
128. Janzen, "Synchronization of Sexual Reproduction."
129. Borchert, "Phenology and Control of Flowering."
130. T. P. Young and Perkocha, "Treefalls."
131. Chapman, Kaufman, and Chapman, "Buttress Formation."
132. Henwood, "Structural Model of Forces."
133. Crook, Ennos, and Banks, "Function of Buttress Roots."
134. Ibid.
135. Chapman, Kaufman, and Chapman, "Buttress Formation."
136. A. R. Lewis, "Buttress Arrangement."
137. Losos and Leigh, *Tropical Forest Diversity.*
138. Cary et al., "Tree Mortality"; Swaine, Lieberman, and Putz, "Dynamics of Tree Populations."
139. Bird, *Sustaining the Yield.*
140. Philips and Gentry, "Increasing Turnover."
141. Condit, "Forest Turnover."
142. Grace et al., "Carbon Dioxide Uptake."
143. Keller et al., "If a Tree Falls."
144. Budowski, "Distribution of Tropical American Rain Forest Species"; Brokaw, "Treefalls"; Finegan, "Pattern and Process"; Whitmore, "Canopy Gaps."

145. Swaine and Whitmore, "On the Definition of Ecological Species Groups."
146. Whitmore, "Canopy Gaps."
147. Renshaw, "Tree Functional Types."
148. Shiel and Burslem, "Disturbing Hypotheses."
149. Friesner, *Hurricanes*.
150. Pavelka and Behie, "Effect of Hurricane Iris."
151. Friesner, *Hurricanes*.
152. Everham and Brokaw, "Forest Damage and Recovery."
153. Ibid.
154. Friesner, *Hurricanes*.
155. Yin et al., "Recovery of the Rain Forest."
156. Walker, "Timing of Post-Hurricane Tree Mortality."
157. Everham and Brokaw, "Forest Damage and Recovery."
158. Ibid.
159. Friesner, *Hurricanes*.
160. Everham and Brokaw, "Forest Damage and Recovery."
161. De Gouvenain and Silander, "Tropical Storm Regimes."
162. Pavelka and Behie, "Effect of Hurricane Iris."
163. Friesner, *Hurricanes*.
164. Burslem, Whitmore, and Brown, "Short-Term Effects of Cyclone Impact."
165. Everham and Brokaw, "Forest Damage and Recovery."
166. Vandermeer et al., "Hurricane Disturbance."
167. Scatena et al., "First Five Years."
168. De Gouvenain and Silander, "Tropical Storm Regimes"; Vandermeer et al., "Hurricane Disturbance"; Brokaw, "Gap-Phase Regeneration."
169. Boucher, "Growing Back."
170. Meerman, Howe, and Arevalo, *Machaca Hill Lodge*.
171. Meerman, *Ecological Assessment*.
172. Bird, *Sustaining the Yield*.
173. Chapela et al., "Evolutionary History of the Symbiosis."
174. Ibid.
175. Dalling and Wirth, "Dispersal of *Miconia argentea* Seeds."
176. Chapela et al., "Evolutionary History of the Symbiosis."
177. Kendrick, *Fifth Kingdom*.
178. Currie, Mueller, and Malloch, "Agricultural Pathology of Ant Fungus Gardens."
179. Rockwood, "Plant Selection."
180. Berish, "Leaf-Cutting Ants."
181. Rockwood, "Plant Selection."
182. T. Lewis, Pollard, and Dibley, "Rhythmic Foraging."
183. Tautz, Roces, and Höllbobler, "Use of Sound-Based Vibratome."
184. Kendrick, *Fifth Kingdom*.
185. Currie, Mueller, and Malloch, "Agricultural Pathology of Ant Fungus Gardens."
186. Ibid.
187. Yu, "Structural Role of Epiphytes."
188. Bawa, "Plant-Pollinator Interactions."
189. Catling, "Evidence of Partitioning"; Catling, "Influence of Aerial *Azteca* Nests."
190. Janzen, "Dissolution of Mutualism."
191. Ibid.
192. Wetterer, "Ants on *Cecropia* Trees."
193. De Andrade and Carauta, "*Cecropia-Azteca* Association."
194. Wetterer, "Ants on *Cecropia* Trees"; Janzen, "Dissolution of Mutualism."
195. Seigler and Ebinger, "Taxonomic Revision."
196. The Ward Ant Lab, "Ants of the Subfamily Pseudomyrmecinae."
197. Janzen, "Coevolution of Mutualism."
198. Keeler, "Infidelity by Acacia Ants."
199. Janzen, "Coevolution of Mutualism."
200. Ibid.
201. Raine, Willmer, and Stone, "Spatial Structuring and Floral Avoidance Behavior."
202. Janzen, "Coevolution of Mutualism."
203. B. E. Young, Kaspari, and Martin, "Species-Specific Nest Selection."

BIBLIOGRAPHY

Able, K. P., ed. *Gatherings of Angels: Migrating Birds and Their Ecology*. Ithaca, NY: Cornell University Press, 1999.

——. "How Birds Migrate: Flight Behavior, Energetics, and Navigation." In Able, *Gatherings of Angels*, 11–26.

Ackerman, J. D. "Specificity and Mutual Dependency of the Orchid-Euglossine Interaction." *Biological Journal of the Linnean Society* 20 (1983): 301–314.

Adams, R. E. W., W. E. Brown, and P. T. Culbert. "Radar Mapping, Archaeology, and Ancient Maya Land Use." *Science* 213 (1981): 1457–1463.

Akers, R. "A Preliminary Checklist of the Vascular Plants of the Cockscomb Basin Wildlife Sanctuary." Master's thesis, Royal Botanic Garden Edinburgh / University of Edinburgh, 2007.

Alianza para un Mundo Justo. *"Growing Together": Xaté in Belize and Guatemala*. Santa Elena, Guatemala: Alianza para un Mundo Justo (AMJ), 2003.

Allen-Wardell, G., P. Bernhardt, R. Bitner, A. Burquez, S. Buchmann, J. Cane, P. A. Cox, et al. "The Potential Consequences of Pollinator Declines on the Conservation of Biodiversity and Stability of Food Crop Yields." *Conservation Biology* 12, no. 1 (1998): 8–17.

Altshuler, D. L. "Flower Color, Hummingbird Pollination, and Habitat Irradiance in Four Neotropical Forests." *Biotropica* 35, no. 3 (2003): 344–355.

Amiguet, V. T., J. T. Arnason, P. Maquin, V. Cal, P. S. Vindas, and L. Poveda. "A Consensus Ethnobotany of the Q'eqchi' Maya of Southern Belize." *Economic Botany* 59, no. 1 (2005): 29–42.

Angiosperm Phylogeny Group (APG). "An Update of the Angiosperm Phylogeny Group Classification for the Orders and Families of Flowering Plants." *Botanical Journal of the Linnean Society* 141 (2003): 399–436.

Anoruo, A. O., and G. O. Berlyn. "Caribbean Pine in Sustainable Tropical Forestry Distribution: Taxonomy, Ecology, Biotechnology and Silvics." 1993. *Journal of Sustainable Forestry* 1, no. 1 (1993): 1–23.

Anwar, M. S. "A Rare Earth and Trace Element Approach to Understanding the Origin of the Santa Rosa Group Sediments, Maya Mountains, Belize." Master's thesis, Department of Geological Sciences, Indiana University, 2004.

Appenzeller, T. "Clashing Maya Superpowers Emerge from a New Analysis." *Science* 266 (1994): 733–734.

Arcadia University. *Biodiversity and Landscape Structure within the Chiquibul Forest Reserve: A Summary Report of Research Activities in 2005*. Report to the Belize Forest Department, 2006.

Arditti, J. *Fundamentals of Orchid Biology*. New York: John Wiley & Sons, 1992.

Arvigo, R. *Sastun: My Apprenticeship with a Maya Healer*. New York: HarperCollins, 1994.

——, and M. Balick. *Rainforest Remedies: One Hundred Healing Herbs of Belize*. Twin Lakes, WI: Lotus Press, 1998.

——, and N. Epstein. *Rainforest Home Remedies: The Maya Way to Heal Your Body and Replenish Your Soul*. San Franciso: Harper, 2001.

Augspurger, C. K. "Morphology and Dispersal Potential of Wind-Dispersed Diaspores of Neotropical Trees." *American Journal of Botany* 73, no. 3 (1986): 353–363.

Baillie, I. C., A. C. S. Wright, M. A. Holder, and E. A. FitzPatrick. *Revised Classification of the Soils of Belize*. Natural Resources Institute Bulletin 59. Chatham, UK: Natural Resources Institute, 1993.

Baker, H. G. "Sugar Concentrations in Nectars from Hummingbird Flowers." *Biotropica* 7, no. 1 (1975): 37–41.

Balick, M. J., R. Arvigo, and L. Romero. "The Development of an Ethnomedical Forest

Reserve in Belize: Its Role in the Preservation of Biological and Cultural Diversity." *Conservation Biology* 8, no. 1 (1994): 316–317.

——, M. H. Nee, and D. E. Atha. *Checklist of the Vascular Plants of Belize with Common Names and Uses.* Memoirs of the New York Botanical Garden 85. New York: New York Botanical Garden, 2000.

Bancroft, E. *Experimenting Researches Concerning the Philosophy of Permanent Colours.* 2 vols. London: T. Cadell and W. Davies, 1831.

Bateson, J. H., and I. H. S. Hall. *The Geology of the Maya Mountains, Belize.* Overseas Memoir 3. London: Her Majesty's Stationery Office, 1977.

Bawa, K. S. "Plant-Pollinator Interactions in Tropical Rain Forests." *Annual Review of Ecology and Systematics* 21 (1990): 399–422.

——, S. H. Bullock, D. R. Perry, R. E. Coville, and M. H. Grayum. "Reproductive Biology of Tropical Lowland Rain Forest Trees: II. Pollination Systems." *American Journal of Botany* 72, no. 3 (1985): 346–356.

——, D. R. Perry, and J. H. Beach. "Reproductive Biology of Tropical Lowland Rain Forest Trees: I. Sexual Systems and Incompatibility Mechanisms." *American Journal of Botany* 72, no. 3 (1985): 331–345.

Beck, M. W. "On Discerning the Cause of Late Pleistocene Megafaunal Extinctions." *Paleobiology* 22, no. 1 (1996): 91–103.

Belize Electrical Company (BECOL) Ltd. *Macal River Upstream Storage Facility Environmental Impact Assessment.* Vol. 4, *Archaeology–Reservoir Area.* Report. Belize City, 2001.

Belize Forest Department / Food and Agricultural Organisation. *Latin American Forestry Sector Network Outlook Study: Working Paper, National Report Belize.* Rome: Food and Agriculture Organization of the United Nations, 2004.

Belize Tourism Board. "Tourism Statistics." http://www.belizetourism.org/content/view/248/295/. Accessed September 11, 2006.

——. *Travel and Tourism Statistics, 2008.* Belize City: Belize Tourism Board, 2008.

Bentley, B. "Nitrogen Fixation by Epiphylls in Tropical Rainforest." *Annals of the Missouri Botanical Garden* 74 (1987): 234–241.

Berish, C. W. "Leaf-Cutting Ants *Atta cephalotes* Select Nitrogen-Rich Foliage." *American Midland Naturalist* 115, no. 2 (1986): 268–276.

Bernhardt, P. "Convergent Evolution and Adaptive Radiation of Beetle-Pollinated Angiosperms." *Plant Systematics and Evolution* 222 (2000): 293–320.

Billings, R. F., S. R. Clarke, V. Espino Mendonza, P. Cordón Cabrera, B. Meléndez Figueroa, J. Ramón Campos, and G. Baeza. "Bark Beetle Outbreaks and Fire: A Devastating Combination for Central America's Pine Forests." *Unasylva* 217, no. 55 (2004): 15–21.

Biodiversity and Environmental Resource Data System of Belize (BERDS). "Welcome to the Biodiversity & Environmental Resource Data System of Beliz." http://www.biodiversity.bz. Accessed May 1, 2008, and May 22, 2008.

Bird, N. M. *Sustaining the Yield: Improved Timber Harvesting Practices in Belize 1992–1998.* Chatham, UK: Natural Resources Institute, 1998.

BirdLife International. "*Amazona oratrix.*" In *2006 IUCN Red List of Threatened Species.* www.iucnredlist.org. Accessed June 12, 2007.

Bloom, P. R., M. Pohl, and J. Stein. "Analysis of Sedimentation and Agriculture along the Rio Hondo." In Pohl, *Prehistoric Lowland Maya Environment,* 21–33.

Blundell, A. G., and B. D. Rodan. "Mahogany and CITES: Moving beyond the Veneer of Legality." *Oryx* 37, no. 1 (2003): 85–90.

Borchert, R. "Phenology and Control of Flowering in Tropical Trees." *Biotropica* 15, no. 2 (1983): 81–89.

——. "Phenology and Flowering Periodicity of Neotropical Dry Forest Species: Evidence from Herbarium Collections." *Journal of Tropical Ecology* 12 (1996): 65–80.

——. "Soil and Stem Water Storage Determine Phenology and Distribution of Tropical Dry Forest Trees." *Ecology* 75, no. 5 (1994): 1437–1449.

Boucher, D. H. "Growing Back after Hurricanes: Catastrophes May Be Critical to Rain Forest Dynamics." *Bioscience* 40 (1990): 163–166.

Brewer, S. W., and M. Rejmánek. "Small Rodents as Significant Dispersers of Tree Seeds in a Neotropical Forest." *Journal of Vegetation Science* 10 (1999): 165–174.

——, M. Rejmánek, M. A. Webb, and P. V. A. Fine. "Relationships of Phytogeography and Diversity of Tropical Tree Species with Limestone Topography in Southern Belize." *Journal of Biogeography* 30 (2003): 1669-1688.

——, and M. A. Webb. "A Seasonal Evergreen Forest in Belize: Unusually High Tree Species Richness for Northern Central America." *Botanical Journal of the Linnean Society* 138 (2002): 275-296.

Bridgewater, S. G. M., D. J. Harris, C. Whitefoord, A. K. Monro, M. G. Penn, D. A. Sutton, B. Sayer, et al. "A Preliminary Checklist of the Vascular Plants of the Chiquibul Forest, Belize." *Edinburgh Journal of Botany* 63, nos. 2 and 3 (2006): 269-321.

——, A. Ibáñez, J. A. Ratter, and P. Furley. "Vegetation Classification and Floristics of the Savannas and Associated Wetlands of the Rio Bravo Conservation and Management Area, Belize." *Edinburgh Journal of Botany* 59, no. 3 (2002): 421-442.

——, P. Pickles, N. C. Garwood, M. G. Penn, R. M. Bateman, H. Porter Morgan, N. Wicks, and N. Bol. "*Chamaedorea* (Xaté) in the Greater Maya Mountains and the Chiquibul Forest Reserve, Belize: An Economic Assessment of a Non-Timber Forest Product." *Economic Botany* 60, no. 3 (2006): 265-283.

——, J. A. Ratter, and J. F. Ribeiro. "Biogeographic Patterns, ß-Diversity, and Dominance in the Cerrado Biome." *Biodiversity and Conservation* 13 (2004): 2295-2318.

Briggs, V. S. "Mating Patterns of Red-Eyed Treefrogs, *Agalychnis callidryas* and *A. moreletii*." *Ethnology* 114, no. 5 (2008): 489-498.

Brokaw, N. V. L. "Gap-Phase Regeneration in a Tropical Forest." *Ecology* 66, no. 3 (1985): 682-687.

——. "Treefalls, Regrowth, and Community Structure in Tropical Forests." In *The Ecology of Natural Disturbance and Patch Dynamics*, edited by S. Pickett and P. White, 53-69. New York: Academic Press, 1985.

Bronstein, J. L. "Maintenance of Species-Specificity in a Neotropical Fig: Pollinator Wasp Mutualism." *Oikos* 48 (1987): 39-46.

Brooks, D. M., R. E. Bodmer, and S. Matola, eds. *Tapirs: Status Survey and Conservation Action Plan*. Gland, Switzerland, and Cambridge, UK: IUCN/SSC Tapir Specialist Group, 1997.

Browder, J. O. "The Limits of Extractivism: Tropical Forest Strategies beyond Extractive Reserves." *BioScience* 42, no. 3 (1992): 174-182.

Brown, N. D., and T. C. Whitmore. "Do Dipterocarp Seedlings Really Partition Tropical Rain Forest Gaps?" *Philosophcal Transactions of the Royal Society of London, Series B, Biological Sciences* 335 (1992): 369-378.

Buchmann, S. L. "The Ecology of Oil Flowers and Their Bees." *Annual Review of Ecology and Systematics* 18 (1987): 343-369.

Budowski, G. "Distribution of Tropical American Rain Forest Species in the Light of Secondary Succession." *Turrialba* 15 (1965): 40-42.

Bullock, S. H. "Wind Pollination of Neotropical Deciduous Trees." *Biotropica* 26, no. 2 (1994): 172-179.

Burslem, D. F. R. P., T. C. Whitmore, and G. C. Brown. "Short-Term Effects of Cyclone Impact and Long-Term Recovery of Tropical Forest on Kolombangara, Solomon Islands." *Journal of Ecology* 88, no. 6 (2000): 1063-1078.

Bush, M. B. "Neotropical Plant Reproductive Strategies and Fossil Pollen Representation." *American Naturalist* 145, no. 4 (1995): 594-609.

Byers, J. A., and M. Bekoff. "Social, Spacing, and Cooperative Behavior of the Collared Peccary, *Tayassu tajucu*." *Journal of Mammalogy* 62, no. 4 (1981): 767-785.

Camargo, J. M. F., and S. R. M. Pedro. "*Meliponini lepeletier*, 1836." In Moure, Urban, and Melo, *Catalogue of Bees*, 272-578.

Cameron, S. A. "Phenology and Biology of Neotropical Orchid Bees (Euglossini)." *Annual Review of Entomology* 49 (2000): 377-404.

Camille, M. A. "Historical Geography of the Belizean Logwood Trade." *Yearbook, Conference of Latin Americanist Geographers* 22 (1996): 77-85.

Campbell, J. A. "Distribution Patterns of Amphibians in Middle America." In *Patterns of Distribution of Amphibians: A Global Perspective*, edited by W. E. Duellman, 111-210. Baltimore: Johns Hopkins University Press, 1999.

Cant, J. G. H. "Feeding Ecology of Spider Monkeys (*Ateles geoffroyi*) at Tikal, Guatemala." *Human Evolution* 5, no. 3 (1990): 269-281.

Caro, T. M., M. J. Kelly, N. Bol, and S. Matola. "Inventorying Mammals at Multiple Sites in the Maya Mountains of Belize." *Journal of Mammology* 82, no. 1 (2001): 43–50.

Cary, E. V., S. Brown, A. J. R. Gillespie, and A. E. Lugo. "Tree Mortality in Mature Lowland Tropical Moist and Tropical Lower Montane Moist Forests of Venezuela." *Biotropica* 26, no. 3 (1994): 255–265.

Castillo Mont, J. J. "The Palms of Guatemala and Their Ornamental Uses." *Acta Horticulturae* 486 (1999): 33–39.

Catling, P. M. "Evidence of Partitioning of Belizean Ant Nest Substrate by a Characteristic Flora." *Biotropica* 27, no. 4 (1995): 535–537.

———. "Influence of Aerial *Azteca* Nests on the Epiphyte Community of Some Belizean Orange Orchards." *Biotropica* 29, no. 2 (1997): 237–242.

Central Statistics Office. *Abstract of Statistics.* Ministry of Natural Development, Government of Belize, 2005.

Chapela, I. H., S. A. Rehner, T. R. Schultz, and U. G. Mueller. "Evolutionary History of the Symbiosis between Fungus-Growing Ants and Their Fungi." *Science* 266 (1994): 1691–1694.

Chapman, C. A., L. M. Fedigan, L. Fedigan, and L. J. Chapman. "Post-Weaning Resource Competition and Sex Ratios in Spider Monkeys." *Oikos* 54, no. 3 (1989): 315–319.

———, L. Kaufman, and L. J. Chapman. "Buttress Formation and Directional Stress Experienced during Critical Phases of Tree Development." *Journal of Tropical Ecology* 14 (1998): 341–349.

Chase, A. F., and D. Z. Chase. "A Mighty Maya Nation: How Caracol Built an Empire by Cultivating Its Middle Class." *Archaeology* 49, no. 5 (1996): 67–72.

Chase, M. W., et al. "Phylogenetics of Seed Plants: An Analysis of Nucleotide-Sequences from the Plastid Gene rbcL." *Annals of the Missouri Botanical Garden* 80 (1993): 528–580.

Chemonics International. *Community Forest Management in the Maya Biosphere Reserve: Close to Financial Self-Sufficiency?* Guatemala BIO-FOR IQC Task Order 815. Washington, DC: USAID, 2003.

Chiappy-Jones, C., V. Rico-Gray, L. Gama, and L. Giddings. "Floristic Affinities between the Yucatán Peninsula and Some Karstic Areas of Cuba." *Journal of Biogeography* 28 (2001): 535–542.

Chittka, L., J. Spaethe, A. Schmidt, and A. Hickelsberger. "Adaptation, Constraint, and Chance in the Evolution of Flower Color and Pollinator Color Vision." In Chittka and Thomson, *Cognitive Ecology,* 106–126.

———, and J. D. Thomson, eds. *Cognitive Ecology of Pollination: Animal Behaviour and Floral Evolution.* Cambridge, UK: Cambridge University Press, 2001.

Clark, C. J., J. R. Poulsen, and V. T. Parker. "The Role of Arboreal Seed Dispersal Groups on the Seed Rain of a Lowland Tropical Forest." *Biotropica* 33 (2001): 606–620.

Colinvaux, P. A. "The History of Forests on the Isthmus from the Ice Age to the Present." In *Central America: A Natural and Cultural History,* edited by A. G. Coates, 123–136. New Haven, CT: Yale University Press, 1997.

Colinvaux, P. A., G. Irion, M. E. Räsänen, M. B. Bush, and J. A. S. Nunes de Mello. "A Paradigm to Be Discarded: Geological and Paleocological Data Falsify the Haffer and Prance Refuge Hypothesis of Amazonian Speciation." *Amazoniana* 16, nos. 3 and 4 (2001): 609–646.

Commission for Environmental Cooperation (CEC). *In Search of a Sustainable Palm Market in North America.* Montreal: CEC, 2002. http://www.cec.org/files/pdf/ECONOMY/PALM-09-02-e.pdf. Accessed July 21, 2005.

Condit, R. "Forest Turnover, Diversity, and CO_2." *TREE* 12, no. 7 (1997): 249–250.

Connell, J. H. "Diversity in Tropical Rain Forests and Coral Reefs." *Science* 199 (1978): 1302–1309.

Conservation International, Mexico and Central American Program. *Ecosystem Profile: Northern Region of the Mesoamerica Biodiversity Hotspot. Belize, Guatemala, Mexico.* Washington, DC: Critical Ecosystem Partnership Fund, 2004.

Convention on Biological Diversity. Article 1. http://www.cbd.int/convention/text/. Accessed December 19, 2010.

Cox, P. A. "Abiotic Pollination: An Evolutionary Escape for Animal-Pollinated Angiosperms. *Philosophical Transactions: Biological Sciences* 333, no. 1267 (1991): 217-224.

——. "Hydrophilous Pollination." *Annual Review of Ecology and Systematics* 19 (1988): 261-280.

——, and M. J. Balick. "The Ethnobotanical Approach to Drug Discovery." *Scientific American* 270, no. 6 (1994): 60-65.

Cracraft, J., and M. J. Donoghue, eds. *Assembling the Tree of Life.* London: Oxford University Press, 2004.

Crane, P. "Phylogentic Analysis of Seed Plants and the Origin of the Angiosperms." *Annals of the Missouri Botanical Garden* 72, no. 4 (1985): 716-793.

——, and R. Scott. "Angiosperm Diversification and Paleolatitudinal Gradients in Cretaceous Floristic Diversity." *Science* 246 (1989): 675-678.

Crook, M. J., A. R. Ennos, and J. R. Banks. "The Function of Buttress Roots: A Comparative Study of the Anchorage Systems of Buttressed (*Aglaia* and *Nephelium ramboutan*) and Non-buttressed (*Mallotus wrayi*) Tropical Trees." *Journal of Experimental Botany* 48, no. 314 (1997): 1702-1716.

Currie, C. R., U. G. Mueller, and D. Malloch. "The Agricultural Pathology of Ant Fungus Gardens." *Proceedings of the National Academy of Sciences of the United States of America* 96, no. 14 (1999): 7998-8002.

Curti, M. "Harpy Eagle Restoration in Belize Begins with Release of Four Birds at Las Cuevas." *Las Cuevas* 11 (2003): 1-3.

Czaplewski, N. J., J. Krejca, and T. E. Miller. "Late Quaternary Bats from Cebada Cave, Chiquibul Cave System, Belize." *Caribbean Journal of Science* 39, no. 1 (2003): 22-33.

Dalling, J. W., and R. Wirth. "Dispersal of *Miconia argentea* Seeds by the Leaf-Cutting Ant *Atta columbica.*" *Journal of Tropical Ecology* 14, no. 5 (1998): 705-710.

Davis, C. C., C. D. Bell, S. Mathews, and M. J. Donoghue. "Laurasian Migration Explains Gondwanan Distributions: Evidence from Malphigiaceae." *Proceedings of the Natural Academy of Sciences* 99 (2002): 6833-6837.

Day, M. "The Conservation of Karst in Belize." *Journal of Cave and Karst Studies* 58, no. 2 (1996): 139-144.

de Andrade, J. C., and J. P. Carauta. "The *Cecropia-Azteca* Association: A Case of Mutualism?" *Biotropica* 14, no. 1 (1982): 15.

De Bodt, S., S. Maere, and Y. van de Peer. "Genome Duplication and the Origin of Angiosperms." *Trends in Ecology and Evolution* 20, no. 11 (2005): 591-597.

de Gouvenain, R. C., and J. A. Silander Jr. "Do Tropical Storm Regimes Influence the Structure of Tropical Lowland Rain Forests?" *Biotropica* 35, no. 2 (2003): 166-180.

de Vivo, M., and A. P. Carmignotto. "Holocene Vegetation Change and the Mammal Faunas of South America and Africa." *Journal of Biogeography* 31 (2004): 943-957.

Del Hoyo, J., A. Elliott, and J. Sargatal, eds. *Handbook of the Birds of the World.* Vol. 1, *Ostrich to Ducks.* Barcelona: Lynx Edicions, 1994.

Delacour, J., and D. Amadon. *Curassows and Related Birds.* Barcelona: Lynx Edicions, 2004.

Dever, J. A. "Examination of Genetic Structure in Wild Populations of Morelet's Crocodile (*Crocodylus moreletii*) in Belize, Central America." PhD diss., Texas Tech University, 2000.

Dillon, A. "*Ocelot Density and Home Range in Belize, Central America: Camera Trapping and Radio Telemetry.*" Master's thesis, Virginia Polytechnic Institute and State University, 2005.

Dixon, C. G. *Geology of Southern British Honduras, with Notes on Adjacent Areas.* Belize City: Government Printer, 1956.

Dobzhansky, T. "Evolution in the Tropics." *American Scientist* 38 (1950): 209-21.

Dressler, R. L. "Pollination by Euglossine Bees." *Evolution* 22 (1967): 202-210.

Dubbin, W. E., M. G. Penn, and M. E. Hodson. "Edaphic Influences on Plant Community Adaptation in the Chiquibul Forest of Belize." *Geoderma* 131, nos. 1 and 2 (2005): 76-88.

Eizirik, E., C. B. Indrusiak, and W. Johnson. "Análisis de la viabilidad de las poblaciones de jaguar: Evaluación de parámetros y estudios de caso en tres poblaciones remanentes del sur de Sudamérica." In *El jaguar en el nuevo millenio,* edited by R. A. Medellín et al., 501–518. Mexico City: Fondo de Cultura Económica, Universidad Nacional Autónoma de México / Wildlife Conservation Society, 2002.

Ellison, A. M., and E. J. Farnsworth. "Seedling Survivorship, Growth, and Response to Disturbance in Belizean Mangal." *American Journal of Botany* 80, no. 10 (1993): 1137–1145.

———, E. J. Farnsworth, and R. R. Twilley. "Facultative Mutualism between Red Mangroves and Root-Fouling Sponges in Belizean Mangal." *Ecology* 77, no. 8 (1996): 2431–2444.

Elphick, J., ed. *The Atlas of Bird Migration*. London: Natural History Museum, 2007.

Endress, B. A., D. L. Gorchov, and M. B. Peterson. "Harvest of the Palm *Chamaedorea radicalis*, Its Effects on Leaf Production, and Implications for Sustainable Management." *Conservation Biology* 18, no. 3 (2004): 822–830.

Engel, S. R., K. M. Hogan, J. F. Taylor, and S. K. Davis. "Molecular Systematics and Paleobiogeography of the South American Sigmodontine Rodents." *Molecular Biology and Evolution* 15, no. 1 (1998): 35–49.

Estrada, A., L. Luecke, S. Van Belle, E. Barrueta, and M. Rosales Meda. "Survey of Black Howler (*Alouatta pigra*) and Spider (*Ateles geoffroyi*) Monkeys in the Mayan Sites of Calakmul and Yaxchilán, Mexico, and Tikal, Guatemala." *Primates* 45, no. 1 (2004): 33–39.

Everham, E. M., and N. V. L. Brokaw. "Forest Damage and Recovery from Catastrophic Wind." *Botanical Review* 62, no. 2 (1996): 113–185.

Fairtrade Labelling Organizations International (FLO). "Facts and Figures." http://www.fairtrade.net/facts_and_figures.0.html Accessed December 29, 2010.

Farjon, A., and B. T. Styles. Pinus (*Pinaceae*). Flora Neotropica Monograph 75. New York: New York Botanical Garden, 1997.

Farnsworth, E. J., and A. M. Ellison. "Global Patterns of Pre-Dispersal Propagule Predation in Mangrove Forests." *Biotropica* 29, no. 3 (1997): 318–330.

Farruggia, F. T. "A Floristic Description of a Neotropical Coastal Savanna in Belize." Master's thesis, Miami University, 2004.

Feller, I. C. "Effects of Nutrient Enrichment on Growth and Herbivory of Dwarf Red Mangrove (*Rhizophora mangle*)." *Ecological Monographs* 65, no. 4 (1995): 477–505.

Finegan, B. "Pattern and Process in Neotropical Secondary Rain Forests: The First 100 Years of Succession." *Trends in Ecology and Evolution* 11, no. 3 (1996): 119–124.

Fischer, A. G. "Latitudinal Variations in Organic Diversity." *Evolution* 14 (1960): 64–81.

Fitzherbert, E., T. Gardner, N. Hill, and L. Williams. "Project Anuran: An Ecological Research Project Concerned with the Assessment and Monitoring of Anuran Populations in the Region around Las Cuevas, Chiquibul Forest Reserve, Belize." Edinburgh University, 2001.

Fleagle, J. G., and R. F. Kay. "Platyrrhines, Catarrhines, and the Fossil Record." In *New World Primates: Ecology, Evolution, and Behavior*, edited by W. G. Kinzey, 3–24. New York: Aldine de Gruyter, 1997.

Flora Mesoamericana. "About Flora Mesoamericana." http://www.mobot.org/mobot/fm/intro.html. Accessed August 1, 2008.

Flores, C. F., and P. M. Ashton. "Harvesting Impact and Economic Value of *Geonoma deversa*, Arecaceae, an Understory Palm Used for Roof Thatching in the Peruvian Amazon." *Economic Botany* 54, no. 3 (2000): 267–277.

Folklore Book Fund Committee. *Characters and Caricatures in Belizean Folklore*. Belize City: Folklore Book Fund Committee, 1998.

Forest Stewardship Council. "FSC Certificate Database." http://info.fsc.org/. Accessed December 20, 2010.

Forshaw, J. M. *Parrots of the World: An Identification Guide*. Princeton, NJ: Princeton University Press, 2006.

Fortey, R. "The Cambrian Explosion Exploded." *Science* 293 (2001): 438–439.

Foster, M. S., and L. S. Delay. "Dispersal of Mimetic Seeds of Three Species of *Ormosia* (Leguminosae)." *Journal of Tropical Ecology* 14 (1998): 389–411.

Fragoso, J. M. V., and J. M. Huffman. "Seed Dispersal and Seedling Recruitment Patterns by the Last Neotropical Megafaunal Element in

Amazonia, the Tapir." *Journal of Tropical Ecology* 16 (2000): 369–385.

Frankie, G. W., H. G. Baker, and P. A. Opler. "Comparative Phenological Studies in Tropical Wet and Dry Forests in the Lowlands of Costa Rica." *Journal of Ecology* 62 (1974): 881–919.

Friesner, J. *Hurricanes and the Forests of Belize*. Belmopan: Belize Forest Department, 1993.

Furley, P. A. "Further Observations on the Nature of the Savanna Vegetation and Soils in Belize." In *Ecology and Management in Belize: An Account of the University of Edinburgh Expedition to Belize, Central America*, edited by D. M. Munro, 9–35. Occasional Publication No. 12. Edinburgh University Geography Department, 1989.

——. "The Significance of the Cohune Palm *Orbignya cohune* (Mart.) Dahlgren, on the Nature and in the Development of the Soil Profile." *Biotropica* 7, no. 1 (1975): 32–36.

——, S. Bridgewater, A. Ibáñez, C. Minty, M. Murray, and J. A. Ratter. "Savannas of the Rio Bravo Conservation Area: Vegetation and Soil-Plant Community Relationships." *Journal of Belizean Affairs*, Special Issue (2001): 64–105.

——, and W. W. Newey. "Variations in Plant Communities with Topography over Tropical Limestone Soils." *Journal of Biogeography* 6 (1979): 1–15.

——, and J. A. Ratter. *Mangrove Distribution, Vulnerability and Management in Central America*. Contract No. R4736. Overseas Development Administration / Oxford Forestry Institute, Forestry Research Programme, Geography Department, Edinburgh University, 1992.

Gauthreaux, S. A., Jr. "Neotropical Migrants and the Gulf of Mexico: The View from Aloft." In Able, *Gatherings of Angels*, 27–49.

Gentry, A. H. "Changes in Plant Community Diversity and Floristic Composition on Environmental and Geographical Gradients." *Annals of the Missouri Botanical Garden* 75 (1988): 1–34.

——. "Neotropical Floristic Diversity: Phytogeographical Connections between Central and South America; Pleistocene Climatic Fluctuations or an Ancient Andean Origin?" *Annals of the Missouri Botanical Garden* 69 (1982): 557–593.

Gibernau, M., D. Barabé, P. Cerdan, and A. Dejean. "Beetle Pollination of *Philodendron solimoesense* (Araceae) in French Guiana." *International Journal of Plant Sciences* 160, no. 6 (1999): 1135–1143.

Gibernau, M., M. Hossaert-MacKey, M. C. Anstett, and F. Kjellberg. "Consequences of Protecting Flowers in a Fig: A One-Way Trip for Pollinators?" *Journal of Biogeography* 23, no. 4 (1996): 425–433.

Gilbert, B. "The 'Little Armored Thing' Doesn't Get By on Looks Alone." *Smithsonian*, October 1995, 142–151.

Godoy, R. A., and K. S. Bawa. "The Economic Value and Sustainable Harvest of Plants and Animals from the Tropical Forest: Assumptions, Hypotheses, and Methods." *Economic Botany* 47, no. 3 (1993): 215–219.

——, R. Lubowski, and A. Markandya. "A Method for the Economic Valuation of Non-Timber Tropical Forest Products." *Economic Botany* 47, no. 3 (1993): 220–233.

Goodban, J. W. D. *The Cohune Palm in British Honduras: Its Occurrence in British Honduras, and Efforts to Exploit Its Nuts*. Belize City: Belize Forest Department, 1955.

Gottsberger, G. "Pollination and Evolution in Neotropical Annonaceae." *Plant Species Biology* 14 (1999): 143–152.

Gould, S. J. *Wonderful Life: The Burgess Shale and the Nature of History*. London: Hutchinson Radius, 1989.

Grace, J., J. Lloyd, J. McIntyre, A. C. Miranda, P. Meir, H. S. Miranda, C. Nobre, et al. "Carbon Dioxide Uptake by an Undisturbed Tropical Rain Forest in Southwest Amazonia, 1992 to 1993." *Science* 270 (1995): 778–780.

Gradstein, F. M., J. G. Ogg, A. G. Smith, eds. *A Geologic Time Scale*. Cambridge, UK: Cambridge University Press, 2004.

Graham, A., and D. L. Dilcher. "Studies in Neotropical Palaeobotany: XII. A Palynoflora from the Pliocene Rio Banano Formation of Costa Rica and the Neogene Vegetation of Mesoamerica." *American Journal of Botany* 85, no. 10 (1998): 1426–1438.

Greenaway, F. *The Bats of Las Cuevas Cave*. London: Natural History Museum, 2003.

Griebel, R., P. E. Gibbs, and A. L. Queiroz. "Flowering Phenology and Pollination Biology of *Ceiba pentandra* (Bombacaceae) in Central Amazonia." *Journal of Tropical Ecology* 15, no. 3 (1999): 247-263.

Gryj, I., C. Martínez del Rio, and I. Baker. "Avian Pollination and Nectar Use in *Combretum fruticosum* (Loefl.)." *Biotropica* 22, no. 3 (1990): 266-271.

Haack, R. A., C. M. Eckelmann, and E. Green. "Southern Pine Beetle Outbreak in Belize." *Newsletter of the Michigan Entomological Society* 45, nos. 3 and 4 (2000): 13-14.

Haffer, J. "Speciation in Amazonian Forest Birds." *Science* 165 (1969): 131-137.

Hall, P., and K. Bawa. "Methods to Assess the Impact of Extraction of Non-Timber Tropical Forest Products on Plant Populations." *Economic Botany* 47, no. 3 (1993): 234-247.

Hardy, L. D. "Pollen Dispersal and the Floral Diversity of Monocotyledons." In *Monocots: Systematics and Evolution*, edited by K. L. Wilson and F. Morrison, 243-257. Melbourne: CSIRO Publishing, 2000.

Harms, K. E., S. J. Wright, O. Calderón, A. Hernández, and E. A. Herre. "Pervasive Density-Dependent Recruitment Enhances Seedling Diversity in a Tropical Forest." *Nature* 404 (2000): 493-495.

Hawksworth, D. L. "The Magnitude of Fungal Diversity: The 1.5 Million Species Estimate Revisited." *Mycological Research* 105, no. 12 (2001): 1422-1432.

Healey, P. F. "An Ancient Maya Dam in the Cayo District, Belize." *Journal of Field Archaeology* 10, no. 2 (1983): 147-154.

——, J. D. H. Lambert, J. T. Arnason, and R. J. Hebda. "Caracol, Belize: Evidence of Ancient Maya Terraces." *Journal of Field Archaeology* 10, no. 4 (1983): 397-410.

Heinzman, R. M., and C. S. Reining. "Commercial Non-Timber Forest Products in Belize." Unpublished report, 1990.

Henderson, A., G. Galeano, and R. Bernal. *Field Guide to the Palms of the Americas*. Princeton, NJ: Princeton University Press, 1995.

Henderson, R. W. "Aspects of the Ecology of the Juvenile Common Iguana (*Iguana iguana*)." *Herpetologica* 30, no. 4 (1974): 327-322.

Henwood, K. "A Structural Model of Forces in Buttressed Tropical Rain Forest Trees." *Biotropica* 5 (1973): 83-89.

Herre, E. A. "An Overview of Studies on a Community of Panamanian Figs." *Journal of Biogeography* 23 (1996): 593-607.

Heyder, H. M. "Sapodilla Tapping in British Honduras." *Empire Forestry* 9 (1930): 107-113.

Hicks, J. "Describing the Plant Diversity of Belizean Savannas: A Floristic Survey of San Pastor Savanna." Master's thesis, University of Edinburgh / Royal Botanic Garden Edinburgh, 2007.

Hill, J., and J. D. Smith. *Bats: A Natural History*. Austin: University of Texas Press, 1992.

Hirth, H. F. "Some Aspects of the Natural History of the Green Iguana on a Tropical Strand." *Ecology* 44, no. 3 (1963): 613-615.

Hodel, D. R. Chamaedorea *Palms: The Species and Their Cultivation*. Lawrence, KS: Allen Press, 1992.

Hodell, D. A., M. Brenner, J. H. Curtis, and T. Guilderson. "Solar Forcing of Drought Frequency in the Maya Lowlands." *Science* 292 (2001): 1367-1370.

Hogarth, P. J. *The Biology of Mangroves*. London: Oxford University Press, 1999.

Horwich, R. H., and J. Lyon. *A Belizean Rain Forest: The Community Baboon Sanctuary*. Gay Mills, WI: Orang-utan Press, 1990.

Howe, H. F., and J. Smallwood. "Ecology of Seed Dispersal." *Annual Review of Ecology and Systematics* 13 (1982): 201-228.

——, and L. C. Westley. *Ecological Relationships of Plants and Animals*. London: Oxford University Press, 1988.

Howell, D. J. "The Bats of Caracol." Unpublished report for the Belize Tropical Forest and Reserve Planning Project, Wildlife Conservation Society, 1990.

Hubbell, S. P. "Seed Predation and the Coexistence of Tree Species in Tropical Forest." *Oikos* 35 (1980): 214-229.

——, S. P., and R. B. Foster. "Biology, Chance, and History and the Structure of Tropical Rain Forest Tree Communities." In *Community Ecology*, edited by J. Diamond and T. J. Case, 314-329. New York: Harper & Row, 1986.

Huber, O. "Neotropical Savannas: Their Flora and Vegetation." *Trends in Ecology and Evolution* 3, no. 3 (1987): 67-71.

Hummel, C. "Sapodilla Trees and Chicle," *The Clarion* (Belize City), September 6, 1923.

Ibarra-Manríquez, G., M. Ricker, G. Angeles, S. Sinaca Colín, and M. A. Sinaca Colín. "Useful Plants of the Los Tuxtlas Rain Forest (Veracruz, Mexico): Considerations of Their Market Potential." *Economic Botany* 51, no. 4 (1997): 362-376.

Iremonger, S., and N. V. L. Brokaw. "Vegetation Classification for Belize." In *Towards a National Protected Area Systems Plan for Belize*, edited by R. Wilson. Belize City: Programme for Belize, 1995.

IUCN. *2001 IUCN Red List Categories and Criteria, Version 3.1.* http://www.iucnredlist.org/technical-documents/categories-and-criteria. Accessed December 30, 2010.

——. *2010 IUCN Red List of Threatened Species.* "Summary Statistics." http://www.iucnredlist.org/about/summary-statistics#How_many_threatened. Accessed December 30, 2010.

——. *2010 IUCN Red List of Threatened Species: Amphibians.* "Analysis of Data: Summary of Key Findings." http://www.iucnredlist.org/initiatives/amphibians/analysis. Accessed December 30, 2010.

Janzen, D. H. "Coevolution of Mutualism between Ants and Acacias in Central America." *Evolution* 20 (1966): 249-275.

——. "Dissolution of Mutualism between *Cecropia* and Its *Azteca* Ants." *Biotropica* 5, no. 1 (1973): 15-28.

——. "Herbivores and the Number of Tree Species in Tropical Forests." *American Naturalist* 104 (1970): 501-528.

——. "How To Be a Fig." *Annual Review of Ecology and Systematics* 10 (1973): 13-51.

——. "Synchronization of Sexual Reproduction of Trees within the Dry Season in Central America." *Evolution* 21 (1966): 620-637.

——, and P. S. Martin. "Neotropical Anachronisms: The Fruits the Gomphotheres Ate." *Science* 215 (1982): 19-27.

Jebb, M., and B. Sayers. *A Survey of the Epiphytes in the Chiquibul Forest Reserve, a Belizean Rain-Forest.* Dublin: National Botanic Gardens, 1994.

Jimenez Perez, J. L., L. Trejo Hernandez, C. E. Gonzalez Romo, E. Jurado Ybarra, H. Villalon Mendoza, and F. Perez Guerrero. *Manejo de palmilla* (Chamaedorea radicalis) *en la Reserva de la Biosfera "El Cielo."* Ciudad Victoria, Tamaulipas, Mexico: Instituto de Ecología y Alimentos, 1999.

Johnson, M. S., and D. R. Chaffey. *An Inventory of the Chiquibul Forest Reserve, Belize.* Land Resource Study 14. London: Land Resources Division, Overseas Development Administration and Foreign Commonwealth Office, 1973.

Johnson, S. D., and T. J. Edwards. "The Structure and Function of Orchid Pollinaria." *Plant Systematics and Evolution* 222 (2000): 243-269.

Jones, H. L. *Birds of Belize.* Austin: University of Texas Press, 2003.

Jordano, P. "Fruits and Frugivory." In *Seeds: The Ecology of Regeneration in Plant Communities*, edited by M. Fenner, 105-156. Wallingford, UK: CAB International, 1992.

Jousselin, E., J. Y. Raspus, and F. Kjellberg. "Convergence and Coevolution in a Mutualism: Evidence from a Molecular Phylogeny of *Ficus.*" *Evolution* 57, no. 6 (2003): 1255-1269.

Kaiser, K. "Evaluation of a Long-Term Amphibian Monitoring Protocol in Central America." *Journal of Herpetology* 42, no. 1 (2008): 104-110.

Kalko, E. K., E. A. Herre, and C. O. Handley Jr. "Relation of Fig Fruit Characteristics to Fruit-Eating Bats in the New and Old World Tropics." *Journal of Biogeography* 23 (1996): 565-576.

Kearns, C. A., and D. W. Inouye. "Pollinators, Flowering Plants, and Conservation Biology." *Bioscience* 47, no. 5 (1997): 297-307.

Keeler, H. K. "Infidelity by Acacia Ants." *Biotropica* 13, no. 1 (1981): 79-80.

Keller, M., D. A. Clark, D. B. Clark, A. M. Weitz, and E. Velkamp. "If a Tree Falls in the Forest." *Science* 273 (1996): 201.

Kellman, M. "Soil Enrichment by Neotropical Savanna Trees." *Journal of Ecology* 67, no. 2 (1976): 565-577.

——. "Synergistic Relationships between Fire and Low Soil Fertility in Neotropical Savannas." *Biotropica* 16, no. 2 (1984): 158-160.

——, and K. Miyanishi. "Forest Seedling Establishment in Neotropical Savannas: Observations and Experiments in the Mountain Pine

Ridge Savanna, Belize." *Journal of Biogeography* 9 (1982): 193–206.

Kelly, M. J. "Jaguar Monitoring in the Chiquibul Forest, Belize." *Caribbean Geography* 13, no. 1 (2003): 19–32.

——, and T. Caro. "Low Density of Small Mammals at Las Cuevas, Belize." *Mammalian Biology* 68 (2003): 372–386.

Kendrick, B. *The Fifth Kingdom*. Sidney, Canada: Mycologue Publications / Focus Publishing, 2000.

Kenrick, P., and P. Davis. *Fossil Plants*. London: Natural History Museum, 2004.

Kiltie, R. A. "Bite Force as a Basis for Niche Differentiation between Rain Forest Peccaries (*Tayassu tajucu* and *T. pecari*)." *Biotropica* 14, no. 3 (1982): 188–195.

King, I. B., I. C. Baillie, T. M. B. Abell, J. R. Dunsmore, D. A. Gray, J. H. Pratt, H. R. Versey, A. C. S. Wright, and S. A. Zisman. *Land Resource Assessment of Northern Belize*. 2 vols. Natural Resource Institute Bulletin 43. London: Natural Resource Institute, 1992.

——, I. C. Baillie, P. G. Bisset, R. J. Grimble, M. S. Johnson, and G. L. Silva. *Land Resource Survey of Toledo District, Belize*. Tolworth, UK: Land Resources Development Centre, 1986.

——, I. C. Baillie, J. R. Dunsmore, R. J. Grimble, M. S. Johnson, and A. C. S. Wright. *Land Resource Survey of Stann Creek District, Belize*. Overseas Development Natural Resources Institute Bulletin 19. Chatham, UK, 1989.

Kirchheimer, W. F., and E. E. Storrs. "Attempts to Establish the Armadillo (*Dasypus novemcintus* Linn.) as a Model for the Study of Leprosy: I. Report of Lepromatoid Leprosy in an Experimentally Infected Armadillo." *International Journal of Leprosy and other Mycobacterial Diseases* 39, no. 3 (1971): 693–702.

Kropp, B. *Historical Biogeography of Fungi from Belize and the Gulf Coast of the US*. Biology Department, Utah State University, 2004.

Lambert, J. D. H., and T. Arnason. "Ramón and Maya Ruins: An Ecological, Not an Economic, Relation." *Science* 216 (1982): 298–299.

——, A. H. Siemens, and J. T. Arnason. "Ancient Maya Drained Field Agriculture: Its Possible Application Today in the New River

Floodplain, Belize, C. A." *Agriculture, Ecosystems, and Environment* 11 (1984): 67–84.

Laughlin, D. C. "Flora of the Pine Savanna at Monkey Bay Wildlife Sanctuary, Belize." *Caribbean Journal of Science* 38, nos. 1 and 2 (2002): 151–155.

Lee, J. C. *The Amphibians and Reptiles of the Yucatán Peninsula*. Ithaca, NY: Cornell University Press, 1996.

Levasseur, V., and A. Olivier. "The Farming System and Traditional Agroforestry Systems in the Maya Community of San Jose, Belize." *Agroforestry Systems* 49 (2000): 275–288.

Levy, D. J. "Tropical Wet Forest Treefall Gaps and Distribution of Understory Birds and Plants." *Ecology* 69 (1988): 1076–1089.

Lewis, A. R. "Buttress Arrangement in *Pterocarpus officinalis* (Fabaceae): Affects of Crown Asymmetry and Wind." *Biotropica* 20, no. 4 (1988): 280–285.

Lewis, T., G. V. Pollard, and G. C. Dibley. "Rhythmic Foraging of the Leaf-Cutting *Atta cephalotes* (L.)(Formicidae: Attini)." *Journal of Animal Ecology* 43, no. 1 (1974): 129–141.

Linhart, Y. B., and J. A. Mendenhall. "Pollen Dispersal by Hawkmoths in a *Lindenia rivalis* Berth. Population in Belize." *Biotropica* 9, no. 2 (1977): 143.

Link, A., and A. Di Fiore. "Seed Dispersal by Spider Monkeys and Its Importance in the Maintenance of Neotropical Rain-Forest Diversity." *Journal of Tropical Ecology* 22 (2006): 235–246.

Listabarth, C. "Insect-Induced Wind Pollination of the Palm *Chamaedorea pinnatifrons* and Pollination in the Related *Wendlandiella* sp." *Biodiversity and Conservation* 1 (1992): 39–50.

Losos, E., and E. G. Leigh Jr. *Tropical Forest Diversity and Dynamism: Findings from a Large-Scale Plot Network*. Chicago: University of Chicago Press, 2008.

Lundell, C. L. "Chicle Exploration in the Sapodilla Forest of the Yucatan Peninsula." *Contributions to American Archaeology* 436 (1933): 15–21.

——. "The 1936 Michigan-Carnegie Botanical Expedition to British Honduras." In *Botany of the Maya Area: Miscellaneous Papers XIV-XXI*, 1–57. Monograph Series 522. Washington, DC: Carnegie Institution of Washington, 1940.

——. "Plants Probably Utilized by the Old Empire Maya of Petén and Adjacent Lowlands." *Papers of the Michigan Academy of Science, Arts, and Letters* 24 (1938): 37–56.

——. *The Vegetation of Peten.* Publication 478. Washington, DC: Carnegie Institution, 1937.

McDade, L. A., and J. A. Weeks. "Nectar in Hummingbird-Pollinated Neotropical Plants: Patterns of Production and Variability in Twelve Species." *Biotropica* 36, no. 2 (2004): 196–215.

McKee, K. L. "Mangrove Species Distribution and Propagule Predation in Belize: An Exception to the Dominance-Predation Hypothesis." *Biotropica* 27, no. 3 (1995): 334–345.

——. "Root Proliferation in Decaying Roots and Old Root Channels: A Nutrient Conservation Mechanism in Oligotrophic Mangrove Forests?" *Journal of Ecology* 89, no. 5 (2000): 876–887.

McKeon, C. S., and I. C. Feller. "The Supratidal Fauna of Twin Cays, Belize." Atoll Research Bulletin 526. Washington, DC: National Museum of Natural History, Smithsonian Institution, 2004.

McKinley, A., and K. Francl. 2006. "*Jabiru mycteria.*" University of Michigan Museum of Zoology, Animal Diversity Web. http://animaldiversity.ummz.umich.edu/site/accounts/information/Jabiru_mycteria.html. Accessed June 13, 2007.

McLoughlin, S. "The Breakup History of Gondwana and Its Impact on Pre-Cenozoic Floristic Provincialism." *Australian Journal of Botany* 49 (2001): 271–300.

Magallon, S., P. R. Crane, and P. S. Herendeen. "Phylogenetic Pattern, Diversity, and Diversification in the Eudicots." *Annals of the Missouri Botanical Garden* 86, no. 2 (1999): 297–372.

Mallory, E. P. *Impacts of Silvicultural Trials on Birds and Tree Regeneration in the Chiquibul Forest Reserve, Belize.* Report to the Forest Planning and Management Project. Manomet, MA: Manomet Observatory for Conservation Sciences, 1996.

Mani, M. S., and J. M. Saravanan. *Pollination Ecology and Evolution in Compositae (Asteraceae).* Enfield, NH: Science Publishers, Inc., 1999.

Marshall, L. G. "Land Mammals and the Great American Interchange." *American Scientist* 76, no. 4 (1988): 380–388.

——. "The Terror Birds of South America." *Scientific American* 270, no. 2 (1994): 64–69.

——, S. S. Webb, J. J. Sepkoski, and D. M. Raup. "Mammalian Evolution and the Great American Interchange." *Science* 215 (1982): 1351–1357.

Martin, P. S. "The Discovery of America." *Science* 179 (1973): 969–974.

Matola, S., ed. *Expedition to Doyle's Delight, Southern Maya Mountains, Belize.* Occasional Series 5. Belmopan: Forest Planning and Management Project, Ministry of Natural Resources, 1995.

Mattheny, R. T. "Maya Lowland Hydraulic Systems." *Science* 193 (1976): 639–646.

Mayer, J. J., and R. M. Wetzel. "*Tayassu pecari.*" *Mammalian Species* 293 (1985): 1–7.

Medellin, R. A., and O. Gaona. "Dispersal by Bats and Birds in Forest and Disturbed Habitats of Chiapas, Mexico." *Biotropica* 31, no. 3 (1999): 478–485.

Meerman, J. *Compilation of Information on Biodiversity in Belize.* Final Report to Inbio and the Belize Forest Department, Ministry of Natural Resources. Belmopan, 2006.

——. *Ecological Assessment of Columbia River Forest Reserve Post Hurricane Iris.* Consultancy Report. Belmopan, 2004.

——. *National List of Critical Species.* Report to the Protected Areas Systems Plan Office. Belmopan, 2005.

——. *National Protected Area Systems Analysis. Case study: The Jaguar.* Belmopan, 2005.

——. *Protected Areas System Assessment and Analysis: Critical Species.* Report to the Protected Areas Systems Plan Office. Belmopan, 2005.

——, A. Howe, and B. Arevalo. *Machaca Hill Lodge Ecosystem Assessment.* Belmopan, 2006.

——, and S. Matola, eds. *Doyle's Delight: The 2004 Expedition.* Belmopan, 2007.

——, and W. Sabido. "Belize Broad Ecosystems Map: 2004 Update." Updated version of Meerman and Sabido, *Central American Ecosystems Map. Belize.* http://biological-diversity.info/images/Articles/bzeecosys04.jpg. Accessed December 29, 2010.

——, and W. Sabido. *Central American Ecosystems Map: Belize. 2 vols.* Programme for Belize, Belize City, 2001.

Mendelsohn, R., and M. J. Balick. "The Value of Undiscovered Pharmaceuticals in Tropical Forests." *Economic Botany* 49, no. 2 (1995): 223–228.

Mendoza-Cuenca, L., and R. Macías-Ordóñez. "Foraging Polymorphism in *Heliconius charitonia* (Lepidoptera: Nymphalidae): Morphological Constraints and Behavioral Compensation." *Journal of Tropical Ecology* 21 (2005): 407–415.

Midtgaard, F., and K. H. Thunes. *Pine Bark Beetles in the Mountain Pine Ridge Forest Reserve, Belize: Description of the Species and Advice on Monitoring and Combating the Beetle Infestations.* Oslo: Norwegian Forestry Group, 2003.

Miller, B. W. "Community Ecology of the Non-Phyllostomid Bats of North-Western Belize, with a Landscape Level Assessment of the Bats of Belize." PhD diss.,University of Kent at Canterbury, Durrell Institute of Conservation and Ecology, 2003.

——. "A Risk Assessment of the Bats of Belize, Phase I, in the Context of the Selva Maya Region." Neotropical Bat Project, Gallon Jug, Belize, 2009.

——, and C. M. Miller. *Biodiversity Reconnaissance in the Chiquibul National Park, Las Cuevas and Puente Natural, 13–19 July 1992.* Belize Tropical Forest and Reserve Planning Project, Wildlife Conservation International, Gallon Jug, Belize, 1992.

Miller, T. E. "Geologic and Hydrologic Controls on Karst and Cave Development in Belize." *Journal of Cave and Karst Studies* 58, no. 2 (1996): 100–120.

——. "Inside Chiquibul: Exploring Central America's Longest Cave." *National Geographic* 197, no. 4 (2000): 55–71.

Milne, R. F. "A Biogeographical and Ecological Study of *Acoelorraphe wrightii.*" Undergraduate thesis, Geography Department, Edinburgh University, 1997.

Minter, D. W., M. Rodríguez Hernández, and J. Mena Portales. *Fungi of the Caribbean: An Annotated Checklist.* London: PDMS Publishing, 2001.

Minty, C. D. *Preliminary Report on the Scientific and Biodiversity Value of the Macal and Raspaculo Catchment: A Wildlife Impact Assessment for the Proposed Macal River Upper Storage Facility.* London: Natural History Museum, 2001.

Mistry, J. *World Savannas: Ecology and Human Use.* Harlow, UK: Prentice Hall, 2000.

Moll, D. "Food and Feeding Behavior of the Turtle, *Dermatemys mawei,* in Belize." *Journal of Herpetology* 23, no. 4 (1989): 445–447.

Moore, F. R. "Neotropical Migrants and the Gulf of Mexico: The Cheniers of Louisiana and Stopover Ecology." In Able, *Gatherings of Angels,* 27–69.

Moritz, C., J. L. Patton, C. J. Schneider, and T. B. Smith. "Diversification of Rainforest Faunas: An Integrated Molecular Approach." *Annual Review of Ecology, Evolution, and Systematics* 31 (2000): 533–63.

Morley, R. J. "Interplate Dispersal Routes for Megathermal Angiosperms." *Perspectives in Plant Ecology, Evolution, and Systematics* 6, nos. 1 and 2 (2003): 5–20.

Morris, S. C. *The Crucible of Creation: The Burgess Shale and the Rise of Animals.* London: Oxford University Press, 1998.

Moure, J. S., D. Urban, and G. A. R. Melo, eds. *Catalogue of Bees (Hymenoptera, Apoidea) in the Neotropical Region.* Curitiba: Sociedade Brasileira de Entomologia, 2007.

Mueller-Dumbois, D., and H. Ellenberg. *Aims and Methods of Vegetation Ecology.* New York: John Wiley, 1974.

Murray, J. L., and G. L. Gardner. "*Leopardus pardalis.*" *Mammalian Species* 548 (1997): 1–10.

Muskin, A., and A. J. Fischgrund. "Seed Dispersal of *Stemmadenia* (Apocynaceae) and Sexually Dimorphic Feeding Strategies by *Ateles* in Tikal, Guatemala." *Biotropica* 13, no. 2 (1981): 78–80.

Myers, R. J., J. O'Brien, and S. Morrison. *Fire Management Overview of the Caribbean Pine (Pinus caribaea), Savannas of the Mosquitia, Honduras.* Global Fire Initiative Technical Report. Arlington, VA: The Nature Conservancy, 2006.

Nature Conservancy. *The Ecological Role and Management of Fire in Caribbean and Central American Pineland Ecosystems: Highlights of a Workshop*

Held at the Rio Bravo Conservation and Management Area, Belize, 07-09 May 2002. Arlington, VA: The Nature Conservancy, 2002.

Nelson, E. C. *Sea Beans and Nickar Nuts: A Handbook of Exotic Seeds and Fruits Stranded on Beaches in North-Western Europe*. London: Botanical Society of the British Isles, 2000.

Newstrom, L. E., G. W. Frankie, H. G. Baker, and R. Colwell. "Diversity of Long-Term Flowering Patterns." In *La Selva: Ecology and Natural History of a Neotropical Rain Forest*, edited by L. A. McDade, K. S. Bawa, H. A. Hespenheide, and G. S. Hartshorn, 142-160. Chicago: University of Chicago Press, 1994.

Noss, A. J., M. J. Kelly, H. B. Camblos, and D. I. Rumiz. "Pumas y jaguares simpátricos: Datos de trampas-cámara en Bolivia y Belize." *Memorias*, 2006, 229-237.

O'Brien, T. G., and M. F. Kinnaird. "The Impact of Harvest on Leaf Development of the Asian Palm *Livistona rotundifolia*." *Conservation Biology* 10 (1995): 53-58.

O'Hara, J. "Potential Effects of Leaf Harvesting on *Sabal morrisiana* in the Rio Bravo Conservation and Management Area." Unpublished report, 1994.

Oliveira, P. E., P. E. Gibbs, and A. A. Barbosa. "Moth Pollination of Woody Species in the Cerrados of Central Brazil: A Case of So Much Owed to So Few?" *Plant Systematics and Evolution* 245 (2004): 41-54.

Ordano, M., and J. F. Ornelas. "The Cost of Nectar Replenishment in Two Epiphytic Bromeliads." *Journal of Tropical Ecology* 21 (2005): 541-547.

Ower, L. H. "The Geology of British Honduras." *Journal of Geology* 36 (1928): 494-509.

Oyama, K. "Conservation and Exploitation of Tropical Resources: The Case of *Chamaedorea* Palms." *Evolutionary Trends in Plants* 6, no. 1 (1992): 17-20.

Paine, R. T. "A Note on Trophic Complexity and Community Stability." *American Naturalist* 103 (1969): 91-93.

Pavelka, M. S. M., and A. M. Behie. "The Effect of Hurricane Iris on the Food Supply of Black Howlers (*Alouatta pigra*) in Southern Belize." *Biotropica* 37, no. 1 (2005): 102-108.

———, O. T. Brusselers, D. Nowak, and A. M. Behie. "Population Reduction and Social Disorganisation in *Alouatta pigra* Following a Hurricane." *International Journal of Primatology* 24, no. 5 (2003): 1037-1055.

———, and K. H. Knopff. "Diet and Activity in Black Howler Monkeys (*Alouatta pigra*) in Southern Belize: Does Degree of Frugivory Influence Activity Level?" *Primates* 45 (2004): 105-111.

Penn, M. G., D. Sutton, and A. Monro. "Vegetation of the Greater Maya Mountains, Belize." *Systematics and Biodiversity* 2 (2004): 21-44.

Pennington, R. T., and C. W. Dick. "The Role of Immigrants in the Assembly of the South American Rainforest Tree Flora." *Philosophical Transactions of the Royal Society of London, Series B, Biological Sciences* 359 (2004): 1611-1622.

———, D. E. Prado, and C. A. Pendry. "Neotropical Seasonally Dry Forests and Quaternary Vegetation Change." *Journal of Biogeography* 27 (2000): 261-273.

Pennington, T. D. "Mahogany: Carving a Future." *Biologist* 49, no. 5 (2002): 204-208.

———. 1981. *Meliaceae*. Flora Neotropica Monograph 28. New York: New York Botanical Garden, 1981. Includes accounts of Swieteniodae by B. T. Styles and Chemotaxonomy by A. D. H. Taylor.

———. *Sapotaceae*. Flora Neotropica Monograph 52. New York: New York Botanical Garden, 1990.

Peters, C. M., A. H. Gentry, and R. O. Mendelsohn. "Valuation of an Amazonian Rainforest." *Nature* 339 (1989): 655-656.

Philbrick, C. T., and A. R. Novelo. "New World Podostemaceae: Ecological and Evolutionary Enigmas." *Brittonia* 47, no. 2 (1994): 210-222.

Philips, O. L., and A. H. Gentry. "Increasing Turnover through Time in Tropical Forests." *Science* 263 (1994): 954-958.

Pitman, N. C. A., J. W. Terborgh, M. R. Silman, P. Núñez, D. A. Neill, C. E. Cerón, W. A. Palacios, and M. Aulestia. "Dominance and Distribution of Tree Species in Upper Amazonian Terra Firme Forests." *Ecology* 82 (2001): 2101-2117.

Platt, S. G. "The Ecology and Status of Morelet's Crocodile in Belize." PhD diss., Clemson University, 1996.

——, T. R. Rainwater, and S. W. Brewer. "Aspects of the Burrowing Ecology of Nine-Banded Armadillos in Northern Belize." *Mammalian Biology* 69, no. 4 (2004): 217–224.

Pohl, M. "An Ethnohistorical Perspective on Ancient Maya Wetland Fields and Other Cultivation Systems in the Lowlands." In Pohl, *Prehistoric Lowland Maya Environment*, 35–45.

——, ed. *Prehistoric Lowland Maya Environment and Subsistence Economy.* Papers of the Peabody Museum of Archaeology and Ethnology 77. Cambridge, MA: Harvard University Press, 1985.

——, and C. H. Miksicek. "Cultivation Techniques and Crops." In Pohl, *Prehistoric Lowland Maya Environment*, 9–20.

Poore, D., J. Burgess, J. Palmer, S. Rietbergen, and T. Synott. *No Timber without Trees: Sustainability in the Tropical Forests.* London: Earthscan Publications, 1989.

Porter Morgan, H. "Thrips as Primary Pollinators of Sympatric Species of *Chamaedorea* (Arecaceae) in Belize." PhD diss., City University of New York, 2007.

Pough, F. H., R. M. Andrews, J. E. Cadle, M. L. Crump, A. H. Savitzky, and K. D. Wells. *Herpetology.* Upper Saddle River, NJ: Prentice Hall, 2000.

Queensborough, S. A. "The Floristics and Phytogeography of Central American Tropical Forests: A Study Based in the Deciduous Forests of Belize." Master's thesis, University of Edinburgh / Royal Botanic Garden Edinburgh, 2001.

Rabinowitz, A. R. *Jaguar: One Man's Struggle to Establish the World's First Jaguar Preserve.* Washington, DC: Island Press, 2000.

——. "Jaguar Predation on Domestic Livestock in Belize." *Wildlife Society Bulletin* 14 (1986): 170–174.

——, and B. G. Nottingham Jr. "Ecology and Behaviour of the Jaguar (*Panthera onca*) in Belize, Central America." *Journal of Zoology* 210 (1986): 149–159.

Radachowsky, J. *Endemism in the Maya Forest.* New York: World Conservation Society, 2002.

Raine, N. E., P. Willmer, and G. N. Stone. "Spatial Structuring and Floral Avoidance Behavior Prevent Ant-Pollinator Conflict in a Mexican Ant-Acacia." *Ecology* 83, no. 11 (2002): 3086–3096.

Rainwater, T. R., B. M. Adair, S. G. Platt, T. A. Anderson, G. P. Cobb, and S. T. McMurray. "Mercury in Morelet's Crocodile Eggs from Belize." *Archives of Environmental Contamination and Toxicity* 42 (2002): 319–324.

Ramírez, W. B. "Fig Wasps: Mechanism of Pollen Transfer." *Science* 163, no. 3867 (1969): 580–581.

Raven, P., and D. I. Axelrod. "Angiosperm Biogeography and Past Continental Movements." *Annals of the Missouri Botanical Garden* 61 (1974): 539–673.

Rengifo, C., L. Cornejo, and I. Akirov. "One Size Fits All: Corolla Compression in *Aphelandra runcinata* (Acanthaceae): An Adaptation to Short-Billed Hummingbirds." *Journal of Tropical Ecology* 22 (2006): 613–619.

Renner, S. S., and J. P. Feil. "Pollinators of Tropical Dioecious Angiosperms." *American Journal of Botany* 80, no. 9 (1993): 1100–1107.

——, and H. Won. "Repeated Evolution of Dioecy from Monoecy in Siparunaceae (Lauraceae)." *Systematic Biology* 55, no. 5 (2001): 700–712.

Renshaw, O. "Are Tree Functional Types Based on Leaf, Seed, and Growth Traits a Useful Tool for Management and Conservation Purposes?" Master's thesis, University of Edinburgh, 2008.

Rhode, K. "Latitudinal Gradients in Species Diversity: The Search for the Primary Causes." *Oikos* 65 (1992): 514–527.

Robbins, C. *Mahogany Matters: The U.S. Market for Big-Leafed Mahogany and Its Implications for the Conservation of the Species.* Washington, DC: TRAFFIC North America, 2000.

Rockwood, L. L. "Plant Selection and Foraging Patterns in Two Species of Leaf-Cutting Ants (*Atta*)." *Ecology* 57, no. 1 (1976): 48–61.

Rogers, A. D. F. *Main Report of the New Millennium Expedition: The Year 2000 Joint Services Expedition to the Upper Raspaculo, Maya Mountains, Belize.* Expedition Report. London: Natural History Museum, 2000.

——, D. A. Sutton, and P. J. Stafford, eds. *Report of the Joint Services Scientific Expedition to the Upper Raspaculo River, Belize, Central America.* Expedition Report. London: Natural History Museum, 1994.

——, eds. *Report of the New Millennium Expedition: The Year 2000 Joint Services Scientific Expedition to the Upper Raspaculo, Maya Mountains, and Limestone Karst of the Western Chiquibul Area, Belize.* London: Natural History Museum, 2000.

Roth Novick, R., C. W. Dick, M. R. Lemes, C. Navarro, A. Caccone, and E. Bermingham. "Genetic Structure of Mesoamerican Populations of Big-Leaf Mahogany (*Swietenia macrophylla*) Inferred from Microsatellite Analysis." *Molecular Ecology* 12 (2003): 2885-2893.

Sakai, S. "*Aristolochia* spp. (Aristolochiaceae) Pollinated by Flies Breeding on Decomposing Flowers in Panama." *American Journal of Botany* 89 (2002): 525-534.

——. "Thrips Pollination of Androdioecious *Castilla elastica* (Moraceae) in a Seasonal Tropical Forest." *American Journal of Botany* 88, no. 9 (2001): 1527-1534.

Sapper, K. "Über Gebirgsbau und Boden des nordlichen Mittelamerika." *Petermanns Mitteilungen* 27, no. 127 (1899).

Sayer, E. J., and D. M. Newbery. "The Role of Tree Size in the Leafing Phenology of a Seasonally Dry Tropical Forest in Belize, Central America." *Journal of Tropical Ecology* 19 (2003): 539-548.

Scarborough, V. L., and G. G. Gallopin. "Water Storage Adaption by the Maya at Tikal." *Science* 251 (1991): 658-662.

Scatena, F. N., S. Moya, C. Estrada, and J. D. Chinea. "The First Five Years in the Reorganization of Aboveground Biomass and Nutrient Use Following Hurricane Hugo in the Bisley Experimental Watersheds, Luquillo Experimental Forest, Puerto Rico." *Biotropica* 28, no. 4a (1996): 424-440.

Schafhauser, A., W. Stinnesbeck, B. Holland, T. Adatte, and J. Remane. "Lower Cretaceous Pelagic Limestones in Southern Belize: Proto-Caribbean Deposits on the Southeastern Maya Block." In *The Circum-Gulf of Mexico and the Caribbean: Hydrocarbon Habitats, Basin Formation, and Plate Tectonics*, edited by C. Bartolini, R. T. Buffler, and J. Blickwede, 624-637. AAPG Memoir 79. Tulsa, OK: American Association of Petroleum Geologists, 2003.

Schopf, J. W., ed. *Major Events in the History of Life.* Proceedings from a symposium convened by the IGPP Center for the Study of Evolution and the Origin of Life, University of California, Los Angeles, January 11, 1991. Sudbury, MA: Jones and Bartlett Publishers, 1992.

Schwartz, N. "Some Notes on the Folklore and Political Economy of La Chicleria." *Revista Española de Antropología Americana* 19 (1989): 169-192.

Scott Mills, L., M. E. Soulé, and D. F. Doak. "The Keystone-Species Concept in Ecology and Conservation." *Bioscience* 43, no. 4 (1993): 219-224.

Sedberry, G. R., and J. Carter. "The Fish Community of a Shallow Tropical Lagoon in Belize, Central America." *Estuaries* 16, no. 2 (1993): 198-215.

Seigler, D. S., and J. E. Ebinger. "Taxonomic Revision of the Ant-Acacias (Fabaceae, Mimosoideae, *Acacia*, series Gummiferae) of the New World." *Annals of the Missouri Botanical Garden* 82 (1995): 117-138.

Shanley, P., A. R. Pierce, S. A. Laird, and A. Guillen. *Tapping the Green Market: Certification and Management of Non-Timber Forest Products.* London: Earthscan, 2002.

Sharer, R. J. *The Ancient Maya.* Stanford, CA: Stanford University Press, 1994.

Shiel, D., and D. F. R. P. Burslem. "Disturbing Hypotheses in Tropical Forests." *Trends in Ecology and Evolution* 18, no. 1 (2003): 18-26.

Silver, S. C., L. E. T. Ostro, L. K. Marsh, L. Maffei, A. J. Noss, M. J. Kelly, R. B. Wallace, H. Gómez, and G. Ayala. "The Use of Camera Traps for Estimating Jaguar *Panthera onca* Abundance and Density Using Capture/Recapture Analysis. *Oryx* 38, no. 2 (2004): 148-154.

Simpson, G. G. "History of the Fauna of Latin America." *American Scientist* 38 (1950): 261-389.

——. "Mammals and Land Bridges." *Journal of the Washington Academy of Sciences* 30 (1940): 137-163.

Snook, L. K. "Catastrophic Disturbance, Logging, and the Ecology of Mahogany (*Swietenia macrophylla* King): Grounds for Listing a Major Tropical Timber Species in CITES." *Botanical Journal of the Linnean Society* 122 (1996): 35-46.

Snow, A. A., and D. W. Roubik. "Pollen Deposition and Removal by Bees Visiting Two Tree Species in Panama." *Biotropica* 19, no. 1 (1987): 57-63.

Sobrado, M. A. "Cost-Benefit Relationships in Deciduous and Evergreen Leaves of Tropical Dry Forest Species." *Functional Ecology* 5 (1991): 608-616.

Sowls, L. K. *The Peccaries.* Tucson: University of Arizona Press, 1984.

Stafford, P. *Annotated Inventory of Amphibians and Reptiles from the Chiquibul Forest, Belize.* London: Natural History Museum, 2009.

——. *Snakes.* London: Natural History Museum, 2000.

——, S. T. McMurry, T. R. Rainwater, D. A. Ray, L. D. Densmore, and B. Barr. "Morelet's Crocodile (*Crocodylus moreletii*) in the Macal River Watershed, Maya Mountains, Belize." *Herpetological Bulletin* 85 (2003): 15-23.

——, P. Walker, P. Edgar, and M. Penn. "Distribution and Conservation of the Herpetofauna of Belize." In *Conservation of Mesoamerican Amphibians and Reptiles,* edited by L. D. Wilson, J. H. Townsend, and J. D. Johnson, 370-406. Eagle Mountain, UT: Eagle Mountain Publications, 2010.

Standley, P. C., and S. J. Record. *The Forests and Flora of British Honduras.* Publication 350, Botanical Series 12. Chicago: Field Museum of Natural History, 1936.

Steiner, K. E. "Nectarivory and Potential Pollination by a Neotropical Marsupial." *Annals of the Missouri Botanical Garden* 68, no. 4 (1981): 505-513.

Styles, F. G. "Ecology, Flowering Phenology, and Hummingbird Pollination of Some Costa Rican *Heliconia* Species." *Ecology* 56, no. 2 (1975): 285-301.

Sunquist, M., and F. Sunquist. *Wild Cats of the World.* Chicago: University of Chicago Press, 2002.

Swaine, M. D., D. Lieberman, and F. E. Putz. "The Dynamics of Tree Populations in Tropical Forest: A Review." *Journal of Tropical Ecology* 3 (1987): 359-366.

——, and T. C. Whitmore. "On the Definition of Ecological Species Groups in Tropical Rain Forests." *Vegetation* 75 (1988): 81-86.

Tautz, J., F. Roces, and B. Höllbobler. "Use of Sound-Based Vibratome by Leaf-Cutting Ants." *Science* 267 (1995): 84-87.

Tavaré, S., C. R. Marshall, O. Will, C. Soligo, and R. D. Martin. "Using the Fossil Record to Estimate the Age of the Last Common Ancestor of Extant Primates." *Nature* 416 (2002): 726-729.

Taylor, B. W. "An Outline of the Vegetation of Nicaragua." *Journal of Ecology* 51 (1963): 27-54.

Taylor, P. E., G. Card, J. House, M. H. Dickinson, and R. Flagan. "High-Speed Pollen Release in the White Mulberry, *Morus alba* L." *Sexual Plant Reproduction* 19 (2006): 19-24.

Terry, I. "Thrips: The Primeval Pollinators?" In *Thrips and Tospoviruses: Proceedings of the Seventh International Symposium on Thysanoptera,* edited by R. Marullo and L. Mound, 157-162. Canberra: Australian National Insect Collection, 2002.

Thomas, W. W. "Conservation and Monographic Research on the Flora of Tropical America." *Biodiversity and Conservation* 8 (1999): 1007-1015.

Thorp, R. W. "The Collection of Pollen by Bees." *Plant Systematics and Evolution* 222 (2000): 211-223.

Tillman, D. "Competition and Biodiversity in Spatially Structured Habitats." *Ecology* 75 (1994): 2-16.

Toledo, V. M. "Pollination of Some Rain Forest Plants by Non-Hovering Birds in Veracruz, Mexico." *Biotropica* 9, no. 4 (1977): 262-267.

Townsend, C. "A Checklist of the Mosses of Belize." *Tropical Bryology* 15 (1998): 89-100.

Turner, B. L. "Prehistoric Intensive Agriculture in the Maya Lowlands." *Science* 185 (1974): 118-124.

——, and P. D. Harrison. "Prehistoric Raised Field Agriculture in the Maya Lowlands." *Science* 213 (1981): 399-405.

——, and C. H. Miksicek. "Economic Plant Species Associated with Prehistoric Agriculture in the Maya Lowlands." *Economic Botany* 38, no. 2 (1984): 179-193.

Twigger, R. *Inflation: The Value of the Pound 1750–1998*. House of Commons Research Paper 99/20. London: House of Commons Library, Economic Policy and Statistics Section, 1999.

Tykot, R. H., N. J. van der Mere, and N. Hammond. "Stable Isotope Analysis of Bone Collagen and Apatite in the Reconstruction of Human Diet: A Case Study from Cuello, Belize." In *Archaeological Chemistry: Organic, Inorganic, and Biochemical Analysis*, edited by M. V. Orna, 116–130. ACS Symposium Series 625. Washington, DC: American Chemical Society, 1996.

Urban, L., S. Bridgewater, and D. Harris. "The Macal River: A Floristic and Phytosociological Study of a Threatened Riverine Vegetation Community in Belize." *Edinburgh Journal of Botany* 63 (2006): 95–118.

Valiela, I., J. L. Bowen, and J. K. York. "Mangrove Forests: One of the World's Threatened Major Tropical Environments." *Biotropica* 51, no. 10 (2001): 807–815.

van der Hammon, T. "The Pleistocene Changes of Vegetation and Climate in Tropical South America." *Journal of Biogeography* 1 (1974): 3–26.

van Schaik, C. P., J. W. Terborgh, and S. J. Wright. "The Phenology of Tropical Forests: Adaptive Significance and Consequences for Primary Consumers." *Annual Review of Ecology and Systematics* 24 (1993): 353–377.

Vandermeer, J., I. Granzo de la Cerda, D. Boucher, I. Perfecto, and J. Ruiz. "Hurricane Disturbance and Tropical Forest Tree Diversity." *Science* 290 (2000): 788–790.

Vander-Wall, S. B., K. M. Kuhn, and M. J. Beck. "Seed Removal, Seed Predation, and Secondary Dispersal." *Ecology* 86, no. 3 (2005): 801–806.

Vaughan, H. H., E. S. Deevey Jr., and S. E. Garrett-Jones. "Pollen Stratigraphy of Two Cores from the Petén Lake District, with an Appendix on Two Deep-Water Cores." In Pohl, *Prehistoric Lowland Maya Environment*, 73–89.

Walker, L. R. "Timing of Post-Hurricane Tree Mortality in Puerto Rico." *Journal of Tropical Ecology* 11 (1995): 315–320.

Wallace, A. R. *Natural Selection and Tropical Nature: Essays on Descriptive and Theoretical Biology*. 2nd ed. London: Macmillan, 1855.

Walter, K. S., and H. J. Gillett, eds. *1997 IUCN Red List of Threatened Plants*. Gland, Switzerland, and Cambridge, UK: IUCN–The World Conservation Union, 1998.

Ward Ant Lab. "Ants of the Subfamily Pseudomyrmecinae: The *Pseudomyrmex ferrugineus* Group." http://entomology.ucdavis.edu/faculty/ward/PsFerGp.html. Accessed November 6, 2007.

Weaver, P. L., and O. A. Sabido. *Mahogany in Belize: A Historical Perspective*. General Technical Report GTR-ITF 2. Rio Piedras, Puerto Rico: USDA Forest Service, International Institute of Tropical Forestry, 1997.

Webb, S. D. "Ecogeography and the Great American Interchange." *Paleobiology* 17, no. 3 (1991): 266–280.

———. "The Great American Faunal Interchange." In *Central America: A Natural and Cultural History*, edited by A. G. Coates, 97–122. New Haven, CT: Yale University Press, 1997.

———, and A. Rancy. "Late Cenozoic Evolution of the Neotropical Mammal Fauna." In *Evolution and Environment in Tropical America*, edited by J. B. C. Jackson, A. F. Budd, and A. G. Coates, 335–358. Chicago: University of Chicago Press, 1996.

Weiblen, G. D. "Phylogenetic Relationships of Functionally Dioecious Ficus (Moraceae) Based on Ribosomal DNA Sequences and Morphology." *American Journal of Botany* 87, no. 9 (2000): 1324–1357.

Weiss, M. R. "Vision and Learning in Some Neglected Pollinators: Beetles, Flies, Moths, and Butterflies." In Chittka and Thomson, *Cognitive Ecology*, 171–190.

Wetterer, J. K. "Ants on *Cecropia* Trees in Urban Costa Rica." *Florida Entomologist* 81, no. 1 (1998): 118–121.

Whitmore, T. C. "Canopy Gaps and the Two Major Groups of Forest Trees." *Ecology* 70, no. 3 (1989): 536–538.

Whittemore, A. T., and B. Allen. "The Liverworts and Hornworts of Belize." *Bryologist* 99, no. 1 (1996): 64–67.

Wicks, N. "Preliminary Fishtail Xaté (*Chamaedorea ernesti-augusti*) Growth Survey Data in the Chiquibul National Forest Reserve,

Belize." Darwin Initiative Report, Conservation of the Diversity of Chamaedorea Palms Project, 2004.

Wikström, N., V. Savolainen, and M. W. Chase. "Evolution of the Angiosperms: Calibrating the Family Tree." *Proceedings of the Royal Society of London; Series B: Biological Sciences* 268 (2001): 2211–2220.

Wilk, R. R. "Dry Season Agriculture among the Kekchi Maya and Its Implications for Prehistory." In Pohl, *Prehistoric Lowland Maya Environment*, 47–57.

Winter, Y., and O. von Helversen. "Bats as Pollinators: Foraging Energetics and Floral Adaptations." In Chittka and Thomson, *Cognitive Ecology*, 148–170.

Wiseman, F. M. "Agriculture and Historical Ecology of the Maya Lowlands." In *Pre-Hispanic Maya Agriculture*, edited by P. D. Harrison and B. L. Turner, 63–115. Albuquerque: University of New Mexico Press, 1978.

——. "Agriculture and Vegetation Dynamics of the Maya Collapse in Central Petén, Guatemala." In Pohl, *Prehistoric Lowland Maya Environment*, 63–71.

——. "Analysis of Pollen from the Fields at Pulltrouser Swamp." In *Pulltrouser Swamp: Ancient Maya Habitat, Agriculture, and Settlement in Northern Belize*, edited by B. L. Turner and P. D. Harrison, 105–119. Austin: University of Texas Press, 1983.

Wolda, H., and C. W. Sabrosky. "Insect Visitors to Two Forms of *Aristolochia pilosa* in Las Cumbres, Panama." *Biotropica* 18, no. 4 (1986): 295–299.

Wright, A. C. S., D. H. Romney, R. H. Arbuckle, and V. E. Vial. *Land in British Honduras: Report of the British Honduras Land Use Survey Team*. Colonial Research Publications 24. 2 vols. London: Her Majesty's Stationary Office, 1959.

Wright, D. H. "Species-Energy Theory: An Extension of Species-Area Theory." *Oikos* 41 (1983): 496–506.

Wright, S. J. "Plant Diversity in Tropical Forests." In *Functional Plant Ecology*, edited by F. I. Pugnaire and F. Valladares, 351–367. New York: CRS Press, 2007.

——, and F. H. Cornejo. "Seasonal Drought and Leaf Fall in a Tropical Forest." *Ecology* 71, no. 3 (1990): 1165–1175.

Wu, T. H., T. R. Rainwater, S. G. Platt, S. T. McMurray, and T. A. Anderson. "Organochlorine Contaminants in Morelet's Crocodile (*Crocodylus moreletii*) Eggs from Belize." *Chemosphere* 40 (2000): 671–678.

Yin, K., D. H. Boucher, J. H. Vandermeer, and N. Zamora. "Recovery of the Rain Forest of Southeastern Nicaragua after Destruction by Hurricane Joan." *Biotropica* 23, no. 2 (1991): 106–113.

Young, A. A. "Belize's Ecosystems: Threats and Challenges to Conservation in Belize." *Tropical Conservation Science* 1, no. 1 (2008): 18–33.

Young, B. E., M. Kaspari, and T. E. Martin. "Species-Specific Nest Selection by Birds in Ant-Acacia Trees." *Biotropica* 22, no. 3 (1990): 310–315.

——, K. R. Lips, J. K. Reaser, R. Ibáñez, A. W. Salas, J. R. Cedeño, L. A. Coloma, et al. "Population Declines and Priorities for Amphibian Conservation in Latin America." *Conservation Biology* 15, no. 5 (2001): 1213–1223.

Young, T. P., and V. Perkocha. "Treefalls, Crown Asymmetry, and Buttresses." *Journal of Ecology* 82 (1994): 319–324.

Yu, D. W. "The Structural Role of Epiphytes in Ant Gardens." *Biotropica* 26, no. 2 (1994): 222–226.

Zerega, N. J. C., W. L. Clement, S. L. Datwyler, and G. D. Weiblen. "Biogeography and Divergene Times in the Mulberry Family (Moraceae)." *Molecular Phylogenetics and Evolution* 37 (2005): 402–416.

Zimmerman, J. K., S. J. Wright, O. Calderón, M. Apomye Pagan, and S. Paton. "Flowering and Fruiting Phenologies of Seasonal and Aseasonal Neotropical Forests: The Role of Annual Changes in Irradiance." *Journal of Tropical Ecology* 23 (2007): 231–251.

Zisman, S. *Mangroves in Belize: Their Characteristics, Use and Conservation*. Technical Report. Forest Planning and Management Project, Belize Forest Department, Belmopan, 1992.

Page numbers in *italics* refer to illustrations and tables.